Lecture Notes in Artificial Intelligε

T0237841

Subseries of Lecture Notes in Computer Science
Edited by J. G. Carbonell and J. Siekmann

Lecture Notes in Computer Science
Edited by G. Goos, J. Hartmanis and J. van Leeuwen

Springer
Berlin
Heidelberg
New York
Barcelona
Budapest
Hong Kong
London
Milan
Paris
Singapore
Tokyo

David Page (Ed.)

Inductive Logic Programming

8th International Conference, ILP-98
Madison, Wisconsin, USA, July 22-24, 1998
Proceedings

Springer

Series Editors

Jaime G. Carbonell, Carnegie Mellon University, Pittsburgh, PA, USA
Jörg Siekmann, University of Saarland, Saarbrücken, Germany

Volume Editor

David Page
Speed Scientific School, University of Louisville
Louisville, KY 40292, USA
E-mail: cdpage@louisville.edu

Cataloging-in-Publication Data applied for

Die Deutsche Bibliothek - CIP-Einheitsaufnahme

Inductive logic programming : 8th international workshop ;
proceedings / ILP-98, Madison, Wisconsin, USA, July 22 - 24, 1998.
David Page (ed.). - Berlin ; Heidelberg ; New York ; Barcelona ;
Budapest ; Hong Kong ; London ; Milan ; Paris ; Santa Clara ;
Singapore ; Tokyo : Springer, 1998
     (Lecture notes in computer science ; Vol. 1446 : Lecture notes in
     artificial intelligence)
     ISBN 3-540-64738-4

CR Subject Classification (1991): I.2, D.1.6

ISBN 3-540-64738-4 Springer-Verlag Berlin Heidelberg New York

© Springer-Verlag Berlin Heidelberg 1998
Printed in Germany

Typesetting: Camera ready by author
SPIN 10638106   06/3142 – 5 4 3 2 1 0   Printed on acid-free paper

Preface

The Eighth International Conference on Inductive Logic Programming was held on the campus of the University of Wisconsin in Madison, Wisconsin, USA, on July 22–24, 1998. The meeting was co-located with the Fifteenth International Conference on Machine Learning (ICML'98), the Fifteenth National Conference on Artificial Intelligence, the Tenth Annual Conference on Innovative Applications of Artificial Intelligence, the Eleventh Annual Conference on Computational Learning Theory (COLT'98), the Third Annual Genetic Programming Conference, the Fourteenth Annual Conference on Uncertainty in Artificial Intelligence (UAI'98), the Twentieth Annual Meeting of the Cognitive Science Society, and the Eighth Annual Meeting of the Society for Text and Discourse. The program included three invited talks, abstracts of which appear at the start of this volume. The invited talks and a joint technical session with ICML'98 took place on July 24, when the program overlapped with the first day of ICML'98, COLT'98, and UAI'98. A joint poster session was held with these conferences as well. Following the three abstracts of invited talks in this volume are six papers accepted for extended presentation, the first two of which also were submitted and accepted to ICML'98.

Many of the papers in this volume are related to one another by more than one theoretical issue, implementation issue, and/or application area. As a result, it is difficult to group them along any one dimension; nevertheless, an attempt has been made to keep highly related papers close to each other within the proceedings.

The chair would like to extend special thanks to the members of the program committee, listed here, for their effort in selecting the papers for the Eighth International Conference on Inductive Logic Programming.

Program Committee

Francesco Bergadano	Peter Flach	Masayuki Numao
Henrik Boström	Alan Frisch	Céline Rouveirol
Ivan Bratko	Nada Lavrač	Claude Sammut
James Cussens	Stan Matwin	Michèle Sebag
Luc De Raedt	Ray Mooney	Ashwin Srinivasan
Sašo Džeroski	Stephen Muggleton	Stefan Wrobel

Table of Contents

Attribute-Value Learning Versus Inductive Logic Programming : The Missing Links
(Extended Abstract)

Luc De Raedt

Department of Computer Science, Katholieke Universiteit Leuven
Celestijnenlaan 200A, B-3001 Heverlee, Belgium
email : Luc.DeRaedt@cs.kuleuven.ac.be

Abstract. Two contributions are sketched. A first contribution shows that a special case of relational learning can be transformed into attribute-value learning. However, it is much more tractable to stick to the relational representation than to apply the sketched transformation. This provides a sound theoretical justification for inductive logic programming. In a second contribution, we show how existing attribute-value learning techniques and systems can be upgraded towards inductive logic programming using the 'Leuven' methodology and illustrate it using the Claudien, Tilde, ICL, Warmr, TIC, MacCent and RRL systems.

1 Introduction

Relational learning and inductive logic programming have received a lot of attention recently, cf. [16, 5]. Also, the field has matured and has been applied to several important practical problems (cf. [3, 18] ...). Despite these successes, some fundamental questions about relational learning and inductive logic programming remain essentially unanswered. The first question concerns the need for relational learning. Though there exist now several impressive applications of relational learning (see e.g. [13]) and inductive logic programming and it is hard to see how these could have been realized with classical attribute value learning techniques, a precise argumentation is often lacking or implicit. The second question concerns the relation among relational learning and attribute value learning. Advocates of attribute-value learning often claim (in corridor discussions) that relational learning can be reduced to attribute-value learning, and hence that inductive logic programming is not (really) needed. Some of these arguments have their roots in database theory, but this author found no track of a precise and general argument in the literature (though many specific results are given in computational learning theory). Furthermore, (as argued in this abstract) the typical argumentation based on the concept of the universal relation is insufficient. It turns out that - under certain (very restrictive) assumptions - inductive logic programming can be reduced to attribute-value learning. However, the transformation is computationally too expensive to be applied on real problems. Thus it is much more effective to stay with the relational representation and apply inductive logic programming systems. This provides a sound theoretical justification for the field of inductive logic programming.

If one is convinced of the use of inductive logic programming, one should also be interested in the development of inductive logic programming techniques and systems. To this aim, we briefly outline the 'Leuven' methodology for upgrading attribute value-learning systems towards using a first order representation. This methodology has its origin in the work by [8] on upgrading Valiant's PAC-learning results for k-CNF towards first order jk-clausal theories. Since then the same techniques has been applied to a number of systems including : the clausal discovery engine Claudien [7], the ICL system for classification [9], the TILDE system for top-down induction of logical decision trees [1], the Warmr system for first order association rules [11], the MacCent system based on the maximum entropy principle [10], the TIC system for top down induction of clustering [2], relational reinforcement learning [14], ...

2 A theoretical justification for ILP

In this abstract, we will use the learning from interpretations approach to inductive logic programming [8, 6]. More specifically, each example corresponds to a set of ground facts (or in relational database terminology, a small relational database in the form of a set of tuples) and are classified into a finite number of classes. E.g. one well-known Bongard problem can be represented as follows :

$$\{object(o1, triangle, red), object(o2, circle, blue), in(o1, o2)\}$$

This example contains a red triangle (referred to as o1) that is inside a blue circle (called o2). Though this example is a toy-problem its structure is very similar to that of well-known applications such as mutagenicity [18]. To represent the same information in a single relational database, one needs to add to each example a unique key which is then used by all relations and predicates.

We will also assume that examples are classified into a finite number of classes. Each class then corresponds to a propositional predicate, e.g. *positive*. The goal of the learning task is then to induce clauses to define these predicates. Such a definition will consist of a set of clauses of the following form :

$$class \leftarrow l_1, ..., l_n$$

where the l_i are different atoms. E.g. a solution to the bongard problem could be:

$$positive \leftarrow object(O1, triangle, X), object(O2, circle, Y), in(O1, O2)$$

To classify an example given a hypothesis H one has to assert H and the example in a Prolog database and run the query $? - positive$. If it succeeds, it is positive, otherwise, it is negative.

This framework corresponds to a simplification of the learning from interpretations setting in inductive logic programming, which was introduced by [8], and which is used in several inductive logic programming systems such as TILDE,

ICL and Claudien. The above framework is also the simplest framework possible for relational learning and inductive logic programming, because classes are propositional, it avoids (and ignores) the difficulties with structured terms, recursion, background knowledge, continuous values and also because it can - under certain conditions - be reduced to the harder (and more popular) learning from entailment setting due to Gordon Plotkin (see [6] for more details). However, it is sufficient for our purposes. If we can justify this simple setting by contrasting it with attribute-value learning, it follows that generalizations of our setting are also justified w.r.t. attribute value learning.

2.1 Parameters of the learning task

We will distinguish the following parameters of the learning task.

Definition 1. Database parameters :

- r is the number of relations (excluding the predicate *positive*)
- i is the maximum number of tuples (facts) an example has in any single relation (or predicate)
- a is the maximum arity of a relation
- d is the maximum number of values of a given attribute
- e is the number of examples

In the above example for a Bongard type problem, $r = 2$, $i = 2$, and $a = 3$. Furthermore, the complexity of the learning task will also depend on the type of clauses and hypotheses searched for. We assume the following normal form for clauses.

$$class : -R_1(t_{1,1}, ..., t_{1,n_1}), ..., R_T(t_{T,1}, ..., t_{T,n_T}), V_1 = U_1, ..., V_J = U_J$$

where the $t_{i,j}$ are either constants or variables, such that each variable $t_{i,j}$ occurs exactly once in $R_1(t_{1,1}, ..., t_{1,n_1}), ..., R_T(t_{T,1}, ..., t_{T,n_T})$, all V_i, U_i are different variables and V_i and U_i appearing in relations R. This type of clause can easily be translated into relational algebra (used in databases). The different literals correspond to cartesian products and the equality literals correspond to possible join operations. E.g. the above clause translates to :

$$positive \leftarrow object(O1, triangle, X), object(O2, circle, Y), in(O3, O4), O1 = O3, O2 = O4$$

So, $T = 3$, and $J = 2$. Here T corresponds to the number of tuple (or relation) variables, and J to the *worst-case* number of joins.

Definition 2. Hypothesis parameters :

- T is the maximum number of tuple variables in a clause of the hypothesis
- J is the maximum number of literals of type $V_i = U_i$ in a clause
- C is the maximum number of rules in a hypothesis.

Though from a theoretical perspective, some inductive logic programming or relational learning systems may search an infinite clause-space, from a practical perspective the search is often restricted to a finite space by restricting the parameters T and J, or variants thereof.

Given a learning problem in the above framework, there are two important questions that characterize the difficulty of the learning task. The first question concerns the complexity of the coverage test. Clearly, the more time it takes to test whether an example is covered by a hypothesis, the more difficult the learning task will be. An adequate measure for our purposes will be the complexity of testing whether a single clause covers an example. The second question concerns the complexity of the search-space. The more hypotheses it contains, the more difficult the learning task will be (generally speaking). An adequate measure for this will be the number of possible clauses allowed in hypothesis[1] Therefore we will be especially interested in the complexity of the following issues :

Definition 3. – Data Complexity : size of the data-set DC
  – Query Complexity : complexity of testing whether a clasue rule covers an example : QC
  – Number of different rules in hypothesis language : HR
  – Number of different hypotheses : H

It is possible to derive some rough estimates of these quantities (full details and proofs will be given in a longer version of this paper).

Lemma 4. – $DC = O(e \cdot i \cdot a \cdot r)$
  – Let $M = min(J+1, T)$, then $QC = O((i^M \cdot a \cdot M) + i \cdot a \cdot (T-M))$
  – $HR = O(r^T \cdot (d+1)^{aT} \cdot (aT)^{2J})$

It turns out that the query complexity is exponential in J and that the hypothesis space complexity is exponential in a, J and T. The size of the data set is less of a problem.

2.2 Special cases

We now consider several special cases of the framework and discuss the relationship among them. All special cases can be obtained by instantiating some of the parameters of the given framework. Corresponding complexity results can be derived from Lemma 4.

Attribute value learning Attribute value learning is the special case of relational learning where $i = 1, r = 1, T = 1, J = 0$.

---

[1] For the sake of simplicity, we will not use more complicated meausures such as the VC-dimension which is common in computational learning theory.

Multi-instance learning Dietterich et al. [12] consider the so-called multi-instance problem, which corresponds to : $r = 1, T = 1, J = 0$.[2] It is easily seen that the number of possible clauses remains unchanged with regard to attribute-value learning. Only the query complexity gets worse by a linear factor i.

It should also be noted that Dietterich et al. view the multi-instance problem as an important extension to the classical attribute-value learning approach. From the framework presented above, it follows that the multi-instance problem can also be regarded as a special case of inductive logic programming. Furthermore, it turns out that several of the topics for future work listed by Dietterich et al. have already been addressed by the inductive logic programming community. For instance, the design of extensions of well-known attribute-value learning systems such as decision trees to the multi-instance problem. Solutions to the multi-instance problem can often be obtained by setting specific (declarative) biases within existing inductive logic programming systems.

On the other hand, it will turn out that the multi-instance problem is at the heart of the difference between attribute-value learning and inductive logic programming. All inductive logic programming problems can easily be transformed into a multi-instance problem, but it is harder to transform the multi-instance problem in a classical attribute-value learning problem.

This touches already at the fundamental question of the relation among multi-instance learning and proper attribute value learning. More specifically, can we transform any multi-instance problem into a corresponding attribute-value learning problem ? The answer to this question is yes. The transformation will contain one (binary) attribute for each rule in the hypotheses space (bounded by the parameters J and T. There will then be one value for each example and attribute that basically expresses whether the clause covers the example or not. Given this transformation, a disjunctive attribute-value learning algorithm can be applied [3].

From a practical perspective, the above transformation is to be avoided because :

- the data-set grows too large.
- even if the attribute-value table would not be generated explicitly, any algorithm working with the attribute-value representation will degenerate into a generate-and-test algorithm at the level of clauses.

On the other hand, it seems hard to find alternative transformations that would not suffer from this problem. Furthermore, it is unnecessary to search for such transformations as it is easy to adapt existing the classical concept-learning algorithms to address this problem. This follows from the observation that the structure on the rule-space does not change, but only the coverage relation changes. Hence, no changes to the search strategy are need, only the point where coverage is tested should be modified in a straightforward manner.

---

[2] In the applications and algorithms of Dietterich et al. hypotheses are further biased by setting $C = 1$.

[3] Disjunctive concepts in this context are of the form $A_1 = true \vee ...A_n = true$ where the A_i are attributes.

Multi-tuple problems The multi-tuple problem is a relaxation of the multi-instance problem where it is no longer required that $T = 1$, i.e. in multi-tuple problems $J = 0, r = 1$.

For the multi-tuple problems, coverage testing grows linearly and the search space exponentially in T as compared to the multi-instance problem.

Multi-tuple problems can easily be transformed into multi-instance problems (and hence also into attribute value format) by computing for each example the cartesian product of the relation with itself (T times). This transformation is again to be avoided because the data-set grows exponentially. A further complication is that it introduces syntactic variants in the hypothesis space. Again, the conclusion is that working with the original representation is more efficient.

Multi-join The multi-join problem is a further relaxation of the multi-tuple problem where it is no longer required that $J = 0$.

Again it is possible to reduce the multi-join problem to the multi-instance problem (and hence to attribute value learning). The reduction involves adding a number of binary attributes to the transformation of the multi-tuple problem. Each binary attribute tests whether two variables are identical.

This transformation inherits its problems from the multi-tuple case.

Multi-relation ($r > 1$ Using the universal relation concept from database theory, any relational learning problem can be transformed into a multi-join learning problem (with a single relation).

The transformation works as follows : Let $R_1, ..., R_r$ be all the relations in the original learning problem (excluding *class*). Then compute for each example e the cartesian product of the R_i', where $R_i' = R_i$ if there are tuples for R_i in e, otherwise $R_i' = (nil, ..., nil)$. It is straightforward to see that the universal relation computed in this way is again exponentially larger than the original one. Therefore it is to be avoided.

Furthermore, notice also that this last transformation *alone* is insufficient to transform an inductive logic programming problem into attribute-value form.

2.3 Conclusions

We have shown that the simplest form of inductive logic programming (or relational learning) can be transformed into an attribute-value form. However, we have also argued that each transformation results in computational problems. Therefore, it is more effective to stick to the original representation. Technically speaking, it seems that the multi-instance problem forms the natural frontier between inductive logic programming and classical attribute-value learning.

3 Upgrading attribute-value learning systems

Given that one is confronted with a true relational learning problem, the question is how to develop learning algorithms for solving it. In recent years, the 'Leuven' team has developed a number of novel inductive logic programming systems using a single methodology.

The methodology is derived from the PAC-learning result for jk-clausal theories by [8]. This result proposes to use Herbrand interpretations (i.e. sets of ground facts as specified above) as the representation of examples. It directly upgrades Valiant's seminal result for k-CNF [19]. This property is important because it means that the original propositional result is obtained as a special case of that for first order logic. Reversing this property is the basis of the methodology: inductive logic programming systems can be obtained by starting from propositional ones and changing the representation from feature-vectors to Herbrand interpretations.

This results in essentially the following 'Leuven' methodology :

1. start from a propositional learning technique and algorithm that matches the problem closest,
2. modify the problem setting of that algorithm as to use examples that are first order (Herbrand) interpretations instead of attribute-value vectors,
3. modify the representation of the hypotheses in the propositional case to a form close to clausal logic (e.g. for the TILDE system, a first order decision tree representation has been developed),
4. modify the generalization and specialization operators of the propositional systems as to use the well-known θ-subsumption framework for generalization [4],
5. retain all other features of the propositional algorithm if possible (this includes : search, heuristics, noise-handling, pruning, ...),
6. implement and evaluate the first order technique.

This methodology has resulted in a number of novel inductive logic programming systems. More specifically, Claudien [7] and the more recent Warmr [11] upgrade the association rule paradigm of data mining, Tilde [1] upgrades Quinlan's C4.5 algorithm [17], ICL [9] upgrades CN2 [4], MacCENT [10] upgrades propositional maximum entropy approaches, and relational reinforcement learning upgrades Q-learning as described by [15].

A more detailed case study with this methodology is in prepartion (in collaboration with Wim Van Laer).

Acknowledgements

This work is supported by the Fund for Scientific Research, Flanders and the ESPRIT project no. 20237 on Inductive Logic Programming. I'd like to thank the members of the 'Leuven' team for their contributions and a long list of other persons for discussions (cf. the longer versions of this paper).

---

[4] Θ-subsumption is sufficient for most purposes in inductive logic programming; problems only arise with recursion or multiple-predicate learning.

References

1. H. Blockeel and L. De Raedt. Top-down induction of first order logical decision trees. *Artificial Intelligence*, 1998. To appear.
2. H. Blockeel, L. De Raedt, and J. Ramon. Top-down induction of clustering trees. In *Proceedings of the 15th International Conference on Machine Learning*, 1998.
3. I. Bratko and S. Muggleton. Applications of inductive logic programming. *Communications of the ACM*, 38(11):65–70, 1995.
4. P. Clark and T. Niblett. The CN2 algorithm. *Machine Learning*, 3(4):261–284, 1989.
5. L. De Raedt, editor. *Advances in Inductive Logic Programming*, volume 32 of *Frontiers in Artificial Intelligence and Applications*. IOS Press, 1996.
6. L. De Raedt. Logical settings for concept learning. *Artificial Intelligence*, 95:187–201, 1997.
7. L. De Raedt and L. Dehaspe. Clausal discovery. *Machine Learning*, 26:99–146, 1997.
8. L. De Raedt and S. Džeroski. First order jk-clausal theories are PAC-learnable. *Artificial Intelligence*, 70:375–392, 1994.
9. L. De Raedt and W. Van Laer. Inductive constraint logic. In *Proceedings of the 5th Workshop on Algorithmic Learning Theory*, volume 997 of *Lecture Notes in Artificial Intelligence*. Springer-Verlag, 1995.
10. L. Dehaspe. Maximum entropy modeling with clausal constraints. In *Proceedings of the 7th International Workshop on Inductive Logic Programming*, volume 1297 of *Lecture Notes in Artificial Intelligence*, pages 109–124. Springer-Verlag, 1997.
11. L. Dehaspe and L. De Raedt. Mining association rules in multiple relations. In *Proceedings of the 7th International Workshop on Inductive Logic Programming*, volume 1297 of *Lecture Notes in Artificial Intelligence*, pages 125–132. Springer-Verlag, 1997.
12. T. G. Dietterich, R. H. Lathrop, and T. Lozano-Pérez. Solving the multiple-instance problem with axis-parallel rectangles. *Artificial Intelligence*, 89(1-2):31–71, 1997.
13. S. Džeroski and I. Bratko. Applications of inductive logic programming. In L. De Raedt, editor, *Advances in inductive logic programming*, volume 32 of *Frontiers in Artificial Intelligence and Applications*, pages 65–81. IOS Press, 1996.
14. S. Džeroski, L. De Raedt, and H. Blockeel. Relational reinforcement learning. In *Proceedings of the International Conference on Machine Learning*. Morgan Kaufmann, 1998.
15. T. Mitchell. *Machine Learning*. McGraw-Hill, 1997.
16. S. Muggleton and L. De Raedt. Inductive logic programming : Theory and methods. *Journal of Logic Programming*, 19,20:629–679, 1994.
17. J. Ross Quinlan. *C4.5: Programs for Machine Learning*. Morgan Kaufmann series in machine learning. Morgan Kaufmann, 1993.
18. A. Srinivasan, S.H. Muggleton, M.J.E. Sternberg, and R.D. King. Theories for mutagenicity: A study in first-order and feature-based induction. *Artificial Intelligence*, 85, 1996.
19. L. Valiant. A theory of the learnable. *Communications of the ACM*, 27:1134–1142, 1984.

Advances in ILP Theory and Implementations

Stephen Muggleton

Department of Computer Science
University of York
Heslington, York, YO1 5DD
United Kingdom

Abstract. A strong linkage exists between advances in applications, implementations and theory within Inductive Logic Programming (ILP). Early ILP systems, such as FOIL, Golem and LINUS learned single predicate definitions from positive and negative examples and extensional background knowledge. They also employed strong learning biases such as ij-determinacy. Although these systems found a number of applications, they had problems in areas such as molecular biology and natural language learning.

General mechanisms for inverting entailment have now been developed which support the use of non-ground background knowledge, and the revision of multiple inter-related predicates. ILP theory results concerning complete refinement graph operators now allow efficient admissible searches. The absolute requirement for negative examples (rare within natural language domains) has been eased by Bayesian analysis of learning from positive-only examples. Bayesian approaches have also supported sample complexity analysis of predicate invention within the framework of repeat learning. In this framework it is assumed that the learner's prior is not equivalent to the distribution from which the teacher is sampling targets. By providing a series of sessions the learner is able to update the initial prior by adding and deleting background predicates. Within the Bayesian framework stochastic logic program representations have been used to estimate the distribution of examples over the instance space. Stochastic logic programs are a generalisation of hidden Markov models and stochastic grammars.

Apart from a few special cases PAC-learning results have been largely negative for ILP. This is in large part due to the fact that testing satisfiability is intractable for most interesting subsets of first-order Horn logic. The development of Bayesian approaches to ILP supported the development of U-learnability, which allows classes of distributions over the hypotheses. Here it was shown that for any exponential-decay distribution the class of time-bounded logic-programs is polynomially U-learnable. The use of such bounds on proof depth is common within ILP systems. Although logically impure, this approach allows general-purpose flexible representations, while maintaining termination guarantees.

Application of ILP to Problems in Chemistry and Biology

A. Srinivasan

Oxford University Computing Laboratory
Wolfson Building, Parks Road, Oxford, OX1 3QD
United Kingdom

Abstract. Machine Learning algorithms are being increasingly used for knowledge discovery tasks. Approaches can be broadly divided by distinguishing discovery of procedural from that of declarative knowledge, with client requirements determining which of these is appropriate. Programs developed under the umbrella of ILP are concerned with the inductive discovery of declarative knowledge, and have been applied with some success in areas of biochemistry and molecular biology. While the experimental studies reported are preliminary, they have at least one commendable feature, namely, they constitute examples of programs participating in true scientific discovery tasks. By "true" here, I mean problems where existing scientific knowledge is incomplete, the descriptions found automatically were unknown to experts in the field, and have been acknowledged by publication in peer-reviewed journals in the field. Which were the really successful applications? Was ILP really necessary? How do results from ILP compare against experts and other prediction techniques? What do experts really think about ILP? Are ILP programs ready for routine use in the pharmaceutical industry? This talk will attempt to answer these questions, and will also describe how listeners can judge some of these matters for themselves in the important area of carcinogenesis prediction by participating in the Predictive Toxicology Evaluation Challenge. This presents a formidable challenge to knowledge discovery programs, with features that include: strong competition from methods used by chemists; participation in objective blind-trials; and an independent evaluation of results by an expert chemist.

Relational Reinforcement Learning*

Sašo Džeroski[1], Luc De Raedt[2], Hendrik Blockeel[2]

[1] J. Stefan Institute, Jamova 39, SI-1000 Ljubljana, Slovenia
[2] K.U.Leuven, Celestijnenlaan 200A, B-3001 Heverlee, Belgium

Abstract. Relational reinforcement learning is presented, a learning technique that combines reinforcement learning with relational learning or inductive logic programming. Due to the use of a more expressive representation language to represent states, actions and Q-functions, relational reinforcement learning can be potentially applied to a new range of learning tasks. One such task that we investigate is planning in the block's world, where it is assumed that the effects of the actions are unknown to the agent and the agent has to learn a policy. Within this simple domain we show that relational reinforcement learning solves some existing problems with reinforcement learning. In particular, relational reinforcement learning allows to employ structural representations, to make abstraction of specific goals pursued and to exploit the results of previous learning phases when addressing new (more complex) situations.

1 Introduction

Within the field of machine learning, both reinforcement learning [8] and inductive logic programming (or relational learning) [12, 10] have received a lot of attention since the early nineties. It is therefore no surprise that both Leslie Pack Kaelbling and Richard Sutton (in their invited talks at IJCAI-97, Nagoya, Japan) suggested to study the combination of these two fields.

From the reinforcement learning point of view, this could significantly extend the application perspective. Most representations used in reinforcement learning are inadequate for describing planning tasks such as the simple block's world. Even reinforcement learning work that involves generalization has by large employed an attribute-value representation. Furthermore, due to the use of variables in relational representations, it is possible to make abstractions of some specific details of the learning tasks, such as the goal pursued. Indeed, when learning to plan in the block's world, one would expect that the results of learning how to stack block a onto block b would be similar to stacking c onto d. Current approaches to reinforcement learning have to retrain from scratch if the goal is changed in this manner. Using relational reinforcement learning retraining is unnecessary. Relational reinforcement learning also allows to exploit the results of one learning task in a simple world when learning in a more complex domain (e.g., going from 3 blocks to 4 blocks in the block's world).

---

* This paper appears in the Proceedings of the Fifteenth International Conference on Machine Learning and is reprinted with permission.

From the inductive logic programming point of view, it is important to address domains such as reinforcement learning. So far, inductive logic programming has mainly studied concept-learning, and largely ignored the rest of machine learning. By demonstrating the potential of relational representations for reinforcement learning, we hope to show that the relational learning methodology does not only apply to concept-learning but to the whole field of machine learning.

With this in mind, we present a preliminary approach to relational reinforcement learning and apply it to simple planning tasks in the block's world. The planning task involves learning a policy to select actions. Learning is necessary as the planning agent does not know the effects of its actions. Relational reinforcement learning employs the Q-learning method [14, 8, 11] where the Q-function is learned using a relational regression tree algorithm (see [6, 9]). A state is represented relationally as a set of ground facts. A relational regression tree in this context takes as input a relational description of a state, a goal and an action, and produces the corresponding Q-value.

This paper is organized as follows. In section 2, we view planning (under uncertainty) as a reinforcement learning task, and in section 3, we briefly review reinforcement and in particular Q-learning. Section 4 introduces relational reinforcement learning that combines Q-learning and logical regression trees. In section 5, we present some experiments, and finally, in section 6, we conclude and touch upon related work.

2 Learning to plan as reinforcement learning

Consider a planning agent with the following task:

Given

- a set of possible states S,
- a set of possible actions A,
- an UNKNOWN function $\delta: S \times A \to A$,
- a function $pre:S \times A \to \{t, f\}$,
- a goal $goal:S \to \{t, f\}$, and
- a starting state $s \in S$,

find a sequence of actions $a_1, ..., a_n$ $(a_i \in A)$ such that

- $goal(\delta(...\delta(s, a_1))...), a_n)) = t$, and
- $pre(\delta(...\delta(s, a_1))...), ...a_i)) = t$.

The agent can be in one of the states of S. It can execute action $a \in A$ in a given state s if the preconditions for a are true in s ($pre(s, a) = t$), e.g., as in STRIPS [7]. Executing an action a in a state s will put the agent in a new state $\delta(s, a)$. When placed in a state s the task of the agent is to find a (shortest) sequence of actions $a_1, ..., a_n$ that will lead it to a goal state. The prototypical AI task belonging to this category is planning.

It is assumed here that the agent does not know the effect of its actions, hence the function δ is unknown to the agent. The above task specification thus contrasts with classical planning in that the δ function is unknown to the agent. Therefore, this task requires a learning component.

Example: The best known (toy)-domain to study planning is the block's world. Consider the situation where we have three blocks called a, b and c, and the floor. Blocks can be on the floor or can be stacked on each other. Each state can be described by a set (list) of facts, e.g., $s_1 = \{clear(a), on(a, b), on(b, c), on(c, floor)\}$. The available actions are then $move(x, y)$ where $x \neq y$ and $x \in \{a, b, c\}$, $y \in \{a, b, c, floor\}$.

It is then possible to define the preconditions and effects of actions. The Prolog code below defines *pre* and δ respectively. The predicate `pre` defines the preconditions for the action `move(X,Y)` while the predicate `delta` defines its effects: `delta(S,A,S1)` succeeds when $\delta(S, A) = S1$. States are represented as lists of facts and the auxiliary predicate `holds(S,Query)` succeeds when `Query` would succeed in the knowledge base containing the facts in S only.

```
pre(S,move(X,Y)) :-
   holds(S,[clear(X), clear(Y), not X=Y, not on(X,floor)]).
pre(S,move(X,Y)) :-
   holds(S,[clear(X), clear(Y), not X=Y, on(X,floor)]).
pre(S,move(X,floor)) :- holds(S,[clear(X), not on(X,floor)]).

holds(S,[]).
holds(S,[ not X=Y | R ]) :- not X=Y, !, holds(S,R).
holds(S,[ not A | R ]) :- not member(A,S), holds(S,R).
holds(S,[A | R]) :- member(A,R), holds(S,R).

delta(S,move(X,Y), NextS) :-
   holds(S,[clear(X), clear(Y), not X=Y, not on(X,floor)]),
   delete([clear(Y),on(X,Z)],S,S1),
   add( [clear(Z),on(X,Y)],S1,NextS).
delta(S,move(X,Y), NextS) :-
   holds(S,[clear(X), clear(Y), not X=Y, on(X,floor)]),
   delete([clear(Y),on(X,floor)],S,S1),
   add([on(X,Y)],S1,NextS).
delta(S,move(X,floor), NextS) :-
   holds(S,[clear(X), not on(X,floor)]),
   delete([on(X,Z)] ,S,S1),
   add([clear(Z),on(X,floor)],S1,NextS).
```

The goal is to stack a onto b, i.e., `goal(S) :- member(on(a,b),S).`   □

3 Reinforcement learning

Planning with incomplete knowledge as outlined above can be recast as a reinforcement learning problem.

3.1 The basics of reinforcement learning

The basic notions of reinforcement learning can be outlined as follows (we follow the notation used by Mitchell [11]).

- The task of the agent is to learn a policy $\pi : S \to A$ for selecting its next action a_t based on the current state s_t; that is $\pi(s_t) = a_t$.
- The reward at time t is $r_t = r(s_t, a_t)$. We will assume here that $r_t = 1$ if $goal(\delta(s_t, a_t)) = t$ and $s_t \neq \delta(s_t, a_t)$; otherwise $r_t = 0$. The reward function r is unknown to the learner as it relies on the unknown δ. The reward function only gives a reward in goal states.
- The state at time $t+1$ is $s_{t+1} = \delta(s_t, a_t)$ if $goal(s_t) = f$; otherwise $s_{t+1} = s_t$. This captures the idea that goal states are absorbing states, i.e., once a goal state is reached the only available action is to stay in the state.
- The learned policy should be optimal, i.e., it should maximize

$$V^\pi(s_t) = \sum_{i=o}^{\infty} \gamma^i r_{t+1}$$

where $0 \leq \gamma < 1$. We will denote the optimal policy by π^*.

The optimal policy π^* allows us to compute the shortest plan to reach a goal state. So, learning the optimal policy (or approximations thereof) will allow us to improve our planning performance.

3.2 Q-learning

It is well-known that under the conditions sketched in the previous subsection, Q-learning allows to approximate the optimal policy.

The optimal policy π^* will always select the action that maximizes the sum of the immediate reward and the value of the immediate successor state, i.e.,

$$\pi^*(s) = argmax_a(r(s, a) + \gamma V^{\pi^*}(\delta(s, a)))$$

The problem with this formulation of π^* is that it requires knowledge of δ and r, which the learner does not have at its disposal.

The Q-function is defined as follows :

$$Q(s, a) = r(s, a) + \gamma V^{\pi^*}(\delta(s, a))$$

Knowing Q allows us to rewrite the definition of π^* as follows :

$$\pi^*(s) = argmax_a Q(s, a)$$

According to Mitchell, this rewrite is important as it shows that if the agent can learn the Q function instead of the V^{π^*} function, it will be able to act optimally. The Q-function for a fixed goal can then be approximated by $\hat{Q}$, for which a look-up table is learned by the following algorithm (cf. [11]).

```
for each s, a do
    initialize the table entry Q̂(s, a) = 0
do forever
    i := 0
    generate a random state s₀
    while not goal(sᵢ) do
        select an action aᵢ and execute it
        receive an immediate reward rᵢ = r(sᵢ, aᵢ)
        observe the new state sᵢ₊₁
        i:=i+1
    for j=i-1 to 0 do
        update Q̂(sⱼ, aⱼ) := rᵢ + γmaxₐ' Q̂(sⱼ₊₁, a')
```

It is common in Q-learning to select action a in state s probabilistically so that $P(a|s)$ is proportional to $\hat{Q}(s,a)$, e.g.,

$$P(a_i|s) = k^{\hat{Q}(s,a_i)} / \sum_j k^{\hat{Q}(s,a_j)} \tag{1}$$

Higher values of k give stronger preference to actions with high values of $\hat{Q}$ causing the agent to exploit what it has learned, while lower values of k reduce this preference allowing the agent to explore actions that currently do not have high values of $\hat{Q}$.

4 Relational reinforcement learning

4.1 The need for relational representations

Given the above classical framework for Q-learning we could now learn to plan in the block's world sketched earlier. Using the approach as it stands we could store all the state-action pairs encountered andmemorize/update the corresponding Q values, having in effect an explicit look-up table for state-action pairs. This has however a number of disadvantages :

- It is impractical for all but the smallest state-spaces. Furthermore, using look-up tables does not work for infinite state spaces which could arise when first order representations are used (e.g., if the number of blocks in the world is unkown or infinite the above method does not work).
- Despite the use of a relational representation for states and actions, the above method is unable to capture the structural aspects of the planning task.
- Whenever the goal is changed from say $on(a, b)$ to $on(b, c)$ the above method would require retraining the whole Q function.
- Ideally, one would expect that the results of learning in a world with 3 blocks could be (partly) recycled when learning in a 4 blocks world later on. It is unclear how to achieve this with the lookup table.

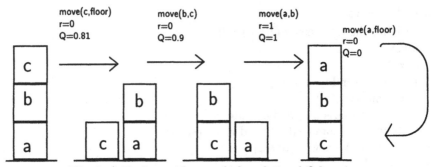

Fig. 1. A blocks-world example for relational Q-learning.

The first problem can be solved by using an inductive learning algorithm (e.g., a neural network) to approximate $\hat{Q}$. The three other problems can only be solved by using a *relational* learning algorithm that can make abstraction of the specific blocks and goals using variables. We now present such a relational learning algorithm.

4.2 The RRL algorithm

The relational reinforcement learning (RRL) algorithm is obtained by combining the classical Q-learning algorithm with stochastic selection of actions and a relational regression algorithm. Instead of having an explicit lookup table, an implicit representation of the Q-function is learned in the form of a logical regression tree, called a Q-tree.

The main point where RRL differs from the algorithm in section 3.2 is in the for-loop where the $\hat{Q}$ function is modified. This for-loop now becomes :

for j=i-1 to 0 **do**
    generate example $(s_j, a_j, \hat{q}_j)$, where $\hat{q}_j := r_i + \gamma max_{a'} \hat{Q}_e(s_{j+1}, a')$
update $\hat{Q}_e$ using TILDE-RT to produce $\hat{Q}_{e+1}$ using the examples $(s_j, a_j, \hat{q}_j)$

TILDE-RT [6] is an algorithm for learning logical regression trees and will be described briefly below.

The initial tree $\hat{Q}_0$ assigns zero value to all state-action pairs. From each goal state g encountered, an example $(g,a,0)$ is generated for each action a whose preconditions are satisfied in g. The rationale for this is that no reward can be expected from applying an action in an absorbing goal state.

Example: A possible initial episode ($e = 0$) in the blocks world with three blocks a, b, and c, where the goal is to stack a on b (i.e., $goal(on(a, b))$) is depicted in Figure 1. The discount factor γ is 0.9 and the reward given is one on achieving a goal state, zero otherwise.

The examples generated by RRL use the actions and the Q-values listed above the arrows representing the actions. The actual format of these examples is listed in Table 1. It is exactly this input that would be used by TILDE-RT to generate the Q-tree Q_1.   □

TILDE-RT is not incremental, so we currently simulate the update of $\hat{Q}$ by keeping all (s, a) pairs encountered and the most recent $\hat{q}$ value for each pair, and inducing a relational regression tree $\hat{Q}_e$ from these examples after each episode e. This tree is then used to select actions in episode $e + 1$.

Table 1. Examples for TILDE-RT generated from the blocks-world Q-learning episode in Figure 1.

qvalue(0.81).	qvalue(0.9).	qvalue(1.0).	qvalue(0.0).
action(move(c,floor)).	action(move(b,c)).	action(move(a,b)).	action(move(a,floor)).
goal(on(a,b)).	goal(on(a,b)).	goal(on(a,b)).	goal(on(a,b)).
clear(c).	clear(b).	clear(a).	clear(a).
on(c,b).	clear(c).	clear(b).	on(a,b).
on(b,a).	on(b,a).	on(b,c).	on(b,c).
on(a,floor).	on(a,floor).	on(a,floor).	on(c,floor).
	on(c,floor).	on(c,floor).	

4.3 Top-down induction of logical regression trees

Logical regression trees are similar to propositional regression trees [3]: leaves predict a value for a continuous class, while internal nodes contain conditions that partition the example space. The difference is that examples here are not feature or attribute-value vectors, but sets of relational facts, representing, e.g., a state of the blocks world, a goal, and an action to be taken, all at the same time. Similarly, internal nodes are not restricted to attribute-value tests but can be first order literals containing predicates, variables and complex terms.

The TILDE-RT system [6] induces such first order logical regression trees (or relational regression trees) from examples (cf. [9] for a related approach). The input for TILDE-RT is a set of state-action pairs together with the corresponding Q-values, represented as sets of facts. From this TILDE-RT induces (using the classical TDIDT-algorithm) a tree in which the classes correspond to real numbers (Q-values).

To illustrate the above notions, consider the episode shown in Figure 1. The examples for TILDE-RT generated by the RRL algorithm are given in Table 1. The relational regression tree induced by TILDE-RT from these examples is shown in Figure 2.

Nodes in the tree correspond to Prolog-queries. If the query succeeds in an example the **yes** subtree is taken, otherwise the **no** subtree. Different nodes in the tree may share variables, e.g., the bottom node in the tree (containing action(move(D,B))) refers to the variable D that first appear in the root of the tree (goal(on(C,D))). The Prolog program corresponding to the tree is shown in the lower part of Figure 2.

The semantics of logical decision trees is extensively discussed in [1], as well as the correspondence between a tree and a Prolog program. The method to induce the trees is described in [6] and is - for the case of regression trees - very similar to Kramer's SRT system [9]. We refer to these papers for more details on the representation and learning of such trees.

```
action(move(A,B)) , goal(on(C,D))
on(C,D) ?
+--yes: [0]
+--no:  action(move(C,D)) ?
        +--yes: [1]
        +--no:  action(move(D,B)) ?
                +--yes: [0.9]
                +--no:  [0.81]
```

```
qvalue(0)    :- action(move(A,B)) , goal(on(C,D)) , on(C,D), !.
qvalue(1)    :- action(move(A,B)) , goal(on(C,D)) , action(move(C,D)), !.
qvalue(0.9)  :- action(move(A,B)) , goal(on(C,D)) , action(move(D,B)), !.
qvalue(0.81).
```

Fig. 2. A relational regression tree generated by TILDE-RT from the examples in Table 1 and its equivalent Prolog program.

To find the Q-value corresponding to a state-action pair, one has to construct a Prolog knowledge base containing the Prolog program (corresponding to the tree), all facts in the state, the action, and the goal. Running the query ?-qvalue(Q) will then return the desired result. E.g., the Q-tree above will return a Q-value of zero for all actions if the goal is on(C,D) and on(C,D) holds in the state (goal states are absorbing). On the other hand, if the goal on(C,D) does not yet hold and the action is move(C,D)), then a Q-value of one is returned (reward of one for achieving a goal state).

5 Experiments

We applied the RRL algorithm described above to learn how to stack one block onto another in worlds with three and four blocks, respectively. In particular, the goal to achieve was $on(a, b)$, the two other blocks being c and d. An example episode in the three blocks world is depicted in Figure 1.

The discount factor γ had the value 0.9. When selecting states stochastically according to equation 1, the constant k was set to $e^{0.2}$. Examples for learning Q-trees were generated after each episode, as described in the section above.

TILDE-RT was used to induce an updated Q-tree after each episode. The minimal number of cases in a leaf was set to one and TILDE-RT generated unpruned trees, which exactly reproduce the Q-values for the state-action pairs seen during the learning phase.

Using the above settings, the RRL algorithm was first run for 10 episodes in the 3 blocks world. The tree shown in Figure 3 was generated by TILDE-RT after the final episode. This tree represents the optimal policy for the given reinforcement learning problem. The top two levels of the tree match those of the tree in Table 1, which was generated from a single episode.

```
action(move(A,B)) , goal(on(C,D))
on(C,D) ?
+--yes: [0]
+--no:  action(move(C,D)) ?
        +--yes: [1]
        +--no:  on(B,C) ?
                +--yes: [0.729]
                +--no:  on(B,D) ?
                        +--yes: [0.729]
                        +--no:  action(move(A,C)) ?
                                +--yes: [0.81]
                                +--no:  action(move(A,D)) ?
                                        +--yes: [0.81]
                                        +--no:  clear(D) ?
                                                +--yes: on(C,B) ?
                                                |       +--yes: on(A,C) ?
                                                |       |       +--yes: [0.9]
                                                |       |       +--no:  clear(C) ?
                                                |       |               +--yes: [0.9]
                                                |       |               +--no:  [0.81]
                                                |       +--no:  [0.9]
                                                +--no:  clear(C) ?
                                                        +--yes: on(C,B) ?
                                                        |       +--yes: [0.9]
                                                        |       +--no:  [0.81]
                                                        +--no:  [0.81]
```

Fig. 3. The Q-tree generated by RRL in the 3 blocks world after 10 episodes.

It is important to note that the individual blocks are not referred to in the tree itself directly, but only through the variables of the goal. This means that the tree represents the optimal policy not only for achieving the goal $on(a, b)$, but also $on(b, c)$ and $on(c, a)$. This is one of the major advantages of using a relation representation for Q-learning.

The Q-tree obtained after 10 episodes in the 4 blocks worlds was much larger (44 nodes as opposed to the 12 nodes of the 3-blocks Q-tree). It also represents an optimal policy: it chooses a shortest path to a goal state from all initial states, if the action with the highest Q-value is always selected.

The 3 top levels of the tree match with the tree from the 3 blocks world. This indicates that the result of learning in the 3 blocks world could be used to bootstrap learning in the 4 blocks world. Indeed, if we take the Q-tree learned in the 3 blocks world shown in Figure 3 and use it to select actions in the 4 blocks world, it selects an optimal path to a goal state from all but 9 of the 73 possible initial states. In 4 of the 9 cases a looping behavior is produced, in the remaining 5 cases one extra action is needed as compared to an optimal plan.

Using the Q-tree from Figure 3 to bootstrap RRL in the 4 blocks world helps improve performance, especially in the initial episodes. Without bootstrapping, after two episodes a tree is learned which produces nonoptimal behavior in 12 of the 73 initial states. With bootstrapping, the behavior of the learned tree is nonoptimal for 8 of the 73 possible initial states. After ten episodes, the learned Q-tree produces optimal behavior and is much smaller (27 nodes) as compared to the Q-tree learned without bootstrapping (44 nodes).

6 Discussion

We have presented an approach to planning with incomplete knowledge that combines reinforcement learning and relational regression into a technique called relational reinforcement learning. The advantages of this approach include the ability to use structured representations, which enables us to also describe infinite worlds, and the ability to use variables, which allows to abstract away from specific details of the situations (such as, e.g., the goal). The ability to use results of simpler tasks to bootstrap learning in more complex tasks is also an advantage worth mentioning. Finally, it is easy to incorporate nondeterministic actions within the proposed approach.

Even for standard reinforcement learning, scaling-up as the dimensionality of the problem increases can be a problem. Using a richer description language may seem to make things even worse. However, there are reasons to expect that using a richer representation actually enables relational Q-learning to scale-up better than standard Q-learning. Let us illustrate these on the blocks world.

First, in the representation employed, the relational theories learned abstract away the specific block names, causing the number of states that are essentially different to decrease. For instance, with $goal(on(a,b))$ the states $\{on(a,c), on(c,b), on(b, floor), on(d, floor)\}$ and $\{on(a,d), on(d,b), on(b, floor), on(c, floor)\}$ are essentially the same as c and d are interchangeable. In standard Q-learning, they would be considered different. In our 4-blocks example, the number of states that essentially differ from one another is 73 for a standard Q-learner, but only 38 for a relational one. This ratio increases combinatorially (since all blocks that do not occur in the goal have no special status and are thus interchangeable, the ratio increases roughly with $(n-2)!$, where n is the total number of blocks).

Second, the use of background knowledge makes it possible to abstract even further from specific situations that do not essentially differ. For instance, when a has to be cleared in order to be able to move it, it is not essential whether there are 1, 5 or 17 blocks above a: the top of the stack on a should be moved. Using background definitions such as $above(X, Y)$ (the recursive closure of $on(X, Y)$) it is possible to state a rule such as "if there are blocks on a, move the topmost of those blocks to the floor" which captures a very large set of specific cases.

However, the exact scale-up behavior of relational reinforcement learning has still to be determined experimentally. The experimental evaluation of our approach done so far is preliminary and is mainly intended to highlight the principal advantages of using a relational representation for reinforcement learning. We hope that this paper will inspire further research into the combination of relational and reinforcement learning, as much work remains to be done. This includes work in the line of proper performance assessment, both in terms of standard performance tests in reinforcement learning fashion (root mean square errors of learned Q-values wrt. the Q-values of the optimal policy) and in considering more complex and demanding planning problems.

More complex problems can be obtained by increasing the number of blocks in the world, considering more complex goals, such as building a stack of all available blocks, and considering problems outside the blocks world.

This work is related to work on generalization in reinforcement learning, which has however mainly addressed the use of neural networks for this purpose [13]. The closest related work is probably Chapman's and Kaelbling's decision tree algorithm that was specifically designed for reinforcement learning [5]. Note however that our approach is distinguished from the mainstream work in reinforcement learning by the use of a relational representation.

Relational representations are commonly used in planning approaches. There have also been some attempts to combine planning with relational learning within those approaches, e.g., within the PRODIGY approach [2]. Our approach is related to them through the use of a relational representation. However, it seems that the combination of planning, reinforcement learning and relational learning has not been addressed so far.

The reinforcement learning part of the work presented in this paper is admittedly simple. We have taken a standard textbook description of reinforcement learning [11] and incorporated an implementation of it within our approach. We have considered a deterministic setting and a goal-oriented formulation of the learning problem. However, both restrictions can be easily lifted to extend to non-zero rewards on non-terminal states (the RRL algorithm actually makes no assumption on the reinforcement received) and nondeterministic actions. To handle nondeterministic actions an appropriate update rule (see page 382 of [11]) has to be used to generate examples for the TILDE-RT algorithm. Other points where the reinforcement learning part can be improved include the initialization of Q values and the exploration strategy.

The current implementation of TILDE-RT is - according to reinforcement standards - not optimal. One of the reasons is that it is not incremental. However, incrementality is not enough, as the (estimated) values of Q are changing with time. These problems are taken care of within the Chapman and Kaelbling's decision tree algorithm that was specifically designed for reinforcement learning [5]. A natural direction for further work is thus to develop a first order regression tree algorithm combining the representations of TILDE-RT with the algorithm and performance measures of the approach by Chapman and Kaelbling. Such an integrated approach, which is currently under development, would not suffer from the abovementioned problems.

Acknowledgements

This work was supported in part by the ESPRIT IV Project 20237 ILP2. Luc De Raedt is supported by the Fund for Scientific Research of Flanders. Hendrik Blockeel is supported by the Flemish Institute for the Promotion of Scientific and Technological Research in Industry (IWT).

References

1. Blockeel, H., and De Raedt, L. (1997) Experiments with Top-down Induction of Logical Decision Trees. *Artificial Intelligence.* Forthcoming.
2. Borrajo, D., and Veloso, M. (1997) Lazy incremental learning of control knowledge for efficiently obtaining quality plans. *AI Review*, 11(1-5): 371–405.
3. Breiman, L., Friedman, J. H., Olshen, R. A., and Stone, C. J. (1984) *Classification and Regression Trees.* Wadsworth, Belmont.
4. Blockeel, H., and De Raedt, L. (1997) Lookahead and discretization in ILP. In *Proc. 7th Intl. Workshop on Inductive Logic Programming*, pages 77–84, Springer, Berlin.
5. Chapman, D., and Kaelbling, L. (1991) Input generalization in delayed reinforcement learning: An algorithm and performance comparisons. In *Proc. 12th Intl. Joint Conf. on Artificial Intelligence*, Morgan Kaufmann, San Mateo, CA.
6. De Raedt, L., and Blockeel, H. (1997) Using logical decision trees for clustering. In *Proc. 7th Intl. Workshop on Inductive Logic Programming*, pages 133–141, Springer, Berlin.
7. Fikes, R.E., and Nilsson, N.J. (1971) STRIPS: A new approach to the application of theorem proving. *Artificial Intelligence*, 2(3/4): 189–208.
8. Kaelbling, L., Littman, M., and Moore, A. (1996) Reinforcement learning: A survey. *Journal of Artificial Intelligence Research*, 4: 237–285.
9. Kramer, S. (1996) Structural regression trees. In *Proc. 13th Natl. Conf. on Artificial Intelligence.* AAAI Press, Menlo Park, CA.
10. Lavrač, N. and Džeroski, S. (1994) *Inductive Logic Programming: Techniques and Applications.* Ellis Horwood, Chichester.
11. Mitchell, T. (1997) *Machine Learning.* McGraw-Hill, New York.
12. Muggleton, S., and De Raedt, L. (1994) Inductive logic programming : Theory and methods. *Journal of Logic Programming* 19/20: 629–679.
13. Tesauro, G. (1995) Temporal difference learning and TD-GAMMON. *Communications of the ACM*, 38(3): 58–68.
14. Watkins, C., and Dayan, P. (1992) Q-learning. *Machine Learning*, 8: 279–292.

Learning First-Order Acyclic Horn Programs from Entailment[*]

Chandra Reddy   Prasad Tadepalli

Dearborn 303
Department of Computer Science
Oregon State University,
Corvallis, OR 97331-3202.
{reddyc,tadepalli}@cs.orst.edu

Abstract. In this paper, we consider learning first-order Horn programs from entailment. In particular, we show that any subclass of first-order acyclic Horn programs with constant arity is exactly learnable from equivalence and entailment membership queries provided it allows a polynomial-time subsumption procedure and satisfies some closure conditions. One consequence of this is that first-order acyclic determinate Horn programs with constant arity are exactly learnable from equivalence and entailment membership queries.

1 Introduction

Learning first-order Horn programs—sets of first-order Horn clauses—is an important problem in inductive logic programming with applications ranging from speedup learning to grammatical inference.

We are interested in speedup learning, which concerns learning domain-specific control knowledge to alleviate the computational hardness of planning. One kind of control knowledge, which is particularly useful in many domains, is represented as goal-decomposition rules. Each decomposition rule specifies how a goal can be decomposed into a sequence of subgoals, given that a set of conditions is true in the initial problem state. Each of the subgoals might in turn have a set of decomposition rules, unless it is a primitive action, in which case it can be directly executed.

Unlike in logical inference, for which Horn clauses are ideally suited, in planning, one needs to keep track of time. In spite of this difference, goal-decomposition rules can be represented as first-order Horn clauses by adding two situation variables to each literal to indicate the time interval in which the literal is true. Hence, the problem of learning goal-decomposition rules for a *single* goal can be mapped to learning first-order Horn definitions—a set of Horn clauses, all having the same head or consequent literal. Learning goal-decomposition rules for *multiple* goals corresponds to learning first-order Horn programs. Henceforth, we omit the prefix "first-order", except when there is a possibility of ambiguity.

---

[*] This paper also appears in the proceedings of 15th International Conference on Machine Learning, 1998. Reprinted here with permission.

In learning from entailment, a positive (negative) example is a Horn clause that is implied (not implied) by the target. Results by Cohen (1995a, 1995b), Dzeroski et al. (1992) and others indicate that classes of Horn programs having a single or a constant number of clauses are learnable from examples. Khardon shows that "actions strategies" consisting of a variable number of constant-size first-order production rules can be learned from examples (Khardon, 1996). However, Cohen (1995a) proves that even predicting very restricted classes of Horn programs (viz. function-free 0-depth determinate constant arity) with variable number of clauses of variable size from examples alone is cryptographically hard.

Frazier and Pitt (1993) first used the entailment setting for learning arbitrary propositional Horn programs. In addition to examples, they also used entailment membership queries ("entailment queries" from now on) which ask if a Horn clause is entailed by the target. Moving to first order representations, Frazier and Pitt (1993) showed that CLASSIC sentences are exactly learnable in polynomial time from examples and entailment queries. A Horn clause is simple if the terms and the variables in the body of the clause are restricted to the terms that appear in the head. Page (1993) considered non-recursive Horn programs restricted to simple clauses and predicates of constant arity, and showed that they are learnable from examples and entailment queries. Arimura (1997) generalized Page's result to acyclic (possibly, recursive) simple Horn programs with constant-arity predicates. Reddy and Tadepalli (1997b) showed that function-free non-recursive Horn definitions are learnable from examples and entailment queries. The result we present here applies to non-generative Horn programs, where the variables and the terms in the head are restricted to those in the body. We show that acyclic non-generative Horn programs with constant arity that have polynomial-time subsumption procedure are learnable from examples and entailment queries when certain closure conditions are satisfied. In particular, the result applies to acyclic Horn programs with constant arity determinate clauses.

Goal-decomposition rules are hierarchical in nature, as are Horn programs. One aspect of learning in hierarchical domains is the hierarchical order of literals (goals or concepts). In many systems, learning hierarchically organized knowledge assumes that the structure of hierarchy or the order of the literals is known to the learner. Examples of such work include Marvin (Sammut & Banerji, 1986) and XLearn (Reddy & Tadepalli, 1997a), on the experimental side; learning from exercises by Natarajan (1989) and learning acyclic Horn sentences by Arimura (1997), on the theoretical side. In fact, Khardon shows that learning hierarchical strategies can be computationally hard when the structure of the hierarchy is not known (Khardon, 1996). Our algorithm also assumes that the hierarchical order of the literals is known.

The rest of the paper is organized as follows. Section 2 provides definitions for some of the terminology we use. Section 3 describes the learning model and the learning algorithm, and proves the learnability result. Section 4 concludes the paper with some discussion on implications and limitations of the work.

2   Preliminaries

In this section, we define and describe some of the terminology we use in the rest of the paper. For brevity, we omit some of the standard terminology (as given in books such as (Lloyd, 1987)). In the following, we use p and its variants, and a and its variants each to stand for a conjunction of literals; and b, q, l and their variants each to stand for a single literal.

Definition 1. A **definite Horn clause** (Horn clause or clause, for short) is a finite set of literals that contains exactly one positive literal—$\{l, \neg l_1, \neg l_2, \ldots, \neg l_n\}$. It is treated as a disjunction of the literals in the set with universal quantification over all the variables. Alternately, it is represented as $l_1, l_2, \ldots, l_n \to l$, where l is called the *head* or *consequent*, and $l_1, l_2, \ldots, l_n$ is called the *body* or *antecedent* and is interpreted as $l_1 \wedge l_2 \wedge \ldots \wedge l_n$. A **unit Horn clause** is a Horn clause with no negative literals and hence no body. A **Horn program** or **Horn sentence** is a set of definite Horn clauses interpreted conjunctively.

Definition 2. Let C_1 and C_2 be sets of literals. We say that C_1 **subsumes** C_2 (denoted $C_1 \succeq C_2$) iff there exists a substitution θ such that $C_1\theta \subseteq C_2$. We also say C_1 is a generalization of C_2.

Definition 3 (Plotkin, 1970). Let C, C', C_1 and C_2 be sets of literals. We say that C is the **least general generalization** (lgg) of C_1 and C_2 iff $C \succeq C_1$ and $C \succeq C_2$, and $C' \succeq C$, for any C' such that $C' \succeq C_1$ and $C' \succeq C_2$.

Definition 4 (Plotkin, 1970). A **selection** of clauses C_1 and C_2 is a pair of literals (l_1, l_2) such that $l_1 \in C_1$ and $l_2 \in C_2$, and l_1 and l_2 have the same predicate symbol, arity, and sign.

If C_1 and C_2 are sets of literals, then $lgg(C_1, C_2)$ is $\{lgg(l_1, l_2) : (l_1, l_2)$ is a selection of C_1 and $C_2\}$. If l is a predicate, $lgg(l(s_1, s_2, \ldots, s_n), l(t_1, t_2, \ldots, t_n))$ is $l(lgg(s_1, t_1), \ldots, lgg(s_n, t_n))$. The lgg of two terms $f(s_1, \ldots, s_n)$ and $g(t_1, \ldots, t_m)$, if $f = g$ and $n = m$, is $f(lgg(s_1, t_1), \ldots, lgg(s_n, t_n))$; else, it is a variable x, where x stands for the lgg of that pair of terms throughout the computation of the lgg of the set of literals.

As an example, let C_1 be $l(a, b), l(b, c), m(b) \to l(a, c)$, and C_2 be $l(1, 2), l(2, 3), m(2) \to l(1, 3)$. $(l(a, c), l(1, 3))$ and $(\neg m(b), \neg m(2))$ are two of the selections of C_1 and C_2. $lgg(C_1, C_2)$ is $l(x, y), l(y, z), l(t, u), l(v, w), m(y) \to l(x, z)$, where x, y, z, t, u, v and w are variables standing for the pairs $(a, 1), (b, 2), (c, 3), (a, 2), (b, 3), (b, 1)$ and $(c, 2)$.

Definition 5. A **derivation** of a Horn clause $p \to q$ from a Horn program H is a finite directed acyclic graph G such that there is a node q, there is no arc (q, r) in G, and for each node l in G, either $l \in p$ or if $(l_1, l), \ldots, (l_d, l)$ are the only arcs of G terminating at l, then $l_1, \ldots, l_d \to l = C\theta$ for some clause $C \in H$ and a substitution θ.

For example, let H be $\{parent(x, y), parent(y, z) \to grandParent(x, z); mother(x, y) \to parent(x, y)\}$. Figure 1 shows a derivation of $mother(a, b), mother(b, c) \to grandParent(a, c)$.

Proposition 6. *In a derivation G of a clause $p \to q$ from a Horn program H, for any node l, either l is in p or $H \models p \to l$.*

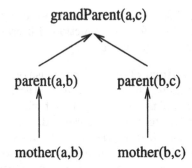

Fig. 1. A derivation of $mother(a, b)$, $mother(b, c) \rightarrow grandParent(a, c)$ from H.

Let P be a set of predicate symbols, and T be a set of terms. Let L be a set of atoms defined using P and T. Let $\mathcal{H}$ be a set of Horn programs using atoms in L only. If k is an integer, then P_k is a subset of P containing only those predicate symbols of arity k or less. Further, L_k is a set of atoms defined using P_k and T, and $\mathcal{H}_k$ is a set of Horn programs using atoms in L_k only. In the following three definitions, we describe a class of Horn programs AH_k for which minimal models are of polynomial size.

Definition 7 (Arimura, 1997). Let $\Sigma \in \mathcal{H}$. Then a binary relation **supported by** (denoted, $\succ$) over atoms in L w.r.t. Σ is such that (1) for all $p \rightarrow l \in \Sigma$, and for all $l_1 \in p$, $l \succ l_1$; (2) for all $l_1, l_2 \in L$ and every substitution θ, if $l_1 \succ l_2$, then $l_1\theta \succ l_2\theta$; and (3) if $l_1 \succ l_2$ and $l_2 \succ l_3$ then $l_1 \succ l_3$.

Definition 8. A Horn program Σ is **acyclic** over L if the relation $\succ$ over L w.r.t. Σ is terminating; i.e., for any $l \in L$, there is no infinite decreasing sequence $l \succ l_1 \succ \ldots$.

In the last example, H is acyclic because $grandParent(x, y) \succ parent(x, y) \succ mother(x, y)$ and there is no cycle formed by the $\succ$ relation.

Following Khardon (1998), we call a definite clause a *non-generative clause* if the set of terms in its consequent are a subset of the set of terms and subterms in its antecedent.

Definition 9. If k is a constant, we define a Horn program $\Sigma \in \mathcal{H}_k$ to be in the class AH_k, if Σ is acyclic over L_k, and each clause is either non-generative or has an empty antecedent.

Definition 10. Let $a \rightarrow b$ be a clause in a Horn program Σ, and $p \rightarrow q$ be a clause. Then, $a \rightarrow b$ is a **target clause** in Σ of $p \rightarrow q$ iff $a \rightarrow b \succeq p \rightarrow q$, i.e., for a substitution θ, $a\theta \subseteq p$, $b\theta = q$. We call $p \rightarrow q$ a **hypothesis clause** of $a \rightarrow b$.

Definition 11. For an antecedent p, q' is a **prime consequent** of p wrt Σ if $\Sigma \models p \rightarrow q'$, $q' \notin p$, and there is no $l \in L$ such that $q' \succ l$, $\Sigma \models p \rightarrow l$ and $l \notin p$.

In the last example, $parent(a, b)$ is a prime consequent of $mother(a, b)$, $mother(b, c)$, but $grandParent(a, c)$ is not—since $parent(a, b) \succ grandParent(a, c)$.

3 Learning Horn Programs

In this section, we show that a subclass of AH_k is exactly learnable, using the exact learning model (Angluin, 1988), in entailment setting. Henceforth, $\Sigma \in AH_k$ denotes a target Horn program.

3.1 The Learning Model

In learning from entailment, an example is a Horn clause. An example $p \to q$ is a positive example of Σ if $\Sigma \models p \to q$; negative, otherwise. An *entailment query* takes as input an example $(p \to q)$, and outputs *yes* if it is a positive example of Σ ($\Sigma \models p \to q$), and *no* otherwise. An *equivalence query* takes as input a Horn program H and outputs *yes* if H and Σ contain (entail) exactly the same Horn clauses; otherwise, returns a *counterexample* that is in (entailed by) exactly one of H and Σ. A *derivation-order query*, $\succ$, takes as input two atoms l_1 and l_2 in L and outputs *yes* if $l_1 \succ l_2$, and *no* otherwise. An algorithm *exactly learns* a Horn program Σ in AH_k in polynomial time from equivalence, entailment, and derivation-order ($\succ$) queries if and only if it runs in time polynomial in the size of Σ and in the size of the largest counterexample, and outputs a Horn program in AH_k such that equivalence query answers *yes*.

3.2 The Learning Algorithm

In this section, we describe the learning algorithm, PLearn, shown in Figure 2. PLearn always maintains a hypothesis H which is entailed by the target, so that every instance of H is also an instance of Σ and all counterexamples are positive.

Suppose that a counterexample $p \to q$ is given to the learner—see Figure 2. Every such counterexample has a derivation from the target theory, Σ. Since this derivation is not possible from the current hypothesis H, there is some clause used in the derivation that has not been learned with sufficient generality. The algorithm tries to identify the antecedent literals of such a clause, $c*$, in the target by expanding the derivation graph from its leaves in p toward the goal using the clauses in H. In other words, PLearn computes the minimal model (p'_f) of H implied by p ("closure" or "saturation") by forward chaining (line 4). To identify the consequent of $c*$, also called the "prime consequent" of p'_f, PLearn calls PrimeCons in line 5. PrimeCons finds the prime consequent of p'_f by tracing the "supported-by" chain starting from q for a literal q_f not in p'_f, but is directly supported by some of the literals in p'_f (lines 13–18). In line 6, PLearn makes use of Reduce to trim away "irrelevant" literals from the antecedent p'_f to form a new clause $p_f \to q_f$ that is also a counterexample to the hypothesis and is subsumed by a single target clause—see Lemmas 20,12,13.

PLearn combines $p_f \to q_f$ with an "appropriate" clause $p_i \to q_i$ in H using *lgg* (lines 7–9). It uses the entailment query to find an appropriate hypothesis clause by checking if the result of *lgg* is implied by the target (line 7). If no such clause exists in H, $p_f \to q_f$ is appended to H as a new clause (line 10).

One problem with this approach is that the size of the *lgg* is a product of the sizes of its two arguments. This causes the size of a hypothesis clause to grow exponentially in the number of examples combined with it in the worst case. To avoid this, the antecedent literals of the clause after lgg are again trimmed using Reduce so that the size of the resulting clause is bounded, while it is still subsumed by the target clause (lines 19–25). The result of Reduce then replaces the original hypothesis clause $p_i \rightarrow q_i$ it is derived from (line 9). After this step, only the antecedents of the target clause and some of their consequents remain in the resulting hypothesis clause—see Lemma 16. This process repeats until the hypothesis H is equivalent to Σ. The algorithm works for unit clauses (which have empty antecedents) without change.

PLearn
Given equivalence, entailment queries, and the derivation order $\succ$
outputs a Horn program H such that equivalent?(H, Σ) is *Yes*.
(1) $H = \{\}$ /* empty hypothesis-clauses set */
(2)   while not equivalent?(H, Σ) do {
(3)   Let $p \rightarrow q$ be the counterexample returned
(4) $p'_f = \{l : H \models (p \rightarrow l)\}$ /* forward chaining */
(5) $q_f = \text{PrimeCons}(p'_f \rightarrow q)$
(6) $p_f \rightarrow q_f = \text{Reduce}(p'_f \rightarrow q_f)$
(7)   if $\exists p_i \rightarrow q_i \in H$ such that $\Sigma \models p_g \rightarrow q_g$,
(8)   where $p_g \rightarrow q_g = lgg(p_i \rightarrow q_i, p_f \rightarrow q_f)$
(9)   then replace first such $p_i \rightarrow q_i$ by $\text{Reduce}(p_g \rightarrow q_g)$
(10)   else append $p_f \rightarrow q_f$ to H
(11) } /* while */
(12) return H

PrimeCons$(p \rightarrow q)$ /* finds prime consequents */
(13) Let L be the set of all possible literals having only those terms that are in p
(14) $q' = q$;
(15) $L' = \{l : l \in L - p \text{ and } \Sigma \models p \rightarrow l\}$
(16) while $\exists l \in L'$ such that $q' \succ l$
(17) $q' = l$;
(18) return q'

Reduce$(p \rightarrow q)$ /* trims irrelevant literals */
(19) $p' = p$
(20) repeat
(21)   for each literal l in p' in sequence do
(22)   if $\Sigma \not\models (p' - \{l\}) \rightarrow l$ and $\Sigma \models (p' - \{l\}) \rightarrow q$
(23)   then $p' = p' - \{l\}$
(24) until there is no change to p'
(25) return $p' \rightarrow q$

Fig. 2. PLearn Algorithm

3.3 An Example

As an example to see how PLearn works, consider $\Sigma = \{l_1(f(x)), l_2(x), l_3(x) \to l_4(x); l_1(f(x)), l_2(x) \to l_5(x); l_4(x), l_5(x) \to l_7(x)\}$ where f is a function symbol. Suppose $H = \{l_1(f(c)), l_2(c) \to l_5(c)\}$. We adopt the convention that the letters such as a, b, c, etc. at the beginning of the alphabet are constants and the letters at the end of the alphabet such as x, y, z, etc. are variables. Let the counterexample be $l_1(f(d)), l_2(d), l_3(d) \to l_7(d)$. In step 4, it does not change. In PrimeCons, since $l_7(d) \succ l_4(d)$ and $l_7(d) \succ l_5(d)$, $l_7(d)$ is not a prime consequent, but any one of $l_4(d)$ and $l_5(d)$ is. Suppose PrimeCons returns $l_5(d)$. Reduce eliminates $l_3(d)$ from the antecedent, because $\Sigma \models l_1(f(d)), l_2(d) \to l_5(d)$, and $\Sigma \not\models l_1(f(d)), l_2(d) \to l_3(d)$. Thus, $p_f \to q_f = l_1(f(d)), l_2(d) \to l_5(d)$. Combining this with the clause in H, we obtain $p_g \to q_g = l_1(f(x)), l_2(x) \to l_5(x)$ is entailed by Σ, new H is $\{l_1(f(x)), l_2(x) \to l_5(x)\}$.

Suppose the next counterexample is $l_1(f(c)), l_2(c), l_3(c) \to l_7(c)$. Then, $q_f = l_4(c)$, and $p'_f = \{l_1(f(c)), l_2(c), l_3(c), l_5(c)\}$. $p_f \to q_f = l_1(f(c)), l_2(c), l_3(c), l_5(c) \to l_4(c)$, since Reduce cannot remove $l_5(c)$, because it is implied by the other literals wrt Σ (line 22). The modified counterexample $p_f \to q_f$ cannot be combined with the clause in H, because the resultant $p_g \to q_g$ after lgg, $l_1(f(x)), l_2(x) \to$, is not entailed by Σ. Hence, it is appended to H to make $H = \{l_1(f(x)), l_2(x) \to l_5(x); l_1(f(c)), l_2(c), l_3(c), l_5(c) \to l_4(c)\}$.

Suppose the next counterexample is again $l_1(f(c)), l_2(c), l_3(c) \to l_7(c)$. After line 4, $p'_f = l_1(f(c)), l_2(c), l_3(c), l_5(c), l_4(c)$. q_f now is $l_7(c)$, because it is a prime consequent of p'_f. After Reduce, $p_f \to q_f = l_5(c), l_4(c)$. $p_f \to q_f$ cannot be combined with the clauses in H, because the resultant lgg's are not entailed by Σ. Again, $p_f \to q_f$ is added to H. This process continues until H and Σ are equivalent.

To bring out the nuances in Reduce, let us revisit the last part of the previous example. Consider the input $l_5(c), l_2(c), l_3(c), l_1(f(c)), l_4(c) \to l_7(c)$ to Reduce. Although $\Sigma \models l_1(f(c)), l_2(c), l_3(c) \to l_7(c)$, since $\Sigma \models l_1(f(c)), l_2(c), l_3(c) \to l_4(c)$ and $\Sigma \models l_1(f(c)), l_2(c) \to l_5(c)$, the literal $l_5(c)$ cannot be removed. This is because $l_5(c)$ is implied by the other literals $(l_1(f(c)), l_2(c))$ wrt Σ. The order in which the literals are removed in Reduce follows the derivation order: if $l_i \succ l_j$, if at all l_i is removed, it is removed after l_j is removed. This can be intuitively imagined in the following way. Consider a derivation tree for a counterexample, with the consequent literal on top and the antecedent literals at the bottom. The above process trims off the literals bottom-up in the tree up to the appropriate level, so that the resulting clause is subsumed by some clause in the target. In the above case, if Reduce removes $l_5(c)$ and leaves over $l_1(f(c)), l_2(c)$, the resulting clause $(l_1(f(c)), l_2(c), l_3(c), l_4(c) \to l_7(c))$ is not subsumed by any clause in Σ.

However, this means that Reduce leaves over literals which are implied by the remaining literals, i.e., l cannot be removed from p' if $\Sigma \models (p' - \{l\}) \to l$ (line 22). Removing such literals could result in hypothesis clauses which are not subsumed by any target clause, as the following example illustrates. Let Σ be $\{l_1(a) \to l_2(a); l_1(x), l_2(x) \to l_3(x)\}$. Suppose the first counterexample is $l_1(a), l_2(a) \to l_3(a)$. Hence $p'_f = \{l_1(a), l_2(a)\}$ and $q_f = l_3(a)$ in line 6. If Reduce were to remove $l_2(a)$ from p'_f because $\Sigma \models l_1(a) \to l_3(a)$, it ends up with a clause that is not subsumed by any target clause. We would like to prevent such redundant hypothesis clauses so that their number is not too high compared to the number of target clauses. (This argument is formalized in Lemmas 17, 18 and 19.)

3.4   Learnability of AH_k

In this section, we prove that PLearn algorithm in Figure 2 exactly learns a subclass of AH_k for which subsumption is of polynomial-time complexity. The plan of the proof is as follows: Through a series of lemmas, we first establish that every hypothesis clause learned has a target clause (Lemma 17). We then show that every target clause has at most one hypothesis clause (Lemma 19). Together, these two lemmas establish that the number of hypothesis clauses is bounded by the number of target clauses. We use this fact and the bounds of the sizes on the hypothesis clauses (established in Lemma 16) to show that PLearn learns successfully in polynomial time (Theorems 21 and 24). We then define a specific hypothesis class that obeys the conditions of these theorems and prove that this class is learnable (Theorem 26).

Lemmas 12 and 13 show that PrimeCons with the input $p \to q$ finds a (prime) consequent q' of p such that $p \to q'$ is subsumed by a clause in Σ.

Lemma 12. *Let $p \to q$ be the input and q' be the output of* PrimeCons. *Assume that $q \not\subseteq p$ and $\Sigma \models p \to q$. Then, (1)* PrimeCons *terminates; (2) q' is a prime consequent of p wrt Σ.*

Proof. (1) Since Σ is acyclic, there is a terminating sequence $q \succ l_1 \succ l_2 \ldots$. Since the loop of lines 16–17 can only iterate as many times as the length of the sequence, PrimeCons terminates.
(2) q' is such that $\Sigma \models p \to q'$, and $q' \not\subseteq p$ (by lines 15–17). Since q' is as in line 17 in the iteration immediately prior to the terminating iteration of lines 16–17, there is no l such that $q' \succ l$, $\Sigma \models p \to l$ and $l \not\subseteq p$. Thus, q' is a prime consequent of p wrt Σ. □

Lemma 13. *If q' is a prime consequent of p wrt Σ, then there is a clause $C \in \Sigma$ such that $C \succeq p \to q'$.*

Proof. Assume that q' is a prime consequent of p wrt Σ. Consider a derivation G of $p \to q'$ in Σ. Let $(l_1, q'), \ldots, (l_d, q')$ be the only arcs of G that terminate at q'. This implies that $q' \succ l_i$ for all $l_i \in \{l_1, \ldots, l_d\}$. It must be that every l_i is in p; otherwise, there is an l (viz. l_i) such that $q' \succ l$, $\Sigma \models p \to l$ and $l \not\subseteq p$— contradicting the assumption that q' is a prime consequent. Thus, $\{l_1, \ldots, l_d\} \subseteq p$. But, $l_1, \ldots, l_d \to q' = C\theta$ for some clause $C \in H$ and a substitution θ, following the definition of derivation. Thus, $C\theta \subseteq p \to q'$, implying that $C \succeq p \to q'$. □

The following definition and Lemmas 15 and 16 help show that Reduce, given a clause $p \to q$ as input, removes irrelevant literals from antecedent p, while maintaining q as a consequent.

Definition 14. *If a is a conjunction, **closure** of a with respect to Σ, denoted by κ_a, is defined as $\{l | \Sigma \models (a \to l)\}$.*

Lemma 15. *If q is a prime consequent of p and $p' \to q = \mathsf{Reduce}(p \to q)$, then q is a prime consequent of p' also.*

Proof. Because q is a prime consequent of p and $p' \subseteq p$, any literal other than the ones in $p - p'$, cannot be prime consequents of p'. By lines 22–23, only those literals l that are not supported by p' are removed. In which case, no literal l in $p - p'$, can be such that $\Sigma \models p' \rightarrow l$. Hence, q is a prime consequent of p' as well. $\square$

Lemma 16. *If the input $p \rightarrow q$ to* Reduce *is s.t. q is a prime consequent of p wrt Σ, then the output $p' \rightarrow q$ is such that $p' \subseteq \kappa_{a\theta}$ where $a \rightarrow b$ is a clause in Σ and $a\theta \subseteq p'$ and $b\theta = q$.*

Proof. Since q is a prime consequent of p, by Lemma 15, q is a prime consequent of p' also. Then, by Lemma 13, there is a clause $a \rightarrow b \in \Sigma$, and a θ such that $a\theta \subseteq p'$ and $b\theta = q$. We now show that $p' \subseteq \kappa_{a\theta}$. Assume that there exists a literal in $p' - \kappa_{a\theta}$. Let $l \in p' - \kappa_{a\theta}$ be a least such literal so that there is no literal l' in $p' - \kappa_{a\theta}$ such that $l \succ l'$. Such a literal must exist, because Σ is acyclic. There are two reasons for l to remain in $p' - \kappa_{a\theta}$: either (a) $\Sigma \not\models (p' - \{l\}) \rightarrow q$ or (b) $\Sigma \models (p' - \{l\}) \rightarrow l$. We disprove both the cases: (a) Since $a\theta \subseteq p'$, and l is not in $\kappa_{a\theta}$ and thus not in $a\theta$, $a\theta \subseteq (p' - \{l\})$. Therefore, $\Sigma \models (p' - \{l\}) \rightarrow q$. (b) The only other reason why l remains in p' is that $\Sigma \models (p' - \{l\}) \rightarrow l$. That means that $p' - \{l\}$ contains literals that imply l. There must be at least one such literal in p' that is not in $\kappa_{a\theta}$, or else $l \in \kappa_{a\theta}$, contradicting $l \in p' - \kappa_{a\theta}$. But then $p' - \kappa_{a\theta}$ contains literals l' such that $l \succ l'$, which contradicts the statement that there is no such l'. Thus, we disprove both the possibilities. Hence, $p' \subseteq \kappa_{a\theta}$. $\square$

Lemmas 17, 18 and 19, below, show that PLearn only maintains right clauses in H.

Lemma 17. *Every clause $p_i \rightarrow q_i \in H$ has a target clause.*

Proof. We first show that each $p_i \rightarrow q_i \in H$ is such that q_i is a prime consequent of p_i. Then, by Lemma 13, $p_i \rightarrow q_i$ has a clause $C \in \Sigma$ such that $C \succeq p_i \rightarrow q_i$.

We show that q_i is a prime consequent of p_i by induction on the number of times a clause at position i in H is updated. It is first introduced by line 10. By Lemmas 12 and 15, q_f is a prime consequent of p_f. This proves the base case. The other way a clause becomes a hypothesis clause is by line 9. The clause at position i in H ($p_i \rightarrow q_i$) is updated by line 9. As inductive hypothesis, assume that each $p_i \rightarrow q_i$ in H is such that q_i is a prime consequent of p_i, at the beginning of an iteration of the loop of lines 2–11 when position i in H is updated. Consider $p_g \rightarrow q_g = lgg(p_i \rightarrow q_i, p_f \rightarrow q_f)$. Suppose q_g is not a prime consequent of p_g, but q_g' such that $q_g \succ q_g'$ is. Let θ_f and θ_i be substitutions such that $p_g\theta_f \subseteq p_f$, $q_g\theta_f = q_f$, $p_g\theta_i \subseteq p_i$, and $q_g\theta_i = q_i$. Let $q_f' = q_g'\theta_f$ and $q_i' = q_g'\theta_i$. Since $q_g \succ q_g'$, by the definition of $\succ$ order, $q_f \succ q_f'$ and $q_i \succ q_i'$. Since q_f is a prime consequent of p_f, q_f' must be in p_f. Similarly, q_i' must be in q_i. Therefore, $lgg(q_i', q_f') = q_g'$ must be in p_g, contradicting the assumption that q_g' is a prime consequent of p_g. Hence, q_g is a prime consequent of p_g. By Lemma 15 if $p_i \rightarrow q_i =$ Reduce$(p_g \rightarrow q_g)$, then q_i is a prime consequent of p_i. So by Lemma 13, $p_i \rightarrow q_i$ has a target clause. $\square$

Lemma 18. *If PLearn combines a modified counterexample $p_f \rightarrow q_f$ with a clause $p_i \rightarrow q_i \in H$, then there is a target clause C s.t. $C \succeq p_f \rightarrow q_f$ and*

$C \succeq p_i \to q_i$. Further, there is no C' s.t. $C' \succeq p_j \to q_j$ and $C' \succeq p_f \to q_f$, for any $j < i$.

Proof. PLearn combines $p_f \to q_f$ with $p_i \to q_i$ only if $\Sigma \models lgg(p_i \to q_i, p_f \to q_f)$. By Lemma 17, q_g is a prime consequent of p_g where $p_g \to q_g = lgg(p_i \to q_i, p_f \to q_f)$. By Lemma 13, there is a $C \in \Sigma$ such that $C \succeq p_g \to q_g$. Hence, $C \succeq p_i \to q_i$ and $C \succeq p_f \to q_f$. Since $p_f \to q_f$ is combined with $p_i \to q_i$, for any $j < i$, $\Sigma \not\models lgg(p_j \to q_j, p_f \to q_f)$. Therefore, there is no C' s.t. $C' \succeq lgg(p_j \to q_j, p_f \to q_f)$. Thus, there is no C' s.t. $C' \succeq p_j \to q_j$ and $C' \succeq p_f \to q_f$. □

Lemma 19. *Every clause $C \in \Sigma$ has at most one hypothesis clause.*

Proof. First, we show that any new hypothesis clause added to H has a target clause distinct from the target clauses of the other hypothesis clauses in H. Next, we show that if two hypothesis clauses do not have common target clauses at the beginning of an iteration of the loop of lines 2–11, then they still have distinct target clauses at the end of the iteration.

When $p_f \to q_f$ is added to H, by Lemma 18, for any clause H_i in H, there is no $C \in \Sigma$ such that $C \succeq H_i$ and $C \succeq p_f \to q_f$. Therefore, $p_f \to q_f$, a new clause added to H, has a target clause distinct from the target clauses of the other hypothesis clauses then in H. Next, at most one of H_i and H_j can change in an iteration of the loop. If neither changes, we are done with the proof. Suppose that H_i changes, without loss of generality. Let C be any target clause of H_j. Assume that H_i and H_j do not have a common target clause at the beginning of an iteration. Hence, C is not a target clause of H_i. That is, $C \not\succeq H_i$. Let e be the counterexample for the current iteration. We first show that $lgg(H_i, e)$ does not have C as a target clause. Since $C \not\succeq H_i$, $C \not\succeq lgg(H_i, e)$. Therefore, C is not a target clause of $lgg(H_i, e)$. Let $lgg(H_i, e)$ be $p_g \to q_g$, and C be $a \to b$. Hence, for every θ, either $a\theta \not\subseteq p_g$ or $b\theta \neq q_g$. If $a\theta \not\subseteq p_g$, $a\theta$ is not a subset of any subset of p_g. Since Reduce outputs a clause with a subset of p_g as the antecedent and q_g as the consequent, $C \not\succeq \mathsf{Reduce}(lgg(H_i, e))$. Therefore, H_j and the new clause in position i, $\mathsf{Reduce}(lgg(H_i, e))$, do not have a common target clause even at the end of the iteration. □

The following lemma shows that even after the modifications due to Prime-Cons and Reduce counterexample remains a counterexample.

Lemma 20. *$p_f \to q_f$ as in line 6 of PLearn is a positive counterexample.*

Proof. First, we show that every counterexample $p \to q$, as in line 3, is a positive counterexample. Then, we argue that $p'_f \to q_f$ (lines 4 and 5) is also a positive counterexample. Finally, we show that $p_f \to q_f$ (line 6) is a positive counterexample.

Since, by Lemma 17, for every $H_i \in H$, there is a clause $C \in \Sigma$ such that $C \succeq H_i$, $\Sigma \not\models H$. Therefore, $p \to q$, as in line 3, is a positive counterexample. Since $p \subseteq p'_f$, $\Sigma \models p'_f \to q$. Since p'_f contains all and only those literals l such that $H \models p \to l$, for any literal $l' \notin p'_f$, $H \not\models p'_f \to l'$. Since q_f (by lines 5 and 15) is not in p'_f, $H \not\models p'_f \to q_f$. By line 15, $\Sigma \models p'_f \to q_f$. Therefore, $p'_f \to q_f$ is also a positive counterexample. Finally, since $p_f \subseteq p'_f$, $H \not\models p_f \to q_f$. By lines 6 and 22, $\Sigma \models p_f \to q_f$. Thus, $p_f \to q_f$ is a positive counterexample. $\square$

Finally, Theorem 21 shows that PLearn exactly learns AH_k when forward chaining using H is of polynomial-time complexity. Theorem 24 identifies conditions on Σ such that PLearn returns an H for which time complexity of forward chaining is polynomial.

Theorem 21. PLearn *exactly learns* AH_k *with equivalence,* $\succ$, *and entailment queries, provided that determining* $H \models p \to l$ *is polynomial in the sizes of* H *and* p.

Proof. By Lemma 20, $p_f \to q_f$ is a positive counterexample. For each counterexample, either a new antecedent is added (line 10) or an existing antecedent is replaced (line 9). In the latter case, the replaced clause $p_i \to q_i$ must be subsumed by the replacing clause $p' \to q_g$, since both lgg and Reduce generalize the original clause by turning constants to variables and dropping literals. On the other hand, the replaced clause must not subsume (and hence be different from) the replacing clause $p' \to q_g = \text{Reduce}(p_g \to q_g)$. If not, that is if $p_i \to q_i \succeq p' \to q_g$, since $p' \to q_g \succeq p_g \to q_g \succeq p_f \to q_f$, $p_i \to q_i \succeq p_f \to q_f$. Since $p_i \to q_i \in H$, $H \models p_f \to q_f$—thus contradicting that $p_f \to q_f$ was a counterexample of H. Hence, the replacement at a position in H changes the clause at that position. The minimum change there can be is either a variablization of a constant or a removal of a literal.

Let n be the number of clauses, and s be the number of distinct predicate symbols in Σ. Further, let the maximum number of terms in any clause be t, and in any counterexample be t_e.

The maximum possible number of literals there can be using t terms is at most st^k. Hence, the maximum number of literals in κ_a, and therefore, by Lemmas 16 and 17, in each clause is at most st^k. This includes all literals and their variablized versions. Hence, we can consider variablization as removing a literal. Thus, we need at most st^k counterexamples for each clause. (This includes one base counterexample to introduce a clause into H.) By Lemmas 17 and 19, there are at most n clauses in H. Hence, we need at most nst^k counterexamples or equivalence queries. A call to PrimeCons from line 5 takes at most st_e^k entailment queries, because the literals we need to try as possible consequents are all in L, and $|L| \leq st_e^k$. PrimeCons is called once for each of the counterexamples.

For each of the nst^k counterexamples, the condition in line 7 is tested at most n times, which needs at most n entailment queries. Reduce is called with the argument $p'_f \to q_f$ once for each of the counterexamples, and with the arguments $p_g \to q_g$ for at most nst^k counterexamples. In Reduce$(p \to q)$, in $|p|$ iterations of the loop of lines 21–23, at least one literal is removed. So, this loop can be tried at most $|p|$ times. Each iteration of the loop of lines 21–23 takes two entailment queries. Therefore, Reduce$(p \to q)$ needs at most $|p|(|p|+1)$ entailment queries. Hence, Reduce$(p'_f \to q_f)$ needs at most $n_f = st_e^k(st_e^k + 1)$ entailment queries. Since $p_i \to q_i$ and $p_f \to q_f$ are outputs of Reduce, the maximum possible number of literals in $p_g \to q_g = lgg(p_i \to q_i, p_f \to q_f)$ is at most s^2t^{2k}. Hence, Reduce$(p_g \to q_g)$ needs at most $n_g = s^2t^{2k}(s^2t^{2k} + 1)$ entailment queries. Thus, the total number of entailment queries is at most $nst^k(st_e^k + n + n_f + n_g)$.

If determining $H \models (p \to l)$ takes $\mathcal{P}(n, l, t_e)$ time where $\mathcal{P}$ is a polynomial, then line 4 takes at most $st_e^k \cdot \mathcal{P}(n, l, t_e)$ time. In the rest, the number of entailment queries dominates the time. Hence, the time taken by PLearn is polynomial in n, s, l, v, t, and t_e. □

Definition 22. Let $p \to q$ be a Horn clause. $p' \to q$ is called its **antecedent expansion** if $p \subseteq p'$ and p' contains only those variables in p. A class $\mathcal{C}$ of Horn sentences is closed under antecedent expansion, if every Horn sentence obtained by selecting a subset of its Horn clauses and replacing them with their antecedent expansions is also in $\mathcal{C}$.

Definition 23. A **subsumption algorithm** takes a clause $a \to b$, a conjunction of literals p, and a ground substitution θ for the variables in b, and returns true if and only if $a\theta \succeq p$.

Theorem 24. PLearn *exactly learns a subclass $\mathcal{C}$ of AH_k with equivalence, $\succ$, and entailment queries, provided that (a) $\mathcal{C}$ is closed under substitution and antecedent expansion and (b) the clauses $a \to b$ of the target concepts in $\mathcal{C}$ have a polynomial-time subsumption algorithm.*

Proof. By Lemma 16, each clause $p_i \to q_i \in H$ in PLearn has a target clause $a \to b$ and a substitution θ such that $a\theta \subseteq p_i \subseteq \kappa_{a\theta}$. Since the target class is closed under substitution and antecedent expansion, the hypothesis clauses have a polynomial-time subsumption algorithm. Hence, the forward-chaining step of computing the consequents of p in line 4 of PLearn can be done in polynomial time by repeatedly checking for a hypothesis clause $a \to b$ whose antecedent subsumes p after a substitution θ of the variables in b, and adding $b\theta$ to p. Hence, by the previous theorem, PLearn exactly learns $\mathcal{C}$. □

The following definition and theorem identify some syntactic restrictions on AH_k such that the resulting subclass satisfies the conditions of the previous theorem.

Definition 25. Let p be a set of literals. A Horn clause $l_1, \ldots, l_n \to q$ is *i*-**determinate** w.r.t. p iff there exists an ordering $l_{o_1}, \ldots, l_{o_n}$ of $l_1, \ldots, l_n$ such that for every $i < j \leq n$ and every substitution θ such that $(l_{o_1}, \ldots, l_{o_{j-1}} \to q)\theta$ is ground and $\{l_{o_1}, \ldots, l_{o_{j-1}}\}\theta \subseteq p$, there is at most one substitution α for the variables in $l_{o_j}\theta$ such that $l_{o_j}\theta\alpha$ is ground and is in p.[2] We call such an ordering of the literals in the clause an *i*-**determinate ordering** w.r.t. p. A Horn program is *i*-determinate w.r.t. p iff each of the clauses in the program is *i*-determinate w.r.t. p.

Theorem 26. *The class of i-determinate Horn programs in AH_k, denoted as $iDetAH_k$, is exactly learnable with equivalence, $\succ$, and entailment queries.*

---

[2] This definition strictly generalizes the standard definition of determinacy (Muggleton & Feng, 1990), in that a Horn clause (program) is determinate w.r.t. a set of literals p when it is 0-determinate w.r.t. p. *i*-determinacy should not be confused with *ij*-determinacy, or constant-depth fixed-arity determinacy, which is more restricted than determinacy.

Proof. First we show that $iDetAH_k$ is closed under substitution and antecedent expansion. Consider a target clause $(l_1, \ldots, l_n \to q)$ for a target program in $iDetAH_k$, whose antecedent literals are sorted in the determinate order. Let $(l_1, \ldots, l_n, l_{n+1}, \ldots, l_m \to q)\beta$ be the target clause after antecedent expansion and substitution. We want to show the new clause to be i-determinate.

For every set of literals p, substitution θ, and j such that $i < j \le m$ and $(l_1, \ldots, l_{j-1})\beta\theta \subseteq p$ is ground, there is a substitution γ which is equivalent to applying β and θ one after another so that $(l_1, \ldots, l_{j-1})\beta\theta = (l_1, \ldots, l_{j-1})\gamma$ and $l_j\beta\theta = l_j\gamma$ for any l_j. Since the target clause satisfies i-determinacy, there must be at most a single ground substitution α for $l_j\gamma$, $j \le n$, so that $l_j\gamma\alpha \in p$, which means that this is true for $l_j\beta\theta$ as well. Since the literals from l_{n+1} through l_m do not have any variables not already in l_1 through l_n, there is at most a single ground substitution for them as well. Hence, $(l_1, \ldots, l_m \to q)\beta$ is also i-determinate.

Now we show that the clauses of the programs in $iDetAH_k$ have a polynomial-time subsumption algorithm. Given a set of literals p and a clause $l_1, \ldots, l_n \to q$ (whose literals have an unknown determinate ordering), consider all possible subsets of $\{l_1, \ldots, l_n\}$ of size i and less. Note that there are at most $O(n^i)$ such subsets. For each such subset, instantiate all the ki variables in that subset in all possible ways. If the total number of terms in p and Σ is t, this gives us t^{ki} different substitutions. For each such substitution, there is at most one substitution for the remaining literals in the clause. The order in which the remaining literals have to be substituted can be determined by sequential search—apply the current substitution to each literal and pick the one that only allows one possible substitution for its remaining variables. This can be done in $O(n^2|p|)$ time. If the antecedent $l_1, \ldots, l_n$ subsumes p, then one of the considered subsets should yield a successful match. Hence, the total time for the algorithm is bounded by $O(n^i t^{ki} n^2 |p|)$, which is polynomial in all variables except k and i which are assumed to be constants.

Since the class $iDetAH_k$ satisfies the two conditions required by Theorem 24 for PLearn to be successful, the result follows. □

4 Discussion and Conclusions

In this paper, we have shown the learnability of certain subclasses of acyclic k-ary Horn programs. More specifically i-determinate Horn programs in AH_k, are exactly learnable with equivalence and entailment queries. Unlike the work of Page (1993) and Arimura (1997), the programs we considered allow local variables in the antecedents. However, the clauses must be non-generative in that the set of terms and variables that occur in the head of the clause must be a subset of those that occur in the body of the clause. This is needed to constrain the forward-chaining inference step to finish in polynomial-time, which could otherwise become unbounded. It appears that simultaneously removing both the non-generative and simplicity restrictions could be difficult when functions are present, due to the unbounded nature of inference in that case.

Learning from entailment and *learning from interpretations* are two of the standard settings for first-order learning (De Raedt, 1997). In learning from interpretations, the learner is given a positive (or negative) interpretation for which the Horn sentence is true (or false). Interpretations can be partial in that the truth values of some ground atoms may be left unspecified. When membership queries are available, learning from entailment and learning from interpretations are equivalent for Horn programs. Hence we can use PLearn to learn from (negative) interpretations as follows. Given a negative interpretation, "minimize" it by removing the negative literals from it and asking membership queries. Since every negative interpretation must violate some Horn clause, this yields an interpretation with a set of positive literals $l_1, \ldots, l_n$ and at most one negative literal q_i. We can convert this into a positive counterexample for PLearn: $l_1 \wedge \ldots \wedge l_n \rightarrow q_i$. Similarly, if PLearn asks an entailment membership query on some clause, say, $l_1 \wedge \ldots \wedge l_n \rightarrow q_i$, we can turn that into a membership query on the interpretation $l_1, \ldots, l_n, \neg q_i$ after substituting a unique skolem constant for each variable in the clause. The answer to the entailment query is *true* iff the answer to the membership query is *false*.

One limitation of our algorithm is that it assumes that the *supported by* relation, $\succ$, is given. While this is a reasonable assumption in some planning domains, where it is known which goals occur as subgoals of which, it is desirable to learn this relation. Unfortunately, this seems difficult due to a number of problems. One of the main difficulties is that it is sometimes not possible to determine which, of the set of consequents of an antecedent, is the prime consequent. For example, consider the target $\Sigma : \{l_1(x) \wedge l_2(x) \rightarrow l_3(x); l_1(x) \wedge l_3(x) \rightarrow l_4(x)\}$. Given the counterexample $l_1(c) \wedge l_2(c) \rightarrow l_4(c)$, the literal $l_4(c)$ is not a correct consequent, but $l_3(c)$ is. Although Lemma 13 says that prime consequent is a right consequent to choose, without knowing the order it is not clear how to identify it. Learning all possible clauses while maintaining all consequents also does not seem to work, resulting in spurious matches between some of these redundant clauses and counterexamples in some cases.

As shown in (Reddy & Tadepalli, 1997b), Horn programs can be used to express goal-decomposition rules (d-rules) for planning using the situation-calculus formalism. We believe that the algorithm discussed here and its extensions can be applied to learn d-rules, which is an important problem in speedup learning. d-rules are a special case of hierarchical task networks or HTNs (Erol, Hendler, & Nau, 1994)—in that HTNs allow partial ordering over subgoals and non-codesignation constraints over variables whereas d-rules do not. Nevertheless, it can be shown that HTNs can be expressed as Horn programs.

Acknowledgments We gratefully acknowledge the support of ONR under grant # N00014-95-1-0557 and NSF under grant # IRI-9520243. We thank Roni Khardon and the anonymous reviewers of ICML-98 and ILP-98 for their insightful comments.

References

Angluin, D. (1988). Queries and concept learning. *Machine Learning, 2,* 319–342.

Arimura, H. (1997). Learning acyclic first-order horn sentences from entailment. In *Proceedings of the Eigth International Workshop on Algorithmic Learning Theory.* Ohmsha/Springer-Verlag.

Cohen, W. (1995a). Pac-learning non-recursive prolog clauses. *Artificial Intelligence, 79*(1), 1–38.

Cohen, W. (1995b). Pac-learning recursive logic programs: efficient algorithms. *Jl. of AI Research*, *2*, 500–539.

De Raedt, L. (1997). Logical settings for concept learning. *Artificial Intelligence*, *95*(1), 187–201.

Džeroski, S., Muggleton, S., & Russell, S. (1992). Pac-learnability of determinate logic programs. In *Proceedings of the Fifth Annual ACM Workshop on Computational Learning Theory*, pp. 128–135.

Erol, K., Hendler, J., & Nau, D. (1994). HTN planning: complexity and expressivity. In *Proceedings of the Twelfth National Conference on Artificial Intelligence (AAAI-94)*. AAAI Press.

Frazier, M., & Pitt, L. (1993). Learning from entailment: An application to propositional Horn sentences. In *Proceedings of the Tenth International Conference on Machine Learning*, pp. 120–127.

Khardon, R. (1996). Learning to take actions. In *Proceedings of the Thirteenth National Conference on Artificial Intelligence (AAAI-96)*, pp. 787–792.

Khardon, R. (1998). Learning first order universal horn expressions. In *Proceedings of the Eleventh Annual Conference on Computational Learning Theory (COLT-98)*.

Lloyd, J. (1987). *Foundations of Logic Programming* (2nd ed.). Springer-Verlag, Berlin.

Muggleton, S., & Feng, C. (1990). Efficient induction of logic programs. In *Proceedings of the First Conference on Algorithmic Learning Theory*, pp. 368–381. Ohmsha/Springer-Verlag.

Natarajan, B. (1989). On learning from exercises. In *Proceedings of the Second Workshop on Computational Learning Theory*, pp. 72–87. Morgan Kaufmann.

Page, C. D. (1993). *Anti-Unification in Constraint Logics: Foundations and Applications to Learnability in First-Order Logic, to Speed-up Learning, and to Deduction*. Ph.D. thesis, University of Illinois, Urbana, IL.

Plotkin, G. (1970). A note on inductive generalization. In Meltzer, B., & Michie, D. (Eds.), *Machine Intelligence*, Vol. 5, pp. 153–163. Elsevier North-Holland, New York.

Reddy, C., & Tadepalli, P. (1997a). Learning goal-decomposition rules using exercises. In *Proceedings of the 14th International Conference on Machine Learning*. Morgan Kaufmann.

Reddy, C., & Tadepalli, P. (1997b). Learning Horn definitions using equivalence and membership queries. In *Proceedings of the 7th International Workshop on Inductive Logic Programming*. Springer Verlag.

Sammut, C. A., & Banerji, R. (1986). Learning concepts by asking questions. In *Machine learning: An artificial intelligence approach*, Vol. 2. Morgan Kaufmann.

Combining Statistical and Relational Methods for Learning in Hypertext Domains

Seán Slattery and Mark Craven

School of Computer Science,
Carnegie Mellon University
Pittsburgh, PA 15213-3891, USA
e-mail: ⟨firstname⟩.⟨lastname⟩@cs.cmu.edu

Abstract. We present a new approach to learning hypertext classifiers that combines a statistical text-learning method with a relational rule learner. This approach is well suited to learning in hypertext domains because its statistical component allows it to characterize text in terms of word frequencies, whereas its relational component is able to describe how neighboring documents are related to each other by hyperlinks that connect them. We evaluate our approach by applying it to tasks that involve learning definitions for (i) classes of pages, (ii) particular relations that exist between pairs of pages, and (iii) locating a particular class of information in the internal structure of pages. Our experiments demonstrate that this new approach is able to learn more accurate classifiers than either of its constituent methods alone.

1 Introduction

In recent years there has been a great deal of interest in applying machine-learning methods to a variety of problems in classifying and extracting information from text. In large part, this trend has been sparked by the explosive growth of the World Wide Web. An interesting aspect of the Web is that it can be thought of as a graph in which pages are the nodes of the graph and hyperlinks are the edges. The graph structure of the Web makes it an interesting domain for relational learning. In previous work [4], we demonstrated that for several Web-based learning tasks, a relational learning algorithm can learn more accurate classifiers than competing propositional approaches. In this paper, we present a new approach to learning hypertext classifiers that combines a statistical text-learning method with a relational rule learner. We present experiments that evaluate one particular instantiation of this general approach: a FOIL-based [14] learner augmented with the ability to invent predicates using a Naive Bayes text classifier. Our experiments indicate that this approach is able to learn classifiers that are often more accurate than either purely statistical or purely relational alternatives.

In previous research, the Web has provided a fertile domain for a variety of machine-learning tasks, including learning to assist users in searches, learning information extractors, learning user interests, and others. Most of the research in this field has involved (i) using propositional learners, and (ii) representing documents by the words that occur in them. Our approach is motivated by two key properties of hypertext:

- Documents (i.e. pages) are related to one another by hyperlinks. Important sources of evidence for Web learning tasks can often be found in neighboring pages and hyperlinks.
- Large feature sets are needed to represent the content of documents because natural language involves large vocabularies. Typically, text classifiers have feature spaces of hundreds or thousands of words.

Because it uses a relational learner, our approach is able to represent document relationships (i.e. arbitrary parts of the hypertext graph) in its learned definitions. Because it also uses a statistical learner with a feature-selection method, it is able to learn accurate definitions in domains with large vocabularies. Although our algorithm was designed with hypertext in mind, we believe it is applicable to other domains that involve both relational structure and large feature sets.

In the next section we describe the commonly used *bag-of-words* representation for learning text classifiers. We describe the use of this representation with the Naive Bayes algorithm, which is often applied to text learning problems. We then describe how a relational learner, such as FOIL, can use this bag-of-words representation along with background relations describing the connectivity of pages for hypertext learning tasks. In Section 3, we describe our new approach to learning in hypertext domains. Our method is based on the Naive Bayes and FOIL algorithms presented in Section 2. In Section 4 we empirically evaluate our algorithm on three types of tasks – learning definitions of page classes, learning definitions of relations between pages, and learning to locate a particular type of information within pages – that we have investigated as part of an effort aimed at developing methods for automatically constructing knowledge bases by extracting information from the Web [3]. Finally, Section 5 provides conclusions and discusses future work.

2 Two Approaches to Hypertext Learning

In this section we describe two approaches to learning in text domains. First we discuss the *Naive Bayes* algorithm, which is commonly used for text classification, and then we describe an approach that involves using a relational learning method, such as FOIL, for such tasks. These two algorithms are the constituents of the hybrid algorithm that we present in the next section.

2.1 Naive Bayes for Text Classification

Most work in learning text classifiers involves representing documents using a *bag-of-words* representation. In this representation, each document is described by a feature vector consisting of one feature for each word in the document. These features can be either boolean (indicating the presence or absence of a word), or continuous (indicating some measure of the frequency of the word). The key assumption made by the bag-of-words representation is that the position of a word in a document does not matter (i.e. encountering the word *machine* at the beginning of a document is the same as encountering it at the end).

One common approach to text classification is to use a Naive Bayes classifier with a bag-of-words representation [12]. Using this method to classify a document with n words $(w_1, w_2, \ldots, w_n)$ into one of a set of classes C, we simply calculate:

$$\arg\max_{c_j \in C} \Pr(c_j) \prod_{i=1}^{n} \Pr(w_i|c_j). \tag{1}$$

In order to make the word probability estimates $\Pr(w_i|c_j)$ robust with respect to infrequently encountered words, it is common to use a smoothing method to calculate them. Once such smoothing technique is to use Laplace estimates:

$$\Pr(w_i|c_j) = \frac{N(w_i, c_j) + 1}{N(c_j) + T} \tag{2}$$

where $N(w_i, c_j)$ is the number of times word w_i appears in training set examples from class c_j, $N(c_j)$ is the total number of words in the training set for class c_j and T is the total number of unique words in the corpus.

In addition to the position-independence assumption implicit in the bag-of-words representation, Naive Bayes also makes the assumption that the occurrence of a given word in a document is independent of all other words in the document. Clearly, this assumption does not hold in real text documents. However, in practice Naive Bayes classifiers often perform quite well [10].

Since document corpora typically have vocabularies of thousands of words, it is common in text learning to use some type of feature selection method. Frequently used methods include (i) dropping putatively un-informative words that occur on a *stop-list*, (ii) dropping words that occur fewer than a specified number of times in the training set, (iii) ranking words by a measure such as their mutual information with the class variable, and then dropping low-ranked words [17], and (iv) *stemming*. Stemming refers to the process of heuristically reducing words to their root form. For example the words *compute, computers* and *computing* would be stemmed to the root *comput*. Even after employing such feature-selection methods, it is common to use feature sets consisting of hundreds or thousands of words.

2.2 Relational Text Learning

Both propositional and relational symbolic rule learners have also been used for text learning tasks [1, 2, 13]. We argue that relational learners are especially appealing for learning in hypertext domains because they enable learned classifiers to represent the relationships among documents as well as information about the occurrence of words in documents. In previous work [4], we demonstrated that this ability enables relational methods to learn more accurate classifiers than propositional methods in some cases.

In Section 4, we present experiments in which we apply FOIL to several hypertext learning tasks. The problem representation we use for our relational learning tasks consists of the following background relations:

- link_to(Hyperlink, Page, Page) : This relation represents Web hyperlinks. For a given hyperlink, the first argument specifies an identifier for the hyperlink, the second argument specifies the page in which the hyperlink is located, and the third argument indicates the page to which the hyperlink points.
- has_*word*(Page) : This set of relations indicates the words that occur on each page. There is one predicate for each word in the vocabulary, and each instance indicates an occurrence of the word in the specified page.
- has_anchor_*word*(Hyperlink) : This set of relations indicates the words that are found in the anchor (i.e., underlined) text of each hyperlink.
- has_neighborhood_*word*(Hyperlink): This set of relations indicates the words that are found in the "neighborhood" of each hyperlink. The neighborhood of a hyperlink includes words in a single paragraph, list item, table entry, title or heading in which the hyperlink is contained.
- all_words_capitalized(Hyperlink) : The instances of this relation are those hyperlinks in which all words in the anchor text start with a capital letter.
- has_alphanumeric_word(Hyperlink) : The instances of this relation are those hyperlinks which contain a word with both alphabetic and numeric characters (e.g., I teach CS760).

This representation for hypertext enables the learner to construct definitions that describe the graph structure of the Web (using the link_to relation) and word occurrences in pages and hyperlinks. The has_*word*, has_anchor_*word*, has_neighborhood_*word* predicates provide a bag-of-words representation of pages and hyperlinks. Note that we do not use theory constants to represent words because doing so would require the relational learner we use (FOIL) to add two literals to a clause for each word test, instead of one as in our representation.

3 Combining the Statistical and Relational Approaches

In this section we present an approach that combines a statistical text learner with a relational learner. We argue that this algorithm is well suited to hypertext learning tasks. Like a conventional bag-of-words text classifier, our algorithm is able to learn predicates that characterize pages or hyperlinks by their word statistics. However, because it is a relational learning method, it is also able to represent the graph structure of the Web, and thus it can represent the word statistics of neighboring pages and hyperlinks.

As described in the previous section, a conventional relational learning algorithm, such as FOIL, can also use employ a bag-of-words representation when learning in hypertext domains. We hypothesize, however, that our algorithm has two properties that make it better suited to such tasks than an ordinary relational method:

Input: uncovered positive examples T^+, all negative examples T^- of target relation R, background relations

1. initialize clause C: $R(X_0, ...X_k)$:- *true*.
2. $T = T^+ \cup T^-$
3. while T contains negative tuples and C is not too complex
4.   call predicate-invention method to get new candidate literals (Figure 2)
5.   select literal (from background or invented predicates) to add to C
6.   update tuple set T to represent variable bindings of updated C
7.   for each invented predicate $P_j(X_i)$
8.   if $P_j(X_i)$ was selected for C then retain it as a background relation

Return: learned clause C

Fig. 1. The inner loop of FOIL-PILFS. This is essentially the inner loop of FOIL augmented with our predicate invention procedure.

- Because it characterizes pages and hyperlinks using a statistical method, its learned rules will not be as dependent on the presence or absence of specific key words as a conventional relational method. Instead, the statistical classifiers in its learned rules consider the weighted evidence of many words.
- Because it learns each of its statistical predicates to characterize a specific set of pages or hyperlinks, it can perform feature selection in a more directed manner. The vocabulary to be used when learning a given predicate can be selected specifically for the particular classification task at hand. In contrast, when selecting a vocabulary for a relational learner that represents words using background relations, the vocabulary is pruned without regard to the particular subsets of pages and hyperlinks that will be described in clauses, since *a priori* we do not know which constants these subsets will include.

We consider our approach to be quite general: it involves using a relational learner to represent graph structure, and a statistical learner with a feature-selection method to characterize the edges and nodes of the graph. Here we present an algorithm, which we refer to as FOIL-PILFS (for FOIL with Predicate Invention for Large Feature Spaces), that represents one particular instantiation of our approach. This algorithm is basically FOIL, augmented with a predicate-invention method in the spirit of CHAMP [9]. Figure 1 shows the inner loop of FOIL-PILFS (which learns a single clause) and its relation to its predicate invention method, which is shown in Figure 2

The predicates that FOIL-PILFS invents are statistical classifiers applied to some textual description of pages, hyperlinks, or components thereof. Currently, the invented predicates are only unary, boolean predicates. We assume that each constant in the problem domain has a type, and that each type may have one or more associated document collections. Each constant of the given type maps to a unique document in each associated collection. For example, the type *page* might

---

Input: partial clause C, document collection for each type, parameter ϵ

1.   for each variable X_i in C
2.   for each document collection D_j associated with the *type* of X_i
3. $S^+ = $ documents in D_j representing constants bound to X_i in pos tuples
4. $S^- = $ documents in D_j representing constants bound to X_i in neg tuples
5.   rank each word in $S^+ \cup S^-$ according to mut. info. w/ class variable
6. $n = |S^+ \cup S^-| \times \epsilon$
7. $F = $ top ranked n words
8.   call Naive Bayes to learn $P_j(X_i)$ w/ feature set F, training set $S^+ \cup S^-$

Return: all learned predicates $P_j(X_i)$

Fig. 2. The FOIL-PILFS predicate invention method.

be associated with a collection of documents that represent the words in pages, and the type *hyperlink* might be associated with two collections of documents – one which represents the words in the anchor text of hyperlinks and one which represents the "neighboring" words of hyperlinks.

Whereas CHAMP considers inventing a new predicate only when the basic relational algorithm fails to find a clause, our method considers inventing new predicates at each step of the search for a clause. Specifically, at some point in the search, given a partial clause C that includes variables $X_1, ..., X_n$, our method considers inventing predicates to characterize each X_i for which the variable's type has an associated collection of documents. If there is more than one document collection associated with a type, then we consider learning a predicate for each collection. For example, if X_i is of type *hyperlink*, and we have two document collections associated with *hyperlink* – one for anchor text and one for "neighboring" text – then we would consider learning one predicate to characterize the constants bound to X_i using their anchor text, and one predicate to characterize the constants using their "neighboring" text.

Once the method has decided to construct a predicate on a given variable X_i using a given document collection, the next step is to assemble the training set for the Naive Bayes learner. If we think of the tuple set currently covered by C as a table in which each row is a tuple and each column corresponds to a variable in the clause, then the training set consists of those constants appearing in the column associated with X_i. Each row corresponds to either the extension of a positive training example or the extension of a negative example. Thus those constants that appear in positive tuples become positive instances for the predicate-learning task and those that appear in negative tuples become negative instances. One issue that crops up, however, is that a given constant might appear multiple times in the X_i column, and it might appear in both positive and negative tuples. We enforce a constraint that a constant may appear only once in the predicate's training set. For example, if a given constant is bound to X_i in multiple positive tuples, it appears as only a single instance in the training set for a predicate. The motivation for this choice is that we want to learn Naive Bayes classifiers that generalize well to new documents. Thus we want the learner to focus on the characteristics that are common to many of the documents in the training set, instead of focusing on the characteristics of a few instances that each occur many times in the training set.

Before learning a predicate using this training set, our method determines the vocabulary to be used by Naive Bayes. In some cases the predicate's training set may consist of a small number of documents, each of which might be quite large. Thus, we do not necessarily want to allow Naive Bayes to use all of the words that occur in the training set as features. The method that we use involves the following two steps. First, we rank each word w_i that occurs in the predicate's training set according to its mutual information with the target class for the predicate. Second, given this ranking, we take the vocabulary for the Naive Bayes classifier to be the n top-ranked words where n is determined as follows:

$$n = \epsilon \times m. \tag{3}$$

Here m is the number of instances in the predicate's training set, and ϵ is a parameter (set to 0.05 throughout our experiments).

The motivation for this heuristic is the following. We want to make the dimensionality (i.e. feature-set size) of the predicate learning task small enough such that if we find a predicate that fits its training set well, we can be reasonably confident that it will generalize to new instances of the "target class." A lower bound on the number of examples required to PAC-learn some target function $f \in F$ is [8]:

$$m = \Omega \left(\frac{\text{VC-dimension}(F)}{\epsilon} \right) \tag{4}$$

where ϵ is the usual PAC error parameter. We use this bound to get a rough answer to the question: *given m training examples, how large of a feature space can we consider such that if we find a promising predicate with our learner in this feature space, we have some assurance that it will generalize well?* The VC-dimension of a two-class Naive Bayes learner is $n + 1$ where n is the number of features. Ignoring constant factors, and solving for n we get Equation 3. Note that this method is only a heuristic. It does not provide any theoretical guarantees about the accuracy of learned clauses since it makes several assumptions (e.g., that the "target function" of the predicate is in F) and does not consider the broader issue of the accuracy of the clause in which the literal will be used.

Another issue is how to set the class priors in the Naive Bayes classifier. Typically, these are estimated by the class frequencies in the training data. These estimates are likely to be biased towards the positive class in our context, however. Consider that estimating the accuracy of a (partially grown) clause by the fraction of positive training-set tuples it covers will usually result in a biased estimate. To compensate for this bias, we simply set the class priors to the uniform distribution. Moreover, when a document does not contain any of the words in the vocabulary of one of our learned classifiers, we assign the document to the negative class (since the priors do not enforce a default class).

Finally, after the candidate Naive-Bayes predicates are constructed, they are evaluated like any other candidate literal. Those Naive-Bayes predicates that are included in clauses are retained as new background relations so that they may be incorporated into subsequent clauses. Those that are not selected are discarded.

Although our Naive Bayes classifiers produce probabilities for each instance, we do not use these probabilities in our constructed predicates nor in the evaluation of our learned clauses. Naive Bayes' probability estimates are usually poor when its independence assumption is violated, although its predictive accuracy is often quite good in such situations [6].

4 Experimental Evaluation

At the beginning of Section 3, we stated that our FOIL-PILFS algorithm has two desirable properties:

- Because it characterizes pages and hyperlinks using a statistical method such as Naive Bayes, its learned rules will not be dependent on the presence or absence of specific key words. Instead, the statistical classifiers used in its learned rules consider the weighted evidence of many words.
- Because it learns each of its statistical predicates to characterize a specific set of pages or hyperlinks, it can perform feature selection in a directed manner. The vocabulary to be used when learning a given predicate can be selected specifically for the particular classification task at hand.

In this section we test the hypothesis that this approach will learn definitions with higher accuracy than a comparable relational method without the ability to use such statistical predicates. Specifically, we compare our FOIL-PILFS method to ordinary FOIL on several hypertext learning tasks.

4.1 The University Data Set

Our primary data set for these experiments is one assembled for a research project aimed at extracting knowledge bases from the Web [3]. This project encompasses many learning problems and we study two of those here. The first is to recognize instances of knowledge base *classes* (e.g. students, faculty, courses etc.) on the Web. In some cases, this can be framed as a page-classification task. We also want to recognize *relations* between objects in our knowledge base. Our approach to this task is to learn prototypical patterns of hyperlink connectivity among pages. For example, a course home page containing a hyperlink with the text `Instructor: Tom Mitchell` pointing to the home page of a faculty member could be a positive instance of the instructors_of_course relation.

Our data set consists of pages and hyperlinks drawn from the Web sites of four computer science departments. This data set includes 4,127 pages and 10,945 hyperlinks interconnecting them. Each of the pages is labeled as being the home page of one seven classes: course, faculty, student, project, staff, department, and the catch-all other class.

The data set also includes instances of the relations between these entities. Each relation instance consists of a pair of pages corresponding to the class instances involved in the relation. For example, an instance of the instructors_of_course relation consists of a course home page and a person home page. Our data set of relation instances comprises 251 instructors_of_course instances, 392 members_of_project instances, and 748 department_of_person instances. The complete data set is available at http://www.cs.cmu.edu/~WebKB/.

All of the experiments presented with this data set use *leave-on-university-out* cross-validation, allowing us to study how a learning method performs on data from an unseen university. This is important because we evaluate our knowledge base extractor on previously unseen Web sites.

4.2 The Representations

For the experiments in Sections 4.3 and 4.4, we give FOIL the background predicates described in Section 2.2. One issue that arises in using the predicates that represent words in pages and hyperlinks is selecting the vocabulary for each one. For our experiments, we remove *stop-words* and apply a stemming algorithm to the remaining words (refer back to Section 2 for descriptions of these processes). We then use frequency-based vocabulary pruning as follows:

- has_word (Page) : We chose words that occur at least 200 times in the training set. This procedure results in 607 to 735 predicates for each training set.
- has_anchor_word(Hyperlink) : The vocabulary for this set of relations includes words that occur at least three times among the hyperlinks in the training set. This results in 637 to 735 predicates, depending on the training set.
- has_neighborhood_word(Hyperlink): The vocabulary for this set of relations includes words that occur at least five times among the hyperlinks in the training set. This set includes 633 to 1025 predicates, depending on the training set.

The FOIL-PILFS algorithm is given as background knowledge the relations listed in Section 2.2, *except for* the three predicates above. Instead, it is given the ability to invent predicates that describe the words in pages and the anchor and neighboring text of hyperlinks. Effectively, the two learners have access to the same information as input. The key difference is that whereas ordinary FOIL is given this information in the form of background predicates, we allow FOIL-PILFS to reference page and hyperlink words only via invented Naive-Bayes predicates.

4.3 Experiments in Learning Page Classes

To study page classification, we pick the four largest classes from our university data set: student, course, faculty and project. Each of these classes in turn is the positive class for four binary page classification problems. For example, we learn a classifier to distinguish student home pages from all other pages. We run FOIL and FOIL-PILFS on these tasks, as well as a Naive Bayes classifier applied directly to the pages.

Table 1. Recall (R), precision (P) and F_1 scores on each of the classification tasks for Naive Bayes, FOIL, and FOIL-PILFS

method	student			course			faculty			project		
	R	P	F_1	R	P	F_1	R	P	F_1	R	P	F_1
Naive Bayes	52.1	42.3	46.7	46.3	29.6	36.1	22.2	20.1	21.1	1.2	16.7	2.2
FOIL	36.0	61.1	45.3	45.5	51.2	48.2	32.7	50.0	39.5	2.4	13.3	4.0
FOIL-PILFS	38.9	66.2	49.0	48.8	59.5	53.6	38.6	45.7	41.8	13.1	17.5	15.0

Table 2. Pairwise comparison of the classifiers. For each pairing, the number of times one classifier performed better than the other on recall (R) and precision (P) is shown.

	R wins	P wins		R wins	P wins		R wins	P wins
Naive Bayes	6	2	Naive Bayes	4	1	FOIL	4	7
FOIL	8	12	FOIL-PILFS	9	14	FOIL-PILFS	10	8

Table 1 shows the recall (R) and precision (P) results on our four classification tasks. Recall and precision are defined as follows:

$$R = \frac{\text{\# correct positive examples}}{\text{\# of positive examples}} , P = \frac{\text{\# correct positive examples}}{\text{\# of positive predictions}} .$$

Also shown is the F_1 score [11, 16] for each algorithm on each task. This is a score commonly used in the information-retrieval community which weights precision and recall equally and has nice measurement properties. It is defined as:

$$F_1 = \frac{2PR}{P + R}.$$

Comparing the F_1 scores first, we see that both FOIL and FOIL-PILFS outperform Naive Bayes on all tasks, except for **student**, where FOIL lags slightly behind. More importantly, we observe that our new combined algorithm outperforms FOIL on all four classification tasks.

Comparing the precision and recall results for FOIL and FOIL-PILFS we see that in all but one case FOIL-PILFS outperforms FOIL. The increased recall performance is not surprising, given the statistical nature of the predicates being produced. They test the aggregate distribution of words in the test document (or hyperlink), rather than depending on the presence of distinct keywords. Apart from the faculty task, we also see an increase in precision. This suggests that our statistical predicates are not only more generally applicable, but they are also better able to describe the concept being learned. However, since FOIL-PILFS can potentially use all the words in the training set, while FOIL can only use the reduced set of words provided to it, the increase in precision may become less pronounced when FOIL is given a larger vocabulary.

Pairwise comparisons of the three algorithms are shown in Table 4.3. Here we see, for each pair of learning methods, how often one of them outperformed the

course_page(A) :- page_naive_bayes_1(A), link_to(B,A,C), anchor_naive_bayes_1(B),
        page_naive_bayes_2(A).

  page_naive_bayes_1 homework, handout, assign, exam, lectur, class, hour, ...
  anchor_naive_bayes_1 assign, homework, lectur, syllabu, project, solution, note, ...
  page_naive_bayes_2 upson, postscript, textbook.

Fig. 3. Clause learned by FOIL-PILFS which covers 43 positive and no negative training examples. On the unseen test set, it covers 16 course pages and 2 non-course pages. Also shown are the words with the greatest log-odds ratios for each invented predicate.

other on one of the cross validation runs. For example, of the 16 cross validation runs performed, FOIL had better recall than Naive Bayes 8 times, and had better precision 12 times. Confirming the results using the F_1 score above, we see that FOIL-PILFS does indeed seem to outperform FOIL which is turn outperforms Naive Bayes on these four problems.

Figure 3 shows one of the most accurate clauses learned by FOIL-PILFS. This clause uses three invented predicates, two which test the distribution of words on the page to be classified (A), and one which tests the distribution of words in a hyperlink on this page (B). The highly weighted words from each of these predicates seem intuitively reasonable for testing whether a page is the home page of a course. Note that the page_naive_bayes_2 predicate uses only six words, and only three of them have positive log-odds ratios.

4.4 Experiments in Learning Page Relations

In this section we consider learning target concepts that represent specific relations between pairs of pages. We learn definitions for the three relations described in Section 4.1. In addition to the positive instances for these relations, each data set includes approximately 300,000 negative examples. Our experiments here involve one additional set of background relations: class(Page). For each class from the previous section, the corresponding relation lists the pages that represent instances of class. These instances are determined using actual classes for pages in the training set and predicted classes for pages in the test set.

As in the previous section, we learn the target concepts using both (i) a relational learner given background predicates that provide a bag-of-words representation of pages and hyperlinks, and (ii) a version of our FOIL-PILFS algorithm. The base algorithm we use here is slightly different than FOIL, however.

In previous work, we have found that FOIL's hill-climbing search is not well suited to learning these relations for cases in which the two pages of an instance are not directly connected. Thus, for the experiments in this section, we augment both algorithms with a deterministic variant of Richards and Mooney's *relational pathfinding* method [15]. The basic idea underlying this method is that a relational problem domain can be thought of as a graph in which the nodes are the domain's constants and the edges correspond to relations which hold among constants. The algorithm tries to find a small number of prototypical paths in

Table 3. Recall (R), precision (P) and F_1 results for the relation learning tasks.

method	department_of_person			instructors_of_course			members_of_project		
	R	P	F_1	R	P	F_1	R	P	F_1
PATH-FOIL	45.7	82.0	58.7	66.5	86.1	75.1	58.2	70.2	63.6
PATH-FOIL-PILFS	81.4	88.3	84.7	58.2	83.9	68.7	55.4	60.1	57.6

Table 4. Recall (R) and precision (P) results for the relation learning tasks.

method	department_of_person		instructors_of_course		members_of_project	
	R wins	P wins	R wins	P wins	R wins	P wins
PATH-FOIL	0	0	2	1	1	1
PATH-FOIL-PILFS	2	3	1	2	2	3

this graph that connect the arguments of the target relation. Once such a path is found, an initial clause is formed from the relations that constitute the path, and the clause is further refined by a hill-climbing search.

Also, like Džeroski and Bratko's m-FOIL [7], both algorithms considered here use m-estimates of a clause's error to guide its construction. We have found that this evaluation function results in fewer, more general clauses for these tasks than FOIL's information gain measure.

As in the previous experiment, the only difference between the two algorithms we compare here is the way in which they use predicates to describe word occurrences. We do not consider directly applying the Naive Bayes method in these experiments since the target relations are of arity two and necessarily require a relational learner.

Table 3 shows recall, precision, and F_1 results for the three target relations. For department_of_person, PATH-FOIL-PILFS provides significantly better recall and precision than PATH-FOIL. For the other two target concepts, PATH-FOIL seems to have an edge in both measures. Table 4, however, shows the number of cross-validation folds for which one algorithm outperformed another. As this table shows, PATH-FOIL-PILFS is decisively better for department_of_person, but that neither algorithm is clearly superior for the other two relations.

4.5 Relational Learning and Internal Page Structure

So far we have considered relational learning applied to tasks that involve representing the relationships *among* hypertext documents. Hypertext documents, however, have internal structure as well. In this section we apply our learning method to a task that involves representing the internal layout of Web pages. Specifically, the task we address is the following: given a reference to a country name in the Web page of a company, determine if the company has operations in that country or not.

Table 5. Recall (R), precision (P), and F_1 results for the node classification task.

method	R	P	F_1	R wins	P wins
FOIL	55.5	64.0	59.5	1	1
FOIL-PILFS	64.4	66.6	65.5	4	4

Our approach makes use of an algorithm that parses Web pages into tree structures representing the layout of the pages [5]. For example, one node of the tree might represent an HTML table where its ancestors are the HTML headings that come above it in the page. In general any node in the tree can have some text associated with it. We frame our task as one of classifying nodes that contain a country name in their associated text.

In our experiments here we apply FOIL and FOIL-PILFS to this task using the following background relations:

- heading(Node, Page), li(Node, Page), list(Node, Page), list_or_table(Node, Page), paragraph(Node, Page), table(Node, Page), td(Node, Page), title(Node, Page), tr(Node, Page): These predicates list the nodes of each given type, and the page in which a node is contained. The types correspond to HTML elements.
- ancestor(Node, Node), parent(Node, Node), sibling(Node, Node), ancestor_heading(Node, Node), parent_heading(Node, Node): These predicates represent relations that hold among the nodes in a tree.

The target relation, has_location(Node, Page), is a binary relation so that the learner can easily relate nodes by their common page as well as by their relationship in the tree. In a setup similar to our previous experiments, we give FOIL a set of has_node_word(Node) predicates, and we allow FOIL-PILFS to invent predicates that characterize the words in nodes. Our data set for this task consists of 788 pages parsed into 44,760 nodes. There are 337 positive instances of the target relation and 358 negative ones. We compare FOIL to FOIL-PILFS on this task using a five-fold cross-validation run.

Table 5 shows the recall, precision and F_1 results for this task. Additionally, the table shows the number of folds for which one algorithm outperformed the other in terms of precision or recall. FOIL-PILFS provides significantly better recall and slightly better precision than ordinary FOIL for this task. For both measures, FOIL-PILFS outperformed FOIL on four out the five folds.

4.6 Varying the Vocabulary Parameter in FOIL-PILFS

As described in Section 3, our FOIL-PILFS algorithm employs a parameter, ϵ, which controls how many words Naive Bayes can use when constructing a new predicate. In contrast to our experiments with ordinary FOIL, where we had to make vocabulary-size decisions separately for the page, anchor and neighborhood predicates, ϵ provides a single parameter to set when using FOIL-PILFS.

Table 6. Recall (R), precision (P) and F_1 scores for FOIL-PILFS on the four page classification tasks as we vary ϵ.

ϵ	student			course			faculty			project		
	R	P	F_1	R	P	F_1	R	P	F_1	R	P	F_1
0.01	35.3	61.8	44.9	61.5	50.7	55.6	36.6	46.7	41.0	20.2	20.5	20.4
0.05	38.9	66.2	49.0	48.8	59.5	53.6	38.6	45.7	41.8	13.1	17.5	15.0
0.10	47.9	63.6	54.6	50.8	55.6	53.1	37.3	51.8	43.4	21.4	22.0	21.7

In all of our experiments so far we have set $\epsilon = 0.05$. In order to assess how FOIL-PILFS's performance is affected by varying ϵ, we rerun the page classification experiment from Section 4.3 with ϵ set to 0.01 and 0.1. The former forces Naive Bayes to work with fewer words, the latter allows it twice as many as in our original experiments. Precision, recall and F_1 scores for this experiment are shown in Table 6. Referring back to Table 1 we see that the general results do not change much with the values of ϵ considered. This seems to indicate that performance is not overly sensitive to the value of ϵ.

5 Conclusions

We have presented a hybrid relational/statistical approach to learning in hypertext domains. Whereas the relational component is able to describe the graph structure of hyperlinked pages or the internal structure of HTML pages, the statistical component is adept at learning predicates that characterize the distribution of words in pages and hyperlinks of interest. We described one particular instantiation of this approach: an algorithm based on FOIL that invents predicates on demand which are represented as Naive Bayes models. We evaluated this approach by comparing it to a baseline method that represents words directly in background relations. Our experiments indicate that our method generally learns more accurate definitions.

Although we have explored one particular instantiation of our approach in this paper, we believe that it is worthwhile investigating both (i) using other search strategies for learning clauses, and (ii) using other statistical methods for constructing predicates. Additionally, we also plan to investigate using the probabilities estimated by our statistical classifiers when evaluating learned clauses.

Finally, we believe that our approach is applicable to learning tasks other than those that involve hypertext. We hypothesize that it is well suited to other domains that involve both relational structure, and potentially large feature spaces. In future work, we plan to apply our method in such domains.

Acknowledgments

Thanks to Dan DiPasquo for his assistance with the experiments reported in Section 4.5. This research was supported in part by the DARPA HPKB program under contract F30602-97-1-0215.

References

1. W. W. Cohen. Fast effective rule induction. In *Proc. of the 12th International Conference on Machine Learning*. Morgan Kaufmann, 1995.
2. W. W. Cohen. Learning to classify English text with ILP methods. In L. De Raedt, editor, *Advances in Inductive Logic Programming*. IOS Press, 1995.
3. M. Craven, D. DiPasquo, D. Freitag, A. McCallum, T. Mitchell, K. Nigam, and S. Slattery. Learning to extract symbolic knowledge from the World Wide Web. In *Proc. of the 15th National Conference on Artificial Intelligence*, Madison, WI, 1998. AAAI Press.
4. M. Craven, S. Slattery, and K. Nigam. First-order learning for Web mining. In *Proc. of the 10th European Conference on Machine Learning*, pages 250–255, Chemnitz, Germany, 1998. Springer-Verlag.
5. D. DiPasquo. Using HTML formatting to aid in natural language processing on the World Wide Web, 1998. Senior thesis, Computer Science Department, Carnegie Mellon University.
6. P. Domingos and M. Pazzani. On the optimality of the simple Bayesian classifier under zero-one loss. *Machine Learning*, 29:103–130, 1997.
7. S. Džeroski and I. Bratko. Handling noise in inductive logic programming. In *Proc. of the 2nd International Workshop on Inductive Logic Programming*, pages 109–125, Tokyo, Japan, 1992.
8. A. Ehrenfeucht, D. Haussler, M. Kearns, and L. Valiant. A general lower bound on the number of examples needed for learning. *Information and Computation*, 82(3):247–251, 1989.
9. B. Kijsirikul, M. Numao, and M. Shimura. Discrimination-based constructive induction of logic programs. In *Proc. of the 10th National Conference on Artificial Intelligence*, pages 44–49, San Jose, CA, 1992. AAAI Press.
10. D. D. Lewis and M. Ringuette. A comparison of two learning algorithms for text categorization. In *Proc. of the 3rd Annual Symposium on Document Analysis and Information Retrieval*, pages 81–93, 1994.
11. D. D. Lewis, R. E. Schapire, J. P. Callan, and R. Papka. Training algorithms for linear classifiers. In *Proc. of the 19th Annual International ACM-SIGIR Conference on Research and Development in Information Retrieval*, pages 298–306. Hartung-Gorre Verlag, 1996.
12. T. Mitchell. *Machine Learning*. McGraw Hill, 1997.
13. I. Moulinier, G. Raškinis, and J.-G. Ganascia. Text categorization: a symbolic approach. In *Proc. of the 6th Annual Symposium on Document Analysis and Information Retrieval*, 1996.
14. J. R. Quinlan and R. M. Cameron-Jones. FOIL: A midterm report. In *Proc. of the 5th European Conference on Machine Learning*, pages 3–20, Vienna, Austria, 1993. Springer-Verlag.
15. B. Richards and R. Mooney. Learning relations by pathfinding. In *Proc. of the 10th National Conference on Artificial Intelligence*, pages 50–55, San Jose, CA, 1992. AAAI Press.
16. C. J. van Rijsbergen. *Information Retrieval*, chapter 7. Butterworths, 1979.
17. Y. Yang and J. Pedersen. A comparative study on feature set selection in text categorization. In *Proc. of the 14th International Conference on Machine Learning*, pages 412–420, Nashville, TN, 1997. Morgan Kaufmann.

Application of Inductive Logic Programming to Discover Rules Governing the Three-Dimensional Topology of Protein Structure

Marcel Turcotte[1], Stephen H. Muggleton[2], and Michael J. E. Sternberg[1]

[1] Imperial Cancer Research Fund, Biomolecular Modelling Laboratory
P.O. Box 123, London WC2A 3PX, UK
{M.Turcotte, M.Sternberg}@icrf.icnet.uk
[2] University of York, Department of Computer Science
Heslington, York, YO1 5DD, UK
stephen@cs.york.ac.uk

Abstract. Inductive Logic Programming (ILP) has been applied to discover rules governing the three-dimensional topology of protein structure. The data-set unifies two sources of information; SCOP and PROMOTIF. Cross-validation results for experiments using two background knowledge sets, global (attribute-valued) and constitutional (relational), are presented. The application makes use of a new feature of Progol4.4 for numeric parameter estimation. At this early stage of development, the rules produced can only be applied to proteins for which the secondary structure is known. However, since the rules are insightful, they should prove to be helpful in assisting the development of taxonomic schemes. The application of ILP to fold recognition represents a novel and promising approach to this problem.

1 Introduction

Classification is an important activity in all scientific areas. In the case of protein structures, the task is complex and at the moment is best performed by human experts. However, the number of known protein structures is increasing rapidly which creates a need for automatic methods of classification. The work presented here focuses on one level of the classification, fold recognition. Inductive Logic Programming (ILP) has been applied to derive new principles governing the formation of protein folds such as common substructures and the relationship between local sequence and tertiary structure.

The tertiary structure of proteins is itself arranged hierarchically. The building blocks, the amino acids, also termed residues, assemble linearly to form the primary structure or sequence. Sequence segments adopt regular conformations, helices and strands, collectively called secondary structures. ILP has previously been applied to prediction of protein secondary structure [1, 2]. Secondary structures form motifs called supersecondary structures. Finally, these interact together to form the tertiary structure.

Protein fold recognition involves finding the fold relationship of a protein sequence of unknown structure. Two proteins have a common fold if they share the same core secondary structures, and the same interconnections. Homologous proteins share the same or similar folds. Protein fold recognition focuses on analogous proteins and remote homologues. It allows the inference of a relationship between two proteins that could not be inferred by direct sequence comparison methods. Thus it allows structural and possibly functional information to inferred for new protein sequences.

Approaches to protein fold recognition can be classified into two broad classes. The first class of approaches considers sequential information, see [3, 4] for a review. Information, often called profile, is derived from the primary sequence, secondary structure and solvent accessibility. A database of target profiles is built for all known folds using experimental data. Dynamic programming algorithm is then used to align two profiles, probe and target. The information about the probe is derived from prediction methods. The second class of approaches uses pair potentials which sums all the propensity scores of residues pairs at a certain distance, see [5] for a review.

Machine learning techniques have been applied to the problem. Hubbard *et al.* [6] used Hidden Markov Models (HMM) to create a model of a multiple sequence alignment which is subsequently used to retrieve related sequences from the protein structure database. The HMM scores are combined with those obtained by comparing the predicted secondary structure, based on the multiple sequence alignment, to the experimental secondary structure. Di Francesco *et al.* [7] also used HMM but at a different stage of the recognition process. They used them to built a model of all observed secondary structures of a given fold. Secondary structure is predicted for the probe and evaluated using the models of all targets. Rost and Sander [8] used neural networks and information from predicted secondary structure plus predicted solvent accessibility. These methods are based on sequence alignment, either of the polypeptide chain, secondary structure or solvent accessibility, they resemble to the first approach mentioned above.

A different approach has been undertaken by Dubchak *et al.* [9], they used neural networks together with global descriptors. The global descriptors are composition, transition and distribution of physico-chemical properties such as hydrophobicity, polarity and predicted secondary structure.

Our approach combines both, sequential and global descriptors. This paper is organised as follows. Section 2 gives the details of the ILP system we used. Section 3 introduces the new data-set. Section 4 presents the results of the learning experiments. We conclude, Section 5, with a discussion of the advantages of ILP to resolve the problem at hand and discuss the anticipated future developments.

2 ILP System

The experimentation was carried out using Progol4.4 which is the latest of the family of Progol ILP systems [10]. Progol4.4 is distinguished from its predecessors

Progol4.1 and Progol4.2 by its use of constraints for numeric parameter estimation. This is an adaptation of the 'lazy-evaluation' mechanism, first proposed by Srinivasan and Camacho. For instance, suppose we want to find upper bounds for the predicate `lessthan/2`. First, use declarations such as the following.

```
:- modeb(1,interval(#float =< +float =< #float))?
:- constraint(interval/1)?
```

The constraint declaration says that any `interval/1` atom in the most-specific clause should have a Skolem constant in place of the upper and lower bound constants (#float's above). In the search, during any refinement which introduces a constraint atom, the flag solving is turned on, and the user-defined predicate is given all substitutions from positive and negative examples as a list of lists of lists (takes the form [P,N] where P is from the positive examples and N from the negatives, and P,N are lists of lists, each list giving all substitutions related to a particular example), and returns an appropriate substitution for the constant. This constant is used in place of the Skolem constant in subsequent testing of the refined clause and its refinements. Thus definitions for constraint predicates have to have at least two clauses, having the guards 'solving' and 'not(solving)' to define respectively the procedure for computing the parameter and the normal application of the predicate.

3 Data-Set

A Prolog database has been constructed by translating automatically the output of the computer program PROMOTIF [11] and the database SCOP [12].

The data-set is meant to be used throughout several projects. The translation retains most of the structure of the data. Program transformations are later applied to reformat the data for each specific project.

In principle, the data-set can be used to learn any feature implemented by SCOP and PROMOTIF. In practice, because learning experiments necessitate supervision, we are aiming at only learning Prolog definition for a limited subset of these features. However, the data are being made available in the hope that it will encourage further experimentation[1].

The data-set should be useful on its own. Prolog has already proven to be an excellent tool to manage protein structure databases [13, 14].

3.1 Structure Classification

The classification of protein structures is a complex task. The main classification schemes are SCOP [12] and CATH [15]. The former classification is performed manually while the second is semi-automated. For this work we refer to SCOP, it is used to relate structures and folds.

---

[1] See http://www.icnet.uk/bmm/people/turcotte/ilp98/

The basic unit in SCOP is a domain, a structure or substructure that is considered to be folded independently. Small proteins have a single domain, for larger ones, a domain is a substructure, also termed region, indicated by a chain id and a sequence interval range. Domains are grouped into families. Domains of the same family have evolved from a common ancestral sequence. In most cases, the relationship can be identified by direct sequence comparison methods. The next level is called a superfamily. Members of a superfamily are believed to have evolved from a common ancestry, but the relationship cannot always be inferred by sequence comparison methods alone; the expert relies on other evidences, functional features for example. The next level is a fold, proteins share the same core secondary structures, and the same interconnections. The resemblance can be attributed to convergence towards a stable architecture. Finally, folds are conveniently grouped into classes (such as all-α and all-β) based on the overall distribution of their secondary structure elements. Figure 1 shows the Prolog representation of a SCOP entry.

```
scop(Class, Fold, Super, Family, Protein, Species, PdbId, Region)
```

Fig. 1. A domain entry in the SCOP database.

A Perl program has been written which creates a Prolog representation from a SCOP HTML file. In this work we used SCOP database 1.35 generated by scopm 1.087. The four major classes contain 9153 domains, covering 630 families and 298 folds.

3.2 Structural Attributes

PROMOTIF is used to calculate the structural attributes used in this work. Given a set of coordinates, PROMOTIF generates a series of files, each containing a particular set of structural features. These features are secondary structure, β- and γ-turns, helical geometry and interactions, β strands and β-sheet topology, β-bulges, β-hairpins, β-α-β units, ψ-loops and main-chain hydrogen bonding patterns [11].

A Perl program has been written that translates these free format files to Prolog clauses, Fig. 2 shows a sub-set of PROMOTIF attributes.

3.3 Selection

Because crystallographers[2] do not select randomly the proteins they study, the databases are biased. Crystallographers select proteins because of their connection to a particular molecular pathway, a particular disease or their overall scientific interest in general.

---

[2] Crystallography, the study of X-ray diffraction patterns, is the main source of our knowledge of protein structure.

```
sst(Pdb, Chain, Pos, Aa, Structure).
helix(Pdb, Num, Chain, Pos, Chain, Pos, Len, Type).
helix_pair(Pdb, Num, Num, Dist, Angle, Region, Region, Num, Num).
strand(Pdb, Num, Sheet, Chain1, Lo, Chain2, Hi, Len).
hairpin(Pdb, Beta1, Beta2, Len1, Len2).
sheet(Pdb, Label, N, Type).
bturn(Pdb, Chain, Pos, Type).
```

Fig. 2. Examples of PROMOTIF attributes represented as Prolog clauses.

To remove redundancy a single representative domain has been selected per protein, as defined in SCOP. The procedure was carried out with the computer system Darwin [16]. All sequences of a protein are gathered and compared all against all. The sequence with maximum average similarity score to all other members of the set is selected as the representative element.

Next, to ensure enough diversity, folds having less than 5 families were removed. Table 1 lists all the selected folds and the cross-validation accuracy measures.

Negative examples were chosen randomly from proteins of the same class but having a different fold. The rational is that it is more difficult to distinguish between two folds of the same class than it is to distinguish between folds of different classes and is justified by the existence of accurate method for class prediction. Finally, in accord with previous experiments we selected the number of negative examples proportional to the number of positive examples.

Rules were learnt that discriminate between members and non-members of a fold. The expected accuracy of a random prediction should be 50%.

4 Learning Experiments

Progol was applied to all folds using two background knowledge sets. The first set involved global attributes of protein structure. The second included constitutional information as well. For each fold, rules were learnt that discriminate between members (positive examples) and non-members (negative examples).

4.1 Global Attributes

We first present a learning experiment that involves only global attributes. Learning here is essentially attribute-value based. We used the total number of residues, total number of secondary structures of both types, β and α, and three different constraints. Figure 3 lists them all. As we will see, it is possible to derive rules that are effective and in some cases provide interesting insights.

For 17 out of 23 folds, Progol produced a descriptive rule; indeed, in this experiment, Progol produced a single rule per fold, with overall cross-validation accuracy of 70.76%, see Table 1. One such rule is that of the Immunoglobulin-like β-sandwich fold. This single rule covers most of the positive examples and

Table 1. Cross-validation predictive accuracy measures for global and combined information for all folds.

Folds	Fam	Dom	Global Acc (%)	Combined Acc (%)
All-α:				
Four-helical bundle	7	12	95.83 ± 4.08	95.83 ± 4.08
EF Hand-like	7	14	78.57 ± 7.75	78.57 ± 7.75
Three-helical bundle	13	27(26)	90.57 ± 4.02	90.57 ± 4.02
All-β:				
Diphtheria toxin	5	6	50.00 ± 14.43	41.67 ± 14.23
Barrel-sandwich	4	8	- ± -	68.75 ± 11.59
beta-Trefoil	5	9	66.67 ± 11.11	66.67 ± 11.11
ConA-like	5	8	75.00 ± 10.83	50.00 ± 12.50
SH3-like barrel	5	13	84.62 ± 7.08	73.08 ± 8.70
OB-fold	9	18	- ± -	61.11 ± 8.12
Immunoglobulin†	13	41	78.75 ± 4.57	71.25 ± 5.06
α/β:				
Restriction endonucleases	5	5	20.00 ± 12.65	80.00 ± 12.65
alpha/beta-Hydrolases	8	9	- ± -	55.56 ± 11.71
Ribonuclease H-like motif	11	16	43.75 ± 8.77	75.00 ± 7.65
Flavodoxin-like	11	14	67.86 ± 8.83	60.71 ± 9.23
P-loop	4	15	- ± -	50.00 ± 9.13
Rossmann-fold	7	20	80.00 ± 6.32	72.50 ± 7.06
(TIM)-barrel†	24	49	80.00 ± 4.22	78.89 ± 4.30
$\alpha + \beta$:				
FAD-linked reductases	5	5	100.00 ± 0.00	90.00 ± 9.49
Lysozyme-like	6	7	92.86 ± 6.88	100.00 ± 0.00
Cystatin-like	5	7	35.71 ± 12.81	71.43 ± 12.07
Metzincin-like	6	11	77.27 ± 8.93	86.36 ± 7.32
beta-Grasp	6	13	- ± -	42.31 ± 9.69
Ferredoxin-like	17	21	- ± -	61.90 ± 7.49
Overall:			70.76 ± 1.79	71.53 ± 1.72

† 10-fold cross validation, other values were obtained by leave-one-out procedure.

Fam is total number of families.

Dom is total number of domains (positive examples), in the case of three-helical bundle, the number of negative examples is one less because of a shortage of data.

Acc is the cross-validation accuracy, defined as the sum of true positives and true negatives over the total. In some cases, Progol was unable to infer any rule, this is indicated with minus sign.

The overall cross-validation accuracy values are calculated from the sum of all the contingency tables, thus it also accounts for cases where Progol was not able to produce any rule. ± values are standard errors of cross-validation accuracy.

```
:- modeh(1,fold(#fold_t,+dom_t))?          % relates folds and domains
:- modeb(1,len(+dom_t,-nat))?              % total number of residues
:- modeb(1,nb_alpha(+dom_t,-nat))?         % total number of helices
:- modeb(1,nb_beta(+dom_t,-nat))?          % total number of strands
:- modeb(1,interval(#nat =< +nat =< #nat))?
:- modeb(1,interval_l(+nat =< #nat))?
:- modeb(1,interval_r(#nat =< +nat))?
```

Fig. 3. Mode declarations.

says that a domain adopts an Immunoglobulin-like β-sandwich fold if its length, measured in number of residues, is between 50 and 173, has one or no α-helix and seven to ten β-strands. The Prolog representation is shown in Fig. 4.

```
fold('Immunoglobulin-like beta-sandwich',A) :-
    len(A,B), interval(50=<B=<173),
    nb_alpha(A,C), interval(0=<C=<1),
    nb_beta(A,D), interval(7=<C=<10).
```

Fig. 4. The rule induced by Prolog for the Immunoglobulin-like β-sandwich fold.

Three rules were produced that are of a particular interest. They say that for these folds there is a significant number of cases where the number of helices and strands is the same. The relation is not trivial as the total number of secondary structures also varies (see Fig. 5). In the case of β/α (TIM)-barrel the rule says that the number of α-helices is the same as the number of β-strands and this number is between eight and sixteen. It suggests that these folds are made of repetitive motifs, this can be programmed in the background knowledge and will be tested in future experiments.

```
fold('Flavodoxin-like',A) :-
    nb_alpha(A,B), nb_beta(A,B), interval_l(B=<6).

fold('NAD(P)-binding Rossmann-fold domains',A) :-
    nb_alpha(A,B), nb_beta(A,B), interval(5=<B=<7).

fold('beta/alpha (TIM)-barrel',A) :-
    nb_alpha(A,B), nb_beta(A,B), interval(8=<B=<16).
```

Fig. 5. Same number of strands and helices. The top rule says that a domain A adopts a Flavodoxin-like fold if it has B helices, B strands and B is less than or equal to 6. All three folds belong to the same class, α/β.

However good these rules are to discriminate between folds, they do not provide much structural insights; although the three rules in Fig. 5 suggest an element of symmetry. We recall that our objective is to derive new principles governing the formation of protein folds and thus we now move on to a more complex representation which facilitates their discovery.

4.2 Combined Attributes

We now present the second learning experiment that incorporates constitutional (relational) as well as global information (attribute-value). New attributes are introduced. The predicate adjacent/6 serves three purposes. First, the predicate is used to introduce two secondary structure identifiers in a rule. Second, the predicate tells us that the two units are consecutive. It gives the location of the first element, the location is allowed to vary slightly and this variation depends on its position in the sequence, the closer to the end the more variation is allowed. Finally, the predicate also indicates the secondary structure type of each unit.

Two consecutive secondary structures are separated by a coil, a sequence of amino acids which varies in length, this information is represented by the predicate coil/3.

Three properties of secondary structures have been considered here: average hydrophobicity, hydrophobic moment and length, respectively represented by ave_h/2, h_mom/2 and unit_len/2. The numerical values of the parameters were substituted by symbolic constants. The constant very_hi was assigned if the value of the parameter was greater than or equal to the mean plus two standard deviations, hi if the value was greater than or equal to the mean plus one standard deviation, very_lo if the value was less than or equal to the mean minus two standard deviations and lo if the the value of the parameter was less than or equal to the mean minus one standard deviation. Values between the mean minus one standard deviation and the mean plus one standard deviation were omitted to speed up the calculations. Following the same line or reasoning as Section 3.3, the mean and standard deviation were calculated for proteins of the same class.

In the previous section, rules were obtained for 17 out of 23 folds. With the new attributes, we now have rules for all the folds. The overall accuracy is not significantly higher, see Table 1. Previously, one rule per fold was produced, we now have some folds having up to three rules.

Figures 7 and 6 illustrate the format of rules produced. We recall that the aim of the learning process is to discriminate between members and non-members of a fold where negative examples are selected from elements of the same class. In the four-helical up-and-down bundle, the distinctive feature is the presence of a rather long helix around position five, followed by another helix. In EF-hand, it is the strand/helix pair located at the start or at the end of the molecule which is the distinctive feature. Finally, in DNA-binding 3-helical bundle, two populations are represented, the largest one is distinguished by its length and the fact that it has exactly three helices. The second population is distinguished by its pair of β-strands, connected by a short coil, located at the beginning of the molecule.

```
fold('Four-helical up-and-down bundle',A) :-
    adjacent(A,B,C,5,h,h), unit_len(B,hi).

fold('EF Hand-like',A) :-
    adjacent(A,B,C,1,h,e), nb_alpha(A,D), interval(4=<(D=<9)).

fold('EF Hand-like',A) :-
    adjacent(A,B,C,9,e,h).

fold('DNA-binding 3-helical bundle',A) :-
    len(A,B), interval(38=<(B=<111)),
    nb_alpha(A,C), interval(3=<(C=<3)).

fold('DNA-binding 3-helical bundle',A) :-
    adjacent(A,B,C,2,e,e), coil(B,C,4).
```

Fig. 6. Prolog representation of the rules of all-α class.

5 Conclusion

We have applied Inductive Logic Programming to the problem of fold recognition. This work is preliminary, but it shows that Progol is capable of producing rules that are both accurate and descriptive. The rules produced are non-trivial. Nevertheless they are easily interpretable by the expert in terms of structural concepts: edge strands, hairpins, etc.

The learning experiment was presented in two steps, global and constitutional attributes, two rather different ways to describe proteins. Attribute learners, such as C4.5 or CART, are suitable for use with global attributes, but it would be difficult to introduce concepts related to constitutional information. Other machine learning techniques address this problem. Hidden Markov Models, for example, are most suitable for this form of information. Here, we have shown an application that integrates both types of information transparently, and often this information has been used in a complementary way.

To tackle this problem a new database has been built that unifies multiple sources of information. The database is general and allows queries that involve structural features and taxonomic information. We hope that it will be useful both inside and outside the machine learning community.

The work presented here also raises interesting questions. It suggests that it is possible to distinguish between folds using small patterns of secondary structure. These patterns are present in most, or all, proteins of a fold but

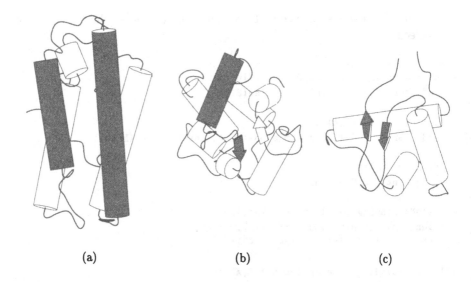

Fig. 7. Schematic representation of the domains of the all-α class. The structural features used for the construction of the rules are shaded. (a) Four-helical up-and-down bundle, (b) EF Hand-like and (c) DNA-binding 3-helical bundle. The cylinders represent α-helices, the arrows represent β-strands and the coil regions are represented as a thin line.

not in others. It would be interesting to know if these also correspond to well defined and predictable segments. Since these patterns are conserved, it is sound to postulate that the multiple sequence alignment in these regions will be well defined as well and should be suitable for evolutionary based secondary structure prediction methods. Such method for fold recognition would depend less on the overall accuracy of the secondary structure prediction program used. The use of experimental secondary structure is justified in the context where it is used as an aid to develop taxonomic schemes. The evaluation of the method using predicted secondary structure is the next step in this project. In addition, for protein fold predictions, these rules could be used in conjunction with other fold recognition methods, based on profiles or pair potentials.

Rules have been learnt independently for each fold. As a result, the fold predictions from different sets of rules are overlapping. We need to quantify this overlap but most importantly we need to consider a resolution mechanism. First-order decision lists paradigm, as described by Mooney and Califf [17], is a good candidate. Rules are ordered in increasing level of coverage. Rules with low coverage are encountered first. They are considered as exception to more general rules. In [17], each rule ends with a cut, hence producing a single answer. In the field of protein recognition it is most common to return the list of all possible folds.

Several developments are planned. The relation between the number of strands and helices detected by Progol suggested that symmetry and segmentation should be added to the background knowledge. Another improvement would be to make a more effective use of the structural information available. For example, we want to make use of structural alignments and equivalence between secondary structures. The richness of this paradigm allows to express hierarchical and non-local information. This is a direction of research that we intend to investigate further. We particularly want to explore the recognition of common substructures.

Acknowledgement

This work is supported by a BBSRC/EPSRC Bioinformatics grant. This work was supported also by the Esprit Long Term Research Action ILP II (project 20237), EPSRC grant GR/K57985 on Experiments with Distribution-based Machine Learning and an EPSRC Advanced Research Fellowship held by the second author. MT receives a fellowship from *Fonds pour la formation de chercheurs et l'aide à la recherche*, Québec, Canada. The authors wish to thank C. Bryant for his careful reading of the manuscript and comments.

References

[1] S. Muggleton, R. King, and M. J. E. Sternberg. Protein secondary structure prediction using logic-based machine learning. *Protein Engineering*, 5(7):647–657, 1992.

[2] M. J. E. Sternberg, R. D. King, R. A. Lewis, and S. Muggleton. Application of machine learning to structural molecular biology. *Philosophical Transactions of the Royal Society of London - Series B: Biological Sciences*, 344(1310):365–71, 1994.

[3] D. Fischer and D. Eisenberg. Protein fold recognition using sequence-derived predictions. *Protein Science*, 5:947–955, 1996.

[4] R. B. Russell, M. A. S. Saqi, P. A. Bates, R. A. Sayle, and M. J. E. Sternberg. Recognition of analogous and homologous protein folds - assessment of prediction success and associated alignment accuracy using empirical substitution matrices. *Protein Engineering*, 11(1):1–9, 1998.

[5] S. H. Bryant. Evaluation of threading specificity and accuracy. *Proteins*, 26(2):172–185, 1996.

[6] T. J. Hubbard and J. Park. Fold recognition and ab initio structure predictions using hidden markov models and beta-strand pair potentials. *Proteins Struct. Funct. Genet.*, 23(3):398–402, 1995.

[7] V. Francesco, Di, J. Garnier, and P. J. Munson. Protein topology recognition from secondary structure sequences: Application of the hidden markov models to the alpha class proteins. *Journal of Molecular Biology*, 267(2):446–463, 1997.

[8] B. Rost, R. Schneider, and C. Sander. Protein fold recognition by prediction-based threading. *Journal of Molecular Biology*, 270:471–480, 1997.

[9] I. Dubchak, I. Muchnik, and S.-H. Kim. Protein folding class predictor for scop: approach based on global descriptors. *ismb*, 5:104–107, 1997.

[10] S. Muggleton, editor. *Inductive Logic Programming*. Academic Press, 1992.

[11] E. G. Hutchinson and J. M. Thornton. PROMOTIF – a program to identify and analyze structural motifs in proteins. *Protein Science*, 5(2):212–20, 1996.

[12] S. E. Brenner, C. Chothia, T. J. Hubbard, and A. G. Murzin. Understanding protein structure: using SCOP for fold interpretation. *Methods in Enzymology*, 266:635–43, 1996.

[13] C. J. Rawlings, W. R. Taylor, J. Fox J. Nyakairu, and M. J. E. Sternberg. Using Prolog to represent and reason about protein structure. In Ehud Y. Shapiro, editor, *Third International Conference on Logic Programming*, volume 225 of *Lecture Notes in Computer Science*, pages 536–543. Springer, 1986.

[14] G. J. Barton and C. J. Rawlings. A Prolog approach to analysing protein structure. *Tetrahedron Computer Methodology*, 3(6C):739–756, 1990.

[15] C.A. Orengo, A.D. Michie, S. Jones, D.T. Jones, M.B. Swindells, and J.M. Thornton. CATH – a hierarchic classification of protein domain structures. *Structure*, 5(8):1093–1108, 1997.

[16] G. H. Gonnet and S. A. Benner. Computational biochemistry research at ETH. Technical report, E.T.H. Department Informatik, March 1991.

[17] R.J. Mooney and M.E. Califf. Induction of first-order decision lists: Results on learning the past tense of english verbs. *Journal of Artificial Intelligence Research*, 3:1–24, 1995.

Term Comparisons in First-Order Similarity Measures

Uta Bohnebeck[1], Tamás Horváth[2], and Stefan Wrobel[2]

[1] University of Bremen,
Center for Computing Technology,
P.O.Box 330 440, D-28834 Bremen,
bohnebec@informatik.uni-bremen.de
[2] German National Research Center for Information Technology,
SET.KI,
Schloß Birlinghoven,
D-53757 Sankt Augustin
{tamas.horvath,stefan.wrobel}@gmd.de

Abstract. The similarity measures used in first-order IBL so far have been limited to the function-free case. In this paper we show that a lot of predictive power can be gained by allowing lists and other terms in the input representation and designing similarity measures that work directly on these structures. We present an improved similarity measure for the first-order instance based learner RIBL that employs the concept of *edit distances* to efficiently compute distances between lists and terms, discuss its computational and formal properties, and show that it is empirically superior by a wide margin on a problem from the domain of biochemistry.

1 Introduction

Instance-based learning (IBL) algorithms have always been a very popular and successful approach for the solution of classification and prediction learning problems (Wettschereck and Aha [17]). For a long time restricted to propositional data, recent work has shown that by devising suitable recursive similarity measures, it is possible to lift the well-known advantages of propositional IBL (excellent prediction performance and high noise tolerance) to the first-order domain, as done e.g. in RIBL (Emde and Wettschereck [6]) and applied successfully to a practical problem in chemistry (Džeroski, Schulze-Kremer, Heidtke, Siems and Wettschereck [5]).

However, the similarity measures used in first-order IBL so far have all been limited to the function-free case, allowing only similarity 1 between identical constants and similarity 0 otherwise, and requiring flattening on representations with non-constant terms. While it might appear that this would in principle be sufficient, in this paper we show that a lot of predictive power can be gained by allowing lists and other terms in the input representation and designing similarity measures that work directly on these structures. We present an improved similarity measure for RIBL that employs the concept of *edit distances* to efficiently compute distances between lists and terms, and show that this new similarity measure empirically beats the previous proposal by a wide margin on a problem from the domain of biochemistry.

The paper is organized as follows. In the next section, we briefly review the basics of IBL and describe the existing function free similarity measure used in RIBL. Section 3 then presents the main technical contribution of the paper, the new similarity measure for constants, lists and terms. We discuss its computational properties and prove that the measure is a semi-metric. Section 4 is devoted to the empirical evaluation on the mRNA signal structure detection problem first presented in Bohnebeck, Sälter, Herzog, Wischnewsky and Blohm [4]. In section 5, we discuss related work, in particular the term distance functions of Hutchinson [7] and Nienhuys-Cheng [11]. We conclude with a summary and open problems. Due to space limitations, proofs are omitted.

2 Instance-based learning and RIBL

In its most simple form (k-nearest neighbor), an IBL algorithm stores all training examples, and when asked to classify an unseen test case, uses a *similarity measure* to retrieve the k training examples that are most similar to the test case. The class values of these nearest neighbors are then combined, e.g. by majority vote for discrete or by averaging for continuous target attributes, to yield the prediction for the unseen test case. More elaborate variants store only selected examples or rely on generalized prototypes instead of individual examples, see [17] for an overview.

The lazy learning method *relational instance-based algorithm* (RIBL) [6] applies the *distance-weighted k-nearest neighbor method* in a relational representation. RIBL's instances are represented as first-order *cases*, i.e., sets of facts about the instance. Exactly one of these facts must be using the designated start or target predicate and contains as one of its arguments an identifier of the instance. The other arguments can be of one of the basic types, namely *number* or *discrete*, or of type *name*. The latter type is used for arguments that contain identifiers representing objects that can be further described by other facts in the case[1].

To compare two cases, the similarity function of RIBL (a modified version of the measure by Bisson [3]) recursively descends into each case, beginning with the two target facts. For arguments of basic types, the corresponding elementary similarity function is called. For arguments of type *name*, all further facts about the respective named objects are collected, and the resulting pairs of facts compared by a recursive call to the similarity measure, and then suitably combined into an overall similarity. The details of all these computations are not central to this paper, and can be found in [6].

---

[1] If RIBL is to be used on a flat theory, it contains a case generation module that recursively collects the literals describing each instance up to a user-specified depth bound, see [6] for details.

For our purposes here, we are interested in the available supply of elementary similarity resp. difference functions[2]. The first version of RIBL (RIBL 1.0) [6] supported only *number* and *discrete* argument types. Difference between arguments of types *number* and *discrete* is computed by

$$\text{DIFF}_{\text{number}}(r_1, r_2) = \left(\frac{r_1 - r_2}{b - a}\right)^2 \qquad (r_1, r_2 \in [a, b]) \quad \text{and}$$

$$\text{DIFF}_{\text{discrete}}(d_1, d_2) = \begin{cases} 0 & \text{if } d_1 = d_2 \\ 1 & \text{otherwise} \end{cases}, \text{ respectively}.$$

In this paper, we significantly extend the power of RIBL's similarity measure by providing appropriate definitions for new basic difference functions $\text{DIFF}_{\text{constant}}$, $\text{DIFF}_{\text{list}}$ and $\text{DIFF}_{\text{term}}$ for arguments of types *constant*, *list*, and *term*, respectively.

3   A Similarity Measure for Lists and Terms

In order to directly compute similarity of cases with non-flat components (lists, terms), we have chosen to rely on the idea of *edit distances* between objects. Intuitively, with an edit distance, we are given a set of edit operations (insert, delete, change) with an associated cost function δ that tells us how expensive it is to delete or insert an element of our alphabet Σ, or how expensive it is to change one into another. The edit distance is given by the smallest cost sequence of such operations that turns the first object into the second, and there are efficient algorithms for computing it (see below).

In the following, we will precisely specify the edit distance measure used in the revised version of RIBL (henceforth referred to as RIBL 2.0). Even though both types constants and list could be considered as terms, we distinguish them from each other for the sake of efficiency.

First, we recall some basic definitions of metrics. Let X be a set and $\delta : X \times X \longrightarrow \mathbb{R}$. δ is a *distance* or *metric* on X if it satisfies the conditions

$$\delta(x, y) \geq 0 \tag{1}$$
$$\delta(x, y) = 0 \text{ iff } x = y \tag{2}$$
$$\delta(x, y) = \delta(y, x) \tag{3}$$
$$\delta(x, y) \leq \delta(x, z) + \delta(z, y) \tag{4}$$

for every $x, y, z \in X$. The pair (X, δ) is called a *metric space*. A metric δ is said to be *trivial* if for every $x, y \in X$

$$\delta(x, y) = \begin{cases} 0 & \text{if } x = y \\ 1 & \text{otherwise} \end{cases}.$$

---

[2] Throughout this paper we use *difference* instead of similarity, because in RIBL both are in the range [0, 1].

δ is a *semi-metric* if Condition (4) (the *triangle inequality*) does not hold. Relaxing Condition (2) to $\delta(x,x) = 0$ for $\forall x \in X$, we get the definition of *pseudo-metric*. A metric, semi-metric or pseudo-metric δ is *r-bounded* for some $r \in \mathbb{R}$ if r is an upper bound on the values of δ.

3.1 Constants

An argument type *constant* is given by a set of constant symbols Σ_{constant} and a 1-bounded semi-metric δ on Σ_{constant}. The *difference* between $a, b \in \Sigma_{\text{constant}}$ is defined then directly by δ, i.e.

$$\text{DIFF}_{\text{constant}}(a,b) = \delta(a,b) \ .$$

We note that the argument type *discrete* can be considered as a special case of this type.

3.2 Lists

Let $\mathcal{L}\left(\Sigma_{\text{list}}\right)$ be the set of finite lists over the alphabet Σ_{list}, and let $\Sigma_{\text{list},\perp} = \Sigma_{\text{list}} \cup \{\perp\}$, where $\perp$ denotes the *empty list*. $|l|$ denotes the *length* of the list $l \in \mathcal{L}\left(\Sigma_{\text{list}}\right)$. Consider the following operations on the elements of $\mathcal{L}\left(\Sigma_{\text{list}}\right)$:

- *insert*(l,i,a): *inserts the symbol* $a \in \Sigma_{\text{list}}$ *before the i-th symbol in* l,
- *delete*(l,i): *deletes the i-th symbol in* l,
- *change*(l,i,a): *changes the i-th symbol in* l *to a new symbol* a

for every $a \in \Sigma_{\text{list}}$, $l \in \mathcal{L}\left(\Sigma_{\text{list}}\right)$ and $i = 1, \ldots, |l|$. Thus, an operation can be considered as an application of a *rewriting rule* $a \to b$ for $a, b \in \Sigma_{\text{list},\perp}$, i.e. insert, delete and change correspond to the application of a rewriting rule $\perp \to a$, $a \to \perp$ and $a \to b$, respectively $(a, b \neq \perp)$. Let $l_1, l_2 \in \mathcal{L}\left(\Sigma_{\text{list}}\right)$. We say that l_2 can be *directly derived* from l_1 (denoted by $l_1 \Rightarrow l_2$) if there exists an operation that produces l_2 from l_1. The *derivation* (denoted by $l_1 \Rightarrow^*_{\sigma_1 \cdots \sigma_n} l_2$) is the *reflexive, transitive closure* of $\Rightarrow$. The index $\sigma_1 \cdots \sigma_n$ denotes the sequence of the applied rewriting rules. A *list type* is given by a 1-bounded metric space $\left(\Sigma_{\text{list},\perp}, \delta\right)$. Here, $\delta(a \to b)$ is considered as the *cost* of the rewriting rule $a \to b$ for every $a, b \in \Sigma_{\text{list},\perp}$. Since δ is a metric, it can be considered as a quadratic symmetrical *cost matrix* with zero elements in its diagonal. The *edit* or *Levenshtein distance*[3] between $l_1, l_2 \in \mathcal{L}\left(\Sigma_{\text{list}}\right)$ is defined by

$$D_{\text{list}}(l_1, l_2) = \min\left\{\sum_{i=1}^{n} \delta(\sigma_i) : \exists \sigma_1, \ldots, \sigma_n \text{ such that } l_1 \Rightarrow^*_{\sigma_1 \ldots \sigma_n} l_2\right\} \ .$$

Since δ is a distance metric on $\Sigma_{\text{list},\perp}$, D_{list} is a distance metric on $\mathcal{L}\left(\Sigma_{\text{list}}\right)$. The next theorem is a special case of Theorems 2 and 3 in Wagner and Fischer [16]:

---

[3] Some authors (e.g. Aho [1]) use different definitions for the edit and for the Levenshtein distances, respectively.

Theorem 1. Let $\left(\Sigma_{\text{list},\perp}, \delta\right)$ be a metric space, and let $l_1 = [a_1, \ldots, a_n]$, and $l_2 = [b_1, \ldots, b_m]$ be lists of $\mathcal{L}\left(\Sigma_{\text{list}}\right)$. Let $D_{i,j} = D_{\text{list}}([a_1, \ldots, a_i], [b_1, \ldots, b_j])$ for $i = 0, \ldots, n$, and $j = 0, \ldots, m$. Then

$$D_{0,0} = 0, \ D_{0,j} = \sum_{k=1}^{j} \delta(\perp \rightarrow b_k), \ D_{i,0} = \sum_{k=1}^{i} \delta(a_k \rightarrow \perp), \ and$$
$$D_{i,j} = \min(D_{i-1,j-1} + \delta(a_i \rightarrow b_j), D_{i-1,j} + \delta(a_i \rightarrow \perp), D_{i,j-1} + \delta(\perp \rightarrow b_j))$$

for every $i, j > 0$. □

By Theorem 1, $D_{\text{list}}(l_1, l_2)$ can be computed in *time* and *space* $O(mn)$.

Example 1. Let $\Sigma_{\text{list}} = \{a, c, g, u\}$, and δ be the trivial metric on $\Sigma_{\text{list},\perp}$. Let $l_1 = [c, c, u, a]$, and $l_2 = [c, u, u, a, g, c, u, c]$. The values of $D_{i,j}$ for $i = 0, \ldots, 4$, and $j = 0, \ldots, 8$ is given in Fig. 1.

	$\perp$	c	u	u	a	g	c	u	c
$\perp$	0	1	2	3	4	5	6	7	8
c	1	0	1	2	3	4	5	6	7
c	2	1	1	2	3	4	4	5	6
u	3	2	1	1	2	3	4	4	5
a	4	3	2	2	1	2	3	4	5

Fig. 1. The distance matrix $D_{i,j}$.

Thus, $D_{4,8} = D_{\text{list}}(l_1, l_2) = 5$. □

An improved algorithm for computing the edit distance between lists and the next theorem can be found in Ukkonen [15].

Theorem 2. *The edit distance* $d = D_{\text{list}}(l_1, l_2)$ *between lists* l_1 *and* l_2 *can be computed in time* $O(d \cdot \min(|l_1|, |l_2|))$ *and in space* $O(\min(d, |l_1|, |l_2|))$. □

We define difference in RIBL as:

$$\text{DIFF}_{\text{list}}(l_1, l_2) = \frac{D_{\text{list}}(l_1, l_2)}{\max(|l_1|, |l_2|)}. \tag{5}$$

Proposition 1. *If* $\left(\Sigma_{\text{list},\perp}, \delta\right)$ *is a 1-bounded metric space then* $\text{DIFF}_{\text{list}}$ *is a 1-bounded semi-metric on* $\mathcal{L}\left(\Sigma_{\text{list}}\right)$. □

3.3 Terms

In RIBL 2.0, terms are considered as *labeled ordered trees* and hence, the distance between terms is computed as the *edit distance* between labeled ordered trees.

Let Σ_{term} be an alphabet. We note that Σ_{term} is not a *ranked* alphabet, i.e. no arity function is assigned to Σ_{term}. The set of all *finite* terms with nodes labeled by the elements of Σ_{term} including the *empty* term ($\bot$), is denoted by $\mathcal{T}(\Sigma_{\text{term}})$. For a given term $t \in \mathcal{T}(\Sigma_{\text{term}})$, the nodes of t are numbered via the *preorder traversal* of t, i.e. the first node in the traversal has number 1 and the last node has number $|t|$, where $|t|$ denotes the number of nodes of t. These numbers are used to identify the nodes of a term.

The following *edit operations* on the elements of $\mathcal{T}(\Sigma_{\text{term}})$ are considered (see Figure 2):

- *insert(t, i, a)*: *inserts* a new node with label a between node i and its children, i.e. the new node inherits the children of node i in their original sequence and the only child of node i will be the new node,
- *delete(t, i)*: *deletes* node i, i.e. this is the inverse of insert,
- *relabel(t, i, a)*: *replaces* the label of node i to label a

for $a \in \Sigma_{\text{term}}$, $t \in \mathcal{T}(\Sigma_{\text{term}})$ and $i = 1, \ldots, |t|$.

The above operations on terms can also be considered as applications of *term rewriting rules* $a \to b$ ($a, b \in \Sigma_{\text{term},\bot}$ and $a \to b \neq \bot \to \bot$). A similar definition and notation of *derivation* between terms can be used as in the case of lists. Let δ be a 1-bounded metric on $\Sigma_{\text{term},\bot}$. As for lists, δ is considered as a *cost matrix* for the term rewriting rules. Taking the same definition of the cost of a sequence of term rewriting rules, the *edit distance* between terms $t_1, t_2 \in \mathcal{T}(\Sigma_{\text{term}})$ is defined by

$$D_{\text{term}}(t_1, t_2) = \min \left\{ \sum_{i=1}^{n} \delta(\sigma_i) : \exists \sigma_1, \ldots, \sigma_n \text{ such that } t_1 \Rightarrow^{*}_{\sigma_1 \ldots \sigma_n} t_2 \right\} .$$

Since $(\Sigma_{\text{term},\bot}, \delta)$ is a metric space, $(\mathcal{T}(\Sigma_{\text{term}}), D_{\text{term}})$ is also a metric space.

Example 2. Consider the terms $t_1 = a(b, c(d))$, and $t_2 = a(b(d))$. Then a sequence of editing operations transforming t_1 to t_2 with minimal cost is one of

$$a(b, c(d)) \Rightarrow_{b \to \bot} a(c(d)) \Rightarrow_{c \to b} a(b(d))$$
$$a(b, c(d)) \Rightarrow_{c \to \bot} a(b, d) \Rightarrow_{d \to \bot} a(b) \quad \Rightarrow_{\bot \to d} a(b(d)) .$$

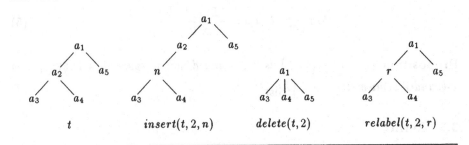

Fig. 2. Editing operations on terms

The first derivation is optimal for the trivial metric. □

The algorithm for computing the edit distance between terms and the following theorem can be found in Zhang and Sasha [18] ($depth(t)$, and $leaves(t)$ denotes the *depth*, and the *number of leaves* of the term t, respectively):

Theorem 3. *The edit distance between terms t_1 and t_2 can be computed in time*

$$O\left(|t_1| \times |t_2| \times \min(depth(t_1), leaves(t_1)) \times \min(depth(t_2), leaves(t_2))\right)$$

and space $O\left(|t_1| \times |t_2|\right)$. □

In contrast to lists, in the next example we show that $\max(|t_1|, |t_2|)$ is not an *upper bound* on D_{term}.

Example 3. Let δ be the trivial metric on $\{\perp, a, b, c\}$, and consider the terms $t_1 = a(a \cdots (a)) \cdots)$ (i.e. a *chain* of a's) and $t_2 = b(c, \ldots, c)$ with $|t_1| = |t_2| = n$. The edit distance is $D_{\text{term}}(t_1, t_2) = 2n - 2$. □

Although $\text{DIFF}_{\text{term}}(t_1, t_2) < |t_1| + |t_2|$ for every 1-bounded metric space $(\Sigma_{\text{term}, \perp}, \delta)$, and $t_1, t_2 \in \mathcal{T}(\Sigma_{\text{term}})$, we normalize with another function measuring the *structural difference* of t_1, and t_2 and giving a tighter upper bound.

Let t_1, and t_2 be terms. A *mapping* from t_1 to t_2 (denoted by $M_{t_1 \to t_2}$) is a one-to-one correspondence between subsets of nodes of t_1, and t_2, respectively, such that by deleting the 'untouched' nodes from t_1 and t_2, respectively, the remaining terms are identical up to relabeling (the formal definition, and properties of mapping can be found in Tai [14]). If there is no confusion we use M instead of $M_{t_1 \to t_2}$.

Example 4. Consider the two terms given in Example 2. $M_1 = \{(a, a), (b, b)\}$ is a mapping from t_1 to t_2, because deleting nodes c, and d in t_1, and d in t_2, we get terms with the same structure, i.e. $a(b)$ for both terms.

$M_2 = \{(a, a), (c, b), (d, d)\}$ is also a mapping, as the resulting terms $(a(c(d))$, and $a(b(d))$ are identical up to relabeling. □

Let $M_{t_1 \to t_2}$ be a mapping. By the definition of mapping, M is a set of ordered pairs. We denote by $\mathcal{U}_1(M)$ (resp. $\mathcal{U}_2(M)$) the set of nodes of t_1 (resp. t_2) *untouched* by M. The *size* of a mapping is defined by

$$size(M) = |M| + |\mathcal{U}_1(M)| + |\mathcal{U}_2(M)| . \tag{6}$$

The *optimal mapping* $M_{t_1 \to t_2}^{\text{OPT}}$ is a mapping with the smallest size.

In RIBL difference between terms is defined by

$$\text{DIFF}_{\text{term}}(t_1, t_2) = \frac{D_{\text{term}}(t_1, t_2)}{size\left(M_{t_1 \to t_2}^{\text{OPT}}\right)} . \tag{7}$$

Example 5. Let t_1, and t_2 be the terms defined in Example 2. $D_{\text{term}}(t_1, t_2) = 2$ using the trivial metric. The optimal mapping is $M_{t_1 \to t_2}^{\text{OPT}} = \{(a, a), (c, b), (d, d)\}$. Since $\mathcal{U}_1\left(M_{t_1 \to t_2}^{\text{OPT}}\right) = \{b\}$, and $\mathcal{U}_2\left(M_{t_1 \to t_2}^{\text{OPT}}\right) = \emptyset$, $size\left(M_{t_1 \to t_2}^{\text{OPT}}\right) = 3 + 1 + 0$ by (6). Applying (7) we get $\text{DIFF}_{\text{term}}(t_1, t_2) = 2/4$. □

Proposition 2. *If $\left(\Sigma_{\text{term},\perp}, \delta\right)$ is a 1-bounded metric space then $\text{DIFF}_{\text{term}}$ is a 1-bounded semi-metric on $\mathcal{T}\left(\Sigma_{\text{term}}\right)$.* □

In RIBL, $size\left(M_{t_1 \to t_2}^{\text{OPT}}\right)$ is computed as follows: let t_1/a (resp. t_2/b) denote the terms obtained from t_1 (resp. t_2) by replacing the label of each node to a (resp. b). Then

$$size\left(M_{t_1 \to t_2}^{\text{OPT}}\right) = D_{\text{term}}(t_1/a, t_2/b)$$

taking the trivial metric on $\{\perp, a, b\}$.

3.4 Lists as Terms

The standard term representation of lists is given by the function symbol ./2, and the empty list $\perp$ (or []). $\text{DIFF}_{\text{list}}$, and $\text{DIFF}_{\text{term}}$ may differ on the same lists, e.g.

$$2/2 = \text{DIFF}_{\text{list}}\left([a,b],[b,a]\right) \neq \text{DIFF}_{\text{term}}\left(.(a,.(b,\perp)),.(b,.(a,\perp))\right) = 2/5$$

using the trivial metric on $\{\perp, a, b\}$.

Let $l = [a_1, \ldots, a_n]$ be a list in $\mathcal{L}\left(\Sigma_{\text{list}}\right)$. The *chain term* representation of l is $a_1(a_2(\cdots(a_n)\cdots))$. Let l_1^c, and l_2^c denote the chain representations of $l_1 = [a_1, \ldots, a_n]$, and $l_2 = [b_1, \ldots, b_m]$, respectively. Since $D_{list}(l_1, l_2) = D_{\text{term}}\left(l_1^c, l_2^c\right)$, and $\max(|l_1|, |l_2|) = size\left(M_{l_1^c \to l_2^c}^{\text{OPT}}\right)$,

$$\text{DIFF}_{\text{list}}\left(l_1, l_2\right) = \text{DIFF}_{\text{term}}\left(l_1^c, l_2^c\right)$$

for every metric used in both representations.

Applying Theorem 3 to l_1^c, and l_2^c, the edit distance of lists in the chain term representation can be computed in $O(mn)$. The reason why we handle lists and terms separately is that the time and space complexity for computing edit distance between lists given in [15] is always as good as the complexity of computing their edit distance in the chain term representation, and the norm function of lists can be computed in linear time.

4 Empirical Evaluation

In this section we discuss the result of the revised version of RIBL (RIBL 2.0) on the *mRNA signal structure detection* problem [4]. For comparison, we have used two older versions of RIBL, RIBL 1.0 (the original variant of [6] described in Section 2), and the intermediate version RIBL 1.5 (RIBL 1.0 extended with the *list* argument type, but lacking the ability of RIBL 2.0 to handle arbitrary terms).

mRNA is a single stranded nucleic acid, copied from the DNA double strand of the cell nucleus. The elements of this sequence are the four bases *adenine* (A), *cytosine* (C), *guanine* (G) and *uracil* (U), which can pair up in three symmetric configurations: the two stable Watson-Crick pairs A-U and G-C and the weak G-U pair. The effect of this intramolecular base pairing is a folding of the mRNA sequence that forms a *secondary structure*. To describe these structures one often uses the abstraction of different building blocks (structure elements) like *stacking regions, hairpin loops, internal loops, bulge loops, multibranch loops* and *dangling ends* (Zuker and Stiegler [19]) and a form of *tree representation* (Shapiro and Zhang [13]). The mRNA molecule can contain interesting substructures called *signal structures* because they are involved in the regulatory machinery. The biological function of each signal structure class is based on the common characteristic binding site of all signal structure elements, which means these structures are not necessarily identical but *very similar*. They can slightly vary in their topology, in the sizes of their structure elements and in their base sequence. The *goal* of the experiments described here was to recognize instances of the given 5 signal structure classes (see below) in mRNA molecules.

4.1 Representation

In the *term* representation, each training instance is described as an example by the ground fact

<signal_structure_class>(struct_id:name),

where <signal_structure_class> is a unique predicate name for each mRNA signal structure class (in the domain, we have investigated, it can be one of ire, tar, secis$_1$, secis$_2$ and histone) and *struct_id* is the identifier of the instance. Structures and structure elements are represented by the background predicates

> structure(*struct_id*:**name**, *topology*:**term**)
>   vertex(*se_id*:**name**)
>   helical(*se_id*:**name**, *type*:**constant**, *size*:**number**, *bases*:**list**, *bases*:**list**)
>   single(*se_id*:**name**, *type*:**constant**, *size*:**number**, *bases*:**list**)

where *topology* is the *topology* (tree structure) of the structure elements and *se_id, size, bases* and *type* represents the *identifier*, the sequence *length*, the amino acid *sequence* and the *type* of the structure elements, respectively (see Figure 3). In our case, *type* is one of {stem, hairpin, bulge5, bulge3, single}. A structure element is described by either a helical or a single predicate.

Since RIBL 1.0 and RIBL 1.5 could not handle terms, two 'flat' (for RIBL 1.0) and two list-based 'non-flat' representations (for RIBL 1.5) were also used:

- *index*: structure elements are represented as ground facts of the form

  <se_type>(struct_id:name, se_ix:number, size:number, bases:discrete),

- *neighbor*: with respect to the representation *index*, it uses additional information about the *next* structure element of *struct_id*.

In the 'non-flat' *alignment* versions of the 'flat' representations, type *bases* has been changed from **discrete** to **list**, i.e. amino acid sequences have been represented as lists.

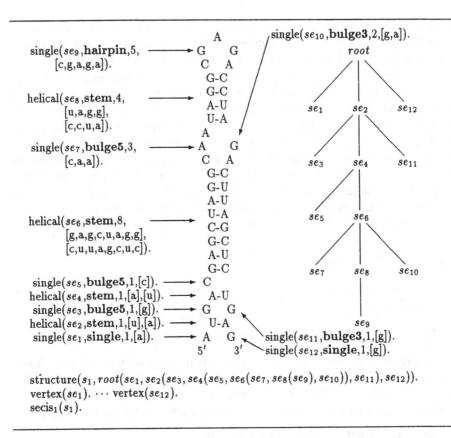

single(se_9,**hairpin**,5, [c,g,a,g,a]).

helical(se_8,**stem**,4, [u,a,g,g], [c,c,u,a]).

single(se_7,**bulge5**,3, [c,a,a]).

helical(se_6,**stem**,8, [g,a,g,c,u,a,g,g], [c,u,u,a,g,c,u,c]).

single(se_5,**bulge5**,1,[c]).
helical(se_4,**stem**,1,[a],[u]).
single(se_3,**bulge5**,1,[g]).
helical(se_2,**stem**,1,[u],[a]).
single(se_1,**single**,1,[a]).

single(se_{10},**bulge3**,2,[g,a]).

single(se_{11},**bulge3**,1,[g]).
single(se_{12},**single**,1,[g]).

structure(s_1, root(se_1, se_2(se_3, se_4(se_5, se_6(se_7, se_8(se_9), se_{10})), se_{11}), se_{12})).
vertex(se_1). ⋯ vertex(se_{12}).
secis$_1$(s_1).

Fig. 3. The representation and the tree structure of a SECIS signal structure.

4.2 Defining δ for the Different Types

In the preceding sections, we have treated constant, list and term differences as basic (non-recursive) difference functions which rely on metrics δ for comparing individual symbols. One possibility is to use user-defined metrics which allows the encoding of additional domain knowledge from the user. Another attractive possibility is to use the basic idea again, and compute the similarity of two symbols by a recursively call to the similarity measure!

In our particular application, we have used a manual definition of δ for constants (referred to as $\delta_{constant}$ in the following), the trivial δ for lists (δ_{list}), and a recursively computed δ for terms (δ_{term}).

The metric δ_{term} between labels of the tree structure is computed in two steps:

1. first, we compute a *semi-metric* on the labels by recursively recalling RIBL's similarity measure,
2. we transform this semi-metric into a *metric* δ_{term}.

In the rest of this subsection we discuss the above two steps in details.

In our representation, each node has a unique label *se_id* of type **name** and for each label a there is a ground fact vertex(a), and another ground fact L_a of the form helical(a, t, n, l_1, l_2), or single(a, t, n, l) (see Section 4.1). Since Σ_{term} is the set of all labels, the metric δ_{term} on $\Sigma_{\text{term}, \perp}$ is based on the *difference* between the *cases* of a, and b. As we use DEPTH = 1, DIFF$_{\text{case}}(a, b) =$ DIFF$_{\text{lit}}(L_a, L_b)$ for every $a, b \in \Sigma_{\text{term}, \perp}$. DIFF$_{\text{lit}}(L_a, L_b)$ is 1 if L_a, and L_b are not compatible atoms (i.e. they have different predicate names and/or arities), and it is the sum of the difference of the non-name arguments dividing by the number of the non-name arguments. The cost of inserting a node with label a is defined as DIFF$_{\text{lit}}(L_a, \perp_{\text{literal}})$, where $\perp_{\text{literal}}$ is either single($\perp, \perp, 0, \perp$), or helical($\perp, \perp, 0, \perp, \perp$) depending on the type of the structure element a, for every $a \in \Sigma_{\text{term}}$.

For computing DIFF$_{\text{constant}}$ we use the semi-metric δ_{constant} for the structure element types (type:**constant**) given in Table 1.

	$\perp$	single	bulge3	bulge5	hairpin	stem
$\perp$	0	0.03	0.03	0.03	0.90	0.03
single		0	0.03	0.03	0.18	1.0
bulge3			0	0.06	0.12	1.0
bulge5				0	0.12	1.0
hairpin					0	1.0
stem						0

Table 1. Semi-metric for structure element types

These are heuristic costs and still under progress. Two properties are essential. First, helical and single stranded regions are morphologically substantially different and should therefore not be mapped. Secondly the hairpin loop takes up an exceptional position because its insertion or deletion produces also a quite substantial morphological difference.

For the comparison of the amino acid sequences (type list), we use the trivial distance δ_{list} on $\{\perp, A, C, G, U\}$.

Since DIFF$_{\text{lit}}$ is a semi-metric, we use δ_{term} obtained from DIFF$_{\text{lit}}$ by

$$\delta_{\text{term}}(a, b) = \min(1, \text{DIFF}_{\text{lit}}(a, b) + C) \tag{8}$$

for every $a, b \in \Sigma_{\text{term}, \perp}$, where C is the maximum of

$$\frac{\text{DIFF}_{\text{lit}}(a, b) - \text{DIFF}_{\text{lit}}(a, c) - \text{DIFF}_{\text{lit}}(c, b)}{2}$$

for every $a, b, c \in \Sigma_{\text{term}, \perp}$ violating the triangle inequality.

4.3 Data and Experiments

The mRNA signal structure domain contains so far only 66 signal structures, composed of 15 IRE (Iron Responsive Element; Klausner, Rouault and Harford [8]), 15 TAR (Trans Activating Region; McCarthy and Kollmus [10]), 2×15 SECIS (Selenocysteine Insertion Sequence; Low and Berry [9], and 6 histone stemloops (Belasco and Brawerman [2]).

The results of the three versions of RIBL (ran on the appropriate representations) are summarized in Table 2. Remember, signal structures have both a

version	representation	DEPTH	accuracy (%)	k	cpu time (sec)
RIBL 1.0	index	1	77	1	0.493
RIBL 1.5	index + alignment	1	79	1	4.343
RIBL 1.0	neighbor	2	83	3	2.772
RIBL 1.5	neighbor + alignment	2	83	1	15.524
RIBL 2.0	**term**	1	**97**	5	32.850

Table 2. Results in different representations.

structural motif and a sequence motif. In the first experiment - representation *index* - the structure is basically described by the membership of the several structure elements, i.e. the neighborship relations respective the topology as whole was neglected. This was improved by the *neighbor* representation. The deficiency consists in its restriction of adjacent elements. The topology as whole may only be described adequately by the *term* representation. The influence of the sequence motif can be seen in the improvement of the alignment versions.

All the experiments were done on a Ultrasparc with OS Solaris 2.5. The optimal number of neighbors (k) has been estimated by the *leave-one-out* evaluation method.

5 Related Work

Two different ways are distinguished in the literature of distance definitions for first order logic: the *semantical* (Sebag [12]) and the *syntactical* ([7,11]) distances. As a first step, the syntactical approaches introduce an appropriate metric or pseudo-metric on ground expressions (i.e. on terms and atoms). In this section we show that the behavior of the term editing distance differs basically from the term distances of [7,11].

For two terms with small edit distance, the pseudo-distance with the size function S on substitutions given in [7] may be too big. Another property of the pseudo-metric in [7] is that the difference between the standard term representations ($n : s^n(\perp)$) of two different natural numbers is always a constant depending on S, while it is a function of n and m, in our case (see Section 5.1).

Considering the term representations of lists, [11] does not take into account the *suffix* of the longer list, i.e. the distance between l_1 and l_2 is equal to the distance between l_1 and $l_2 + l$, for every lists l_1, l_2, l with $|l_1| \leq |l_2|$. Furthermore, it may happen that terms with big and other terms with small edit distances may have very close distances by [11]. In the case of distance between different natural numbers, the result is independent of the greater number (see Section 5.1).

5.1 Quantitative Comparison of Metrics on Examples

Since D_1 is a pseudo-metric with no upper bound, and D_2 is a 1-bounded metric on terms, we compare D_1 and D_2 with D_{term} and DIFF_{term}, respectively. We consider the following three cases:

1. Let $f, a_1, \ldots, a_n$ $(n > 1)$ be different symbols and consider the terms

$$t_{1,1} = f(a_1, f(a_2, \cdots f(a_{n-1}, a_n) \cdots)) \text{ and}$$
$$t_{1,2} = f(a_2, f(a_3, \cdots f(a_{n-1}, a_n) \cdots)) .$$

2. Let f, a_1, a_2 be different symbols and consider the terms

$$t_{2,1} = f(a_1, f(a_1, \cdots f(a_1, a_1) \cdots)) \text{ and } t_{2,2} = f(a_2, f(a_2, \cdots f(a_2, a_2) \cdots))$$

with $|t_{2,1}| = |t_{2,2}| = 2n - 1$ $(n > 1)$.

3. Let $s^n(\perp)$ denote the n applications of the unary function symbol s (successor) to $\perp$, i.e. $s^n(\perp)$ denotes the integer n $(n > 0)$. Let $t_{3,1} = s^n(\perp)$ and $t_{3,2} = s^m(\perp)$ for some $n > m \geq 0$ (all the distances are 0 for $n = m$).

Using the size function S of [7] with $wt_\perp = 0$ and $wt_{a_i} = 1$ for $i = 1, \ldots, n$ and the trivial metrics for the edit distances, we get

	D_1	D_{term}	D_2	DIFF_{term}
$(t_{1,1}, t_{1,2})$	$2n+1$	2	$\frac{1+2^{5-2n}}{3}$	$\frac{2}{2n-1}$
$(t_{2,1}, t_{2,2})$	2	n	$\frac{1+2^{3-2n}}{3}$	$\frac{n}{2n-1}$
$(t_{3,1}, t_{3,2})$	2	$n-m$	2^{-m}	$\frac{n-m}{n+1}$

We note that $\lim_{n \to \infty} D_2(t_{1,1}, t_{1,2}) = \lim_{n \to \infty} D_2(t_{2,1}, t_{2,2})$.

6 Summary, Open Problems, and Future Works

In this paper we have shown that lists and terms with similarities based on edit distance improves the accuracy of RIBL 1.0 on the mRNA signal structure detection problem. We think that an appropriate distance is strongly application dependent, e.g. the nature of the mRNA signal structure detection problem requires such a syntactical distance that is not sensitive to the depth of the differences and is *stable*, i.e. small changes on a term do not cause big distances. Therefore, the distances on terms given in [7, 11] are not appropriate for this application. However, we do not state in general that the proposed edit distance on terms was *better* than other existing metrics, e.g. [7] or [11].

Below we list some of the open problems, and future works.

- Throughout this paper terms have been considered as labeled ordered trees, i.e. the arities of the function symbols (labels) have not been taken into account. Hence, the method assumes implicitly that a label f corresponds to the set of function symbols f/n for $n \geq 0$ and the cost of a rewriting rule is independent on the arities of its symbols. If the ranked alphabet is not previously given (which corresponds to the most practical cases), how can we extend automatically a metric δ on $\Sigma_{\text{term}} = \{\perp, f, g, \ldots\}$ to a metric δ' on

$$\Sigma'_{\text{term}} = \{\perp, f/0, f/1, f/2, \ldots, g/0, g/1, g/2, \ldots\}$$

by using an *appropriate* function of $\delta(f, g)$, n and m for $\delta'(f/n, g/m)$?

- The size of an optimal mapping between terms t_1, and t_2 is computed in RIBL by $D_{\text{term}}(t_1/a, t_2/b)$ using the trivial metric on $\{\perp, a, b\}$. As it is a special case of Theorem 3, is there a *better* algorithm to this problem?

- We get 1-bounded *semi-metrics* from *metrics* by dividing with $\max(|l_1|, |l_2|)$ and with the size of an optimal mapping in (5) and (7), respectively. Are there other expressions $N_{\text{list}}(l_1, l_2)$ and $N_{\text{term}}(t_1, t_2)$ such that

$$\frac{D_{\text{list}}(l_1, l_2)}{N_{\text{list}}(l_1, l_2)} \text{ and } \frac{D_{\text{term}}(t_1, t_2)}{N_{\text{term}}(t_1, t_2)},$$

remain 1-bounded *metrics* with *supremum* 1?

- In this paper, lists and terms have been defined above alphabets consisting of only *constants*. However, even in the mRNA signal structure application the labels of the terms were not constants. Since they were previously given, we could compute first a distance δ by a recursive manner and in a second step we had to adjust the values of δ by (8) in order to get a metric. Is it possible to extend the method to *arbitrary* lists and terms (i.e. where the alphabet belongs to an *aggregate* type) if the alphabet is not previously given?

- Distances between clauses are defined by either a semantical way ([12]) or by an extension of distances on to *Hausdorff metrics* ([7, 11]). We are going to investigate other kind of approach based on *combinatorial optimization* methods, e.g. the *weighted matching* problem, where the *weight* of an edge can be defined as *edit distance* between literals.

Acknowledgments

We thank János Csirik and Dietrich Wettschereck for useful discussions and Mathias Kirsten for technical support of the implementation. The second and the third authors were partially supported by the ESPRIT IV Long Term Research Project ILP II (No. 20237).

References

1. A. Aho. Algorithms for Finding Patterns in Strings. In J. van Leeuwen, editor, *Handbook of Theoretical Computer Science, Volume A: Algorithms and Complexity*, pages 255–300. The MIT Press, 1990.

2. J. G. Belasco and G. Brawerman. *Control of messengerRNA Stability*. Academic Press, 1993.
3. G. Bisson. Conceptual Clustering in a First-Order Logic Representation. In B. Neumann, editor, *Proceedings of the 10th European Conference on Artificial Intelligence*, pages 458–462. John Wiley, 1992.
4. U. Bohnebeck, W. Sälter, O. Herzog, M. Wischnewsky, and D. Blohm. An Approach to mRNA Signalstructure Detection through Knowledge Discovery. In *Proceedings of GCB'97*, pages 125–126, 1997.
5. S. Džeroski, S. Schulze-Kremer, K. Heidtke, K. Siems, and D. Wettschereck. Applying ILP to Diterpene Structure Elucidation from ^{13}C NMR Spectra. In S. Muggleton, editor, *Proceedings of the 6th International Workshop on Inductive Logic Programming*, pages 14–27. Stockholm University, Royal Institute of Technology, 1996.
6. W. Emde and D. Wettschereck. Relational Instance-Based Learning. In L. Saitta, editor, *Proceedings of the 13th International Conference on Machine Learning*, pages 122–130. Morgan Kaufmann, 1996.
7. A. Hutchinson. Metrics on Terms and Clauses. In M. Someren and G. Widmer, editors, *Proceedings of the 9th European Conference on Machine Learning*, volume 1224 of *LNAI*, pages 138–145. Springer-Verlag, 1997.
8. R. D. Klausner, T. A. Rouault, and J. B. Harford. Regulating the Fate of mRNA: The Control of Cellular Iron Metabolism. *Cell*, **72**:19–28, 1993.
9. S. L. Low and M. J. Berry. Knowing When Not to Stop: Selenocysteine Incorporation in Eukaryotes. *Trends in Biochemistry Sciences*, **21**:203–208, 1996.
10. J. E. G. McCarthy and H. Kollmus. Cytoplasmic mRNA-Protein Interactions in Eukaryotic Gene Expression. *Trends in Biochemistry Sciences*, pages 191–197, 1995.
11. S.-H. Nienhuys-Cheng. Distance Between Herbrand Interpretations: A Measure for Approximations to a Target Concept. In N. Lavrač and S. Džeroski, editors, *Proceedings of the 7th International Workshop on Inductive Logic Programming*, volume 1297 of *LNAI*, pages 213–226. Springer-Verlag, 1997.
12. M. Sebag. Distance Induction in First Order Logic. In N. Lavrač and S. Džeroski, editors, *Proceedings of the 7th International Workshop on Inductive Logic Programming*, volume 1297 of *LNAI*, pages 264–272. Springer-Verlag, 1997.
13. B. A. Shapiro and K. Zhang. Comparing Multiple RNA Secondary Structures Using Tree Comparisons. *CABIOS*, **6**(4):309–318, 1990.
14. K. Tai. The Tree-to-Tree Correction Problem. *Journal of the ACM*, **26**(3):422–433, 1979.
15. E. Ukkonen. Algorithms for Approximate String Matching. *Inform. and Control*, **64**:100–118, 1985.
16. R. Wagner and M. Fischer. The String-to-String Correction Problem. *Journal of the ACM*, **21**(1):168–173, 1974.
17. D. Wettschereck and D. Aha. Weighting Features. In M. Veloso and A. Aamodt, editors, *Proceedings of the 1st International Conference on Case-Based Reasoning*, volume 1010 of *LNAI*, pages 347–358. Springer-Verlag, 1995.
18. K. Zhang and D. Shasha. Simple Fast Algorithms for the Editing Distance Between Trees and Related Problems. *SIAM J. Computing*, **18**(6):1245–1262, 1989.
19. M. Zuker and P. Stiegler. Optimal Computer Folding of Large RNA Sequences Using Thermodynamics and Auxiliary Information. *Nucleic Acids Research*, **9**(1), 1980.

Stochastic Propositionalization of Non-determinate Background Knowledge

Stefan Kramer[1], Bernhard Pfahringer[1], and Christoph Helma[2]

[1] Austrian Research Institute for Artificial Intelligence,
Schottengasse 3, A-1010 Vienna, Austria
{stefan,bernhard}@ai.univie.ac.at
[2] Institute for Tumor Biology – Cancer Research
University of Vienna,
Borschkegasse 8a, A-1090 Vienna, Austria
Christoph.Helma@univie.ac.at

Abstract. Both propositional and relational learning algorithms require a good representation to perform well in practice. Usually such a representation is either engineered manually by domain experts or derived automatically by means of so-called constructive induction. Inductive Logic Programming (ILP) algorithms put a somewhat less burden on the data engineering effort as they allow for a structured, relational representation of background knowledge. In chemical and engineering domains, a common representational device for graph-like structures are so-called non-determinate relations. Manually engineered features in such domains typically test for or count occurrences of specific substructures having specific properties. However, representations containing non-determinate relations pose a serious efficiency problem for most standard ILP algorithms. Therefore, we have devised a stochastic algorithm to automatically derive features from non-determinate background knowledge. The algorithm conducts a top-down search for first-order clauses, where each clause represents a binary feature. These features are used instead of the non-determinate relations in a subsequent induction step. In contrast to comparable algorithms search is not class-blind and there are no arbitrary size restrictions imposed on candidate clauses. An empirical investigation in three chemical domains supports the validity and usefulness of the proposed algorithm.

1 Introduction

A very large number of algorithms require a propositional representation, whereas many real-world learning problems are essentially relational. To bridge this gap, various researchers (e.g., [11]) have proposed a transformational approach. This type of transformation is called propositionalization.

Propositionalization is also a necessity for types of background knowledge that even full-fledged ILP learners cannot handle efficiently, namely background knowledge "containing" non-determinate literals. Literals are non-determinate if they introduce new variables that can be bound in several alternative ways.

Non-determinate literals often introduce additional parts of a structure like adjacent nodes in a graph. (Other examples are "part-of"-literals.) Non-determinate background knowledge poses a serious problem for greedy hill-climbing search, since non-determinate literals in themselves do not provide any gain. On the other hand, complete search needs some arbitrary length restriction on clauses to make induction practical due to the extremely large search spaces encountered otherwise. Current solutions either rely on manually engineered features or employ solutions based on look-ahead, for instance by so-called relational cliches [18].

In general, full equivalence between the original and the transformed problem can only be achieved for certain subsets of first-order logic and certain types of background knowledge ([11], [3], [4]). But even if an equivalent transformation exists theoretically, its size (measured as the number of propositional features generated) is usually huge in most interesting application domains. Thus, any subsequent propositional learner will need to employ some form of feature subset selection. So for pragmatic reasons we should not expect the transformed problem to be equivalent to the original problem. Note that such a transformation may also be viewed as a kind of *constructive induction*, i.e., as a representational change for improved learning performance.

It should be clear that the *problems* of propositionalization and of concept learning are not the same, even if there are similarities in the *solutions* to these problems. Firstly, constructing new features should best be viewed as a preparatory step prior to learning. Propositional learning algorithms heavily rely on "good" features. Secondly, most learning tasks involve solving the set-cover problem. During feature construction we do not have to bother about coverage. Rather, we have to strive for features that help to create useful *partitions* of the examples. Thirdly, concept learning is supervised, while feature construction can be supervised or unsupervised (concept formation). Fourthly, in practice we often know some expert-provided features (such as the so-called "Hansch attributes" or "structural alerts" in toxicology), and we are interested in finding features that complement them.

Since we have to select from a large number of features, we have to specify preferences. We used the following constraints that should be fulfilled by features constructed from background knowledge. The constructed features should be

- (**C1**) not too specific and not too general.
- (**C2**) not too complex. (So they have at least a potential for being comprehensible.)
- (**C3**) different from one another.
- (**C4**) different from existing, expert-provided features.

In the next section we describe a new algorithm for propositionalization which considers the above constraints in a rather straight-forward fashion. In section 3, we will present experimental results from chemical domains. In section 4, we will review related work. Section 5 is devoted to discussion.

2   Description of the Method

In this section we describe a new algorithm for propositionalization. The algorithm stochastically conducts a top-down search for first-order clauses, where each clause represents a binary feature. It differs from existing algorithms in that its search is not class-blind, and that it is capable of considering clauses of arbitrary length (size).

First we give a brief overview of the algorithm as it is described in Figure 1. In the following, the algorithm will be referred to as SP.

The algorithm maintains three sets of clauses. One set (*CurrentClauses*) contains the clauses of the current generation. This set (of fixed size *NrClauses*) is developed over a predefined number of generations (*NrGenerations*). Another set of what we will call "parent clauses" (*ParentClauses*) contains the clauses which are the basis for specializations. The third set (*BestClauses*) is simply the set of the best clauses found so far.

The algorithm proceeds in the following way: in each step, the set of *CurrentClauses* is obtained by stochastically removing the *NrClausesToReplace* clauses from the set of best clauses so far. Note that the starting point for refinements is always the best theory so far, which is intended to focus search. The probability of removing a clause is proportional to $1/fitness(Clause)$ (the fitness function is defined below). The same number of clauses, *NrClausesToReplace*, is generated stochastically in each step, and added to the set of current clauses. After that, the current set of clauses is compared with the best set of clauses so far. If the current set is better than the best set so far, it is remembered as the new best set so far. After *NrGenerations* generations of clauses, the best set of clauses up to then is returned.

Every newly generated clause is a candidate for being a parent clause, but only a subset of parent clauses is actually kept. The reason for this is that the chance of selecting a good parent clause decreases with an increase in the number of parent clauses. Only those candidate parent clauses with the best expected fitness of refinements are kept. In contrast to all other parent clauses, the most general clause can never be discarded. This enables recovery from too many overly specific clauses in the population.

The algorithm that generates new clauses can be found in Figure 2: it randomly selects a parent from the set of potential parents with a probability proportional to the *expected fitness of all possible refinements*. Subsequently, a literal is selected for refining the chosen parent clause with a probability proportional to the fitness of the resulting clause. The refinement operator is defined in terms of schemata [1].

The definition of the fitness of a clause is shown in Figure 3. The fitness (1) is based on the *Minimum Description Length* (MDL) principle [16]. This principle allows taking into account a model's accuracy and its complexity simultaneously. The key idea is to measure the joint cost of coding a model (in our case a clause) and of coding the data in terms of that model. The main motivation for employing an MDL-based measure is the need for a penalty for overly complex

Fig. 1. Pseudocode of the algorithm for stochastic propositionalization.

---

procedure *stochastic_propositionalization*

Input:
Target:	target literal
NrGenerations:	number of steps to be performed
NrClauses:	number of clauses in the "population"
NrClausesToReplace:	number of clauses to be replaced in each step
NrParentClauses:	number of parent clauses to keep

Output:
BestClauses:	set of clauses corresponding to binary features

$BestClauses \leftarrow randomly\_refine\_parent\_clauses(NrClauses, \{Target \; : - \; true\})$

$ParentClauses \leftarrow select\_best\_parent\_clauses(NrParentClauses - 1, BestClauses)$
$\qquad\qquad\qquad \cup\{Target \; : - \; true\}$

for $i \leftarrow 2$ **to** *NrGenerations* **do**

$\quad CurrentClauses \leftarrow$
$\quad randomly\_remove\_clauses(NrClausesToReplace, BestClauses)$
$\quad$ /*
$\quad$ Randomly remove clauses from the set of best clauses, with a
$\quad$ probability proportional to the inverse of the fitness of the
$\quad$ respective clause.
$\quad$ */
$\quad NewClauses \leftarrow$
$\quad randomly\_refine\_parent\_clauses(NrClausesToReplace, ParentClauses)$
$\quad CurrentClauses \leftarrow CurrentClauses \cup NewClauses$
$\quad ParentClauses \leftarrow select\_best\_parent\_clauses(NrParentClauses - 1,$
$\qquad\qquad\qquad\qquad ParentClauses \setminus \{Target \; : - \; true\} \cup NewClauses)$
$\qquad\qquad\qquad \cup\{Target \; : - \; true\}$

$\quad$ **if** $fitness(CurrentClauses) > fitness(BestClauses)$ **then**
$\qquad BestClauses \leftarrow CurrentClauses$

return *BestClauses*
end procedure

---

clauses (see **C2** above). The coding cost of a clause (2) is the sum of the coding costs of the selections made from all possible refinements while building the clause. In (2), $poss(i)$ is the number of possible refinements when selecting literal l_i. In effect, we encode the "history" of the clause construction. The coding cost of the errors (3) uses an encoding of selections of subsets of a set that is due to Cameron-Jones [15]. In (3), $eoc(cl)$ is the number of errors of commission of the clause in question, and $eoo(cl)$ is the number of errors of omission. $ce(cl)$ is the number of examples covered by the clause, and $ne(cl)$ is the number of examples that are not covered by the clause. So, negative examples covered by a clause are encoded as well as positive examples not covered. Basically, the Cameron-Jones encoding (4) maps the respective subsets to integers, such that subsets of the same size have the same coding length. This coding scheme is quite redundant, but it has the nice property that the coding length increases monotonically with the number of errors.

The expected fitness of a parent clause is obtained by evaluating all possible refinements r_i of the parent clause p. Given that the refinements are selected proportional to their fitness, the expected fitness can be calculated as follows:

$$exp.\ fitness(p) = \frac{\sum_{r_i \in refinements(p)} fitness(r_i)^2}{\sum_{r_i \in refinements(p)} fitness(r_i)}$$

Sets of clauses are evaluated in the following way: we construct a decision table using all binary features corresponding to the given clauses, and apply it to the training set. The accuracy figure obtained in this way is used as a quality estimate for the respective sets of clauses. The rationale for this procedure is as follows: a decision table is the most extreme way of combining all features for generating a global partitioning all of examples. Sets of features of strong discriminatory ability should lead to decision tables exhibiting small resubstitution error.

The overall approach would not work, if the clauses in the population were the same extensionally. In other words, there would be no "division of labour" among the clauses (**C3**). (This is also the motivation for the universal suffrage selection algorithm presented in [8].) We took a simple *extension-driven approach* to solve this problem: the algorithm considers only those refinements that yield clauses with an extension different from the extensions of clauses in the current population. The extension has to differ in at least one example to make it different. This (extensional) restriction can also be used to enforce the construction of features that are different from expert-provided features (**C4**). As expert-provided features are a form of established knowledge, the extension-driven approach enables discoveries: the new features have to complement the existing ones.

Finally, the rest of the above constraints are addressed: **C1** is fulfilled by parameters for the required minimum and maximum coverage of clauses. **C2** requires restrictions concerning the complexity of clauses. First, we restrict the maximum number of variables of certain user-defined types, as the number of variables is crucial for the comprehensibility and for the feasibility of search in

Fig. 2. Pseudocode of the procedure for random refinements of given parent clauses.

---

procedure *randomly_refine_parent_clauses*

Input:
NrNewClauses: number of new clauses to be generated as refinements
                            of some of the given parent clauses
ParentClauses: clauses used as basis for refinements

Output:
NewClauses: newly generated clauses

NewClauses ← {}

for i ← 1 **to** *NrNewClauses* **do**
   ParentClause ← *randomly_select_parent_clause*(*ParentClauses*)
   /*
     Selects a parent clause with a probability proportional
     to the expected fitness of all possible refinements.
   */

   NewClause ← *randomly_refine_clause*(*ParentClause*)
   /*
     Selects a refinement of the chosen parent clause with a
     probability proportional to the fitness of the resulting clause.
   */

   NewClauses ← *NewClauses* ∪ {*NewClause*}
return *NewClauses*
end procedure

---

general. Second, no negation is used in the clauses, since it often is detrimental to comprehensibility.

3 Experimental Results

In the following experiments, we applied C4.5 [14] in the learning step after propositionalization.

3.1 Family Domain

We conducted experiments in the family domain [13] with the relations son(A,B) and niece(A,B). Although the family domain is determinate, it helped us see which things work and which do not.

Fig. 3. Definition of the coding cost of a clause and its error on the training data

---

$$fitness(cl) = \frac{1}{c\_clause(cl) + c\_errors(cl)} \qquad (1)$$

$$c\_clause(cl) = \sum_{l_i \in cl} log_2(poss(i)) \qquad (2)$$

$$c\_errors(cl) = cj\_c\_sel(eoc(cl), ce(cl)) + \qquad (3)$$
$$cj\_c\_sel(eoo(cl), ne(cl))$$

$$cj\_c\_sel(E, N) = log^*(\sum_{i=0}^{E} \binom{N}{i}) + c \qquad (4)$$

SP consistently found correct solutions for both relations. (Correct in the sense that the subsequent learning step induced 100% accurate theories.) However, due to the probabilistic nature of the algorithm, there is no guarantee for that. These are a few features found for the relation **son(A,B)**:

```
new_f1(A, B)  :- father(B, A),
                 brother(A, _).

new_f2(A, B)  :- mother(B, A),
                 husband(A, _).

new_f3(A, B)  :- nephew(A, C),
                 brother(B, C).
```

Note that the predicate **male** is not available, so that the algorithm tries to approximate it by **brother(A,_)**, **husband(A, _)** and **nephew(A, C)**. These features are not as trivial as it may seem. They are all more specific than the target concept, but together they are sufficient to learn it correctly. For **niece**, SP generates features like the following:

```
new_f4(A, B)  :- aunt(B, A).

new_f5(A, B)  :- daughter(A, _).
```

Since the family domain is very simple, all the work is already done in the propositionalization step. In most real-world domains, however, the chance of finding the correct concept during propositionalization is very small. So usually the work is divided by the propositionalization algorithm and by the subsequently applied learning algorithm.

3.2 Experiments in Three Chemical Domains

Table 1. Performance of the compared methods in three chemical domains in terms of predictive accuracy

	Mutag. Acc. Mean (σ)	Biod. Acc. Mean (σ)	Carc. Acc. Mean (σ)
SP+C4.5	0.89 (0.06)	0.71 (0.12)	0.65 (0.06)
ProgolFC+C4.5	0.80 (0.10)	0.64 (0.15)	0.46 (0.06)
C4.5	0.89 (0.07)	0.78 (0.21)	0.65 (0.02)
Progol r. BK	0.70 (0.10)	0.55 (0.16)	0.43 (0.07)
Progol f. BK	0.89 (?)	0.59 (0.15)	0.63 (?)

Table 2. Performance of the compared methods in three chemical domains in terms of complexity and the number of constructed features. Note that the number of features constructed by SP is a parameter of the algorithm.

	Mutagenicity		Biodegradability		Carcinogenicity	
	Tree size	# features	Tree size	# features	Tree size	# features
SP+C4.5	11.4	10	4	10	14.6	15
ProgolFC+C4.5	14.5	20	5.8	6.5	59	52.4
C4.5	29	–	16.3	–	50	–

We conducted experiments in three chemical domains to validate the usefulness of the approach. In the first domain, the goal is to predict whether or not a chemical is mutagenic, i.e., if it is harmful to DNA. (For details see [21] and [20]). We used the dataset containing 188 instances (compounds) and performed 10-fold cross-validation. In the second domain, we are trying to predict the half-rate of surface water aerobic aqueous biodegradation in hours [6]. The class to learn is whether this quantity exceeds a certain threshold. The dataset contains 62 chemicals, and we performed 6-fold cross-validation in our tests. The third database, provided by King and Srinivasan [9], contains information about the carcinogenicity of 330 compounds, as classified by the National Institute of Environmental Health Sciences (NIEHS). The NIEHS has classified these chemicals as non-carcinogenic, equivocal and carcinogenic. Here, we performed 5-fold cross-validation for a two-class problem (equivocals are counted as non-carcinogenic).

All compounds are described at the atom-and-bond level, i.e., the chemical structure of a compound is described by the atoms it contains (the relation **atm**) and by a specification of the bonds between the atoms (the relation **sym_bond**). (Both relations are used in the examples below.) All atoms are characterized by their element, their atom type according to the molecular modeling package QUANTA, and their partial charge. The bonds are defined as relations between atoms, and also have types (according to QUANTA).

In the experiments, we compared SP with the currently only other general method for propositionalization of non-determinate background knowledge that has been presented in [19]. This method constructs features based on hypotheses returned by Progol [12]. For each clause, each input-output connected subset of literals is used to define a feature. In the following, we will refer to that method as ProgolFC (Progol feature construction). All experiments except those for Progol with full background knowledge in the mutagenicity domain and in the carcinogenicity domain have been carried out by the authors of this paper. After propositionalization through ProgolFC, we applied C4.5.

The second major reference method is C4.5 run on manually engineered features provided by a domain expert. The manually engineered features have been defined by one of the authors, who is an expert in toxicology. The basis for these features was a Prolog program defining functional groups provided by Srinivasan and King. We refined and extended these definitions to obtain a high-level description of the chemicals in terms of features, each feature counting the occurrences of a type of some functional group. One of the additionally defined groups describes a double bond between a carbon and a nitrogen atom:

```
c2n(Drug,Group,Connections) :-
        atm(Drug,N,n,_,_),
        sym_bond(Drug,N,C,2),
        atm(Drug,C,c,_,_),
        sort([N,C],Group),
        non_ring_non_h_connections(Drug,Group,Connections).
```

Due to lack of space, we cannot include the complete group definitions here. The complete program is available upon request.

The parameter of SP were set as follows in the experiments: $NrGenerations = 100$, $NrClauses = 10$ (for carcinogenicity $NrClauses = 15$), $NrClausesToReplace = 2$, and $NrParentClauses = 20$ (for carcinogenicity $NrParentClauses = 25$). The parameter settings are motivated as follows: the number of binary features is related to the number of examples in the data set. Roughly speaking, the more features there are, the higher the granularity of the partitionings of the examples. More precisely, the largest number of partitions achievable with $NrClauses$ clauses is $2^{NrClauses}$. Note that the subsequent learning algorithm cannot distinguish between any two examples in the same partitioning. So, one should choose the parameter setting dependent on the number of example and on the supposed noise level. The precise theoretical foundation for this intuitive rationale is subject of further work.

The overall settings for carcinogenicity are slightly larger than for the other problems, as this learning problem is more complex.

In Table 1, we summarize the accuracy results of the compared methods in the three domains. In all three domains, SP+C4.5 performed better than ProgolFC+C4.5[1], the only other general-purpose algorithm for propositionalization.

---

[1] Note, however, that ProgolFC is targeted at constructing features for multiple linear regression and does perform well in that context.

The differences are significant in the mutagenicity and the carcinogenicity domain, but not in the biodegradability domain. For biodegradability, only the differences between the best and the worst results are significant. This domain may be the hardest domain for relational learning algorithms and algorithms for propositionalization, because it contains relatively few, structurally diverse examples.

The entries for 'Progol r. BK' are the accuracies achieved by Progol theories given *only* relational background knowledge. These theories are the basis for the subsequent feature construction by ProgolFC. The entries for 'Progol f. BK' are the results by Progol with the full available background knowledge, including global features describing the molecule such as the molecular weight. The results for mutagenicity and for carcinogenicity have been taken from [20] and [9], respectively.

In general, the reason for the performance of ProgolFC is that it heavily relies on the quality of the Progol theories induced from relational background knowledge only. As can be seen in Table 1 (in the entries for 'Progol r. BK'), the accuracies of these theories are quite low. Progol seems to be unable to find compressive clauses given this kind of background knowledge.

Another major observation is that SP-constructed features are competitive with expert-provided features in two of the three domains. Actually, they perform equally well for carcinogenicity and for mutagenicity. Biodegradability is the only domain where SP+C4.5 is worse than C4.5 with expert-provided features.

In the most complex domain, carcinogenicity, the time per generation is approximately 600 seconds on a ultraSPARC workstation with 167 MHz. The runtime of Progol on this workstation is about the same as the one of 15 generations of SP. After 15 generations, SP+C4.5 achieves an accuracy of 64.48%, which is slightly better than the one of the Progol-generated theory given full background knowledge. This accuracy only improves minimally in subsequent generations.

Table 2 shows the results of the methods in these domains with respect to complexity. The sizes of the learned decision trees and the number of generated features are averaged over the cross-validation folds. SP constructs a fixed number of features (this is a user-specified parameter), whereas ProgolFC constructs features depending on the theories returned by Progol. In two of the three domains, SP constructs less features than ProgolFC. When looking at the tree sizes, SP's features tend to allow for the formulation of the most compact trees. Surprisingly, even the trees induced with expert-provided features are larger.

Obviously, the definitions of the generated features increase the overall complexity of a theory, but the features usually are of reasonable size. An example of a clause defining a feature in the mutagenicity domain looks like this:

```
new_f6(A) :- atm(A, B, _, 27, _),
             sym_bond(A, B, C, _),
             atm(A, C, _, 29, _).
```

This means that an atom of type 29 occurs connected to an atom of type 27, where types 27 and 29 designate different kinds of aromatic carbon atoms.

A sample of example features from a successful generation of features in the carcinogenicity domain looks like this:

```
new_f7(A) :- atm(A, _, _, 29, _),
             atm(A, _, n, _,  _).


new_f8(A) :- atm(A, _, br, _, _).


new_f9(A) :- atm(A, B, _, 21, _),
             sym_bond(A, B, C,_),
             atm(A, C, _, 3, _).
```

new_f7 means a carbon atom in a benzene ring connected to another aromatic or heteroaromatic ring and the presence of nitrogen in the compound. This feature covers mainly benzidine compounds which are well known for their carcinogenic activity.

new_f8 covers bromine-containing compounds, mainly carcinogenic brominated aliphatic hydrocarbons.

new_f9 points to a carbon atom in an aromatic five-membered ring with an hydrogen attached to it. It is interesting that the presence of hydrogen excludes substituted and conjugated carbons.

Summing up, SP appears to construct features that allow for the formulation of small and accurate decision trees. Features are constructed automatically, and yet are of a quality comparable to expert-provided features.

4 Related Work

In this section we briefly review related work on propositionalization and stochastic search in machine learning and Inductive Logic Programming.

LINUS [11] was the first system to transform a relational representation into a propositional representation. The hypothesis language of LINUS is restricted to function-free constrained DHDB (deductive hierarchical database) clauses. This implies that no recursion is allowed, and that no new variables may be introduced.

DINUS [11] weakens the language bias of LINUS so that the system can learn clauses with a restricted form of new variables, namely determinate variables. This allows for the same transformation approach as the one taken in LINUS.

Cohen [3] introduces a new restriction on non-determinate free variables called "locality constraint". This can be thought of in terms of schemata [1] or clichés [18] of literals. Newly introduced non-determinate variables may only be reused in literals within the same instantiated schema or cliché.

Turney [22] described a *special-purpose* program for translating the "trains" problem of the East-West challenge into a propositional representation. Zucker and Ganascia [23] proposed to decompose structured examples into several learning examples, which are descriptions of parts of what they call the "natural example". Cohen [4] introduced the notion of "set-valued features", which can be used to transform certain types of background knowledge.

Geibel and Wysotzki [7] propose a method for feature construction in a graph-based representation. The features are obtained through fixed-length paths in the neighborhood of a node in the graph. The constructed features are either "context-dependent node attributes of depth n" or "context dependent edge attributes of depth n". This method is restricted to graphs, and using all fixed-length paths obviously becomes prohibitive for large n.

Srinivasan and King [19] presented a method for feature construction based on hypotheses returned by Progol [12]. For each clause, each input-output connected subset of literals is used to define a feature. In contrast to all previously discussed methods, this method works for all types of background knowledge. Besides, this approach could be applied to any ILP algorithm. SP differs in that it tries to approach the problem of propositionalization directly, without the "help" of an ILP algorithm.

In contrast to SP, REGAL [8] is a *concept learning* algorithm. It is a full-fledged genetic algorithm. REGAL's universal suffrage selection algorithm is the first extension-driven approach to stochastic search in machine learning.

MILP [10] is an ILP algorithm that performs stochastic search for single clauses to overcome the myopic behavior of greedy search. The outer loop of the algorithm still employs the more conventional separate-and-conquer strategy.

In principle, SP is capable of exploring features of arbitrary length, but in practice the constraints are strong enough to keep search focused. The only other algorithm capable of efficiently exploring arbitrary-length features is STILL [17]. Interestingly, STILL is also a stochastic algorithm, but stochastic search is applied in a totally different manner in STILL, namely in the matching phase between features and examples. STILL also uses a totally different representation, which effectively yields black-box classifiers instead of intelligible features.

SUBDUE [5] is an MDL-based algorithm for substructure discovery in graphs. It differs from SP in that its search is class-blind, and that it basically performs a beam search (the current clauses are the parent clauses of the next generation).

5 Discussion

There are quite a few design decisions in SP that at first glance might seem ad-hoc. In the following we will explain some of these decisions. First of all stochastic search is an effective compromise between two extremes, namely greedy search and exhaustive search. Whereas the former considers too few clauses, the latter is overwhelmed by too many of those. Stochastic search is a little less myopic than greedy search while still being tractable.

Search in SP proceeds in a top-down fashion, because better control seems possible when simple clauses are generated first. A similar approach in a bottom-up fashion would have to apply feature subset selection rigorously from an early stage on.

The parent generation is kept separately from the children generation as both roles rely on different evaluation criteria. Whereas parent clauses are judged by the estimated fitness of their possible children, child clauses are judged by their actual own fitness. Obviously a good "child" (i.e. a good feature) need not be a good "parent" (i.e. a good source for refinement), as there may not exist better refinements of an already good feature. Vice versa, clauses with a bad actual fitness may lead to excellent refinements, therefore their expected fitness values can still qualify them as good parent clauses.

Feature search must necessarily take into account the extensions of features both predefined and constructed, as otherwise identical features could not be prevented from entering a generation. Such features would lead to unwanted redundancy and would occupy valuable space in a generation which is of limited size.

The chance of probabilistically selecting a good parent decreases with an ever increasing number of parent clauses, therefore we restrict the set of parent clauses to a small set of clauses of high expected fitness. The only exception to this rule is the most general clause, which will never be discarded, no matter how bad its expected fitness value might be. Refinements of this clause enable recovery from sets of overly complex clauses.

The type of search used in SP is not a genetic algorithm in the strict sense, since no cross-over operator is defined and since the refinement operator is a rather restricted form of mutation allowing only for specializations. Still, the presented search algorithm definitely belongs to the wider range of evolutionary algorithms and therefore shares some of their properties. For instance, it can be viewed as a kind of "anytime" algorithm: the user can choose the currently best set of features and quit the search. On the other hand, evolutionary algorithms tend to be computationally expensive, and our specialized search algorithm is no exception to this general rule. Its total runtimes for constructing a reasonable number of feature generations, translating the examples using the best features, and the subsequent induction step are of the same order as the runtimes of the Progol system [12].

Although SP belongs to the family of evolutionary algorithms, its runtimes need to be improved. This can be achieved by applying approximations instead of precise operations and calculations. For instance, one of the most costly operations is the computation of the expected fitness of all refinements of a candidate parent clause. A suitable approximation of this should be able to speed up the process and still perform well. Secondly, building a decision table may not be necessary to evaluate the performance of a complete set of features. A less time-consuming computation could be performed instead.

6   Conclusion and Further Work

In this paper we presented a stochastic approach to propositionalization of relational background knowledge. In summary, the approach appears to construct features that allow for the formulation of small and accurate decision trees. In experiments in three chemical domains, the constructed features exhibited a quality comparable to manually engineered features.

One can envision transforming SP into a full-fledged self-contained ILP algorithm capable of inducing complete theories. The necessary changes would include a built-in bias towards clauses with a high coverage of positive examples and the addition of a noise-handling mechanism.

Currently, there exists no fully worked-out theory of propositionalization in general and of the stochastic approach in particular. For the set-valued feature approach, [4] employed Blum's infinite attribute model [2] as a theoretical basis. We conjecture that this model could serve as a basis for certain other types of propositionalization as well.

Acknowledgements

This research is part of the project "Carcinogenicity Detection by Machine Learning" supported by the Austrian Federal Ministry of Science and Transport. Partial support is also provided by the "Jubiläumsfond der Österreichischen Nationalbank" under grant number 6930. The Austrian Federal Ministry of Science and Transport provides general financial support for the Austrian Research Institute for AI. We would like to thank Ross King and Ashwin Srinivasan for providing the carcinogenicity data, definitions for functional groups, and the program for feature extraction from Progol-induced theories. We are also indebted to Sašo Džeroski for making the biodegradability data available to us.

References

1. H. Blockeel and L. DeRaedt. Top-down induction of logical decision trees. Technical Report CW 247, Katholieke Universiteit Leuven, Belgium, 1997.
2. A. Blum. Learning boolean functions in an infinite attribute space. *Machine Learning*, 9(4), 1992.
3. W.W. Cohen. Pac-learning nondeterminate clauses. In *Proc. Twelfth National Conference on Artificial Intelligence (AAAI-94)*, 1994.
4. W.W. Cohen. Learning trees and rules with set-valued features. In *Proceedings of the Thirteenth National Conference on Artificial Intelligence (AAAI-96)*, pages 709–716, 1996.
5. D.J. Cook and L.B. Holder. Substructure discovery using minimum description length and background knowledge. *Journal of Artificial Intelligence Research*, 1:231–255, 1994.
6. S. Džeroski and B. Kompare, 1995. Personal Communication.
7. P. Geibel and F. Wysotzki. Relational learning with decision trees. In *Proc. Twelfth European Conference on Artificial Intelligence (ECAI-96)*, pages 428–432, 1996.
8. A. Giordana, L. Saitta, and F. Zini. Learning disjunctive concepts by means of genetic algorithms. In *Proceedings of the Eleventh International Conference on Machine Learning*, pages 96–104, 1994.
9. R.D. King and A. Srinivasan. Prediction of rodent carcinogenicity bioassays from molecular structure using inductive logic programming. *Environmental Health Perspectives*, 1997.
10. M. Kovačič. MILP: a stochastic approach to Inductive Logic Programming. In *Proceedings of the Fourth International Workshop on Inductive Logic Programming (ILP-94)*, GMD-Studien Nr. 237, pages 123–138, 1994.

11. N. Lavrac and S. Džeroski. *Inductive Logic Programming*. Ellis Horwood, Chichester, UK, 1994.

12. S. Muggleton. Inverse Entailment and Progol. *New Generation Computing*, 13:245–286, 1995.

13. J.R. Quinlan. Learning logical definitions from relations. *Machine Learning*, 5:239–266, 1990.

14. J.R. Quinlan. *C4.5: Programs for Machine Learning*. Morgan Kaufmann, San Mateo, CA, 1993.

15. J.R. Quinlan. The minimum description length principle and categorical theories. In *Proceedings of the Eleventh International Conference on Machine Learning*, San Mateo, CA, 1994. Morgan Kaufmann.

16. J. Rissanen. Modeling by shortest data description. *Automatica*, 14:465–471, 1978.

17. M. Sebag and C. Rouveirol. Tractable induction and classification in first order logic via stochastic matching. In *Proc. Fifteenth International Joint Conference on Artificial Intelligence (IJCAI-97)*, pages 888–893, San Mateo, CA, 1997. Morgan Kaufmann.

18. G. Silverstein and M.J. Pazzani. Relational clichés: Constraining constructive induction during relational learning. In L.A. Birnbaum and G.C. Collins, editors, *Machine Learning: Proceedings of the Eighth International Workshop (ML91)*, pages 203–207, San Mateo, CA, 1991. Morgan Kaufmann.

19. A. Srinivasan and R.D. King. Feature construction with Inductive Logic Programming: a study of quantitative predictions of chemical activity aided by structural attributes. In *Proceedings of the 6th International Workshop on Inductive Logic Programming (ILP-96)*, 1996.

20. A. Srinivasan, S. Muggleton, and R.D. King. Comparing the use of background knowledge by Inductive Logic Programming systems. In *Proceedings of the 5th International Workshop on Inductive Logic Programming (ILP-95)*, pages 199–230. Katholieke Universiteit Leuven, 1995.

21. A. Srinivasan, S. Muggleton, R.D. King, and M. Sternberg. Mutagenesis: ILP experiments in a non-determinate biological domain. In *Proceedings of the Fourth International Workshop on Inductive Logic Programming (ILP-94)*, GMD-Studien Nr. 237, pages 217–232, 1994.

22. P. Turney. Low size-complexity Inductive Logic Programming: the East-West challenge considered as a problem in cost-sensitive classification. In *Proceedings of the 5th International Workshop on Inductive Logic Programming (ILP-95)*, pages 247–263. Katholieke Universiteit Leuven, 1995.

23. J.D. Zucker and J.G. Ganascia. Representation changes for efficient learning in structural domains. In *Proceedings of the Thirteenth International Conference on Machine Learning*, pages 543–551, 1996.

A Stochastic Simple Similarity

Michèle Sebag

LMS, Ecole Polytechnique, F-91128 Palaiseau
LRI, Université Paris-Sud, F-91405 Orsay
Michele.Sebag@polytechnique.fr

Abstract. This paper continues a previous work using stochastic heuristics to extract and exploit knowledge with no size restrictions, with polynomial complexity.

A simplified relational framework is described; within this framework, one basic learning component, the generalization operator, is reconsidered.

Stochastic heuristics are combined with Plotkin's least general generalization to derive a stochastic generalization operator and a simple stochastic similarity function with controllable complexity.

Preliminary experiments on the well-studied mutagenesis problem (regression-friendly and regression-unfriendly datasets) demonstrate the potential and the limitations of this similarity.

1 Introduction

First Order Logic (FOL) Languages, say Prolog, allow one to accurately model and handle complex problem domains: natural language is adequately represented by sequences of words, and relations among them; chemical molecules are sets of atoms, connected by simple or double bonds. Learning in Logic Programming, termed Inductive Logic Programming (ILP) [13] receives an ever growing attention, as it appears a royal road for learning in complex domains [10,20]. Nevertheless, ILP is hindered by the fact that FOL inference is exponential in the length of the knowledge[1]. For instance, consider a clause stating that a chemical molecule is toxic if it contains a given pattern of atoms: checking whether this clause matches an actual molecule amounts to graph matching, which is exponential in the size of the pattern.

To sum up, Machine Learning faces the following dilemma: if a programming framework allows the description of graphs (and many complex domains are described in terms of graphs), deductive inference must support graph matching, which is NP-complete in the general case. And inductive inference cannot be less complex than deductive inference. The complexity of inference gets tractable iff clauses only involve small-size patterns.

This dilemma is classically addressed in ILP by learning short clauses [12,15].

---

[1] Another weakness of Logic Programming, not discussed hereafter, regards the handling of numerical information.

Another possibility, first investigated in [19], is to reconsider inductive and deductive inference. A "resource-bounded inference" has been proposed to extract and exploit knowledge with *no size restrictions and polynomial complexity*. The approach is based on stochastic heuristics; the quality of learning/classification is controlled by user-supplied parameters, and the computational cost is polynomial in these parameters.

In the same line, we investigate in the present paper a simplified relational framework (section 2). Within this framework, the least general generalization defined by Plotkin [14] is combined with stochastic heuristics, to derive a resource-bounded generalization operator and a similarity function (section 3). The approach is experimentally validated on the mutagenesis dataset, which has been extensively studied [21, 19]; the results obtained on the easy "regression-friendly" and on the difficult "regression-unfriendly" datasets, are compared in section 4. Some perspectives for further research are last presented.

2   A Simplified Relational Framework

This paper considers a learning from entailment setting [16], where positive and negative examples are represented as definite or constrained clauses. We restrict ourselves to non-recursive clauses.

$$
\begin{aligned}
active(m) \quad &: - \; atom(m, m_1, hydrogen), atom(m, m_2, carbon), \\
&\quad atom(m, m_3, carbon), bond(m_2, m_1, 1) \\
inactive(m') &: - \; atom(m', m'_1, oxygen), atom(m', m'_2, carbon), \\
&\quad atom(m', m'_3, chlore)
\end{aligned}
$$

It is worth noting that the arguments of predicates can be divided into two categories depending on the nature of their domain of instantiation.

Some domains could be modified without affecting in any way the information contained in the examples. For instance, the second argument of predicate *atom*, and the first and second arguments of predicate *bond* have $\{m_1, m_2, m_3, ...\}$ for domain of instantiation. These constants stand for the "names" of the atoms in the molecules. However, even a chemistry-illiterate knows that the semantics of a molecule is invariant up to a consistent renaming of its atoms: actually, any constant in domain $\{m_1, m_2, m_3, ...\}$ could be replaced by any new constant without affecting the information of the examples. In other words, the grounding of arguments with such domains of instantiation does not convey any intrinsic information. These arguments are called *relational*.

Other arguments are called *valued*: e.g. the third argument of predicate *atom* indicates the element of the atom and has $\{carbon, hydrogen, oxygen, ..\}$ for domain of instantiation.

The category of the predicate arguments is given by explicit declarations, similar to the *mode* declarations used in PROGOL [12] :

$$
category(atom(Relational, Relational, Valued))
$$

Two further assumptions are made.

• If a predicate does not involve any relational argument, there exists at most one literal built on this predicate in each example. In other words, this predicate encodes one or several attributes.

• If a predicate involves relational argument(s), there does not exist two literals built on this predicate, with same instantiation of the relational arguments, and different instantiations of the valued arguments (e.g. one does not have $atom(m, m_1, carbon)$ and $atom(m, m_1, oxygen)$). In other words, valued arguments in a predicate encode functions of the relational arguments of this predicate.

These assumptions do not hold for all ILP problems; typically, the case of recursive clauses has been excluded. Still, these assumptions fit one most famous domain of application of ILP, that is chemistry. Actually, the "objects" of chemistry are the atoms; any molecule is described by some attributes (*lumo* or *logp*), functions of its atoms (*element, element-type*, and *electrical-charge*) and functions of pairs or tuples of atoms (*bond-type, methanol-radical*).

These assumptions are also satisfied in the Finite Element Methods problem [3]: the objects here are the vertices of the finite elements. Last, these assumptions are satisfied in all "family" problems (discovery of the "grand-parent" or "ancestor" relations).

These assumptions altogether allow one to reformulate any constrained or definite clause E as:

• a set $\mathcal{O}(E)$ of objects $o_1, \dots o_k$,

• a set of constraints of the type $\quad [f(o_{i_1}, \dots, o_{i_L}) = V] \quad$ where $(o_{i_1}, \dots, o_{i_L})$ is a L-uple of objects, f is a function of arity L, and V is a subset of the domain of value of f. In the particular case $L = 0$, the constraint just is a selector [9].

This change of representation is to some extent the opposite of the flattening operator [17]. Flattening gets rid of function symbols by "promoting" them to predicate symbols:

$$p(X, blue) \qquad \text{reformulates as} \qquad p(X, Y), \; blue_p(Y)$$

This way, the non-decidability of inference with function symbols is set aside the scope of learning.

The above change of representation rather provides a simpler formalization of the pattern-matching task [7,1]: any pattern-matching between two clauses E and F can be represented as a mapping from $\mathcal{O}(E)$ to $\mathcal{O}(F)$.

3 Resource Bounded Generalization and Similarity

This section describes a new generalization operator, combining Plotkin's least general generalization [14] with stochastic heuristics. This operator relies on an unsophisticated similarity function, which is compared to the similarity functions used in KBG [2] and RIBL [5].

3.1 Stochastic Least General Generalization

The least general generalization (lgg) operator has been defined by Plotkin [14] (see [11] for a detailed presentation). One drawback is the size of the output (product of the sizes of the input in the worst case)

This drawback is overcome by a new generalization operator, defined as follows. Let E and F be two examples described as in section 2, respectively involving the set of objects $\mathcal{O}(E)$ and $\mathcal{O}(F)$.

$E : \mathcal{O}(E) = (m_1, m_2)$
$\qquad [el(m_1) = carbon], [el(m_2) = hydrogen], [bond\_type(m_1, m_2) = 1]$
$F : \mathcal{O}(F) = (n_1, n_2, n_3)$
$\qquad [el(n_1) = hydrogen], [el(n_2) = carbon], [el(n_3) = carbon]$

Let Σ denote the set of mappings from $\mathcal{O}(E)$ onto $\mathcal{O}(F)$.
Let $d_E = [f(m_{i_1}, \ldots m_{i_L}) = V]$ and $d_F = [g(n_{j_1}, \ldots n_{j_K}) = W]$ respectively be two constraints in E and F.
For any σ in Σ, we define the σ-generalization of d_E and d_F, noted $gen_\sigma(d_E, d_F)$ as follows:

$$gen_\sigma(d_E, d_F) = \begin{cases} d_E & \text{if } f = g, \ \sigma(m_{i_k}) = n_{j_k} \text{ for } k = 1 \ldots L \text{ and } V = W \\ \text{undefined} & \text{otherwise} \end{cases}$$

The σ-generalization of examples E and F, noted $gen_\sigma(E, F)$ is defined as the conjunction of the σ-generalization of their constraints whenever these are defined. For instance, if σ maps m_1 onto n_2 and m_2 onto n_1, the σ-generalization of E and F is:

$$gen_\sigma(E, F) : (m_1, m_2) \qquad [el(m_1) = carbon], [el(m_2) = hydrogen]$$

Note that, up to a renaming of the objects, $gen_\sigma(E, F) = gen_\sigma(F, E)$. For each mapping σ in Σ, let $n(\sigma)$ denote the number of constraints in $gen_\sigma(E, F)$: the greater $n(\sigma)$, the most specific $gen_\sigma(E, F)$.

A resource-bounded generalization operator called K-generalization, is defined as follows. Let $\sigma_1, \ldots \sigma_K$ be K mappings drawn in Σ with uniform probability, and let σ_i be such that $n(\sigma_i)$ is the maximum of $n(\sigma_j)$ for $j = 1 \ldots K$ (selected at random in case there is a tie). Then, the K-generalization of E and F, noted $gen_K(E, F)$, is set to $gen_{\sigma_i}(E, F)$. A resource-bounded similarity function noted $sim_K(E, F)$ is defined as the number of constraints in $gen_K(E, F)$.

The complexity of K-generalization and sim_K is in $\mathcal{O}(K \times |E| \times |F|)$, where $|E|$ and $|F|$ respectively denote the number of constraints in E and F.

3.2 Discussion

The advantages and limitations of sim_K are situated with respect to some related work. KBG [1] computes the similarity of all pairs of examples/hypotheses, and uses this similarity function to guide the generalization. RIBL [5] computes the similarity of the instance to classify with all training examples, and classifies the instance at hand by means of a standard k-nearest neighbor approach.

Both KBG and RIBL require elementary distances to be defined on the domains of instantiation of the arguments. These distances are used to compute the elementary similarity of non-valued constants (called "objects" within our framework) that respectively appear in examples E and F. For instance, let example E describe "objects" *John* and *Ann*, who are cousins, with *John* being 24 year old and *Ann* living in *New - York*. Let example F describe "objects" *Peter*, *Marc* and *Jane*, such that *Marc* and *Jane* are cousins, *Jane* lives in *San-Francisco* and *Peter* is 20-year old. The similarity between *John* and *Marc* depends on the similarity between their respective cousins *Ann* and *Jane*, which itself depends on the similarity between *John* and *Marc* and on the distance between *New-York* and *San-Francisco*.

KBG and RIBL compute the similarity between objects in different ways. KBG involves user-supplied weights; e.g. depending on the relative weight of predicates *age* and *cousin*, one finds that *John* is most similar to *Peter* or *Marc*. The similarity of all pairs of objects is then determined by resolving a set of linear equations. In opposition, RIBL automatically determines the predicate weights[2], and computes the similarity of any two objects by an iterative method.

Both KBG and RIBL use these elementary similarities to define a mapping σ from E on F, by repeatedly mapping each object m_i in E onto the object n_j in F most similar to m_i when possible. Such a σ induces an attribute-value "alignment" of E and F. Thereby the generalization step in KBG is brought back to attribute-value generalization, and the global similarity of E and F in RIBL proceeds like a weighted Euclidean-like distance.
In other words, KBG and RIBL attempt to find a global optimum (the best σ) by combining locally optimal choices; the elementary similarity function must then capture information as global as possible. For instance, RIBL sets an upper-bound on the number ℓ of links examined: if ℓ is set to 3, cousins *Ann* and *Jane* are considered when computing the similarity of *John* and *Peter*, as they are directly linked to *John* and *Peter*; the similarity of *Ann*'s and *Jane*'s respective daughters, (and there can be many of them), would also be considered; but the similarity of their daughters' dogs would be discarded.
The ability of the elementary similarity function to evaluate whether *John* resembles *Peter* from a global point of view certainly increases with ℓ ; unfortunately the complexity of elementary similarity is exponential in ℓ.

On the opposite, K-generalization attempts to find a "rather good" σ: it uniformly selects a bunch of mappings in Σ and retains the mapping σ optimizing the *very poor, but global* criterion $n(\sigma)$. To sum up, all approaches are myopic in some sense: KBG and RIBL approaches rely on detailed local points of view; K-generalization uses a global but very approximative point of view.

---

[2] The accuracy of weights is evaluated from the rate of test examples correctly classified; finding a good set of weights then reformulates as an optimization problem.

K-generalization is to be more general than KBG-like generalization. In the same line, the similarity function sim_K is to be poorer than that used in RIBL: it gives the maximum size of the set of constraints shared by E and F, estimated from a Monte-Carlo process. Still, K-generalization is more and more specific as K goes to infinity; for large enough values of K, K-generalization should be equal or more specific than KBG-generalization; and the neighborhoods based on the RIBL similarity should be close to those based on sim_K.

This raises the question of whether K-generalization or sim_K could achieve reasonable results, *for reasonable values of K*.

4 Experimental validation

This section first describes the goal of the experimentation, then the mutagenesis domain considered [6]. The results obtained are then discussed.

4.1 Goal of the experiments

This paper only studies the relevance of the similarity function defined by sim_K. This relevance is evaluated from the predictive accuracy of two similarity-based classifiers [4].

The first one is the well-known k-nearest neighbor classifier (kNN) (see [22] for a comprehensive discussion). One computes the similarity between the case C at hand and any training example, and classifies C according to the majority vote of the k training examples most similar to C. The complexity of classification is in $\mathcal{O}(N \times |sim|)$, if N denotes the number of training examples and $|sim|$ the complexity of one similarity calculation. Apparently, kNN does not involve any learning stage; however, the adjustment of parameter k should be viewed as a hidden learning stage. Anyway, it should be taken into account for fair algorithmic comparisons [18]; as this adjustment relies in any case on the classification of the training examples themselves [8], its complexity is in $\mathcal{O}(N^2 \times |sim|)$.

A variant of the k-nearest neighbor algorithm, termed *consistent nearest neighbor* (cNN) and not involving any parameter, is defined as follows. For each training example E, let F_E be a "near-miss" of E, i.e. a training example most similar to E such that it does not belong to the same class as E. One computes the similarity between the case C at hand and any training example; then, one classifies C according to the majority vote of all training examples E such that C is closer to E than its near-miss ($sim_K(C, E) > sim_K(E, F_E)$). The complexity of classification is also in $\mathcal{O}(N \times |sim|)$. The learning stage includes the computation of the near-misses of the training examples, in $\mathcal{O}(N^2 \times |sim|)$.

4.2 The domain

The problem is to classify chemical organic molecules into two classes, *active* and *inactive* [6]. Several descriptions of the molecules are considered. The first one, noted $\mathcal{B}_0$, is an attribute-value description which was used by propositional classifiers, e.g. linear regression (REG), decision tree (DT), neural nets with 3 hidden units (NN). A basic FOL description, noted B_1, only contains the description of the atoms and the bonds in the molecules. The most complete FOL description, noted B_4, is B_1 completed with expert attributes (e.g. hydrophobicity) and chemical concepts (e.g. methyl groups, benzenic rings).

The total dataset includes 230 molecules, which are decomposed into a 188 molecule dataset called "regression-friendly" and a 42 molecule dataset called "regression-unfriendly". Table 1 reports the average predictive accuracy together with the standard deviation, measured from a 10-fold cross-validation on the 188 dataset (respectively by leave-one-out validation on the 42 dataset), found in [21, 19].

Algorithm	188 data set			42 data set	
Default class	66 ±3			69 ±7	
Description	B_0	B_1	B_4	B_0	B_4
REG	89 ±2			67 ±7	
DT	85 ±3			67 ±7	
NN	89 ±2			64 ±7	
Progol [12]		76 ±3	88 ±2		83 ±6
Foil [15]		61 ±6	86 ±3		
Still [19]		83 ±4	93 ±4		

Table 1: Reference results on the mutagenesis domain.

4.3 Experimental setting

As recommended for stochastic methods, our approach is evaluated from the average result of 15 independent runs, i.e. with different random seeds; for a fair comparison, each run is a 10-fold cross-validation for the 188 dataset, and a leave-one-out validation for the 42 dataset.

We used two stochastic mechanisms to sample the matching space Σ. The unbiased sampling mechanism (US) uses a uniform distribution: while possible, one selects a non yet selected object m_i with uniform probability in $\mathcal{O}(E)$, and then selects a non yet selected object n_j with uniform probability in $\mathcal{O}(F)$; the sample σ is iteratively defined by $\sigma(m_i) = n_j$.

The biased sampling mechanism (BS) differs from the previous one in the selection of object n_j, which depends on m_i: atom m_i in E is mapped onto the atom n_j in F most similar to m_i and non yet selected. The description of the dataset makes this bias rather straightforward: two atoms can have same description (same atom-element, same atom-type and same electric-charge); otherwise, they can be very similar (same atom-element and same atom-type); otherwise, they are similar (same atom-element); otherwise, they are different.

Only the B_1 description of the examples will be considered, for the following reason. As such, similarity sim_K does not take much advantage from the expert attributes; even if two examples had same hydrophobicity, this would only increase their similarity by 1, which is nothing compared to the number of constraints in a molecule (3 times the number of atoms plus the number of bonds). The fact that having same hydrophobicity is more important than having two atoms with same element should be acknowledged, e.g. by means of weights. But our goal here is to study the general behavior of sim_K and how it depends on the number of samples K or on the sampling mechanism — rather than how this behavior could be improved by weights.

4.4 Results

Table 2 summarizes the results obtained by k-nearest neighbors (kNN with $k = 1, 3$) and consistent nearest neighbors (cNN), based on the similarity sim_K. For each experiment, the predictive accuracy averaged over 15 independent runs, is reported, together with the standard deviation measured on each run (10-fold cross validation or leave-one-out), itself averaged on all 15 runs.

Learning is linear in the number of samples K and quadratic in the number of training examples. On a Pentium 120, the learning time for $K = 100$ is 31 minutes for biased sampling and 21 minutes for unbiased sampling on the 188 dataset, and 80 seconds for biased sampling on the 42 dataset. The classification time is negligible.

The results obtained on the 188 dataset when sim_K is constructed with biased and unbiased sampling are respectively shown in Table 2.a and Table 2.b. K varies in $\{2, 10, 50\}$ for the biased sampling, and in $\{100, 200, 300\}$ for the unbiased sampling.

| | | 188 data set | | | | | 42 dataset | |
| 2.a Biased sampling | | | 2.b Unbiased sampling | | | 2.c Biased sampling | | |
Alg.	K	Pred. acc		K	Pred. acc		K	Pred. acc
cNN		87 ± 7	cNN		80 ± 9	cNN		74 ± 14
1NN	2	89 ± 6	1NN	100	78 ± 8	1NN	100	73 ± 17
3NN		85 ± 8	3NN		78 ± 10	3NN		79 ± 12
cNN		89 ± 6	cNN		79 ± 8	cNN		75 ± 14
1NN	10	89 ± 6	1NN	200	79 ± 8	1NN	500	74 ± 18
3NN		86 ± 8	3NN		79 ± 10	3NN		79 ± 11
cNN		89 ± 5	cNN		79 ± 9	cNN		75 ± 14
1NN	50	89 ± 7	1NN	300	80 ± 8	1NN	1000	74 ± 18
3NN		86 ± 8	3NN		80 ± 10	3NN		80 ± 9

Table 2: *Predictive accuracy of sim_K with description $\mathcal{B}_1$.*

The results obtained on the 42 dataset when sim_K is constructed with biased sampling are reported in Table 2.c. K varies in $\{100, 500, 1000\}$ for the biased sampling. The results of unbiased sampling are not shown as they are comparable to the default rate for reasonable values of K.

4.5 Discussion

On both datasets, the biased sampling leads to results significantly better than those of unbiased sampling. This could have been expected, as biased sampling achieves a partial alignment of the examples, and sim_K just estimates the maximum number of parts in the examples which can be aligned. In particular, biased sampling strongly decreases the standard deviation of the results obtained for a given number K of samples.

On the 188 dataset with biased sampling, competitive results are obtained for low values of K, and no improvement is obtained by increasing K. Further, there exist almost no variation (not shown here) between the runs. With respect to computational cost, this approach needs less than 900 seconds on Pentium-120, which is much faster than PROGOL (46 000 seconds on HP-735) and much slower than STILL (120 seconds on HP-735).

What is surprising is the fact that despite sim_K uses the basic B_1 description of the data, it obtains same results as FOIL or PROGOL using the much richer B_4 description (circa 89%). As a matter of fact, FOIL or PROGOL obtain *significantly worse* results than sim_K when they consider description B_1 (respectively 61% or 76%).

On the whole, the 188 dataset seems to be rather clean and regular; the absence of noise is witnessed by the fact that better results are obtained when fewer neighbors are considered to classify the examples.

The 42 data set is clearly more difficult. Similarity sim_K with unbiased sampling is not significantly different from the default classifier. With biased sampling, the predictive accuracy slowly increases as K increases, but the trend is not statistically significant given the high standard deviation. On this dataset, sim_K using description B_1 stays behind PROGOL using description B_4. It would be interesting to see how PROGOL performs with description B_1.

Note that the information captured by sim_K reflects the FOL nature of examples, but not that much: the bonds between atoms are responsible for about 30% of $sim_K(E, F)$, the remaining 70% coming from the comparison of the distribution of atom properties (elements, types and electric charges) in E and F, which could be accommodated within an attribute-value description.

5 Conclusion and Perspectives

An alternative to soundly learn and use a concise optimal knowledge is to learn and use "as well as possible" an imperfect knowledge. The former approach is indeed the best one, when it is applicable; but the latter approach remains the only applicable when the domain is ill-observed, or ill-described, or when the computational resources are limited.

For this reason, our goal is to be able to accommodate relational knowledge with no size restrictions and still with polynomial complexity. In this line, this paper first describes a simple relational framework, where the pattern-matching task is brought back to find an element in a set of mappings Σ.

Within this framework, we construct a stochastic similarity function which estimates the maximum number of parts of two examples which can be "aligned", by sampling Σ in a Monte-Carlo like approach.

Unexpectedly, this approach leads to results comparable to those of prominent ILP learners on an "easy" ILP problem — despite the fact it uses a much poorer description of the examples. Actually, the results obtained by ILP learners with the same poor description are significantly worse. This seems to confirm that different learning strategies should be adopted depending on the quality of the background knowledge.

Further perspectives of research are concerned with improving this similarity, in particular with respect to numerical information. So far, the comparison of two constraints or selectors is boolean: $n(\sigma)$ is incremented iff $V = W$. This could be refined in various ways, inspired from data analysis techniques.

Another perspective is to study the K-generalization operator, estimating the least general generalization operator and based on this similarity.

References

1. G. Bisson. KBG: A knowledge base generalizer. In B. Porter and R. Mooney, editors, *Proceedings of the 7th International Conference on Machine Learning*, pages 9–15. Morgan Kaufmann, 1990.

2. G. Bisson. Learning in FOL with a similarity measure. In *Proceedings of 10th AAAI*, 1992.

3. D. Dolsak and S. Muggleton. The application of ILP to finite element mesh design. In S. Muggleton, editor, *Proceedings of the first International Workshop on Inductive Logic Programming*, pages 453–472, 1991.

4. R.O. Duda and P.E. Hart. *Pattern Classification and scene analysis*. John Wiley and sons, Menlo Park, CA, 1973.

5. W. Emde and D. Wettscherek. Relational instance based learning. In L. Saitta, editor, *Proceedings of the 13th International Conference on Machine Learning*, pages 122–130, 1996.

6. R.D. King, A. Srinivasan, and M.J.E. Sternberg. Relating chemical activity to structure: an examination of ILP successes. *New Gen. Comput.*, 13, 1995.

7. Y. Kodratoff and J.-G. Ganascia. Improving the generalization step in learning. In R.S. Michalski, J.G. Carbonell, and T.M. Mitchell, editors, *Machine Learning : an artificial intelligence approach*, volume 2, pages 215–244. Morgan Kaufmann, 1986.

8. R. Kohavi and G.H. John. Automatic parameter selection by minimizing estimated error. In A. Prieditis and S. Russell, editors, *Proceedings of ICML-95, International Conference on Machine Learning*, pages 304–312. Morgan Kaufmann, 1995.

9. R.S. Michalski. A theory and methodology of inductive learning. In R.S Michalski, J.G. Carbonell, and T.M. Mitchell, editors, *Machine Learning : an artificial intelligence approach*, volume 1, pages 83–134. Morgan Kaufmann, 1983.

10. R. Mooney. ILP for natural language processing. In S. Muggleton, editor, *Inductive Logic Programming, ILP96 — Selected papers*. Springer-Verlag LNAI 1314, 1997.

11. S. Muggleton. Inductive logic programming. In S. Muggleton, editor, *Inductive Logic Programming*. Academic Press, 1992.

12. S. Muggleton. Inverse entailment and PROGOL. *New Gen. Comput.*, 13:245–286, 1995.

13. S. Muggleton and L. De Raedt. Inductive logic programming: Theory and methods. *Journal of Logic Programming*, 19:629–679, 1994.

14. G. Plotkin. A note on inductive generalization. In *Machine Intelligence*, volume 5. Edinburgh University Press, 1970.

15. J.R. Quinlan. Learning logical definition from relations. *Machine Learning*, 5:239–266, 1990.

16. L. De Raedt. Induction in logic. In *Proceedings of 3nd International Workshop on Multistrategy Learning*, pages 29–38. AAAI Press, 1996.

17. C. Rouveirol. Flattening and saturation: Two representation changes for generalization. *Machine Learning*, 14:219–232, 1994.

18. T. Scheffer and R. Herbrich. Unbiased assessment of learning algorithms. In *Proceedings of IJCAI-97*, pages 798–803. Morgan Kaufmann, 1997.

19. M. Sebag and C. Rouveirol. Tractable induction and classification in FOL. In *Proceedings of IJCAI-97*, pages 888–892. Morgan Kaufmann, 1997.

20. A. Srinivasan. The predictive toxicology evaluation challenge. In *Proceedings of IJCAI-97*, pages 4–8. Morgan Kaufmann, 1997.

21. A. Srinivasan, S.H. Muggleton, M.J.E. Sternberg, and R.D. King. Theories for mutagenicity: a study in first order and feature-based induction. *Artificial Intelligence*, 85:277–299, 1996.

22. D. Wettscherek and T.G. Dietterich. An experimental comparison of the nearest-neighbor and nearest hyperrectangle algorithms. *Machine Learning*, 19:5–27, 1995.

Using Prior Probabilities and Density Estimation for Relational Classification

James Cussens

Department of Computer Science
University of York
Heslington, York YO10 5DD, UK
Tel: +44 1904 434732
Fax: +44 1904 432767
jc@cs.york.ac.uk

Abstract. A Bayesian method for incorporating probabilistic background knowledge into ILP is presented. Positive only learning is extended to allow density estimation. Estimated densities and defined prior are combined in Bayes theorem to perform relational classification. An initial application of the technique is made to part-of-speech (POS) tagging. A novel use of Gibbs sampling for POS tagging is given.

1 Introduction

ILP is often situated within a concept learning framework, where a concept definition is to be induced from background knowledge and positive and negative examples. Unfortunately, in most applications the assumption that there is a target concept is untenable. A more realistic model of a domain will be probabilistic, where examples have a certain probability of being positive or negative. This motivates using ILP to build probabilistic models from data.

There has been much successful work in this direction already, often using ILP for feature construction. A theory is induced by an ILP system in the standard way and then parts of it are used as features. The parts are generally clauses and/or variable connected literals from clauses. Srinivasan and King [13] used Progol to construct relationally defined boolean features and then used these in linear regression. Pompe and Kononenko [10] used ILP-R to build an hypothesis and then used a Bayesian approach involving splitting and merging clauses to do classification. Dehaspe [5] explicitly constructs a conditional probability distribution using a maximum entropy approach with clausal constraints. In all these cases, experimental results demonstrate the effectiveness of a probabilistic approach.

In this paper we use a particular application of Bayes theorem which allows a user to incorporate probabilistic domain knowledge. Making this possible is the main aim of the presented method. The positive only framework of Muggleton [8] is extended to allow *density estimation*. The prior information and density estimates are then bolted together in Bayes theorem to calculate posterior probabilities for atoms in the test set. We report on some initial experiments using this approach in the domain of part-of-speech (POS) tagging [4].

The structure of the paper is as follows. In Section 2, we modify the standard example-level use of Bayes theorem to allow the user to define a prior distribution. In Section 3 a meta-predicate is introduced which can be used to define this prior in the background knowledge. The extension of positive only learning to density estimation is covered in Section 4 and Section 5 describes how the previously defined approach is applied to part-of-speech tagging.

2 Bayes Theorem and Classification

Bayes theorem can be used in two ways for classification. In the first, given a prior distribution over classification models, the data is used directly to find a posterior distribution.

$$P(\text{model}|\text{data}) = \frac{P(\text{data}|\text{model})}{P(\text{data})} P(\text{model}) \tag{1}$$

Individual examples are then given class labels using $P(\text{model}|\text{data})$. In the second, Bayes theorem is applied on the level of the example:

$$P(\text{class}|\text{example}) = \frac{P(\text{example}|\text{class})}{P(\text{example})} P(\text{class}) \tag{2}$$

In (1), the likelihood $P(\text{data}|\text{model})$ is known—the model space is generally chosen to ensure this. Difficulty rests with the choice of the prior $P(\text{model})$—the user is faced with defining the probability of every model before considering the data. This is often done using priors where the prior probability of a model is a convenient function of its syntactic description, with a bias towards simpler models [8, 2]. Continuous model parameters are often given "non-informative" priors.

In (2), the prior $P(\text{class})$ can be often estimated easily and accurately by simply counting the proportion of examples of each class in the data. Here it is the class-conditional likelihoods $P(\text{example}|\text{class})$ that are generally unknown, and which must be estimated from the data. These densities, $P(\text{example}|\text{class})$ for each class, can be estimated using a variety of parametric and nonparametric approaches. See [7] for a survey and experimental comparison. The resulting estimate of $P(\text{class}|\text{example})$ is then used to classify examples.[1]

In many applications it will be easier to define the prior probability of particular sorts of examples being in particular classes than to define a prior over the model space. This motivates modifying (2) to incorporate such prior information. We split the information contained in each example into two parts: example $= (I_1, I_2)$. I_1 is the information which the user wishes to use to directly

---

[1] In both (1) and (2), the value of the denominators $P(\text{data})$ and $P(\text{example})$ are irrelevant, since they are constant for each model and class respectively.

define a distribution $P(\text{class}|I_1)$. I_2 is the remaining information. Either I_1 or I_2 can be empty. We then alter (2), to get

$$P(\text{class}|I_1, I_2) = \frac{P(I_2|\text{class}, I_1)}{P(I_2|I_1)} P(\text{class}|I_1)$$

and then assuming: $P(I_2|\text{class}, I_1) = P(I_2|\text{class})$ we get

$$P(\text{class}|I_1, I_2) = \frac{P(I_2|\text{class})}{P(I_2|I_1)} P(\text{class}|I_1) \propto P(I_2|\text{class})P(\text{class}|I_1)$$

The assumption made by (2) is the naive Bayes assumption of class conditional independence of our "attributes" I_1 and I_2. The assumption is made, since estimating $P(I_2|\text{class}, I_1)$ will generally be infeasible.

The more information the user is prepared to allow in I_1, the harder it is to define accurate estimates of $P(\text{class}|I_1)$, but the easier it is to estimate the density $P(I_2|\text{class})$. If we were doing attribute value learning, then $\{I_1, I_2\}$ would be a partition of the attributes, and reducing the size of I_2 reduces the dimensionality of the space over which the densities $P(I_2|\text{class})$ are defined. Reducing dimensionality makes density estimation considerably easier.

In this paper, (2) is used within an ILP setting. Definition of the prior $P(\text{class}|I_1)$—prior to I_2 that is—and estimation of the likelihood density $P(I_2|\text{class})$ can both be carried out in a logical setting. Section 3 describes the former and Section 4 the latter.

3   Using Prior Probabilistic Information in ILP

Our approach demands that the user defines the prior class probabilities for each example. Since these prior probabilities will be "plugged in" to Bayes theorem to classify test examples, we can define them however is easiest for the process which uses the posteriors to classify test examples.

One natural method in an ILP setting is to use Prolog to define the prior distributions. A major advantages of the ILP approach to machine learning is that it allows the user to include complex information about the domain in the form of relational background knowledge expressed as a logic program. This can be extended to include *relational probabilistic* information. Probabilistic information is meta-information and so we take the natural approach of using a probabilistic meta-predicate $w/2$.

Defining a distribution using the $w/2$ meta-predicate is straightforward. All that is required is that for each atom, a single probability value is computed, and the logic program used for this can be as complex as the user requires, for example using recursion and non-logical predicates.

In the following example the odds of a train being eastbound triple for each closed car in the train. It is often simpler to use odds rather than actual probabilities to define $w/2$ (See [3] for examples and discussion.) Note how the use of quantified expressions makes it easy to assign a particular probability to a set of examples having certain logically defined properties.

```
w(eastbound([Car]),0.75) :- closed(Car).
w(eastbound([Car]),0.25) :- not(closed(Car)).
w(eastbound([Car|Cars]),P) :-
        (closed(Car) -> Factor=3 ; Factor=1),
        w(eastbound(Cars),P2),
        Odds2 is P2/(1-P2),
        Odds is Factor*Odds2,
        P is Odds/(1+Odds).
```

Using $w/2$ is analysed in considerable detail in [3]. In that report, a formal semantics is given to $w/2$ which identifies it with the possible worlds probability semantics of Halpern [6]. Such theoretical underpinning is crucial. For example, it allows us to distinguish between the probability that a particular atom $bird(tweety)$ is true and the probability that some randomly chosen object is a bird (there is a difference!). Connections with previous related work such as Ng and Subrahmanian's Probabilistic Logic Programming [9] are also given.

4 Relational Density Estimation by Positive Only Learning

4.1 Positive Only Learning

The ILP system Progol can induce definitions of a target predicate using only positive examples of that predicate.[2] Positive only learning is explained in [8], where Muggleton follows a concept learning framework. Positive examples in a domain X are members of a target concept $T \in 2^X$, and negative examples are in $X \setminus T$. We denote the unknown sampling distribution on X as D_X, so that the positive examples are drawn according to $D_{X|T}$. From these an estimate H of T must be constructed.

Muggleton uses a Bayesian framework with an MDL prior to obtain the log posterior probability of an hypothesis H which is consistent with the positive examples E. Let $|E| = m$, $D_X(H)$ be the *generality of H* and let $sz(H)$ be the size of H. Then, where d_m is a value independent of H, we have:

$$\ln P(H|E) = m \ln \left(\frac{1}{D_X(H)} \right) - sz(H) + d_m$$

Probable hypotheses are those that do not cover too many other examples in addition to E (so $g(H)$ is low) and are not too complex (so $sz(H)$ is low). The examples covered by H in addition to E play a role similar to that of negative examples in standard ILP.

Generality is estimated using a Stochastic Logic Program (SLP). An SLP is range-restricted logic program *Prog* with a stochastic selection rule based on clause labels, which can be used to define and sample from distributions such as

---

[2] CProgol4.2 and later, P-Progol2.5 and later

D_X. With a target predicate p/n, Progol constructs an SLP for a new predicate $*p/n$ which defines all the tuples **a** which are of the right type to satisfy p/n. The SLP is used to estimate generality as follows. To estimate, say $g(H_i)$, we use the SLP to generate atoms $*p(\mathbf{a}_1), *p(\mathbf{a}_2), \ldots, *p(\mathbf{a}_s)$, then if B is background knowledge and $s' = |\{\mathbf{a}_j, 1 \le j \le s | B \wedge H_{i-1} \models p(\mathbf{a}_j)\}$, $g(H_i)$ is estimated (using a Laplace correction) as $(s' + 1)/(s + 2)$.

Although Progol's type declarations determine the clauses of the SLP, there remains the question of finding clause labels so that the SLP approximates D_X well. One possibility is to use the positive examples themselves to estimate D_X, as in [8]. Sampling from $D_{X|T}$ to estimate D_X may lead to a poor estimate in some cases though. Another possibility is to use an SLP with uniformly valued clause labels. In the tagging application described below, we actually have a sample from D_X, and so this is used.

4.2 Positive Only Learning for Density Estimation

In positive only learning we only need to decide whether an example x is in T, i.e. whether $D_X(x|T) > 0$. In density estimation we are after the actual probability $D_X(x|T)$. This motivates using a theory induced from positive examples as a *model* for a density, where we have to estimate parameters for the model from the data.

If x is covered by H, then let C_x be some clause that covers x. We have that $D_X(x|T) = D_X(C_x|T)\frac{D_X(T|x)}{D_X(T|C_x)}D_X(x|C_x)$. $D_X(C_x|T)$ can be estimated by simply counting the proportion of positives in the training set covered by C_x. $D_X(x|C_x)$, on the other hand, does not need to be estimated here, since it will "cancel out" when we classify examples. However, if we were doing density estimation in isolation, one sensible estimate of $D_X(x|C_x)$ would be $k/D_X(C_x)$, where $D_X(C_x)$, the generality of C_x, can be estimated by simply counting the proportion of training examples covered by C_x. We would then have an estimate of $D_X(x|T)$ up to a factor k, which is sufficient for most purposes.

We can estimate $D_X(x|T)$ by $D_X(C_x|T)D_X(x|C_x)$ using that clause C_x where $D_X(T|x)$ is closest to $D_X(T|C_x)$. We choose the most specific clause covering x, i.e. that C_x that minimises $D_X(C_x)$, on the basis that the distribution $D_X(T)$ will be more uniform over "smaller" areas of X than larger ones, where D_X is the measure of size.

If no clause in H covers x, we estimate $D_X(x|T)$ as 0, on the assumption that H covers all the positives. This is entirely reasonable when H is generated by Progol, since Progol errs on the side of over-generalisation when learning from positives only.

5 Application: Part-of-Speech Tagging

Here we continue the work done in [4], where data from the pre-tagged Wall Street Journal corpus was used by Progol to construct a tagger. Lexical information is readily extracted from the tagged corpus: we just count how often words are given particular tags. Here is the lexical information for the word "New", showing that it almost always a "np" (singular proper noun).

```
New nps 2 jj 61 nn 1 np 2501
```

Similarly to [4], Progol was used to find contextual rules which predict the occurrence of tags based on an already tagged left and right context. For each tag, Progol did positive only learning using examples of that tag with its contexts. Here is one of the examples Progol used to construct a theory for *nns/2*.

```
%tag2(Left,Right).
nns2([dt,in,nns,np,cd,cd,cma,cd,to,cd,in],[vbd,vbn,cma,dt,nn,vbd,stp]).
```

Since induced clauses tended to be over-general, we induced clauses for *nns2/2* which represents (left,right) contexts which make an nn tag *likely*. Learning *nns/2* precisely from positive examples only is over-ambitious.

As we had access to examples of all classes, we were able to construct that SLP which estimated D_X as closely as possible by conditioning on a large set of examples. X is the set of all (left,right) contexts for ambiguous words. A set of 30,574 randomly selected examples from X were used. We simply count how often each clause is used in proving that all 30,574 examples are domain members. (1.2% of the examples did not satisfy context/2 due to a small error in the type definitions.) Some of the resulting counts are given in Fig 1 together with the clause labels they define.

```
30219 1.00 context(A,B):-taglist(B),taglist1(A).
398213 0.93 taglist1([A|B]):-tag(A),taglist1(B). 30219  0.07 taglist1([]).
440693 0.94 taglist([A|B]):-tag(A),taglist(B). 30378 0.06 taglist([]).
82258 0.10 tag(np). 15231 0.02 tag(vbz).
```

Fig. 1. Fragment of the SLP constructed prior to positive only learning. The first figure for each clause gives the number of times the clause was used to prove context(A,B) where A and B are left and right contexts. The second figure gives the resulting clause selection probability.

With this SLP in place to generate elements of X, Progol did positive only learning for each of the 43 tags using 8000 positive examples for that tag. (Not all tags had as many as 8000 positive examples.) Constructing all the theories took 47 minutes of CPU time on a Sparc Ultra 1. A small amount of time is also used in reading the examples into Progol. P-Progol Version 2.5 was used running under Yap Prolog 4.1.1. The P-Progol implementation of positive only learning follows the method given by Muggleton [8]. The speed of learning is impressive since 129,850 positive training examples were used in total and 1418 clauses were constructed. (The limit of 8000 examples had to be imposed due to a problem with Yap4.1.1, not because of time constraints.)

These tagging theories contained clauses such as `nn(A,B):-adjp1(A,C).` and `cd(A,B):-adjp1(A,C).` which claim that a word preceded by an adjectival phrase is, respectively, a singular common noun and a number. Background predicates such as adjp1/2 are defined by a rough grammar in the background knowledge where the tags are terminals. Both of these are clearly over-general and if we were purely doing positive only learning this would need addressing. However we are using the induced clauses as structural features with which to build a probability distribution useful for classification.

With this in mind, the head predicate functor of all 1418 clauses was changed to `context/2` and the theories concatenated. After eliminating duplicates this lead to a theory of 618 clauses. Then, using a set of 160,000 training examples, these clauses where parameterised. For each clause, we found (1) the proportion of examples covered by the clause and (2) the proportion of examples of each class (tag) covered by the clause. This gave us estimates of (1) the generality and (2) the class conditional likelihoods for each clause. The parameterisation was done in parallel, 80,000 examples were used on a Sparc Ultra 1 and another 80,000 on an SGI O2. The time taken was 14.8 hours and 22.6 hours of CPU time respectively. The final parameters were a simple average of those found on each run.

The second clause in Fig 2 shows that 22.6% of nn-tagged words and 6.8% of cd-tagged words appeared after an adjectival phrase, and that 6.9% of all words occurred in such a context.

```
lclause((context(A,B):-sverb(A,C),nounp1(C,D)),1(0.0561622,0.101476,
... ,0.0572671),0.0619875).
lclause((context(A,B):-adjp1(A,C)),1(0.015625,0.0684997, ... 0.226359,
... ,0.0,0.00862323),0.0696563).
```

Fig. 2. 1st argument of lclause/3 is a context, the term in the 2nd argument contains 32 class conditional likelihoods, 3rd argument is the generality

Our aim is to allow different sources of information to be combined in a principled way in an ILP environment. Here, we combine lexical and contextual information to tag words. We have $P(Tag|Word, Context)$ proportional to $P(Tag|Word)P(Context|Tag, Word)$ and estimate $P(Context|Tag, Word)$ by $P(Context|Tag)$ using the naive Bayes assumption. $P(Tag|Word)$ is estimated directly from the lexicon using relative frequency, so we do not need a formalism as expressive as Prolog to define the priors: each word in a sentence is just replaced by a representation of its entry in the lexicon. This is equivalent to having vast numbers of ground meta-facts in the background such as:

```
w(np('New'),0.975). w(jj('New'),0.024). w(nps('New'),0.001).
```

If a word's context is already disambiguated, we estimate $P(Context|Tag)$ by finding the most specific clause that covers that context and then pull out the Tag-conditional likelihood attached to that clause. In other words we use the most specific generalisation of a word's context for which we have collected statistics. If no clause covers the context the posterior is estimated using the prior.

In general, a word's context will in fact contain many ambiguous words. We address this by using Gibbs sampling [11] to find a Markov chain of disambiguated sentences, and choose the most frequently occurring element in this chain. We initialise by guessing tags for all ambiguous words based on their prior lexical probabilities. We then work left to right along the sentence, using the current guessed context (and lexical prior) to construct a posterior distribution for each ambiguous word, and then replace the current guess for the focus word by a tag drawn at random from this posterior. Doing this for the entire sentence gives us a new guess for the disambiguated sentence and completes one step of the Markov chain. This procedure is iterated and the frequency of the various guesses is recorded. Our final answer for the sentence is the modal value of the Markov chain.

Figure 3 shows the 7 most common disambiguations for "A House-Senate conference last week accepted the provision with no discussion of the potential cost to the government." in a Markov chain of 50 iterations. 50 iterations were used in all cases. The correct disambiguation is the last one which only occurs 3 times. The problem here is the high lexical prior for "House-Senate" to be a noun: we have w(np('House-Senate'),0.732).

```
count([dt,np,nn,jj,nn,vbd,dt,nn,in,dt,nn,in,dt,jj,nn,to,dt,nn,stp],13)
count([dt,np,nn,jj,nn,vbd,dt,nn,in,dt,nn,in,dt,jj,vb,to,dt,nn,stp],4)
count([dt,np,nn,jj,nn,vbd,dt,nn,in,dt,nn,in,dt,nn,nn,to,dt,nn,stp],4)
count([dt,np,nn,jj,nn,vbd,dt,nn,in,dt,nn,in,dt,jj,vbd,to,dt,nn,stp],3)
count([dt,jj,nn,jj,nn,vbn,dt,nn,in,dt,nn,in,dt,jj,nn,to,dt,nn,stp],3)
count([dt,np,nn,jj,nn,vbd,dt,nn,in,dt,nn,in,dt,nn,vb,to,dt,nn,stp],3)
count([dt,jj,nn,jj,nn,vbd,dt,nn,in,dt,nn,in,dt,jj,nn,to,dt,nn,stp],3)
```

Fig. 3. Counts from a Markov chain for tagging

Results from this initial experiment are unspectacular. On an independent test set of 5000 sentences composed entirely of "known words", a per-word accuracy of 103961/109177 = 95.22 ± 0.06% and a per sentence accuracy of 2025/5000 = 40.5 ± 0.7% was achieved. Better results have been achieved using similar data elsewhere. Also using 50 iterations of the Markov chain meant that the tagging was slow. Perhaps unsurprisingly, more work is needed for good tagging results. Effort will be directed into a number of areas:

1. Both the lexical prior probabilities and the contextual likelihoods are estimated probabilities, and there is no consideration of the uncertainty in these estimates. For example, "babble" is seen only once in the training set, where

it is tagged nn (singular common noun). On the basis of this single example it will have zero prior and hence zero posterior probability of being a verb, no matter what context it is found in. A more sophisticated approach would be to replace point-estimates of probabilities by Dirichlet posterior distributions.

2. Using the most specific clause may result in "overfitting" although the fact that these rules were constructed by Progol should guard against this. One could prune the parameterised theory by only using clauses above a certain generality, with the optimal value of this threshold being found by cross-validation or using a validation set as in CART.

3. One might be able to calculate modal values exactly and efficiently, perhaps using a generalisation of the Viterbi algorithm.

4. Only known words were considered, but we could easily use morphological information and $w/2$ to define a prior for unknown words.

6 Conclusion

Separating the construction of a logical theory from its parameterisation, as is done here, has a number of advantages. The theory can be induced from a modest number of examples (i.e. 8000), and parameterisation of the theory can then be done in a single pass through a large example set. This is a little like the sampling technique of Srinivasan [12], where a theory is induced on a sample of the training data and then the whole training set is used to knock out clauses which turn out to be less accurate than they appeared to be according to the sample. Here, instead of knocking out clauses, we attach a probabilistic score to each clause. Since we can rely on the very large amounts of data available in tagging to find accurate parameters, we do not have to worry too much about inducing "bad" clauses—they will get suitable parameters later.

Given the generality of the probabilistic method given here one would expect it to have applications where we need to combine probabilistic and logical information such as in POS tagging. POS tagging was chosen here since it is (i) a real application and (ii) hard. It would have been possible to demonstrate our approach on a toy domain such as that of the "trains", complete with a convoluted prior using recursive clauses, but it is doubtful what such "applications" prove.

Future work will involve other applications of probabilistic ILP including further experimental work on POS tagging. The technique is not Progol specific, we could also use it with the MERLIN system [1] which learns from positives only. It would also be interesting to parameterise theories learnt from positive *and* negative examples, when the latter are available.

One possible criticism of a probabilistic approach is that the resulting model is unintelligible. This could be addressed by using the probabilistic model as a noise-free oracle which will label any desired example as positive or negative, depending on which is more probable. A standard ILP system could then be used to construct a more intelligible theory, with a possible trade-off between intelligibility and expected accuracy.

Acknowledgements

I would like to thank Gillian Higgins for her support during the writing of this paper. Ashwin Srinivasan helped with the P-Progol implementation of positive only learning and with useful discussions. Thanks also to Stephen Muggleton for discussions on positive only learning, and also to two anonymous referees.

References

1. Henrik Boström. Predicate invention and learning from positive examples only. In *Proceedings of the 10th European Conference on Machine Learning (ECML-98)*. Springer, 1998.
2. Wray Buntine. Learning classification trees. In D.J. Hand, editor, *Artificial Intelligence Frontiers in Statistics: AI and Statistics III*, chapter 15, pages 182–201. Chapman & Hall, London, 1993.
3. J. Cussens. Bayesian Inductive Logic Programming with explicit probabilistic bias. Technical Report PRG-TR-24-96, Oxford University Computing Laboratory, 1996.
4. James Cussens. Part-of-speech tagging using Progol. In *Inductive Logic Programming: Proceedings of the 7th International Workshop (ILP-97)*. *LNAI 1297*, pages 93–108. Springer, 1997.
5. Luc Dehaspe. Maximum entropy modeling with clausal constraints. In *Inductive Logic Programming: Proceedings of the 7th International Workshop (ILP-97)*. *LNAI 1297*, pages 109–124. Springer, 1997.
6. Joseph Y. Halpern. An analysis of first-order logics of probability. *Artificial Intelligence*, 46:311–350, 1990.
7. D. Michie, D.J. Spiegelhalter, and C.C. Taylor. *Machine Learning, Neural and Statistical Classification*. Ellis Horwood, Hemel Hempstead, 1994.
8. S. Muggleton. Learning from positive data. In S. Muggleton, editor, *Inductive Logic Programming: Proceedings of the 6th International Workshop (ILP-96)*. *LNAI 1314*, pages 358–376. Springer, 1996.
9. Raymond Ng and V.S. Subrahmanian. Probabilistic logic programming. *Information and Computation*, 101(2):150–201, 1992.
10. Uroš Pompe and Igor Kononenko. Probabilistic first-order classification. In *Inductive Logic Programming: Proceedings of the 7th International Workshop (ILP-97)*, pages 235–243, 1997.
11. A.F.M. Smith and G.O. Roberts. Bayesian computation via the Gibbs sampler and related Markov chain Monte Carlo methods. *Journal of the Royal Statistical Society B*, 55(1):3–23, 1993.
12. A. Srinivasan. Sampling methods for the analysis of large datasets with ILP. Technical Report PRG-TR-27-97, Oxford University Computing Laboratory, Oxford, 1997.
13. A. Srinivasan and R.D. King. Feature construction with inductive logic programming: A study of quantitative predictions of biological activity aided by structural attributes. In S. Muggleton, editor, *Inductive Logic Programming: Proceedings of the 6th International Workshop (ILP-96)*. *LNAI 1314*, pages 89–104. Springer, 1996.

Induction of Constraint Grammar-Rules Using Progol

Martin Eineborg[1] and Nikolaj Lindberg[2]

[1] Telia Research AB,
Spoken Language Processing,
SE-123 86 Farsta, Sweden,
Martin.E.Eineborg@telia.se
[2] Centre for Speech Technology,
Royal Institute of Technology,
SE-100 44 Stockholm, Sweden,
nikolaj@speech.kth.se

Abstract. The paper reports a pilot study aiming at inducing rules for disambiguating words with different possible part of speech readings in unrestricted Swedish text. The rules, which are inspired by Constraint Grammar, are learnt using the Progol inductive logic programming system. The training data is sampled from the part of speech tagged one million word Stockholm-Umeå Corpus. The results show that the induction of disambiguation rules using Progol is a realistic way of learning rules of good quality with a minimum of manual effort. When tested on unseen data, 97% of the words retain the correct reading after tagging leaving an ambiguity of 1.15 readings per word.

1 Introduction

The Constraint Grammar (CG) approach to part of speech tagging and surface syntactic dependency parsing has attracted a lot of attention in recent years. Its success is due to the minutely hand-crafted two-level morphology lexicon (TWOL) and grammar (CG). There is as yet a fully mature version for English only (EngCG), but CGs for other languages are being developed. EngCG is claimed, by its developers, to be superior to stochastic taggers [9].

Generating CG rules automatically could be helpful and time saving when developing systems for new languages. Rules have the advantage over for example statistical methods that they can be interpreted in a meaningful way by a linguist and that they can be evaluated, modified or serve as a base for further manual refinement. Promising experiments of inducing CG inspired rules [2] as well as CG rules proper [8] have been reported.

In the current study, Progol [6] was used to induce rules from a one million word part of speech tagged corpus of Swedish. A lexicon was created based on the corpus, and disambiguation rules ('constraints') were learnt for tags in the corpus. Over 7 000 rules were induced, and when tested on unseen data, 97%

of the words retained the correct tag. There were still ambiguities left in the output, on an average 1.15 readings per word.

The rest of the paper is organised as follows: some background information about Constraint Grammar, the Stockholm-Umeå Corpus and previous work is given in Section 2. The approach taken in this paper is described in Section 3 along with some results in Section 4. Finally, in Section 5 the result is discussed, and in 6 some conclusions are made.

2 Background

In this section, the Constraint Grammar framework and the corpus, from which training and testing material is sampled, will be presented briefly. Two previous studies on rule induction are also presented.

2.1 Constraint Grammar POS tagging

The Constraint Grammar (CG) is a system for automatic part of speech tagging and shallow syntactic dependency analysis of unrestricted text [4], [10]. CG is 'reductionistic', since a big part of the rules discards ambiguous readings rather than states what readings are the correct ones. In the following, only the part of speech tagging step will be considered (however, the CG approach to syntactic tagging is in nature similar to the part of speech tagging step). The tagging is done in three steps: preprocessing of text, lexicon look-up and rule application.

The preprocessing includes the identification of 'idioms' which are assigned a single, unambiguous part of speech reading. For example, the three-word sequence *in order to* would be given one single part of speech reading (the infinitive marker).

All words in the input text are looked up in a lexicon, which renders the text morphologically ambiguous.

The text is passed on to the tagger, which discards incorrect readings among the ambiguities, according to contextual constraints.

- *Local-context rules* discard readings given that the conditions on the surrounding words are satisfied.
- *Lexical rules* discard readings given that the conditions on the *target* word (the word to disambiguate) are satisfied.
- *Barrier rules* allow arbitrarily long context between a context word and the word to disambiguate, given that the words in between do not have certain features.
- *Select rules* are used when the correct reading has been identified and all other readings should be removed.

For example, a local-context rule discarding a verbal (V) reading of a word following a word unambiguously (-1C) tagged as determine (DET) can be expressed as [10]:

```
REMOVE (V) (-1C (DET));
```

A CG rule can refer to part of speech tags and to word tokens as well as to sets of tags. A full-scale CG consists of hundreds, if not thousands, of rules. The developers of EngCG report that 99.7% of the words retain their correct reading, and that 93-97% of the words are unambiguous after tagging [4, page 186]. The Constraint Grammars, parsers and TWOL lexica are commercial products.

2.2 The Stockholm-Umeå Corpus

The training material is sampled from a pre-release of the Stockholm-Umeå Corpus (SUC)[3]. SUC covers just over one million words of part of speech tagged Swedish text, sampled from different text genres.

The SUC tagset has 146 different tags, and the tags consist of a part of speech tag, e.g. VB (the verb) followed by a (possibly empty) set of morphological features, such as PRS (the present tense) and AKT (the active voice), etc. There are 25 different part of speech tags. Thus, many of the 146 tags represent different inflected forms. Examples of the tags are found in Table 1 and Table 2.

2.3 Samuelsson et al. (1996)

Samuelsson et al. [8] describe experiments of inducing English CG rules. The training corpus consisted of some 55 000 words of English text, morphologically and syntactically tagged according to the EngCG tagset.[1]

Local-context, lexical and barrier rules were induced based on bigram statistics. While the induced local-context and lexical rules look only at bigrams, the barrier rules utilize longer contexts.

When tested on a 10 000 word test corpus, the recall of the induced grammar was 98.2% with a precision of 87.3%, which means that some of the ambiguities were left pending after tagging (1.12 readings per word).

2.4 Cussens (1997)

Cussens [2] describes a project in which CG inspired rules for tagging English text were induced using Progol. The training examples were sampled from the 3 million word tagged Wall Street Journal corpus and consisted of the tags of all of the words on each side of the word to be disambiguated (the target word). Constraints were learnt separately for each of the tags in the corpus using a small hand-crafted syntactic grammar as background knowledge.

A lexicon consisting of all word forms with their ambiguity class (all possible readings for a word form) and a per word frequency score for each tag was built from the training corpus.

In the final tagger, the rules were applied to the text after lexicon look-up. If no rules were applicable, but there still were ambiguities left in the input, the

---

[1] The EngCG tagset has 17 different part of speech tags.

tagger discarded the most unlikely tag for a word, and continued doing so until some constraint was applicable or the input was unambiguously tagged.

Given no unknown words and a tag set of 43 different tags, the system tagged 96.4% of the words correctly.

3 Present work

The current work is inspired by [2] as well as [8], but departs from both in some respects.

Following Samuelsson et al. we induced local-context and lexical rules. In the present work, no barrier rules were induced. In contrast to their study, a TWOL lexicon and an annotated training text using the same tagset were not available. Instead, a lexicon was created from the training corpus.

Just as Cussens, we use Progol to induce tag elimination rules from an annotated corpus. In contrast to his study, no grammatical background knowledge is given to the learner and also word tokens, and not only part of speech tags, are in the training data. Furthermore, the tags in the training data are split into two parts, the part of speech category (e.g. VB or PP) and the set of morphological features (e.g. PRS AKT), which makes it possible for the Progol system to generalize over sets of tags by referring to only part of speech (e.g. VB) and not only to fully specified readings (e.g. VB PRS AKT).

In the present work, the context has been limited to a window of maximally seven words, with the target word to disambiguate in the middle. This restriction is not inherent in the method, but was applied in order to reduce the search space in the initial experiments. A further motivation for this strategy is that sensible constraints referring to a position relative to the target word utilize close context, typically 1-3 words [4, page 59].

A pre-release of the Stockholm-Umeå Corpus was used. Some 10% of the corpus was put aside to be used as test data, and the rest of the corpus made up the training data. The test data files were evenly distributed over the different text genres.

3.1 Preprocessing

Before starting the learning of constraints, the corpus material was pre-processed in different ways: A lexicon based on the corpus was created, lexical rules and unambiguous bi- and trigrams were extracted from the corpus.

Following [2], a lexicon was produced from the training corpus. All different word forms in the corpus were represented in the lexicon by one look-up word and an ambiguity class (the set of different tags which occurred in the corpus for the word form). Each reading in the ambiguity class was assigned a per word frequency figure. The lexicon ended up just over 86 000 entries big. A few sample entries are found in Table 1.

Similar to [4], the first step of the tagging process was to identify 'idioms', although we use the term differently. We decided to search the training text

Table 1. *Lexicon. Tags are flanked with a per word frequency figure, ambiguous readings delimited by a colon.*

Word Form	POS Readings
beståndsdelar	NN UTR PLU IND NOM 9
poppelved	NN UTR SIN IND NOM 1
att	SN 10023 : UO 1 : IE 10749
så	KN 382 : SN 201 : AB 3122 : VB INF AKT 1 : IN 16

for bi- and trigrams which were often tagged with one specific tag sequence (unambiguously tagged, i.e.). The bi- and trigrams should have a frequency of at least 20, and a given word sequence should be assigned the same reading in at least 90% of the cases. 1 253 bigrams and 577 trigrams were found. Example 'idioms' are given in Table 2.

Table 2. *'Idioms': unambiguous word sequences found in the training data.*

Bi- and Trigrams	POS Readings (unambiguous tag sequence)
ett par	ett/DT NEU SIN IND par/NN NEU SIN IND NOM
det är	det/PN NEU SIN DEF SUB/OBJ är/VB PRS AKT
i samband med	i/PP samband/NN NEU SIN IND NOM med/PP
på grund av	på/PP grund/NN UTR SIN IND NOM av/PP

Following [8], a list of very unlikely readings for certain words was produced ('lexical rules'). For a word form plus tag to qualify as a lexical rule, the word form should have a frequency of at least 100 occurrences in the training data, and the word should occur with the tag to discard in no more than 1% of the cases. 355 lexical rules were produced this way.

3.2 Rule induction

The aim of this study was to investigate the feasibility of the method rather than to create a complete tagger. This means that rules were learnt for only 45 of the 146 possible readings of the SUC tagset. Rules were induced for all of the part of speech categories, but not for all of the possible inflected forms. In other words, there might be ambiguities which we cannot yet disambiguate. As an illustration, consider this example: If there exist rules discarding any verbal reading (VB), but there are no rules discarding e.g. verbs of the infinite form, active voice (VB INF AKT), a word assigned the ambiguity class {VB INF AKT, VB IMP AKT} would be impossible to correctly disambiguate whenever VB INF AKT is the wrong reading.

A different set of training data was produced for each tag to discard. The training data was pre-processed by applying the bi- and trigrams and the lexical rules, described above (Section 3.1). This step was taken in order to reduce the amount of training data — rules should not be learnt for ambiguities which could easily be taken care of anyway. The size of the data sets varied considerably, both due to experimenting and the number of available examples. Some sets had only a few hundred positive and a few hundred negative examples. Other sets had over 6 000 examples of each type.

We also experimented with different noise values, allowing different percentages of negative examples to be covered by the induced rules. A few of the rule sets had a noise value of 10% while others had less. A reason for allowing some noise was that there could be faulty tags in the data.

Since we are inducing tag eliminating rules, an example is considered positive when a word is incorrectly tagged and the reading should be discarded. A negative example is a correctly tagged word where the reading should be retained.

For such a hard task as learning tagging rules for unrestricted text, several thousand examples are needed for each tag, in order to produce rules of high quality.

3.3 Rule formalism

The format of the induced rules is

```
remove(LHS, RHS) :-
        left_context(LHS, Cond).
remove(LHS, RHS) :-
        right_context(RHS, Cond).
remove(LHS, RHS) :-
        left_context(LHS, Cond1),
        right_context(RHS, Cond2).
```

where the second arguments of left_context/2 and right_context/2 are the constraints on the context, such as part of speech tags, word forms or a combination of both. Since rules are induced for each tag individually, no information about which tag the rules refer to is present in the output from Progol.

Cond is actually a structure where the functor describes the position and content of the condition. The content is described by the letters w (word), p (part-of-speech) and m (morphology). The position of a constraint is given by the position of the letter within the functor where x is a skipped word. For example

```
remove(vb, A,B) :-
        left_context(A,wpm_x(vet,vb,prs_akt)),
        right_context(B,p(pn)).
```

is a rule which discards the vb reading of a word if the second word to the left is the word *vet* ('know'), has the part-of-speech tag vb, and the features (prs akt), and where the first word to the right has part-of-speech tag pn. More examples of induced rules can be seen i Table 3.

Table 3. *Example of induced vb rules (randomly picked).*

---

remove(vb, A,B) :- left_context(A,wpm_x(var,vb,prt_akt)),
         right_context(B,x_pm(ab,")).
remove(vb, A,B) :- left_context(A,wpm_x(en,dt,utr_sin_ind)),
         right_context(B,x_wpm(och,kn,")).
remove(vb, A,B) :- left_context(A,wpm_x(en,dt,utr_sin_ind)),
         right_context(B,x_pm(vb,prs_akt)).
remove(vb, A,B) :- left_context(A,wpm_x(de,dt,'utr/neu_plu_def')),
         right_context(B,p_p(nn,vb)).

By using Progol's prune feature, hypotheses of unwanted properties can be avoided. For example, it is not desirable that Progol looks twice into the same context or that a context is seen as both a right and a left context at the same time.

```
prune(remove(_, _), (right_context(_, _),
   right_context(_, _))).
prune(remove(_, _), (left_context(_, _),
   left_context(_, _))).
prune(remove(_, _), (left_context(A, _),
   right_context(B, _))) :- A == B.
```

4 Results

More than 7 000 rules were induced using CProgol Version 4.2. The tagger was tested on a subset of the unseen data. Only sentences in which all words were in the lexicon were allowed.

The test data consisted of 4 193 sentences and 48 408 words, including punctuation marks. After lexicon look-up the words were assigned 105 828 readings, i.e., on average 2.19 readings per word. 46 942 words retained the correct reading after disambiguation, which means that the correct tag survived for 97.0% of the words. After tagging, there were 55 464 readings left, 1.15 readings per word. The remaining ambiguities were left as further disambiguating would contrast with the CG philosophy, which rather leaves an ambiguity pending than gives a guess.

As a comparison to these results, a preliminary test of the Brill tagger [1], also trained on the Stockholm-Umeå Corpus, tagged 96.9% of the words correctly, and Oliver Mason's QTag [5], a probabilistic tagger, got 96.3% on the same data [7]. Neither of these two taggers leave ambiguities pending.

The different training sets (of different sizes) were run on a couple of different machines, which makes it hard to present any results on processing times. However, as an illustration, 493 rules were induced from a file of 1 284 positive and 419 negative examples in 11 785 seconds (on a Sparc Ultra 2).

5 Discussion and future work

The figures of the experimental tagger are not optimal, but not a disappointment either. The correctness figure would have been better if we did not accept as much as 10% noise for some of the training sets. Furthermore, we have not eliminated the worst rules. These could easily be identified by testing all rules against the training data.

The figure of ambiguities left pending after tagging is rather small given the fact that we did not learn rules for all of the 146 possible readings of the words in the corpus. We did learn rules for 24 part of speech categories, but not for all their possible inflexions. Thus, there are ambiguities that our rules cannot solve. Considering this fact, and that we so far have induced only one kind of rule, `remove/3`, we do find the result of this pilot study encouraging.

It should be pointed out that there are some ambiguity classes which are very hard to deal with. For example, there is a tag for the adverb, AB, and one tag for the verbal particle, PL. In the lexicon built from the corpus, there are 83 word forms which can have at least both these readings. (After tagging, there were 483 words in the test data which had both tags.) Thus, turning a corpus into a lexicon might lead to the introduction of ambiguities hard to solve.

Future work includes learning rules for disambiguating all ambiguity classes in the lexicon. A lexicon better tailored to the task would be of much use. Another important issue is that of handling unknown words.

So far only a subset of the rule types of CG has been induced. A next step will be to learn also select and barrier rules.

The rules induced in this study cannot refer to e.g. 'noun in the plural' but only either 'noun' or a full morphological reading. This means that the rules are less general than they should have to be. This can be fixed by making it possible for Progol to refer to individual morphological features of the context words.

6 Conclusions

Using the Progol ILP system, more than 7 000 tag eliminating rules were induced from the Stockholm-Umeå Corpus. A lexicon was built from the corpus, and after lexicon look-up, test data (including only known words) was disambiguated with the help of the induced rules. Of 48 408 words, 46 942 (97%) retained the correct reading after disambiguation. Some ambiguities remained in output: on an average 1.15 readings per word. Considering the experimental status of the tagger, we find the results encouraging.

Acknowledgments

We would like to thank Henrik Boström for helpful discussions and clarifications and also Britt Hartmann who answered many corpus related questions.

References

1. Eric Brill. Some advances in transformation-based part of speech tagging. In *Proceedings of the Twelfth National Conference on Artificial Intelligence (AAAI-94)*, Seattle, Wa., 1994.
2. James Cussens. Part of speech tagging using Progol. In *Proceedings of the 7th International Workshop on Inductive Logic Programming (ILP-97)*, pages 93–108, 1997.
3. Eva Ejerhed, Gunnel Källgren, Wennstedt Ola, and Magnus Åström. *The Linguistic Annotation System of the Stockholm-Umeå Project*. Department of General Linguistics, University of Umeå, 1992.
4. Fred Karlsson, Atro Voutilainen, Juha Heikkilä, and Arto Anttila, editors. *Constraint Grammar: A language-independent system for parsing unrestricted text*. Mouton de Gruyter, Berlin and New York, 1995.
5. Oliver Manson. *QTAG—A portable probabilistic tagger*. Corpus Research, The University of Birmingham, U.K., 1997.
6. Stephen Muggleton. Inverse entainment and Progol. *New Generation Computing Journal*, 13:245–286, 1995.
7. Daniel Ridings. SUC and the Brill tagger. Technical Report GU-ISS-98-1, Department of Swedish, Göteborg University, 1998.
8. Christer Samuelsson, Pasi Tapanainen, and Atro Voutilainen. Inducing Constraint Grammars. In Miclet Laurent and de la Higuera Colin, editors, *Grammatical Inference: Learning Syntax from Sentences*, pages 146–155. Springer Verlag, 1996.
9. Christer Samuelsson and Atro Voutilainen. Comparing a linguistic and a stochastic tagger. In *Proceedings of the 35th Annual Meeting of the Association for Computational Linguistics and 8th Conference of the European Chapter of the Association for Computational Linguistics (ACL-EACL'97)*, pages 246–253, 1997.
10. Pasi Tapanainen. *The Constraint Grammar Parser CG-2*. Department of General Linguistics, University of Helsinki, 1996.

A Hybrid Approach to Word Segmentation

Dimitar Kazakov[1] and Suresh Manandhar[2]

University of York, Heslington, York YO10 5DD, UK,
{kazakov,suresh}@cs.york.ac.uk,
WWW home page: [1] http://www.cs.york.ac.uk/mlg/ and
[2] http://www.cs.york.ac.uk/~suresh/

Abstract. This article presents a combination of unsupervised and supervised learning techniques for generation of word segmentation rules from a list of words. First, a bias for word segmentation is introduced and a simple genetic algorithm is used for the search of segmentation that corresponds to the best bias value. In the second phase, the segmentation obtained from the genetic algorithm is used as an input for two inductive logic programming algorithms, namely FOIDL and CLOG. The result is a logic program that can be used for segmentation of unseen words. The learnt program contains affixes which are characteristic for the given language and can be used in other morphology tasks.

1 Introduction

Word segmentation is an important subtask of natural language processing with a range of applications from hyphenation to more detailed morphological analysis and text-to-speech conversion. Several approaches based on learning aiming at word segmentation and morphology have been published recently. Some of them, as in Brill [2] and van den Bosch et al. [15] make use of prepocessed data—a text corpus tagged with the corresponding part of speech in the first case or morphologically analysed words in the second one. At the same time, algorithms for unsupervised learning that use plain text [5] or lists of words are also known. A series of works is based on the notion of *analogy* introducing a bias for word segmentation [13]. This principle has also been used for text-to-speech conversion rules [16].

Inductive logic programming (ILP) [10] has proved to be a feasible way to learn linguistic knowledge in different domains, such as morphological analysis [1], part-of-speech taging [4] and parsing [8]. Unlike statistical or connectionist approaches, these results are comprehensible and a human expert can easily interpret or modify them. However, ILP remains within the supervised learning paradigm and requires preprocessed (classified) input data. Another possible limitation of ILP approach in the field of linguistics is the very large search space that is to be explored. A typical illustration of the pros and cons of the use of ILP for natural language processing is the learning of the past tense of English verbs [12]. When compared to neural networks and decision trees a more accurate knowledge in the form of decision lists is obtained [12]. Top-down learning algorithms such as FOIDL require theory constants which in our task are the relevant affixes. These constants are generated by exploring the exhaustive set of possible affixes, which slows down the algorithm and limits the size of the input data the system can handle.

In this work, we describe a hybrid approach combining unsupervised and supervised learning techniques for generation of word segmentation rules from a list of words. A bias for word segmentation introduced in our previous work [9] is reformulated as a fitness function of a simple genetic algorithm, which is used for the search of a word list segmentation that corresponds to the best bias value. In the second phase, the list of segmented words obtained from the genetic algorithm is used as an input for two decision list learning algorithms, namely FOIDL and CLOG [11]. The result is a logic program in a decision list representation that can be used for segmentation of unseen words. This program also contains a number of constants, which are characteristic for the given language and can be used in other learning tasks related to word morphology.

2 Prerequisites

2.1 Genetic Algorithms

Genetic algorithms (GA) [7] are often used as an alternative approach to tasks with a large search space where greedy search methods would often get stuck in local maxima. Genetic algorithms are inspired from Darwinian evolution. A GA maintains a set of candidate solutions (called *chromosomes* or *individuals*) and applies the natural selection operators of *crossover* and *mutation* to successively generate new candidate solutions from existing ones. A *fitness function* is employed to rank the individuals to determine their goodness. The chromosomes are represented as a sequence of characters (or a bit vector). The *crossover* operation constructs two new child chromosomes by splicing two parent chromosomes at *n* points. The *mutation* operator creates a new chromosome from a single parent by randomly changing a single character (or flipping a bit) of the parent chromosome. Chromosomes are mutated according to some mutation probability known as *mutation rate*. The following algorithm is known as a *simple genetic algorithm*:

1. Initialization
   (a) Create a random population of candidate solutions (*individuals*) of *popsize* size.
   (b) Evaluate all individuals using the fitness function.
   (c) Store the best evaluated individual as *best-ever* individual.
2. Generation and Selection
   (a) Sample the individuals according to their fitness, so that in the resulting *matching pool* those with higher fitness appear repeatedly with a higher probability.
   (b) Apply crossover with probability *crossover_rate*.
   (c) Apply mutation with probability *mutation_rate*.
   (d) Evaluate all individuals using the fitness function.
   (e) Update the best-ever individual.
3. If the stopping condition is satisfied, provide the *best-ever* individual as a solution. Otherwise go to step 2.

There are two characteristics that are typical for all GA: 1. they are indeterministic and 2. they provide a solution, which may be not optimal.

2.2 Decision list learning in FOIDL

FOIDL [12] is a system for learning first-order decision lists from examples and is closely related to FOIL[14]. One of the main reasons that a system such as FOIDL is a good candidate for NLP applications is that it can be used to learn from positive examples only. FOIDL uses an assumption known as *output completenes* to generate implicit negative examples from positive data. The notion of *output completenes* can be best explained by an example. Let the database (in Prolog form) consist of the following positive examples: `past(sleep,slept)`, `past(like,liked)`, `past(walk,walked)`.

Assuming that this database is queried using the mode `past(+,-)` the query corresponding to the example `past(sleep,slept)` will be `past(sleep,X)`. Then the implicitly assumed negative examples will consists of all instantiations of `X` such that `past(sleep,X)` is *false* in the database.

Such a closed-world assumption is quite reasonable in the morphology tasks and provides a method for inducing rules from positive only examples. FOIDL learns a given target predicate from a set of examples by following a greedy top-down hill-climbing strategy by starting from the most general hypothesis and by successively refining the hypothesis by adding body literals which match the user supplied mode declarations.

2.3 Decision list learning in CLOG

CLOG is another system for learning of first-order decision lists. CLOG shares a fair amount of similarity with FOIDL [3]. Like FOIDL, CLOG can learn first-order decision lists from positive examples only using the *output completeness* assumption. The main difference is that CLOG only considers generalisations that are relevant to an example. In the current implementation these generalisations are supplied by a user-defined predicate which takes as input an example and generates a list of all generalisations that cover that example. The reader is referred to [11] for more detailed discussion of CLOG .

For the task of learning segmentation rules described in this paper we coded our own clause generator that took as input an example and generated as output all clauses whose body contained at most two **append/3** clauses and covered the example. The generated clauses included all possible variable binding patterns that were consistent with the mode declarations. CLOG treats the set of generalisations of an example as a *generalisation set*. It then cycles every input example through the generalisation set in a single iteration checking whether a candidate generalisation covers the example positively or negatively. Once this process is complete the "best" candidate generalisation is chosen. The example set is pruned using this candidate and the cycle repeats.

The *gain* function currently used in CLOG is user-defined. For the segmentation problem we chose the following simple gain function: $gain = QP - SN - C$

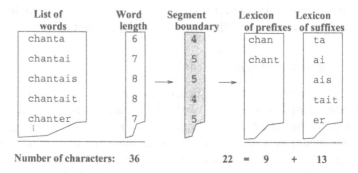

Fig. 1. A naïve theory of word morphology

where QP denotes the number of new examples covered positively, SN denotes the number of previously covered examples that are covered negatively and C is the number of literals in the clause body.

3   Word Segmentation Bias

The segmentation model accepted here limits the number of word segments up to two. These segments will be called further 'prefixes', resp. 'suffixes' where the terms correspond to their etymological meaning rather than to the one used by linguists. In other words, any left/right substring of the word characters is seen as a prefix/suffix. There are two reasons for this assumption. For practical purposes, such as on-line morpho-lexical analysis, a higher number of word constituents either produces a lot of spurious analyses or requires the use of some additional constraints, which slows down the algorithm and increases the cost of the system development. On the other hand, some of the limitations of the assumption that we make can be overcome by the repeated use of our approach.

For a given set of words the segment boundary positions correspond to a vector of integers, each of them between zero and the word length. The word set along with an arbitrary vector of that kind introduces a *naïve theory of morphology* [9]. Every such theory defines two lexicons where prefixes, resp. suffixes are enumerated without repetition (see fig.1). The quality of the theory will be estimated by the number of characters $N = P + S$ in the prefix lexicon (P) and the suffix one (S)—the smaller that number, the better the theory. The upper bound N_{max} of that measure is given by the number of characters W in the word list. This case is reached when no prefix nor suffix has been generated twice by the theory. Now, the word segmentation bias can be formulated.

Word Segmentation Bias: *among a set of naïve theories of word morphology, select the one with the lowest number of characters in the corresponding pair of lexicons.*

The Naïve Theory of Morphology (NTM) bias is based on the hypothesis that substrings composed out of real morphemes occur in the words with a frequency higher than any other left or right substrings.[1] In that way, a theory with a low

---

[1] This presumption is limited to the languages in which the main operator used in derivational and inflectional morphological rules is concatenation.

N would produce lexicons where 'prefixes' and 'suffixes' correspond very often to single morphemes or their combinations. Since the word list can be stored as a list of pairs of indices <prefix,suffix> along with the two lexicons of affixes, the bias described can be seen as using Occam's razor to choose the simplest theory corresponding to the given dataset.

4 GA Representation of the Learning Task

The approach is straight-forward, making use of a simple genetic algorithm, where the vector of integers corresponding to the theory is directly used as an individual (chromosome) and its fitness function is $N_{max} - N$. The fitness function defined in that way does not take negative values and the GA searches for individuals with maximal fitness. In the context of individuals with non-binary features, mutation is defined either as a shift of the morpheme boundary with one position to the left or right, or, as a random choice of a new boundary position from the allowed interval. The mutation rate is set by the user and is increased by 20% after 10 generations with the same best-ever individual. The higher mutation rate is kept until a better individual is produced and then changed back to its original value. A 1-point crossover is applied. The fittest individual is kept through the generations and is finally given as a result of the learning after a certain number of generations.

5 Results of Unsupervised Learning

A list containing many forms of the same lexical entry or its entire paradigm is suitable for the learning since the difference between N_{max} and N of the best solution is very great. A possible way to obtain such a word list while remaining within the framework of unsupervised learning is to sort the words of a large corpus and remove all duplicates. With the increasing corpus size, the word list converges on an exhaustive lexicon of word forms. A chunk of 700 different word forms from a very large alphabetically ordered French lexicon of word forms was actually used for our experiments.

ébarb+e	ébatt+irent	ébouillant+erez	ébourgeonn+ée
ébarb+ent	ébatt+issent	ébouillant+eriez	ébourgeonn+és
ébarb+erai	ébatt+ra	ébouillant+erions	éb+ouriffais
ébarb+erez	éborgn+es	ébouillant+ez	ébouriff+ait
ébarb+ez	éborgn+ons	ébouillant+ions	ébouriff+asse
ébarb+iez	éborgn+ées	ébouillant+ât	ébouriff+ent
ébarb+ons	ébouillant+assent	éboul+ait	ébouriff+er

Table 1. GA output sample

Two experiments were carried out. In the first, the list of words was randomly sampled and divided into a training set of 200 words and a test set containing

500 words. The genetic algorithm was applied on the training set for 1500 generations.[2] A sample of the NTM obtained is shown in table 1. For the second experiment, the list of words was divided into a training set of 500 words and a 200-word test set. The training set was randomly split into 5 disjunctive sets of 100 words and the genetic algorithm was separately run on each of them. Then the NTM found were merged and evaluated in the same way as described above. This technique proved to be a feasible trade-off between the input data size and the time needed to find an NMT of high quality. It also makes the GA time complexity linear w.r.t. the input size.

A quantitative description of the first experiment is given in table 2. With regard to the different theoretical approaches [6], it is difficult to give an exact linguistic evaluation of the acquired results. Nevertheless, the quality of the results can be judged by two criteria, namely, whether the segments produced have a linguistic interpretation and whether that interpretation is consistent for the whole set of words. The training data contains a large percentage of inflected

	Experiment 1		Experiment 2	
	Items	Characters	Items	Characters
GA input	**200**	1943	**500**	4855
Generated prefixes	43	259	75	454
Generated suffixes	64	252	131	638
$(P + S)/W$	0.535	**0.263**	0.412	**0.225**

Table 2. Results of GA segmentation

verb forms, which is typical for the Roman languages. The fragment of the GA output in table 2 displays some of them. The verb stems (*ébarb-*, *ébatt-*, *éborgn-*, *ébouillant-*, *éboul-*, *ébourgeonn-* and *ébouriff-*) have been reliably identified most of the time, therefore many endings corresponding to these verb paradigms have also been enumerated[3]. The proposed segments do not have equal value. The results confirmed that, in general, the more frequently an affix appears in the derived theory, the higher is the probability that the affix is really a morpheme or a concatenation of morphemes.

6 Induction of Procedural Rules for Segmentation

Regardless of the quality of the GA results, their reusability is limited by two factors: 1. when several affixes are present in the processed word, there is no way to choose among the possible segmentations, and 2. the segmentation derived by GA is most probably not optimal, i.e., some of the segmentations can be seen as "wrong" w.r.t. the given bias. The first problem can be addressed by the

---

[2] For *popsize* = 1400 the algorithm ran for about 8 hours on Pentium 200Mhz PC.
[3] The affixes generated are saved along with their frequency in separate files.

application of some simple statistical measure, so that, for instance, for a given word and prefix/suffix lexicons containing the relative frequency of the items, the segmentation which maximizes the probability $P_{seg} = Freq_p * Freq_s / W^2$ is selected. However, this criterion needs the prefix *and* the suffix of the best segmentation to be present in the lexicons.

6.1 Setting

The output of GA is represented as clauses of the predicate seg(W,P,S), for instance: seg([â,n,o,n,n,e,r,a,s],[â,n,o,n,n],[e,r,a,s]). Then seg/3 is used as a target predicate with mode seg(+,?,?) of two inductive learning algorithms: FOIDL and CLOG. In both cases, the predicate append(P,S,W) is used as intentional background knowledge and the range of the theory constants is limited to the set of prefixes and suffixes that appear in seg/3 predicate. As a matter of fact, either of the last two arguments of seg/3 is redundant and one of them was omitted in the real input dataset. The preliminary tests showed that seg(Word,Preffix) and seg(Word,Suffix) settings resulted in almost equal theories and only the latter was used further on.

6.2 Results

The result of ILP learning is an ordered list of rules (logic clauses) preceded by a list of exceptions represented as ground facts, e.g. seg([â,m,e],[m,e]). The latter do not have any impact on the segmentation of unseen words. If these exceptions correspond to individual word segmentations from the GA output which are not optimal w.r.t. the NTM bias, the application of the rules on them should result in more uniform (and compact) segmentation than the one produced by the GA. The exceptions that are not covered by any rule can be seen as segmented at their very end or beginning. They can be added to one of the two lexicons and the ratio $(P + S)/W$ [chars] can be computed for the whole dataset in the same way as for the GA evaluation. The results of this

	Algorithm	Elapsed time	Rules	Test data		Training data	
				Coverage [items]	$(P+S)/W$ [chars]	Coverage [items]	$(P+S)/W$ [chars]
Exp. 1	FOIDL	15'	29	85%	0.21	92.0%	0.257
200 words	CLOG	1' 35"	40	89%	0.30	95.5%	0.276
Exp. 2	FOIDL	4h 28'	50	98.0%	0.390	98.2%	0.227
500 words	CLOG	13' 31"	71	95.5%	0.410	97.2%	0.170

Table 3. Results of ILP learning

experiment[4] are shown in the "training data" column of table 3. Indeed, for the

---

[4] The tests had to be run on different hardware—FOIDL on Sun Ultra Sparc 256MB RAM and CLOG on Sun 4 128MB RAM

500 words the 83.0% $= \frac{1-0.170}{100}$ compression reached by the CLOG "rule-only" theory on the training data is better than the 77.5% $= \frac{1-0.225}{100}$ of GA (see table 2). The difference between the 77.3% compression rate of the FOIDL theory and the 77.5% GA performance approximately corresponds to the worse score of the 9 exceptions not covered by any rule. The remaining 87 exceptions have been segmented in a different way by the rules and the GA, yet the compression rate has not changed. That means that many regular patterns have not been learnt from the GA output but treated as exceptions and some of them have probably been segmented by the rules in a worse manner.

In the second evaluation step, the rules induced were used to generate the segmentation of unseen words (the test dataset) and the results were evaluated as above (see the "test data" column of table 3). The 500-word test dataset for experiment 2 contains 2.5 times more words than the test dataset for experiment 1 when the affixes present in the data remain almost the same. That results in lower compression rates for the second experiment as compared to the first one. The rules derived correspond to four basic patterns:

1. seg(A,B) :- append([é,c,a,r,t,e,l],B,A),!. 2. seg(A,[e,r,e,z]) :- append(_,[e,r,e,z],A),!.
3. seg(A,B) :- append([é,b,l,o,u,i,s,s],B,A), 4. seg(A,B) :- append([é,b,l,o,u,i],B,A),
      append(C,[o,n,s],A),!.   append([é,b,l,o,u,i,s,s],C,A),!.

Rules of the first type look for a particular prefix. For the given data, most of the prefixes correspond to a word stem. Such rules have a limited scope given by the number of word forms that can be derived from the same stem. The rules of the second type are based on suffixes and are essential for languages such as French and English, in which a closed set of derivational or inflexional suffixes is used. As a result, for any representative dataset the rules based on such suffixes should cover a stable percentage of examples, i.e., the absolute number of words covered by them should increase approximately linearly with the lexicon size.

The last two rule patterns can be a result of the insufficient number of examples or the noise in the data where learning from a larger or less noisy dataset would result in rules of the first two types. However, these rules are of real interest when they identify substrings (morphemes) that have not been or cannot be derived by the GA within the given setting. For instance, the example shown for the third pattern covers two words: *éblouissons* and *éblouissions* where the alternation -∅-/-i- is typical for some verb forms and corresponds to the opposition between the indicative present tense and other verb tenses. Similarly, in the fourth example the pattern ⟨stem⟩-/⟨stem⟩-ss- is characteristic for the French verb conjugation.

The theory that CLOG learnt from in the second experiment contains 32 rules based on suffixes (as compared to 3 learnt by FOIDL). Thirty-one of these endings can be found in any standard grammar book and the last one (-r) still has a clear linguistic interpretation. This theory was used to segment an unseen example of the "-er" verb paradigm covering the large majority of French verbs. Out of 48 word forms, 37 have been consistently split into the verb stem *aim-* (not present in the theory) and the corresponding ending. In five more cases two suffixes corresponding to the imperfect tense of subjunctive -ass- or future -er- have been shown as a part of the stem. Only four different word forms have not been covered at all. The example follows where the endings produced are in bold face.

aime	aimais	aimai	aimerai	aime	aimasse	aimerais	aimé
aimes	aimais	aimas	aimeras	aimes	aimasses	aimerais	aimés
aime	aimait	aima	aimera	aime	aimât	aimerait	aimée
aimons	aimions	aimâmes	aimerons	aimions	aimassions	aimerions	aimées
aimez	aimiez	aimâtes	aimerez	aimiez	aimassiez	aimeriez	aimant
aiment	aimaient	aimèrent	aimeront	aiment	aimassent	aimeraient	aimer

7 Conclusions

The hybrid approach to word segmentation described in this paper is an efficient combination of GA and ILP. The former provides a first approximation of the concept learnt and reduce dramatically the search space. The latter, on its turn, refines the target concept reformulating it as intentional rules, so that no other words are necessary to provide the segmentation context for later use. The results of the tests show that a set of rules for word segmentation can be learnt from a *limited* amount of *unanotated* words, as opposed to other approaches where very large and/or tagged corpora are used.

Comparison to other learning strategies shows that some of them [16] use small subsets of data to derive "microtheories" that are independent from the rest of the data. For instance, in the cited work, $P_1 + S_1$ is a legal word segmentation if the words $P_1 + S_2$, $P_2 + S_1$ and $P_2 + S_2$ can be found in the lexicon.[5] On the other hand, the best segmentation choice can be based on some integral criterion, such as the constituent relative frequency [5]. The NTM bias chooses a single segmentation that is related to the segmentation of most of the other words. In the limit, when only words with the same prefix (or suffix) are provided, the NTM bias, unlike the analogy principle [13], [16] is still able to produce the segmentation. Also, NTM does not need to impose a limitation on the length of the affixes as other approaches [2], [5] do.

Possible limitations of the approach are the computational complexity of the NTM search and the restricted number of constituents derived in each learning step. The time efficency that CLOG provided is a good premise for experimentation with larger datasets. In our future research, we intend to modify the NTM bias so that it will take into account the amount of information needed to reconstruct the dataset from the NTM. We also intend to explore the possibility to use our approach as a preprocessing phase of other morphology learning tasks in order to provide them with a feasible set of theory constants.

For instance, the Brill part-of-speech tagger [2] derives part-of-speech prediction rules for unknown words from tagged corpora (typically of size 10^5). If only the affixes derived by the GA+ILP approach are used during the search of rules instead of the blind use of all affixes up to a given size present in the words, this should result in a manyfold speed-up.

---

[5] There might be several such segmentations.

8 Acknowledgements

The authors wish to thank Stephen Muggleton, James Cussens and the two anonymous reviewers for their thoughtful comments. The first author also wishes to thank Olga Štěpánková for a number of improvements suggested. He has been supported by ESPRIT Long Term Research Action No 20237 on Inductive Logic Programming II and part of this research was carried out by him in CTU Prague.

References

1. H. Blockeel. Application of inductive logic programming to natural language processing. Master's thesis, Katholieke Universiteit Leuven, 1994.
2. E. Brill. Some advances in transformation-based part of speech tagging. In *Proceedings of AAAI-94*, pages 748–753. AAAI Press/MIT Press, 1994.
3. Mary Elaine Califf and Raymond J. Mooney. Advantages of decision lists and implicit negatives in inductive logic programming. Technical report, University of Texas at Austin, 1996.
4. James Cussens. Part-of-speech tagging using Progol. In *Inductive Logic Programming: Proceedings of the 7th International Workshop (ILP-97)*, pages 93–108, 1997.
5. Sabine Deligne. *Modèles de séquences de longueurs variables: Application au traitement du langage écrit et de la parole.* PhD thesis, ENST Paris, France, 1996.
6. Bernard Fradin. L'approche à deux niveaux en morphologie computationnelle et les développements récents de la morphologie. *Traitement automatique des langues*, 35(2):9–48, 1994.
7. David E. Goldberg. *Genetic Algorithms in Search, Optimization, and Machine Learning.* Addison-Wesley, 1989.
8. Dimitar Kazakov. An inductive approach to natural language parser design. In Kemal Oflazer and Harold Somers, editors, *Proceedings of Nemlap-2*, pages 209–217, Ankara, Turkey, September 1996. Bilkent University.
9. Dimitar Kazakov. Unsupervised learning of naïve morphology with genetic algorithms. In W. Daelemans, A. van den Bosch, and A. Weijters, editors, *Workshop Notes of the ECML/MLnet Workshop on Empirical Learning of Natural Language Processing Tasks*, pages 105–112, Prague, April 1997.
10. Nada Lavrač and Sašo Džeroski. *Inductive Logic Programming Techniques and Applications.* Ellis Horwood Ltd., Campus 400, Maylands Avenue,Hemel Hempstead, Herdfortshire, HP2 7EZ, England, 1994.
11. Suresh Manandhar, Sašo Džeroski, and Tomaž Erjavec. Learning Multilingual Morphology with CLOG. In *The Eighth International Conference on Inductive Logic Programming (ILP'98)*, Madison, Wisconsin, USA, 1998.
12. Raymond J. Mooney and Mary Elaine Califf. Induction of first–order decision lists: Results on learning the past tense of English verbs. *JAIR*, June 1995.
13. Vito Pirelli. *Morphology, Analogy and Machine Translation.* PhD thesis, Salford University, UK, 1993.
14. J.R. Quinlan. Learning logical definitions from relations. *ML*, 5:239–266, 1990.
15. Antal van den Bosch, Walter Daelemans, and Ton Weijters. Morphological analysis as classification: an inductive learning approach. In Kemal Oflazer and Harold Somers, editors, *Proceedings of Nemlap-2*, pages 79–89, Ankara, Sep. 1996.
16. François Yvon. *Prononcer par analogie: motivations, formalisations et évaluations.* PhD thesis, ENST Paris, France, 1996.

Learning Multilingual Morphology with CLOG

Suresh Manandhar,* Sašo Džeroski,† Tomaž Erjavec†

* Intelligent Systems Group, Department of Computer Science, University of York
YO10 5DD, York, U.K.
Suresh@cs.york.ac.uk

† Department for Intelligent Systems, Jožef Stefan Institute
Jamova 39, SI-1000 Ljubljana, Slovenia
Saso.Dzeroski@ijs.si, Tomaz.Erjavec@ijs.si

Abstract. The paper presents the decision list learning system CLOG and the results of using it to learn nominal inflections of English, Romanian, Czech, Slovene, and Estonian. The dataset used to induce rules for the synthesis and analysis of the inflectional paradigms of nouns and adjectives of these languages is the MULTEXT-East multilingual tagged corpus. The ILP system FOIDL is also applied to the same dataset, and this paper compares the induction methodology and results of the two systems. The experiment shows that the accuracy of the two systems is comparable when using the same training set. However, while FOIDL is, due to efficiency reasons, severely limited in the size of the training set, CLOG does not suffer from such limitations. With the increase of the training set size possible with CLOG, it significantly outperforms FOIDL and learns highly accurate morphological rules.

1 Introduction

Machine learning methods been recently applied to a variety of tasks within the area of natural language processing [2]. Inductive logic programming (ILP) systems have been applied to tasks such as learning to parse [6] and learning part-of-speech tagging [1]. Learning of morphological structure has also been attempted with the ILP system FOIDL [7], with the original experiment focused on relatively small samples of English. In subsequent work, FOIDL was used to learn the synthesis and analysis rules for Slovene nouns [3]. Here, the system was used to learn morphological rules for producing the inflectional forms of nouns given the base form (the *lemma*) as well as for deducing the lemma from these inflectional forms. Thus, rules for both morphological synthesis and analysis were learned. While these rules induced by FOIDL had a relatively high accuracy on smaller datasets, we were severely hampered by the fact that we were unable to train on larger datasets. This bottleneck is due to the training inefficiency of FOIDL.

In this paper we present a new decision list learning system, CLOG, which is similar to FOIDL but with a much greater training efficiency, enabling it to train on larger datasets, and thus achieve significantly better results. Furthermore, we extend the scope of the experiments to encompas adjectives and nouns of English, Romanian, Czech, Slovene, and Estonian.

The aim of the paper is to empirically demonstrate that it is possible to extend current ILP techniques to realistic NL tasks such as morphological rule learning that require processing of large amounts of data by the use of more efficient algorithms.

The training and testing data was taken from the MULTEXT-East tagged corpus [4], and converted to Prolog encoding, as explained in Section 2. CLOG and FOIDL are used to learn rules for synthesizing and analyzing the noun and adjective forms of the five languages. An overview of CLOG and a comparison with FOIDL is given in Section 3. Section 4 describes the MULTEXT-East corpus experiments with CLOG and FOIDL. Discussed here are the experimental setup, the induced rules of both systems for the synthesis and the analysis tasks, and their performance on unseen text. Section 5 concludes with a discussion and some directions for further work.

2   The Data

The EU MULTEXT-East project [4] developed corpora, lexica and tools for six Central and East-European languages; the project reports and samples of results are available at *http://nl.ijs.si/ME/*. The centerpiece of the corpus is the novel *"1984"* by George Orwell, in the English original and translations. For the experiments reported here, the first three parts of the *"1984"* were taken for training, and the fourth part (Appendix: *"The Principles of Newspeak"*) for testing.

The *"1984"* corpus is tokenised, and its words labelled with linguistic annotations both in context disambiguated and non-disambiguated forms. The linguistic annotation of a word contains its lemmas and morphosyntactic descriptions (MSDs). So, for example, the lexical annotation of the Slovene word *članki* contains two lemma/MSD pairs: *članek*/Ncmpi and *članek*/Ncmpn.

The MSDs are structured and more detailed than is commonly assumed for part-of-speech tags; they are compact string representations of a simplified kind of feature structures — the formalism and MSD grammar for the MULTEXT-East languages is defined in [5]. The first letter of a MSD encodes the part of speech (Noun, Adjective), while the letters following give the value of the position determined attribute. Each part of speech defines its appropriate attributes and their values, acting as a kind of feature-structure type or sort. So, for example, the MSD Ncmpi expands to PoS:Noun, Type:common, Gender:masculine, Number:plural, Case:instrumental. It should be noted that in case a certain attribute is not appropriate (1) for a language, (2) for the particular combination of features, or (3) for the the word in question, this is marked by a hyphen in the attribute's position. Estonian nouns, for example, are not marked for gender and a 'Noun common (no gender) singular translative' is written as Nc-s4.

For our experiments triplets were extracted from the tagged corpus, consisting of the word-form itself, and the lexical, undisambiguated lemmas with their accompanying MSDs, thus using a setting similar to the one prior to tagging. As mentioned, we considered only the triples with noun and adjective MSDs.

Each triplet gives rise to two examples, one for synthesis and one for analysis. The examples have the form `syn_msd(lemma,orth)` and `ana_msd(orth,lemma)`. Within the learning setting of inductive logic programming, `syn_msd` and `ana_msd` are relations or predicates, that consist of all pairs (lemma, word-form), resp. (word-form, lemma) that have the same morphosyntactic description [1]. A set of rules has to be learned for each of these predicates or concepts.

Encoding-wise, the MSD's part-of-speech is decapitalised and hyphens are converted to underscores. The word-forms and lemmas are encoded as lists of characters, with non-ASCII characters encoded as SGML entities. In this way, the generated examples comply with Prolog syntax. For illustration, the orthography/lemma/MSD triplet *članki*/*članek*/Ncmpn gives rise to the following two examples:

```
syn_n0mpn([ccaron,l,a,n,e,k],[ccaron,l,a,n,k,i]).
ana_n0mpn([ccaron,l,a,n,k,i],[ccaron,l,a,n,e,k]).
```

Certain attributes have (almost) no effect on the inflectional behaviour of the word. We generalise over their values in the predicates, and indicate this by a 0 for the value of the vague attribute, as seen above for the collapsing of proper and common nouns (Nc, Np) to n0.

Below we give the numbers of these generalised MSDs for the complete noun and adjective paradigms for each of the five languages:

```
en:    1 MSD  =  1 N +  0 A
ro:   30 MSDs = 15 N + 15 A
et:   58 MSDs = 29 N + 29 A
cs:   91 MSDs = 45 N + 46 A
sl:  108 MSDs = 54 N + 54 A
```

In English the plural of nouns to account for in both the Noun and the Adjective paradigms, and only this MSD was used for the dataset. For the other languages complete paradigms were modeled, including the base forms themselves. The languages have a varying numbers of MSDs, depending on their inflectional complexity and the particular choices made in the MSD grammar. Lowest is Romanian; next comes Estonian, which has a large number of cases but does not distinguish gender. The two Slavic languages, known for their heavy inflection (on gender, number, case, animacy and definiteness) are highest.

3 CLOG and Learning of Morphological Rules

CLOG is a system for learning of first-order decision lists. CLOG shares a fair amount of similarity with FOIDL [7]. Like FOIDL, CLOG can learn first-order decision lists from positive examples only — an important consideration in NLP applications. CLOG inherits the notion of *output completeness* from FOIDL to generate implicit negative examples (see [7]). Let E be an example and Q be the corresponding *query* whose refutation should result in an answer substitution

---

[1] We need two different relations because the decision list representation restricts the modes of the predicates to `syn_msd(+,?)` and `ana_msd(+,?)`.

that would make $Q = E$. Let Q' be the actual result of executing Q. Then Q' is considered to be a negative example if the training set does not contain Q'. Output completeness is a form of closed world assumption which assumes that every related "variant" of an example is included in the training set.

```
Let PTC be the (positive) examples to be covered
Let CPE be the set of covered (positive) examples initially empty
Let DL be the decision list being learnt initially empty
While PTC not empty
    DO
        Let x be an (arbitrary) example in PTC
        Let GC = { (G,0,0,0,0) | G is a clause that covers x }
        For each example e in PTC
            For each (G,SP,SN,QP,QN) in GC
                if G covers e positively
                    then (G,SP,SN,QP,QN) := (G,SP,SN,QP+1,QN)
                    else if G covers e negatively
                        then (G,SP,SN,QP,QN) := (G,SP,SN,QP,QN+1) endif
                endif
        For each example e in CPE
            For each (G,SP,SN,QP,QN) in GC
                if G covers e positively
                    then (G,SP,SN,QP,QN) := (G,SP+1,SN,QP,QN)
                    else if G covers e negatively
                        then (G,SP,SN,QP,QN) := (G,SP,SN+1,QP,QN) endif
                endif
        Let Best ∈ GC be such that gain(BEST) is maximum
        For each example e in PTC
            if Best covers e positively
                then
                    CPE := CPE ∪ {e}
                    PTC := PTC − {e}
            endif
        For each example e in CPE
            if Best covers e negatively
                then
                    CPE := CPE − {e}
                    PTC := PTC ∪ {e}
            endif
        Add Best to top of DL
    ENDDO
```

Fig. 1. CLOG algorithm

Our experiments show that CLOG is significantly more efficient than FOIDL in the induction process. On the task of analysis of the plural of English nouns, we ran FOIDL and CLOG on subsets of the training set of size 100, 200, 300, 400, 500, 600, 700, 800, 900 and the whole set of 1063 examples. The running times for CLOG were 21, 61, 112, 204, 277, 477, 646, 941, 1198, and 1771 seconds, respectively. For FOIDL the running times of up to 700 examples were 254, 1290, 2191, 5190, 9521, 18353, and 33915 seconds, respectively (all times on a SUN SPARC 10).

With FOIDL we were therefore forced to cut the training set example sizes (to 200 per concept — even so, learning of all 576 concepts still took about 5 days CPU time), while we were able to run CLOG on the whole dataset (on average 317 examples per concept, 751 max, 1 min). This gave us a rule set with significantly more predictive accuracy. Although a detailed analysis of the reasons behind CLOG's efficiency is beyond the scope of the current paper, we believe there are two contributing reasons.

Firstly, CLOG only considers generalisations that are relevant to an example (cf. Progol [8]). This helps in focussing the search to only those clauses that are relevant with respect to an example. In the current implementation these generalisations are supplied by a user-defined predicate `generate_clauses(+Example, -Clauses)` which takes as input an example and generates a list of all generalisations that cover that example. An alternative would have been to provide mode declarations (cf. Progol [8]) which could then be used to build clauses incrementally. However, since our primary aim was to build a system for learning morphological relations this generality was not essential and we chose the simplest approach.

Secondly, CLOG treats the set of generalisations of an example as a *generalisation set*. It then cycles every input example through the generalisation set in a single iteration checking whether a candidate generalisation covers the example positively or negatively. Once this process is complete the "best" candidate generalisation is chosen. The example set is pruned using this candidate and the cycle repeats. There are two advantages of this approach - **1.** Every example is accessed once (and used many times) and **2.** The example set is accessed sequentially. This means that the example set can be kept in a file as opposed to being kept in memory. This allows CLOG to handle large training sets.

The algorithm (see fig. 1) maintains two sets — namely examples yet to be covered and examples already covered. The examples which have already been covered can get "uncovered" by subsequent rules which results in such examples needing to be covered again. This is important since CLOG uses a hill-climbing strategy (as does FOIDL) and hence is sensitive to the example order. However, this sensitivity is avoided if generalisations from subsequent examples override a previously learnt rule by providing better *gain*. This turns out to be usually the case given enough redundancy in the training data.

The *gain* function currently used in CLOG is user-defined. For the morphology learning problem we used a simple function that maximises the number of new positive examples covered against the sum-total of implicit negatives covered:

$$gain((G, SP, SN, QP, QN)) = QP - QN - SN$$

where: G is the clause being learnt,
  QP,QN: number of new examples covered positively and negatively
  SP,SN: number of already covered examples covered positively and negatively

3.1 Problem representation

A morphological transformation rule transforms a word in one form to another form. For example, the past morphological rule in English would transform the word *sleep* (resp. *walk*) to the word *slept* (resp. *walked*). For languages that employ *concatenative* morphology such as the majority of European languages, different forms of the same word are realised by changing the *prefix* and *suffix* of words. Thus, *slept* (resp. *walk*) can be derived from *sleep* (resp. *walked*) by changing the suffix *-ep* (resp. *-∅*) to the suffix *-pt* (resp. *-ed*).

We chose the following morphological rule representation:

```
past(A,B) :- mate(A,B,[],[],[e,p],[e,t]),!.
...
past(A,B) :- mate(A,B,[],[],[e],[e,d]),!.
past(A,B) :- mate(A,B,[],[],[],[e,d]),!.
```

where the auxilliary predicate mate/6 is defined by:

```
mate(W1,W2,[],[],Y1,[]):- split(W1,W2,Y1).
mate(W1,W2,[],[],[],Y2):- split(W2,W1,Y2).
mate(W1,W2,[],[],Y1,Y2):- split(W1,X,Y1),    split(W2,X,Y2).
mate(W1,W2,P1,P2,Y1,Y2):- split(W1,P1,W11), split(W2,P2,W22),
                          split(W11,X,Y1),   split(W22,X,Y2).
split([X,Y|Z],[X],[Y|Z]).
split([X|Y],[X|Z],W) :- split(Y,Z,W).
```

This representation contrasts with the representation used in [7, 3]:

```
past(A,B) :- split(A,C,[e,p]), split(B,C,[e,t]),!.
...
past(A,B) :- split(B,A,[d]), split(A,C,[e]),!.
past(A,B) :- split(B,A,[e,d]),!.
```

Essentially, the predicate mate(W1,W2,P1,P2,S1,S2) is true if P1 and S1 is the prefix and the suffix of W1 respectively and similarly for P1, S1 and W2. Although, this representation is restrictive in that it can handle only prefixation and suffixation operations we consider it to be sufficient for our task taking advantage of the linguistic fact that the languages we are dealing with employ concatenative morphology. Our representation has the benefit that it can easily be understood by linguists.

The *generalisation set* is constructed by the following predicate which generates the set of all prefixes and suffixes of a morphologically related pair of words.

```
generate_clauses(past(U,V),Clauses):-
     bagof( ( past(X,Y) :- (mate(X,Y,P1,P2,S1,S2), !)),
            mate(U,V,P1,P2,S1,S2),
            Clauses).
```

One limitation of the current implementation is that the size of the generalisation set cannot be too large. For the morphology task the size of the generalisation set ranged from **7** to **61** per example averaging between **22-35** for a typical example. However, this limitation can be avoided by a top-down search of the hypothesis space (*cf.* Progol [8]). We hope to address this in our future implementation.

4 Experiments and Results

In our experiments we used FOIDL and CLOG to perform two sets of experiments, the first concerning synthesis and the second analysis of word-forms. For each MSD, a set of rules for the predicate syn_msd was induced: the induced rules generate the oblique form from a given lemma. The input and output arguments of the syn_msd predicate are switched for the ana_msd predicate: the task of FOIDL/CLOG was to learn rules that produce the base form of the word given the oblique form. Apart from exchanging the input and the output, the set-up for the synthesis and analysis experiments was identical. There were altogether 288 MSDs in the five languages.

As has been mentioned, the training sets were taken from the first three parts of "*1984*". Due to FOIDL's computational efficiency limits and the large number of relations to be induced, the 200 (most frequent) examples were chosen for training for each MSD, where more than 200 were available. CLOG, on the other hand, does not have efficiency problems, so the complete training set could be used. In order to compare CLOG with FOIDL fully, we ran CLOG twice, once on the same training set as FOIDL (i.e. cut at 200 examples), and once on the full training sets. The Appendix of the novel was used for the test set. While the whole "*1984*" has approx. 100,000 words, the Appendix has only approx. 4,000. It therefore happens that a few rare MSDs were not represented in the test set (6 for Romanian, 8 for Slovene).

The set-up for the experiment was as for the orthographic past tense learning experiment: for synthesis the training data were encoded as Prolog facts of the form syn_msd(lemma, oblique) and for analysis as Prolog facts of the form ana_msd(oblique, lemma). In both cases, the first argument of each target predicate is an input argument and the second is an output argument. The predicate split was used as background knowledge with FOIDL, and mate with CLOG. Constant prefixes and suffixes were allowed in the rules.

4.1 Results

For a start, let us take a look at the sets of rules induced for the particular task of synthesising the genitive singular of Slovene feminine nouns. The complete training set for this concept contained 608 examples, which were cut to the most frequent 200. The testing set contained 313 examples.

Comparing FOIDL with CLOG on the same training and test set shows that FOIDL slightly outperforms CLOG on the nOfsg concept, with a 97.4% accuracy (8 errors) for the former vs. 96.2% (12 errors) for the latter. In all cases, the errors of FOIDL were due to a wrong lemma being proposed, while the errors of CLOG were caused by the predicate failing.

The rule set induced by FOIDL consists of five exceptions and three generalizations; the generalizations are listed below.

```
nOfsg(A,B) :- split(A,C,[e,n]), split(B,C,[n,i]).
nOfsg(A,B) :- split(A,C,[a]),   split(B,C,[e]).
nOfsg(A,B) :- split(B,A,[i]).
```

From the bottom up, the first rule describes the formation of genitive for feminine nouns of the canonical second declension where -*i* is added to the nominative singular (lemma) to obtain the genitive. The second rule deals with the canonical first declension, where the lemma ending -*a* is replaced by -*e* to obtain the genitive. Finally, the third rule deals with nouns of the second declension that exhibit a common morpho-phonological alteration in Slovene, the schwa elision. Namely, if a schwa (weak -*e*-) appears in the last syllable of the word when it has the -*0* ending, this schwa is dropped with non-null endings: *bolezen-0*, but *bolezn-i*. However, this alternation does not affect only second declension feminine nouns but practically all inflecting words of Slovene. FOIDL attempts to deal with other examples of this alternation on a case by case basis: of the five exceptions, three exhibit this alternation.

An analysis of FOIDL's test set errors on nOfsg reveals that all bar one are due to a noun exhibiting schwa elision, which incorrectly triggers the default second declension +*i* rule, e.g., *vrnitevi instead of *vrnitve*, from the base form *vrnitev*.

Running CLOG on the same training set (CLOG 200), the induced rules set is somewhat larger, and consists of eleven exceptions and six generalizations, with the generalzations listed below:

```
nOfsg(A,B) :- mate(A,B,[],[],[e,d],[e,d,i]),!.
nOfsg(A,B) :- mate(A,B,[],[],[e,n],[n,i]),!.
nOfsg(A,B) :- mate(A,B,[],[],[ccaron],[ccaron,i]),!.
nOfsg(A,B) :- mate(A,B,[],[],[r],[r,i]),!.
nOfsg(A,B) :- mate(A,B,[],[],[t],[t,i]),!.
nOfsg(A,B) :- mate(A,B,[],[],[a],[e]),!.
```

All the FOIDL exceptions are also included in the exceptions of CLOG. Additionally, the first two of FOIDL's generalisations are also induced by CLOG. But where FOIDL differs from CLOG is in the second declension default discussed above; while FOIDL posits the default rule, CLOG is more conservative and attempts to model it by a series of exceptions and partial generalisations. Ultimately, neither method is sufficient to correctly predict all the cases, as neither is able to successfully model the schwa elision. While FOIDL errors are all due to schwa elision, the CLOG errors are due to a combination of schwa elision errors and second declension errors. Although the number of errors is here slightly greater, the errors of CLOG are less severe; as has been mentioned, CLOG fails on its errors, while FOIDL proposes an incorrect lemma.

We next give the average overall results on all the languages of the dataset. The 288 programs learned by FOIDL and CLOG for the synthesis and analysis concepts show varying degrees of success in capturing the relevant morphological generalizations. Table 1 gives an overview of the results obtained by testing the induced programs. Three tests were performed; one for FOIDL, with the training sets, where necessary, cut to 200 examples, then for CLOG on the same training sets, and finally for CLOG on the full training sets.

For each experiment and for each language, the results on the synthesis and analysis tasks are listed, first for nouns and adjectives separately (*n and *a) (except for English, where there is only one MSD), then aggregated (*). The

			FOIDL 200		CLOG 200		CLOG	
	syn	*	94.07%	21/6	94.73%	19/6	98.02%	38/17
	ana	*	93.85%	22/5	93.42%	21/3	96.05%	65/9
English	*	*	93.96%	43/11	94.07%	40/9	97.03%	103/26
		a*	95.91%	91/32	95.33%	103/33	97.23%	135/41
	syn	n*	92.00%	298/99	89.87%	382/100	93.77%	500/140
		*	93.01%	389/131	91.28%	485/133	94.66%	635/181
		a*	94.89%	101/27	94.60%	115/29	96.35%	159/38
	ana	n*	86.89%	422/144	86.84%	476/120	91.24%	724/181
		*	88.95%	523/171	88.84%	591/149	92.56%	883/219
Romanian	*	*	90.98%	912/302	90.06%	1076/282	93.61%	1518/400
		a*	98.98%	144/76	98.97%	155/79	98.77%	276/112
	syn	n*	93.85%	865/326	93.22%	1087/415	95.67%	1615/562
		*	96.61%	1009/402	96.32%	1242/494	97.34%	1891/674
		a*	98.90%	178/96	98.90%	197/93	99.06%	375/110
	ana	n*	92.53%	1054/375	91.14%	1285/375	94.76%	1909/550
		*	95.96%	1232/471	95.32%	1482/468	97.08%	2284/660
Czech	*	*	96.29%	2241/873	95.82%	2724/962	97.21%	4175/1334
		n*	95.92%	819/323	96.21%	904/305	97.78%	1114/372
	syn	a*	77.49%	1675/877	82.26%	1741/729	86.79%	3983/1106
		*	85.48%	2494/1200	88.31%	2645/1034	91.56%	5097/1478
		n*	95.01%	1014/404	95.76%	1001/371	97.12%	1194/457
	ana	a*	90.19%	1530/822	92.90%	1610/635	96.81%	2043/966
		*	92.28%	2544/1226	94.14%	2611/1006	96.95%	3237/1423
Slovene	*	*	88.88%	5038/2426	91.22%	5256/2040	94.25%	8334/2901
		a*	88.5%	512/181	85.51%	639/186	88.03%	771/230
	syn	n*	73.24%	1463/396	65.44%	1915/415	81.53%	3691/981
		*	78.19%	1975/577	71.94%	2554/601	83.64%	4462/1211
		a*	87.97%	520/223	86.45%	616/207	89.13%	756/260
	ana	n*	76.32%	1235/376	74.60%	1680/382	86.29%	3084/758
		*	80.10%	1755/599	78.45%	2296/589	87.21%	3840/1018
Estonian	*	*	79.14%	3730/1176	75.20%	4850/1190	85.42%	8302/2229

Table 1. Accuracy and complexity of FOIDL and CLOG rules

induced rules for each MSD are applied to the testing cases of that MSD and the incorrectly predicted cases recorded. The number of test cases and incorrectly predicted cases are then summed over all noun MSDs, all adjective MSDs, and all MSDs. On the basis of these sums we then compute the percentage of the correctly predicted cases in the test set, which is given as the first entry in each cell of the table. The second cell entry gives the total number of clauses in the concept decision list and the number of generalisations that appear in it, e.g. 21/6. This is an estimate of the complexity of the rules induced by FOIDL and CLOG.

Comparing FOIDL 200 with CLOG 200 we can see that there is no great systematic difference between the accuracies: the difference in all cases, except Estonian, is around 1%. However, FOIDL is somewhat more compact in expressing the concepts, having smaller theory sizes, both with exceptions and generalisation. Unsurprisingly, CLOG run on the complete training set greatly outperforms FOIDL. As has been mentioned, speed of induction is the main advantage of CLOG over FOIDL: even with full training sets, CLOG needs only a fraction of the time that FOIDL does with the reduced training sets.

5 Conclusions

We have presented the ILP system CLOG and used it to learn rules for synthesizing and analyzing inflectional forms of nouns and adjectives for English, Romanian, Czech, Slovene, and Estonian. The accuracy of the obtained rule-sets was evaluated and compared to the rule-sets obtained with the FOIDL system. The two systems have comparative performance given the same training set. However, while FOIDL is limited as to the ammount of training data it can handle due to it's computational efficiency, CLOG suffers no such bottleneck. Tests on the full training set show that CLOG can outperform FOIDL significantly.

Further work will focus on improving the induced rules by using additional linguistic background knowledge, esp. for capturing (morpho-)phonological regularities and on using the improved rules to perform preliminary analysis of word forms appearing in corpora, producing input for further text processing, e.g., part-of-speech tagging.

Acknowledgements
The authors would like to thank Alan Frisch and two anonymous reviewers for useful comments. This work was supported in part by the project ESPRIT IV 20237 ILP2.

References

1. J. Cussens. Part-of-speech tagging using Progol. In *Proc. 7th Intl. Wshp. on Inductive Logic Programming*, pages 93–108. Springer, Berlin, 1997.
2. W. Daelemans, T. Weijters, and A. van der Vosch, editors. *Proc. ECML-97 Workshop on Empirical Learning of Natural Language Processing Tasks*. Prague, Czech Republic, 1997.
3. S. Džeroski and T. Erjavec. Induction of Slovene nominal paradigms. In *Proc. 7th Intl. Wshp. on Inductive Logic Programming*, pages 141–148. Springer, Berlin, 1997.
4. T. Erjavec, N. Ide, V. Petkevič, and J. Véronis. MULTEXT-East: Multilingual text tools and corpora for Central and Eastern European languages. In *Proc. 1st TELRI European Seminar*, pages 87–98. Tihany, Hungary, 1995.
5. T. Erjavec, M. Monachini (eds.). Specifications and Notation for Lexicon Encoding. MULTEXT-East Final Report D1.1F, Ljubljana, IJS, 1997.
6. R. J. Mooney. Inductive logic programming for natural language processing. In *Proc. 6th Intl. Wshp. on Inductive Logic Programming*, pages 3–22. Springer, Berlin, 1997.
7. R. J. Mooney and M.-E. Califf. Induction of first-order decision lists: Results on learning the past tense of English verbs. *Journal of Artificial Intelligence Research*, (3):1–24, 1995.
8. S. Muggleton. Inverse entailment and Progol, *New Generation Computing*,(13):245–286, 1995.

Using ILP-Systems for Verification and Validation of Multi-agent Systems

Nico Jacobs, Kurt Driessens, Luc De Raedt

K.U. Leuven, Dept. of Computer Science,
Celestijnenlaan 200A, B-3001 Heverlee, Belgium
{nico, kurtd, lucdr}@cs.kuleuven.ac.be

Abstract. Most applications of inductive logic programming focus on prediction or the discovery of new knowledge. We describe a less common application of ILP namely verification and validation of knowledge based systems and multi-agent systems. Using inductive logic programming, partial *declarative* specifications of the software can be induced from the behaviour of the software. These rules can be readily interpreted by the designers or users of the software, and can in turn result in changes to the software. The approach outlined was tested in the domain of multi-agent systems, more in particular the RoboCup domain.

1 Introduction

Most applications of inductive logic programming (ILP) focus on prediction tasks or the discovery of new knowledge. But the basic idea of inductive learning (learning general hypotheses from specific examples) can also be used to verify the correctness of software systems, especially in complex domains like knowledge based and multi-agent systems where regular techniques are harder to apply.

Most approaches to verification and validation (V&V) of knowledge based systems employ deductive reasoning techniques in order to check whether a knowledge based system is conform with some (possibly partial) specifications. There is however some inherent limitation of the deductive approach. The deductive approach relies on the ability to specify the intended behaviour of the knowledge base. For complex systems, such as multi-agent systems operating in complex environments, this is a very hard task; one might even argue that for certain applications (such as RoboCup) designing the specifications of the overall multi-agent system is almost as hard as implementing the individual agents.

Inductive V&V methods take a different approach. Rather than starting from the specification and testing whether it is consistent with an implementation, inductive reasoning methods start from an implementation, or more precisely, from examples of the behaviour of the implementation, and produce a (partial) specification. Provided that the specification is declarative, it can be interpreted by the human expert. This machine generated specification is likely to give the expert new insights into the behaviour of the complex system he wants to verify. If the induced behaviour is conform with the expert's wishes, this will (partly) validate the system. Otherwise, if the expert is not satisfied with the induced specification, he or she may want to modify the knowledge based system and reiterate the verification or validation process.

This work is related to the work of William Cohen [4] on construction of high-level specifications of large software systems. However, we use different systems (Grendel2 versus CLAUDIEN and TILDE) on a different problem (database views versus multi agent systems), which makes it necessary to construct hypotheses that describe relations between the behaviour of multiple programs. Also, in V&V it is necessary to be able to 'zoom in' on certain aspects of the behaviour of a program when an error in the software is expected.

This paper addresses the use of ILP-techniques for knowledge base verification and validation. The sketched techniques are tested in a multi-agent setting, i.e. that of RoboCup. In such complex multi-agent systems, it is very hard to see the impact of changes in one agent on the overall behaviour of the environment. This paper is organised as follows: in section 2, we briefly introduce the inductive logic programming techniques and systems used in this paper; next we show how this techniques can be used for verification. We give an example of a multi-agent system and how we used our technique to verify this, after which we conclude.

2 Inductive Logic Programming

An ILP system takes as input examples and background knowledge and produces hypotheses as output. There are two common used ILP settings which differ in the representation of these data: learning from entailment ([7] compares different settings) and learning from interpretation [10]. In this paper we will use the second setting. In learning from interpretations, an example or observation can be viewed as a small relational database, consisting of a number of facts that describe the specific properties of the example. In the rest of the paper, we will refer to such an example as a model. Such a model may contain multiple facts about multiple relations. This contrasts with the attribute value representations where an example always corresponds to a single tuple for a single relation.

The background knowledge takes the form of a Prolog program. Using this Prolog program, it is possible to derive additional properties (through the use of Prolog queries) about the examples.

There are also two forms of induction considered here: predictive and descriptive induction. Predictive induction starts from a set of classified examples and a background theory. The aim is to induce a theory that will classify all the examples in the appropriate class. On the other hand, descriptive induction starts from a set of unclassified examples, and aims at finding a set of regularities that hold for the examples. In this paper, we will use the TILDE system [2] for predictive induction, and the CLAUDIEN system [9] for descriptive induction.

TILDE induces logical decision trees from classified examples and background theory. An example of such models and background knowledge can be found in paragraph 5.2, while examples of resulting trees are in paragraph 5.3.

CLAUDIEN induces clausal regularities from examples and background theory. E.g. consider the single example consisting of the following facts and empty background theory:

`human(an). human(paul). female(an). male(paul).`

The induced theory found by CLAUDIEN is:

human(X) ← female(X). human(X) ← male(X).
false ← male(X) ∧ female(X). male(X) ∨ female(X) ← human(X).

Details of the TILDE and CLAUDIEN system can be found in [2, 9].

3   ILP for Verification and Validation

Given an inductive logic programming system, one can now verify or validate
a knowledge based or multi-agent system as follows. One starts constructing
examples (and possibly background knowledge) of the behaviour of the system
to be verified. E.g. in a knowledge based system for diagnosis, one could start
by generating examples of the inputs (symptoms) and outputs (diagnosis) of the
system. Alternatively, in a multi-agent system one could take a snapshot of the
environment at various points in time. These snapshots could then be checked
individually and also the relation between the state an agent is in and the action
he takes could be investigated.

Once examples and background knowledge are available one must then formulate verification or validation as a predictive or descriptive inductive task.
E.g. in the multi-agent system, if the aim is to verify the properties of the states
of the overall system, this can be formulated as a descriptive learning task. One
then starts from examples and induces their properties. On the other hand, if
the aim is to learn the relation among the states and the actions of the agent, a
predictive approach can be taken.

After the formulation of the problem, it is time to run the inductive logic
programming engines. The results of the induction process can then be interpreted by the human verifiers or validators. If the results are in agreement with
the wishes of the human experts, the knowledge based or multi-agent system
can be considered (partly) verified or validated. Otherwise, the human expert
will get insight into the situations where his expectations differ from the actual
behaviour of the system. In such cases, revision is necessary. Revision may be
carried out manually or it could also be carried out automatically using knowledge revision systems (see e.g. Craw's KRUST system [5], or De Raedt's Clint
[6]). After revision, the validation and verification process can be repeated until
the human expert is satisfied with the results of the induction engines.

Very simple verification tasks can be handled by propositional systems (e.g.
C4.5 [14] or CN2 [3]). However, in most cases the power of an ILP-system is
necessary. First because the input for the system may contain multiple facts
about multiple relations (e.g. an agent may not know in advance the number
of active and passive objects it will observe in it's environment). Second, agent
environments can be very complex and it only very rarely happens that a situation re-occurs (e.g. in RoboCup a player almost never stands at exact the same
field-position twice during a game). This makes it necessary to have hypotheses
that can have variables in it (e.g. "if there is an agents which holds the same

believes as I do then ..." without the need to specify all possibles believes an agent can have). Finally there is flexibility of ILP-systems. With the approach sketched above it is possible to build specifications for the complete system or to focus on smaller parts of the system. ILP systems allow this by changing the background theory and language bias used for constructing the specification.

4 Complexity of Multi Agent Systems

Recently a lot of attention has been devoted to intelligent agents. A number of promising agent applications exists in domains such as information filtering and electronic commerce. Although the concept of an intelligent agent is not yet clearly defined there are diverse aspects re-occuring in numerous agents. We briefly mention some of those and study their consequences for the V&V process.

A number of 'agent features' such as reactiveness (react to a changing environment) and pro-activeness (take the initiative to perform some action when necessary) will probably become standard practice in future software agent development. These features are intended to result in a more robust software product but at the same time make it more complex to implement such an agent. As a result of reactiveness an agent can change it's behaviour based on observations. Some agents even learn and incrementally adapt their behaviour. Pro-activeness has as a consequence that the functional view of software (transform a certain input into a desired output) does not hold for agents. Agents can act even if there was no (explicit) input; agents can act 'spontaneously'.

An other aspect in which agents differ from regular software applications is that they often have incomplete and/or incorrect information concerning the environment in which they operate. This is due to the fact that agents most of the time operate in complex and dynamic environments like the Internet or environments with real world interaction. Because we are never certain of the precise result of an action, we can never get an 100% accurate system. With agents, one should cope with systems that perform well most of the time.

Finally agents also act and by this influence their environment. Take for instance a factory work flow scheduling agent. If at a certain point the agent notices that some decisions were bad it can't roll back the environment; it has to live up to the effects of the actions it did or proposed. An agent continuously produces possible side-effects which irreversibly change the agent's environment.

A number of agent applications is based on multiple agents cooperating to achieve a common goal. In this case, the changes made to the environment are not a result of the behaviour of a single agent, but of the interaction of the agents with each other and the world they act upon. As a consequence, the emergent behaviour of the system is hard to understand. Furthermore, the system is very hard to specify (or verify) at the overall level. The global behaviour is not the sum of the local behaviours of the agents. Also, agent implementations are designed and implemented at this local level. It is then hoped that this will work as desired at the global level. This is e.g. the case in RoboCup. Further complications arise because the agent designer may not exercise total control over the environment, e.g. in Robocup one only controls one team. Because of this situation, a global V&V approach can benefit from using induction.

5 Experiments in RoboCup

5.1 RoboCup

We now perform experiments with the sketched approach to V&V in order to demonstrate the promise of the technique. As a test bed we choose RoboCup [13], which is a standard problem for many fields of AI and Robotics research of which multi agent systems is only one. The challenge consist of various competitions such as the real robot league, the software league and the special skills competition. Most of the multi agent research is done in the simulator league.

In the simulator league, the object of the challenge is to build eleven software agents that together form a soccer playing team. The agents' environment is defined by the soccer-server supplied by the RoboCup competition. It creates the world in which the agents act and artificially supplies the researchers with real world problems such as uncertainties, noise, an obstructive environment — consisting of the simulated field and the opposing team —, limited communication and a high degree of dynamics, all in a controlled environment. The various uncertainties — e.g. a well kicked ball can still not be guaranteed to reach it's destiny, but can be intercepted by another player or simply deviate from it's course — result in a complex environment with complex, hard to verify behaviour of the agents. This forms an ideal test bed for our ideas.

For the experiments, a reactive agent was used. Each time new sensory information was processed, the agent evaluated the believed state of the world and returned the appropriate action. There was no internal reference to prior actions of the agent or to long term plans. Two threads were used in the agent. One to process the sensory information and one to analyse the believed information and select the appropriate actions.

5.2 Modelling the Information

We supplied the agents with the possibility to log their actions and the momentary state of the world as perceived by them. This way we were able to study the behaviour of the agents starting from their beliefs about the world. Because all agents of one team were identical except for their location on the playing field, the log files were joined to form the knowledge base used in the experiments. A sample description of one state from the log-files looks as follows:

```
begin(model(e647)).
    player(my,1,-43.91466,5.173167,3352).
    player(my,2,-30.020395,7.7821097,3352).
    ...
    player(other,10,14.235199,15.192206,2748).
    player(other,11,0.0,0.0,0).
    ball(-33.732,10.014,3352).
```

```
   mynumber(5).
   bucket(1).
   rctime(3352).
   moveto(-33.732,10.014).
   actiontime(3352).
end(model(e647)).
```

The different predicates have the following meaning:

player(T, N, X, Y, C) the agent has last seen the player with number N from
   team T at location (X, Y) at time C.

ball(X, Y, C) the agent has last seen the ball at location (X, Y) at time C.

mynumber(N) this state was written by the agent with number N. It thus
   corresponds to the observation of agent N.

bucket(N) the bucket used for bringing the agent back to his home position. The
   bucket-value was lowered every input/output cycle and forced the agent to
   his home-location and reset when it reached zero.

rctime(C) the time the state was written.

actiontime(C) the time the action listed was executed.

moveto(X, Y), *shoottogoal*, *passto*(X, Y), *turn*(X), *none* the action performed by
   the agent.

The *rctime*(C) predicate was used to judge the age of the information in the
model as well as to decide how recent the action mentioned in the model is. This
was done by comparing the *rctime*(C) with *actiontime*(C). Logging was done
at regular time intervals instead of each time an action was performed, to be
able to use the inactivity of the agent or his passed actions as information also.

Some of the actions that were used while logging were already higher level
actions than the ones that are sent to the soccer-server. However these actions,
such as *shoottogoal* for example, were trivial to implement. To make the results
of the tests easier to interpret an even higher level of abstraction was introduced
in the background knowledge used during the experiments. Actions that are
known to have a special meaning were renamed. For instance a soccer-player that
was looking for the ball always used the *turn*(85) command, so this command
was renamed to *search_ball*. An other example of information defined in the
background knowledge is the following rule:

   action(movetoball):- validtime, moveto(X1,Y1), ball(X2,Y2),
   distance(X1,Y1,X2,Y2,Dist), Dist $\leq$ 5 .

in which the *moveto*(X, Y) command was merged with other information in
the model to give it more meaning. For instance, *moveto*$(-33.732, 10.014)$ and
ball$(-33.732, 10.014, 3352)$ in the model shown above, would be merged into
movetoball by this rule. Often a little deviation was permitted to take the dynamics and noise of the environment into account. The actions used to classify
the behaviour of the agent were: *search_ball*, *watch_ball*, *moveto*, *movetoball*,
moveback, *shoottogoal*, *passto*, *passtobuddy* and *none*. Some of these actions
were not used in the implementation of the agent but were included anyway
for verification purposes. For instance, although — according to specifications

— an agent should always "move to the ball" or "move back", the possible classification *moveto* was included in the experiments anyway.

Other background knowledge included the playing area's of the soccer-agents and other high level predicates such as *ball_near_othergoal, ball_in_penaltyarea, haveball* etc. Again, not all of these concepts were used when implementing the agent. This illustrates the power of using background knowledge. Using background knowledge, it is possible for the verifier to focus on high-level features instead of low-level ones.

5.3 Verifying Single Agents

The first tests were performed with TILDE, which allowed the behaviour of the agent to be classified by the different actions of the agent.

The knowledge base used was the union of the eleven log-files of the agents of an entire team. The agents used in the team all had the same behaviour, except for the area of the playing field. The area the agent acted in depended on the number of the agent and also was specified in the used background knowledge. The resulting knowledge base consisted of about 17000 models, collected during one test-game of ten minutes. The first run of TILDE resulted in the following decision tree

```
seeball ?
+--yes: ball_in_my_area ?
|       +--yes: haveball ?
|       |       +--yes: ball_near_othergoal ?
|       |       |       +--yes: action(shoottogoal) [15 / 15]
|       |       |       +--no:  action(passtobuddy) [122 / 124]
|       |       +--no:  action(movetoball) [1007 / 1015]
|       +--no:  bucket_was_empty ?
|               +--yes: action(moveback) [342 / 347]
|               +--no:  action(watch_ball) [2541 / 3460]
+--no:  action(search_ball) [7770 / 7771]
```

Only ± 12000 models were classified. We did not include the action *none* as a classification possibility because although a lot of models corresponded to this action, it's selection was a result of the delay in processing the input information instead of depending on the state of the agent's world.

Most of the classifications made by TILDE were very accurate for the domain. However, the prediction of the *action(watch_ball)* only reached an accuracy of 73.4%. Since the system was provided with all concepts used to express the specifications of the agent, the system should find a very accurate hypothesis[1]; a low accuracy indicates that the behaviour of the implemented agent isn't easy to represent with the concepts of the specification: the implementation does not fit the specification.

To get a better view on the behaviour of the agent in the given circumstances CLAUDIEN was used to describe the behaviour of the agent in case "*seeball,*

---

[1] however not 100% accurate due to noise present in the environment.

not(ball_in_my_area), not(bucket_was_empty)." CLAUDIEN found two rules that describe these circumstances.

> action(watch_ball) :- seeball, not(ball_in_my_area), not(bucket_was_empty).
> action(moveback) :- seeball, not(ball_in_my_area), not(bucket_was_empty).

The first rule was the one TILDE used to predict the *watch_ball* action. CLAUDIEN discovered the rule had an accuracy of 73%. The second rule reached an accuracy of 26%. It states that the agent would move back to his home location at times he was not supposed to. Being forced to go back to its home-location every time the bucket was emptied, this behaviour was a result of the bucket getting empty while the player was involved in the game and therefore not paying immediate attention to the contents of the bucket.

To gain more consistency in the agents behaviour, the bucket mechanism was removed and replaced by a new behaviour where the agent would move back when it noticed that it was to far from its home location. The new behaviour, after being logged and used in a TILDE-run resulted in the following tree :

```
seeball ?
+--yes: ball_in_my_area ?
|       +--yes: haveball ?
|       |       +--yes: ball_near_othergoal ?
|       |       |       +--yes: action(shoottogoal) [48 / 48]
|       |       |       +--no:  action(passtobuddy) [85 / 85]
|       |       +--no:  action(movetoball) [796 / 810]
|       +--no:  at_place ?
|               +--yes: action(watch_ball) [3826 / 3840]
|               +--no:  action(moveback) [384 / 394]
+--no:  action(search_ball) [7180 / 7318]
```

in which the *action(watch_ball)* was predicted with an accuracy of 99,6 %. The increase in consistency in the behaviour in the agent, improved its performance in the RoboCup environment. Because the agent did not move back to his home-location at moments it wasn't necessary he could spend more time tracking the movement of the ball and fellow agents.

5.4 Verifying Multiple Agents

In agent applications it is often important that not only all agents individually work properly, the agents also have to cooperate correctly. One important point in this is to check if the beliefs of the different agents more or less match. In the case of our RoboCup agents we want to know for instance if there is much difference between the position where player A sees player B and the position where player B thinks it is[2]. So first we used CLAUDIEN to find out how often agents have different believes about there positions, and how much their beliefs differ.

---

[2] it is impossible to know what the real position of a player is, so we can only compare the different believes the agents have.

To do these tests, we transformed the data-file so that one model contains the believes of multiple agents at the same moment in time. CLAUDIEN found multiple rules like the one below:

Dist < 2 :- mynumber(A,Nr), vplayer(A,my,Nr,X1,Y1), vplayer(B,my,Nr,X2,Y2), mynumber(B,Nr2), vplayer(B,my,Nr2,X3,Y3), not(A=B), distance(X1,Y1,X2,Y2,Dist), distance(X2,Y2,X3,Y3,Dist2), Dist2 < 10.

This rule, which has an accuracy of 78% states that if two players are less then 10 units apart, the difference in the believes of the position of one of those two players is less then 2 units. From all the rules we could conclude useful information, for instance, we found out that our agents can best estimate a teammate's position from distance 10. All rules found were 'acceptable' rules (e.g. for distances larger than 10, the error is positively correlated with the distance between the players), so we can conclude from the observed behavior that the beliefs of the different agents do not differ much.

6 Related work

This work builds upon earlier ideas on combining V&V with inductive logic programming [8]. It is also related to other approaches applying machine learning with validation and verification. This includes the work of Susan Craw on her KRUST system for knowledge refinement [5], the work by Bergadano et al. and the work by De Raedt et al. [11]. The approach taken in KRUST is complementary to ours. Rather than starting from examples of the actual behaviour of the system, KRUST starts from examples of the desired behaviour of the system. Whenever the two behaviours do not match, KRUST will automatically revise the knowledge based system. It is clear that the KRUST approach could also be applied within our methodology, at the point where the human discovers inconsistencies between the two behaviours. If the human then specifies examples of the intended behaviour, KRUST might help revising the original knowledge base. The approach of Bergadano et. al. [1] and De Raedt et. al. both use inductive machine learning to automatically and systematically generate a test set of examples that can be used for verification or validation. Finally, our work is also related to the work by William Cohen [4] on recovering software specifications from examples of the input-output behaviour of the program.

7 Conclusions

We briefly sketched a novel approach to V&V that is based on inductive reasoning rather than deductive reasoning. We also reported a number of experiments in the domain of multi-agent systems (RoboCup) which prove the concept of the approach. Further work on this topic could involve applying the verification and validation technique to more complex RoboCup-agents or other multi-agent systems (such as e.g. DESIRE [12]), and also to extend the inductive method to other representations. For instance, it seems very well possible to apply inductive techniques in order to automatically construct decision tables starting from the knowledge base. Such decision tables are already popular in V&V, but they are

typically made by the human expert (in collaboration with the machine), see
e.g. [15].

Acknowledgements: The authors wish to thank Hendrik Blockeel and Luc
Dehaspe for their help with the TILDE and CLAUDIEN system. Nico Jacobs is
financed by a specialisation grant of the Flemish Institute for the promotion
of scientific and technological research in the industry (IWT). Luc De Raedt is
supported by the Fund for scientific research, Flanders. This work is supported
by the European Community Esprit project no. 20237 (ILP 2).

References

1. F. Bergadano and D. Gunetti. Testing by means of inductive program learning.
   ACM Transactions on Software Engineering and Methodology, 5(2):119–145, 1996.
2. H. Blockeel and L. De Raedt. Lookahead and discretization in ILP. In *Proceedings
   of the 7th International Workshop on Inductive Logic Programming*, volume 1297
   of *Lecture Notes in Artificial Intelligence*, pages 77–85. Springer-Verlag, 1997.
3. P. Clark and T. Niblett. The CN2 algorithm. *Machine Learning*, 3(4):261–284,
   1989.
4. W. Cohen. Recovering Software Specifications with ILP. In *Proceedings of the 12th
   National Conference on Artificial Intelligence (AAAI-94)*, pages 142–148, 1994.
5. S. Craw and D. Sleeman. Knowledge-based refinement of knowledge based systems. Technical Report 95/2, The Robert Gordon University, Aberdeen, UK, 1995.
6. L. De Raedt. *Interactive Theory Revision: an Inductive Logic Programming Approach.* Academic Press, 1992.
7. L. De Raedt. Logical settings for concept learning. *Artificial Intelligence*, 95:187–
   201, 1997.
8. L. De Raedt. Using ILP for verification, validation and testing of knowledge based
   systems, 1997. invited talk at EUROVAV 1997.
9. L. De Raedt and L. Dehaspe. Clausal discovery. *Machine Learning*, 26:99–146,
   1997.
10. L. De Raedt and S. Džeroski. First order jk-clausal theories are PAC-learnable.
    Artificial Intelligence, 70:375–392, 1994.
11. L. De Raedt, G. Sablon, and M. Bruynooghe. Using interactive concept learning
    for knowledge-base validation and verification. In *Validation, Verification and Test
    of Knowledge-based Systems*, pages 177–190, 1991.
12. B. Dunin-Keplicz and J. Treur. Compositional formal specification of multi-agent
    systems. In *Proceedings of the ECAI'94 Workshop on Agent Theories, Architec-
    tures and Languages*, pages 102–117, 1995.
13. H. Kitano, M. Veloso, H. Matsubara, M. Tambe, S. Coradeschi, I. Noda, P. Stone,
    E. Osawa, and M. Asada. The robocup synthetic agent challenge 97. In *Proceed-
    ings of the 15th International Joint Conference on Artificial Intelligence*, pages
    24–29. Morgan Kaufmann, 1997.
14. J. Ross Quinlan. *C4.5: Programs for Machine Learning.* Morgan Kaufmann series
    in machine learning. Morgan Kaufmann, 1993.
15. J. Vanthienen, C. Mues, and C. Wets. Inter-tabular verification in an interactive
    environment. In *Proceedings of the '97 European Symposium on the Validation and
    Verification of Knowledge Based Systems (EUROVAV-97)*, pages 155–165, 1997.

Inducing Shogi Heuristics
Using Inductive Logic Programming

Tomofumi Nakano, Nobuhiro Inuzuka, Hirohisa Seki and Hidenori Itoh

Nagoya Institute of Technology
Gokiso-cho, Showa-ku, Nagoya 466-8555, Japan
E-mail: {tnakano,inuzuka,seki,itoh}@ics.nitech.ac.jp

Abstract. This paper reports the results of an inductive logic programming (ILP) application to solve shogi or Japanese chess mating problems, which are puzzles using shogi rules. The problems can be solved by heuristic search of AND-OR trees. We propose a method of using the ILP technique to generate heuristic functions, which are automatically tuned according to the confidence of the knowledge induced by ILP. Experiments show that the method prunes search space compared with a naive search.

1 Introduction

Chess applications of machine learning methods have focused attention on important issues. [1] investigated an EBL-like learning algorithm by chess concepts that represent the roles of particular chess pieces. In [2], a feature generation method is inspected with chess games. Chess endgames, such as KRK (King and Rook against King), in particular provide a continuing challenge as a benchmark for the study of concept learning especially by ILP algorithms [3, 4].

In this paper we deal with *shogi mating problems*, i.e. puzzles using the rules of shogi, or Japanese chess. The problem is for the player to obtain continuous checking moves from a given board situation. These can be regarded as problems of searching for a path in a state space consisting of board situations and checking moves. We focus on heuristic functions to search for solutions in this state space.

Learning methods have often been applied to problem solving. LEX[5] learns heuristic rules that indicate which operators should be used in given situations, from the experience of solving problems. Explanation-based learning[6] makes a problem-solving process shorter by generating shortcut rules.

Attempts to use ILP for problem solving include DOLPHIN[7] and SCOPE[8]. DOLPHIN, using EBL, learns conditions to make non-deterministic programs deterministic. SCOPE, also using EBL, learns control rules for partial order planning. These methods all work to complete each production rule given, using history to solve problems by acquiring macro operators, or by adding conditions to rules. They are, however, not applicable to domains that do not have explicit production rules. Instead of completing rules, the method presented in this paper directly constructs heuristic functions using logic programs induced by ILP systems, which extends our previous method[9] in a procedure to generate heuristic functions.

2   Shogi mating problems

Shogi is a board game similar to chess, played on a 9 × 9 square board, with eight kinds of pieces: King, Gold General, Silver General, Knight, Rook, Bishop, Lance and Pawn. The *capture* and *drop* rules lead to a high level of complexity in shogi. When a piece is captured, the captured piece becomes part of the captor's force and can be dropped in a later move. Another difference from chess is the *promotion* rule. When a piece reaches the enemy area it can be promoted up a level in mobility. A short survey of shogi rules is in [10].

A shogi mating problem is a puzzle using shogi rules. To solve a problem is to find moves to mate from a given board position. The first player has to continue checking the opponent's King. The opponent has all pieces which are not shown explicitly in the problem. A problem is given as a board and has to satisfy:

1. **(Unshakeable win)** The first player has to be able to win against the second player, that is, the first player can checkmate no matter what the next move of the opponent might be.
2. **(Unique solution)** When the opponent does its best, the move to bring checkmate has to be unique for each opponent's move, that is, the opponent can make the first player fail to checkmate if a wrong move is once taken.

The solver of a shogi mating problem has to answer with the sequence of moves

$$m = (m_1, M_1, m_2, M_2, \cdots, m_{n-1}, M_{n-1}, m_n),$$

in which $m_1, m_2, \cdots$ are moves of the first player and $M_1, M_2, \cdots$ are the opponent's moves. $m_i (i = 1, \cdots, n)$ check the opponent's King and m_n makes checkmate. The opponent's best moves mean that the length n of the sequence of checking moves is longer than that for any other opponent's moves M_i. We call m a *solution* of the problem with the *length* $2n - 1$.

A shogi mating problem can be given as an initial board state. We treat a move m as an operator that maps a board b to another board $m(b)$, which is the board position after the move is taken.

To solve a problem we use an extension of the best-first search algorithm to search the AND-OR tree or game tree, where a board and a move are treated as a node and an arrow, respectively. The algorithm is shown in Fig. 1, where branch_cut procedure prunes unnecessary branches. The heuristic function h uses knowledge induced by the ILP system. This is discussed in later sections.

3   An ILP problem in shogi

We treat this problem as an ILP application for the following reasons:

– Unique solution: it is easy to generate positive and negative examples.
– Relatively small search space: because of a restriction that a player has to continue checking, the number of moves for a board is not large.

global *found_solution* # TRUE for solution found or FALSE for not.
       Open   # Open list of boards to be visited.
       Solutions   # List of boards found to be checkmated.
                 # A board is expressed as a sequence of moves.
       root   # The root of AND-OR tree, or the initial board.

<u>main</u>

input *board$_{init}$*   # an initial board
        h   # a heuristic function

found_solution := FALSE ; *Solutions*:= ϕ ; *Open*:= {*board$_{init}$*} ; *root* := *board$_{init}$*
while *found_solution* = FALSE
    board$_{first}$:= (the first element of *Open* sorted by heuristic function *h*)
    Open := *Open* − {*board$_{first}$*}
    expand *board$_{first}$* to *Boards*
    if *Boards* is empty   # *board$_{first}$* is a leaf of AND-OR tree
        if *board$_{first}$* is the first player's
            flag := OK ; *Solutions* := *Solutions* ∪ {*board$_{first}$*}
        else
            flag := NG
        branch_cut(*board$_{first}$*, *flag*)
    else   # *board$_{first}$* is not a leaf of AND-OR tree
        Open := *Boards* ∪ *Open*
end while

<u>branch_cut(*board*, *flag*)</u>

input *board*   # a board visited currently
       flag   # OK or NG

board$_{parent}$:= (the parent node of *board*)
if *board$_{parent}$* = root
         found_solution := TRUE
else **if** *flag* = NG   # found *board* not to be checkmated
        if *board* is the second player's
            Cut := (a set of descendent nodes of *board*)
            Open := *Open* − *Cut* ; *Solutions* := *Solutions* − *Cut*
            branch_cut(*board$_{parent}$*, *flag*)
        else
            if there exists a descendant of *board$_{parent}$* in *Open* ∪ *Solutions*
                branch_cut(*board$_{parent}$*, *flag*)
      else # *flag* = OK   # found *board* to be checkmated
        if *board* is the first player's
            Cut := (a set of descendent nodes of *board*)
            Open := *Open* − *Cut* ; *Solutions* := *Solutions* − *Cut*
            branch_cut(*board$_{parent}$*, *flag*)
        else
            if there exists a descendant of *board$_{parent}$* in *Open* ∪ *Solutions*
                branch_cut(*board$_{parent}$*, *flag*)
return

Fig. 1. An algorithm to search an AND-OR tree of mating problems.

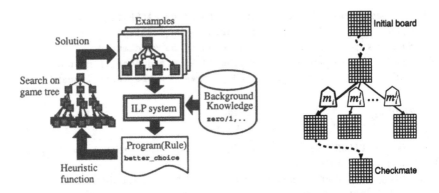

Fig. 2. Outline of the method.   **Fig. 3.** Solution and wrong moves

– Abundant number of problems: shogi mating problems have a long history and many problems at any level can easily be prepared.

We here propose a method to search mating problems with ILP, as outlined in Fig. 2. We discuss the method in this and the next section.

Noting the uniqueness of a solution, we use solutions as examples to induce a predicate on shogi. Let us consider a shogi mating problem b and its solution:

$$m = (m_1, M_1, \cdots, m_{n-1}, M_{n-1}, m_n).$$ (1)

For each board state $M_{i-1}(m_{i-1}(\cdots M_1(m_1(b))\cdots))$, there may be several checking moves $m_i^1, \cdots, m_i^{j_i}$ other than m_i. From the uniqueness, $m_i^1, \cdots, m_i^{j_i}$ cannot lead to checkmate. Only m_i is correct (See Fig. 3). So, we can use m_i as a positive example and $m_i^1, \cdots, m_i^{j_i}$ as negative ones for a selection predicate. However, we do not take this selection predicate itself as a target for ILP learning. The predicate has to choose a move from many other moves and it is difficult to induce such a predicate. Instead of the selection predicate we take as the target a comparison predicate between two moves, which we name better-choice.

better-choice(b, m, m') is true when a move m is better than a move m' on a board b. Please note that we can not only be certain that the correct move is better than others but also expect this predicate on all possible moves.

We return to the mating problem b and its solution (1). Then for each board state $M_{i-1}(m_{i-1}(\cdots \cdots M_1(m_1(b))\cdots))$ and checking moves $m_i^1, \cdots, m_i^{j_i}$,

$$\text{better-choice}(M_{i-1}(m_{i-1}(\cdots M_1(m_1(b))\cdots)), \ m_i, \ m_i^k), \ k = 1, \cdots, j_i$$

are positive examples and

$$\text{better-choice}(M_{i-1}(m_{i-1}(\cdots M_1(m_1(b))\cdots)), \ m_i^k, \ m_i), \ k = 1, \cdots, j_i$$

are negative ones. All examples for every move in the solution are joined and are used to induce definition of better-choice by ILP. Section 4 explains the method of generating a heuristic function from better-choice.

4 better-choice relation to a heuristic function

Although better-choice is a local relation among possible checking moves, the search algorithm needs a global heuristic function which selects a board among all possible boards in a search tree. The method proposed here makes a heuristic function from the better-choice relation. The method consists of two steps:

1. For a board b and possible checking moves $m^1, \cdots, m^j$ on it, assign a value $v_b(m^i)$ $(0 < v_b(m^i) < 1)$, where the order of the values for moves is consistent with the better-choice relation as much as possible.
2. Assign a heuristic value $h(b')$ for a board situation b' as follows:

$$h(b') = \begin{cases} 1 & \text{if } b' \text{ is an initial board} \\ v_b(m) \cdot h(b) & \text{if } b' = m(b) \end{cases} \tag{2}$$

As a result the heuristic function $h(\cdot)$ has the following properties:

1. When m_1 and m_2 are both moves on a board b and m_1 is better than a move m_2 in the sense of better-choice, the value $h(m_1(b))$ is greater than $h(m_2(b))$.
2. If a board b' follows a board b after several moves, $h(b')$ is less than $h(b)$.

To construct the local values $v_b(m)$, we use an idea of *plausibility flow* among moves. The plausibility of a move means a likelihood that the move leads to the solution. If better-choice(b, m_1, m_2) is true, the plausibility of m_1 should be higher than m_2 and so we can imagine a flow of plausibility from m_2 to m_1. The resulting plausibility should be a stationary state calculated on the basis of the flow.

Four steps are necessary to achieve the result. We assume that $\mathcal{M}$ is a set of possible checking moves on a board b and m_1 and m_2 are in $\mathcal{M}$. Though all values appearing in Step 1 to Step 4 relate to a board b, we omit the board b in their descriptions.

Step 1 *Plausibility points* Two functions are defined by:

$$\text{Out}(m_1, m_2) = \begin{cases} p_L & \text{if better-choice}(m_1, m_2) \text{ holds} \\ p_H & \text{otherwise} \end{cases}$$

$$\text{Stay}(m_1, m_2) = \begin{cases} p_H & \text{if better-choice}(m_1, m_2) \text{ holds} \\ p_L & \text{otherwise} \end{cases},$$

where $m_1 \neq m_2$ and $p_L < p_H$[1]. To express plausibility flowing out from m_1 to m_2 for the case that better-choice(m_1, m_2) is true, we give a smaller value p_L to $\text{Out}(m_1, m_2)$, and a larger value p_H to $\text{Stay}(m_1, m_2)$.

The plausibility points $Pl(m_1, m_2)$ are defined by these functions as follows:

$$Pl(m_1, m_2) = \begin{cases} \text{Out}(m_1, m_2) & m_1 \neq m_2 \\ \sum_{m' \in \mathcal{M} - \{m_1\}} \text{Stay}(m_1, m') & m_1 = m_2 \end{cases}$$

---

[1] In our implementation $p_L = 1$ and $p_H = 2$.

Table 1. A better-choice relation matrix.

	m_1	m_2	m_3	m_4
m_1	–	0	0	0
m_2	1	–	0	1
m_3	1	1	–	0
m_4	1	1	1	–

Table 2. A plausibility point matrix.

	m_1	m_2	m_3	m_4
m_1	3	2	2	2
m_2	1	5	2	1
m_3	1	1	5	2
m_4	1	1	1	6

Table 3. A transition probability matrix.

	m_1	m_2	m_3	m_4
m_1	0.33	0.22	0.22	0.22
m_2	0.11	0.56	0.22	0.11
m_3	0.11	0.11	0.56	0.22
m_4	0.11	0.11	0.11	0.67

Table 4. Stationary probability.

m_1	0.14
m_2	0.23
m_3	0.27
m_4	0.35

Table 5. Local heuristic values induced.

m_1	0.43
m_2	0.49
m_3	0.52
m_4	0.57

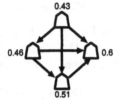
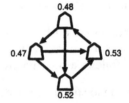

Fig. 4. Two cases of better-choice relation and local heuristic values.

Step 2 *Transition probability* By regarding each move as a state, we can use the plausibility flow to decide transition probability among states. By dividing 1 (the total probability of transition from a state to others) in proportion to the plausibility points, we define transition probability from one move (state) to another.

$$Tr(m_1, m_2) = \frac{Pl(m_1, m_2)}{\sum_{m' \in \mathcal{M}} Pl(m_1, m')}$$

Step 3 *Stationary probability* Stationary probability $St(m)$ of each state or a move $m \in \mathcal{M}$ is defined as probability after many iterations of transition according to the transition probability. It satisfies:

$$St(m) = \sum_{m' \in \mathcal{M}} St(m')\, Tr(m', m)$$

Step 4 *Local heuristic values* Because $\sum_{m \in \mathcal{M}} St(m) = 1$, the stationary probability of each move is relatively small when a board has many checking moves. Then, we tune the stationary probability to give local heuristic evaluation $v(m)$ for each move m by lifting the average of $St(m)$ to a constant value C_{ave}. Hence, the value $v(m)$ should satisfy:

$$(1 - v(m)) = a(1 - St(m)) \tag{3}$$

$$\sum_{m \in \mathcal{M}} v(m) = N \cdot C_{\text{ave}} \qquad (4)$$

We can obtain the coefficient a by: $a = \frac{N}{N-1}(1 - C_{\text{ave}})$, where N is the number of moves in $\mathcal{M}$. We denote $v(m)$ for a board b as $v_b(m)$ in Equation (2). See Appendix for derivation of a and a proof of $0 \le v_b(m) \le 1$.

Tables 1, 2, 3, 4 and 5 show examples of each of the steps. In Table 1, a numeral 1 (0) to the right of m_i and below m_j means that better-choice(m_i, m_j) does (does not, respectively) hold. To obtain Table 5 we let $C_{\text{ave}} = 0.5$.

The values generated accord with the better-choice relation. When better-choice is not a partial order on moves, the values are only slightly different from each other, while if it gives a total order the difference is relatively large. Fig. 4 illustrates these cases, which depend on the induced knowledge. The search process using the values is also reflected by the knowledge.

5 Implementation and experiments

We have performed experiments to confirm (1) generality of knowledge induced by ILP and (2) efficiency of search with heuristic functions constructed from the knowledge.

For the experiments we prepared 40 shogi mating problems of several levels of difficulty, or several lengths of solutions. Ten of the problems were reserved for induction, called *training problems*, and the others were used to check results, called *test problems*.

Any given mating problem can be transformed into a problem of a lower level. When we have a problem b with solution $(m_1, M_1, m_2, M_2, \cdots, m_{n-1}, M_{n-1}, m_n)$, whose length is $2n - 1$, we can regard $M_i(m_i(\cdots(M_1(m_1(b)))\cdots)))$ as another easier problem with length $2(n-i)-1$, the problem whose solution is $(m_{i+1}, M_{i+1}, \cdots, m_{n-1}, M_{n-1}, m_n)$. So, we increased the number of test problems by shortening them.

We used a version of FOIL-I[11, 12], which is a derivative of an ILP system FOIL[13]. The system is extended to work on incomplete examples and to be able to work with any prolog programs as background knowledge.

We prepared background knowledge including the moves of the pieces in shogi rules, basic concepts of shogi and arithmetic predicates. The background knowledge and the examples used in the experiments may be found in the following URL: "http://www-itolab.ics.nitech.ac.jp/research/ilp/shogi/".

The experiments were performed as follows:

1. Prepare sets of examples by choosing 1, 2, 3, 5 or 8 training problem(s) randomly, 10 of each, and by generating positive and negative examples from them. A total of 50 sets of examples was prepared.
2. Induce a logic program defining better-choice from each of the 50 sets of examples, using background knowledge of shogi.
3. Generate 30 easier test problems of length 3, and another 30 problems of length 5, from the 30 test problems.

Table 6. Average accuracy of programs induced and the number of clauses included.

The number of training problems to induce	Average accuracy for training problems	Average accuracy for test problems	Average of the number of clauses induced
1 problem	92.1±1.9%	55.5±3.5%	6.2±3.3
2 problems	90.5±2.2%	62.1±3.5%	13.3±4.3
3 problems	87.6±3.0%	61.7±4.1%	18.9±5.8
5 problems	85.4±3.2%	66.4±3.8%	28.2±12.8
8 problems	84.1±2.4%	68.5±1.5%	39.6±8.3

4. Attempt to solve the 60 test problems using the heuristic function generated from each of the 50 logic programs. Thus a total of 3000 trials of execution (1500 of length 3 and 1500 of length 5) were performed.

Table 6 shows the accuracy of induced programs against training problems used in induction and against test problems. The average accuracy is calculated for the groups of 10 based on 1, 2, 3, 5 and 8 training problem(s), respectively. We can observe that the accuracy for test problems increases with the number of problems used to induce programs, although the accuracy for training problems decreases. This demonstrates an increase of the generality of programs with larger training sets.

Fig. 5 focuses on the number of nodes visited during search. For each trial in 3000 executions, we observed the percentage of nodes visited during search with heuristics against search without knowledge. The no-knowledge case is identical to using a breadth-first search. Each graph in Fig. 5 combines five histograms for problem sets consisting of 1, 2, 3, 5 and 8 problem(s), respectively. The histograms show the number of trials in each 10% range class, and the mean and median of the percentage are also shown. A small percentage means the search is much faster than the no-knowledge case. The graph demonstrates increasing speed-up for searches with heuristics induced from many problems.

6   Conclusion and further work

This paper reports an ILP application to shogi mating problems. Because of the complex rules of shogi it is very difficult to obtain information on strategies from board status. We chose background knowledge that concerns only superficial information of board status, that is, the knowledge does not plan ahead. In our previous work that treats eight puzzles[9] we allowed knowledge to plan ahead and to induce recursive clauses. As a result the ILP system induced a recursive program to plan ahead. To use the induced knowledge was the same as to search without knowledge. Our experiment shows that ILP technique can give heuristic functions using only a limited set of background knowledge.

In our results, the mean proportion of nodes visited by the heuristic functions, relative to the no-knowledge or breadth-first case, is higher than the median

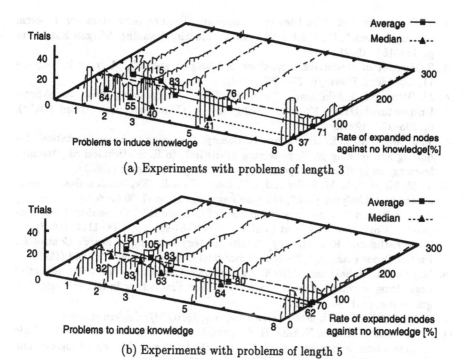

(a) Experiments with problems of length 3

(b) Experiments with problems of length 5

Fig. 5. Histograms of proportion of expanded nodes in search relative to no-knowledge cases.

proportion. This is because the proportions are very large (higher than 1000%) in rare cases, which lifts the average. We also need to take into account the overhead involved in calculating the heuristic functions. In our implementation, a heuristic search with approximately 65% reduction has the same runtime as the no-knowledge cases. This, however, depends on the nature and number of clauses and background knowledge in programs induced.

To refine the method we need to investigate several things. Induced knowledge depends on which mating problems are to be used. We have to consider the generality of the knowledge: if problems and knowledge can be classified into discrete types or areas, induction based on more types should give more effective knowledge. We can also tune the parameters p_L, p_H and C_{ave} used to calculate the heuristic functions. These parameters decide how severely to treat induced knowledge. Selection of background knowledge is another important issue, and re-implementation of the method by more efficient language will also be necessary.

References

1. N. S. Flann and T. G. Dietterich: "Study of Explanation-Based Methods for Inductive Learning", Machine Learning, Vol.4, pp.187–226 (1989).

2. T. E. Fawcett and P. E. Utogoff: "Automatic Feature Generation for Problem Solving Systems", Proc. 9th Int'l Conf. on Machine Learning, Morgan Kaufmann pp.144–153 (1992).
3. S. Muggleton: "Inductive Acquisition of Chess Strategies", Machine Intelligence 11, Clarendon Press, pp. 375–387 (1988).
4. M. Bain and A. Srinivasan: "Inductive Logic Programming With Large-Scale Unstructured Data", Machine Intelligence 14, Clarendon Press Oxford (OUP), pp.235–274 (1995).
5. T. M. Mitchell, P. E. Utogoff and R. Banerji: "Learning by Experimentation: Acquiring and refining problem- solving heuristics", In R. S. Michalski ed., Machine learning: an artificial intelligence approach, Tioga Publishing (1983).
6. T. M. Mitchell, R. M. Keller and S. T. Kedar-Cabelli: "Explanation-Based Generalization: A Unifying View", Machine Learning, 1, pp.47–80 (1986).
7. J. M. Zelle and R. J. Mooney: "Combining FOIL and EBG to speed-up Logic Programs", Proc. 13th Int'l Joint Conf. on AI (IJCAI-93), pp. 1106–1111, (1993).
8. T. A. Estlin and R. J. Mooney: "Multi-Strategy Learning of Search Control for Partial-Order Planning", Proc. 13th National Conf. on AI, pp. 843-848 (1996).
9. N. Inuzuka, H. Seki and H. Itoh: "An intelligent search method using Inductive Logic Programming", Proc. IJCAI97 Workshop Frontiers of Inductive Logic Programming, pp.115-120 (1997).
10. SHOGI-RULES, URL:http://www.ricoh.co.jp/SHOGI/rules/erules.html.
11. N. Inuzuka, M. Kamo, N. Ishii, H. Seki and H. Itoh: "Top-down induction of logic programs from incomplete samples", Proc. 6th Int'l Inductive Logic Programming Workshop (LNAI 1314, Springer-Verlag), pp.265-282 (1996).
12. N. Inuzuka, H. Seki and H. Itoh: "Efficient induction of executable logic programs from examples", Proc. Asian Computing Science Conference (LNCS 1345, Springer-Verlag), pp.212-224 (1997).
13. J. R. Quinlan: "Learning logical definitions from relations", Machine Learning, 5, pp.239–266 (1990).

Appendix

A.1 Derivation of local heuristic values from stationary probability

From Equation (3), the local heuristic value $v(m)$ is expressed as $v(m) = -a + 1 + a \cdot St(m)$. By substituting this into Equation (4), we have $\sum_{m \in \mathcal{M}} (-a + 1 + a \cdot St(m)) = N \cdot C_{ave}$ This can be transformed to $\sum_{m \in \mathcal{M}} (1-a) + a \sum_{m \in \mathcal{M}} St(m) = N \cdot C_{ave}$. Then $N \cdot (1-a) + a = N \cdot C_{ave}$ by $\sum_{m \in \mathcal{M}} St(m) = 1$. As a result we have $a = \frac{N}{N-1}(1 - C_{ave})$.

A.2 Proof of $0 \leq v(m) \leq 1$

The conditions $1/N \leq C_{ave} \leq 1$ and $N \geq 2$ are assumed. Obviously $v(m) \leq 1$, because $N/(N-1) \geq 0$, $1 - C_{ave} \geq 0$ and $1 - St(m) \geq 0$. By the assumption, $0 \leq 1 - C_{ave} \leq 1 - 1/N$. So, we have the following inequality, which yields $0 \leq v(m)$.

$$1 - v(m) = \frac{N}{N-1}(1 - C_{ave})(1 - St(m)) \leq \frac{N}{N-1}(1 - 1/N)(1 - St(m)) \leq 1 - St(m) \leq 1.$$

Repeat Learning Using Predicate Invention

Khalid Khan[1,2], Stephen Muggleton[1], and Rupert Parson[2]

[1] Department of Computer Science, University of York
{kmk,stephen}@cs.york.ac.uk
[2] Oxford University Computing Laboratory
rupert.parson@comlab.ox.ac.uk

Abstract. Most of machine learning is concerned with learning a single concept from a sequence of examples. In *repeat learning* the teacher chooses a series of related concepts randomly and independently from a distribution $\mathcal{D}$. A finite sequence of examples is provided for each concept in the series. The learner does not initially know $\mathcal{D}$, but progressively updates a posterior estimation of $\mathcal{D}$ as the series progresses. This paper considers *predicate invention* within Inductive Logic Programming as a mechanism for updating the learner's estimation of $\mathcal{D}$. A new predicate invention mechanism implemented in Progol4.4 is used in repeat learning experiments within a chess domain. The results indicate that significant performance increases can be achieved. The paper develops a Bayesian framework and demonstrates initial theoretical results for repeat learning.

1 Introduction

Predicate Invention (PI) has been investigated for some time within Inductive Logic Programming (ILP) [7, 11, 3, 9, 4, 10]. The literature describes various mechanisms for the introduction of new predicates into the learner's vocabulary, as well as conditions under which this is necessary. However, surprisingly little, if any, experimental evidence exists to indicate that learners which employ PI perform better than those which do not. On the face of it, there are good reasons to believe that since increasing the learner's vocabulary expands the hypothesis space, PI could degrade both the learner's predictive accuracy and learning speed. Indeed in the experiments described in Sect. 3 PI does not significantly increase accuracy during the training sessions in which it is employed.

However, the situation is different in the case in which the learner is allowed to repeatedly employ PI to discover background definitions for a series of related concepts. In this case predicates which successfully help describe one concept may decrease the sample requirements for subsequent concepts. This idea was tested in the experiments described in Sect. 3. The experimental domain, chess moves on the open board, was chosen because of the ease of data generation and analysis of results. Unlike many recursive domains in which PI has previously been demonstrated, it is not *necessary* for the learner to invent vocabulary in order to learn in this domain. However, without invention the learnt definitions are far more complex than when a few simple auxiliary monadic predicates are added. The results show that the invented predicates significantly increase accuracy on *subsequent* sessions involving the same, or related concepts.

In this paper we suggest a theoretical framework for *Repeat Learning* (RL) over a series of inter–related concepts. This framework is related to existing theoretical results of Baxter [1].

The paper is organized as follows. Section 2 introduces the experimental domain involving moves of the various chess pieces on the open board. The experiments described in Sect. 3 indicate that a) PI *does not* reduce sample requirements for learning a single concept and b) does significantly reduce sample requirements when successful invented predicates are provided as background knowledge for subsequent concepts. Section 4 describes how constraint solving in Progol4.4 was used to carry out PI in the experiments. A framework for RL is described in Sect. 5. Future directions for the research are discussed in Sect. 6. Pointers to an FTP site containing the experimental materials used in this paper are given in Sect. 7.

2 Examples

Consider the problem of repeat learning the definitions of legal moves on the open board for chess pieces. A concept will be associated with each piece to represent its legal moves. For example Fig. 1. shows the legal moves which can be made by a King and a Knight. Note the symmetries common to the legal moves of the pieces. In the experiment (Sect. 3) the initial background knowledge does not take account of symmetries. However once a predicate related to symmetry for one piece has been learnt it reduces the sample complexity of the learning in the second.

If we label the squares on a chess board according to *file* (column letter a–h) and *rank* (row number 1–8), we can then define two predicates fdiff/2 and rdiff/2 which compute the difference in file and rank for a move. All the legal chess piece moves can be defined entirely using these two predicates. However the size of the resulting theories is large. Both the King and Knight predicates would need 8 clauses to be defined in this way for each of the 8 possible directions (see Table 1). We therefore attempt to introduce symmetry predicates into our definitions. This is done via PI and is used to demonstrate the general principle of RL — that a set of related concepts can better be learnt by also learning a common bias in which to represent those concepts. In the chess setting we might start off learning one piece, then use bias shift operations such as PI in order to help in the learning of subsequent pieces.

3 Experiments

3.1 Training Data

The training data was generated by hand–coding a definition of the move for each piece, then using Progol's built in sample/3 predicate to generate random

a) The King

b) The Knight

Fig. 1. The legal moves of the pieces

Table 1. Move definitions — with and without Symmetry Predicates. Length is the number of literals in a clause. Total is the total number of literals in a predicate definition

	King			Knight		
	No. Clauses	Length	Total	No. Clauses	Length	Total
Without Symmetry Predicates	8	3	24	8	3	24
With Symmetry Predicates	2	5,2	7	4	5,5,2,2	14

examples. In this domain purely random training data will result in (typically 8 times) more negative examples than positive examples. Given this the positive and negative examples were generated separately and combined in a ratio of 1:1 in the training sets. For each piece the training sets contained 5,10,15,20,30,40 and 80 positive and negative examples. For each training set size, 20 random and independent example sets were generated. The results were then averaged over these 20 example sets to reduce variance.

3.2 Test Data

One of the advantages of using a well defined enclosed domain such as chess is the ability to obtain a perfect testing metric, based on the fact that there are only a finite number of possible moves. In particular there are 64 squares on a chess board, so this gives us a total of 64×64=4096 possible moves, most of which will clearly be negative examples for any given piece. The total error was re-weighted to be the average of the errors of commission and omission. Also, in the interests of simplicity, each piece was allowed to stay still in its definition of move. It is easy to compensate for this mis-specification simply by introducing an additional predicate. If we are trying to build up a move generator as in [2], we would want to state such a predicate only once, so it would be piece independent.

3.3 Runs

For each piece there were 4 trials conducted. In the first trial, "Ordinary Learning", Progol was given the opportunity to learn the definition of the piece without any predicate invention, and with only the `fdiff/2` and `rdiff/2` predicates as background knowledge. In the second trial, "Predicate Invention", Progol was supplied with the same background knowledge, but this time allowed to invent new predicates. This process is described fully in Sect. 4. In the third trial "*Intra*–Repeat Learning", Progol was supplied with the successful invented predicates from the second trial as background knowledge. Finally in the fourth trial "*Inter*–Repeat Learning", the learning of each piece was helped with the invented predicates from the other piece. This is how it is hoped RL would work in general. Similar concepts would share common defining predicates and predicate invention performed on some of them could be used to help the learning of others.

The accuracy results for Ordinary Learning, Predicate Invention and Intra–Repeat Learning are plotted in Fig. 2 (standard deviations for the sample mean over 20 runs are shown as error bars). Finally a comparison of Inter–Repeat Learning to Ordinary Learning is given in Fig. 3.

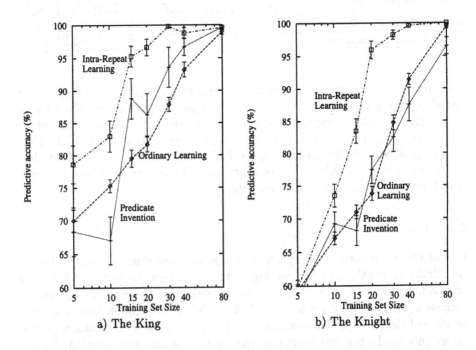

a) The King   b) The Knight

Fig. 2. Learning curves for each piece (with standard deviations of sample means)

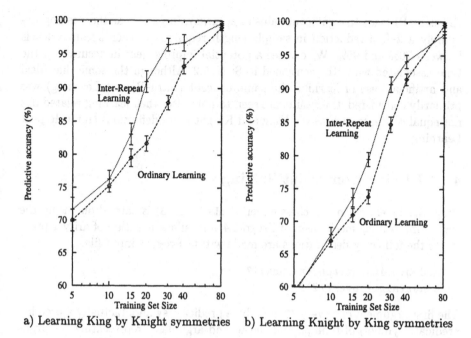

a) Learning King by Knight symmetries   b) Learning Knight by King symmetries

Fig. 3. The Inter–Repeat Learning Setting

3.4 Repeat Learning Setting

The above experiments can be formulated in terms of the RL framework described in Sect. 5 as follows. The learner $\mathcal{L}$ is Progol 4.4. The learner's (initial) distribution D_1 over hypotheses is the distribution induced by L_1, the initial language described in Sect. 2. The teacher's distribution, D_T is some distribution over the possible targets, i.e. King, Knight. The first learning session is the ordinary learning of the target chess move. The role of the *repeat–adjustment* operator is taken by the Predicate Invention phase. If this achieves a low enough error ($\epsilon < 0.05$) then the learner updates its hypothesis language L_1 to L_2 by adding any used invented predicates, inducing a new distribution D_2 over the hypotheses. This occurs at 80 examples in all our experiments. The Intra or Inter Repeat learning takes place in the second learning session. Note that in the experiments we try all possible pairs of target concept (inter–repeat: king then knight, knight then king and intra–repeat: king then king, knight then knight). It is also important to note that in the RL framework the number of learning sessions is unrestricted, but that in the experiments we have conducted 2 learning sessions.

3.5 Evaluation of Results

The results obtained clearly show that PI on its own does not significantly increase accuracy. Taken within a RL setting however, the results indicate that

RL using PI leads to significant gains in accuracy. In particular there is approximately a 2–fold reduction in sample length required to reach accuracy levels between 70% and 95%. We can see a potential improvement in accuracy of the type associated with RL mentioned in Sect. 5.2. Although the somewhat ideal and artificial case of learning the same concept (Intra–Repeat Learning) was primarily considered, the results are seen to hold also when learning related but not equal concepts such as the King and Knight move definitions (Inter–Repeat Learning).

4 PI Using Constraint Solving

Predicate invention in the chess experiments (Sect. 3) is carried out using the constraint–solving mechanism of Progol4.4[1]. To allow invention of arity 1 predicates the following declarations are made within Progol's input file.

```
:- modeb(1,invent(#pn,+pmrank))?
:- constraint(invent/2)?
```

The first argument of invent/2 must be a predicate symbol (actually a pseudo–predicate symbol) of type pn and the second argument (representing the argument of the invented predicate) is a variable of type pmrank. The constraint declaration says that any invent/2 atom in the most–specific clause should have a Skolem constant in place of the predicate symbol to be invented (#pn above). In the search, during any clause refinement which introduces a constraint atom, the flag 'solving' is turned on, and invent/2 is called with the second argument bound to a term representing all substitutions for this variable from the positive and negative examples. The bound term is given as a list of lists of lists(takes the form [P,N] where P is from the positive examples and N from the negatives, and P,N are lists of lists, each list giving all substitutions related to a particular example). The predicate invent/2 returns an appropriate substitution for the constant, which will be either an existing predicate symbol or a new predicate symbol created using gensym/1. This predicate symbol replaces the Skolem constant in subsequent testing of the clause and its refinements. Definitions for constraint predicates have at least two clauses, with guards 'not(solving)' and 'solving' to define respectively the normal application of the predicate and the procedure for computing the constant. The following is the user–defined definition of invent/2 used for the experiments.

```
invent(P,X) :-              % Non-solving clause
      not(solving),
      !, defn(P,X), !.      % Simply use definition of P
invent(P,[PosA,_]) :-
      solving,              % Solving clause,
      flatten(PosA,PosA1),  % Flatten pos substs.
```

---

[1] This is an adaptation of Srinivasan and Camacho's lazy evaluation, originally devised to allow the estimation of numerical constants within clauses

```
       sort(PosA1,PosA2),        % Make normal form model for P.
       not(element(X,PosA2),not(number(X))),
                                 % Check no Skolem constants.
       (clause(model(P,PosA2),true);        % Already exists?
        (gensym(P),              % Create new pred. symbol P.
         asserta(model(P,PosA2)), % Assert the model of P.
         assertdef(P,PosA2))).   % Assert the definition of P.
```

The auxiliary predicates defn/2 and model/2 store the definitions and models of invented predicates respectively. The definition has a set of clauses associated with each invented symbol while the model has a single clause containing a list of all ground instances of a particular invented predicate. For instance, q8 might have a definition and model as follows.

```
defn(q8,-1).  defn(q8,0).  defn(q8,1).
model(q8,[-1,0,1]).
```

The model can be used to check whether a new predicate has already been invented. The definition allows for further generalization of the invented predicate (given appropriate mode declarations).

Despite the apparent simplicity of the approach, the predicate invention technique allows simultaneous invention of multiple predicates, and also allows user choice of arity and argument typing for invent-able predicates. In fact, the technique appears to be at least as powerful as anything in the literature. For instance, in the release examples of Progol4.4 (available by anonymous ftp from ftp.cs.york.ac.uk in directory pub/ML_GROUP/progol4.4), it is shown how append1/3 can be invented when learning a recursive definition of naive reverse.

5 A Framework for Repeat Learning

The following describes a framework for the Repeat Learning setting, similar to one described by Baxter in [1]. This framework is then applied to ILP. This setting is a natural extension of the U–learnability model [8], [5]. The framework is a generalization of the setting used in the experiments.

5.1 Repeat Learning

The teacher starts by choosing a distribution D_T over the target space $\mathcal{H}$, and a distribution D_X over the instance space X, where $\mathcal{H} \subseteq \mathcal{P}(X)$.

The learner $\mathcal{L}$ is given the distribution D_X, and is given a *prior distribution* D_1 over the target space $\mathcal{H}$. $\mathcal{L}$ is also equipped with a *repeat–adjustment* operator $r_{\mathcal{L}}$ that produces a refined posterior distribution D_{n+1} on the basis of all the data received by $\mathcal{L}$ so far.

The teacher uses D_T and D_X to carry out an infinite series of teaching sessions, starting with session 1. In session $n \geq 1$ the teacher chooses a target concept $T_n \in \mathcal{H}$ according to D_T. T_n is used to provide labels from $\{true, false\}$

for a new sequence of instances $\langle x_1, x_2, \ldots \rangle$ chosen randomly and independently from X according to D_X. An instance x_i is labelled true if $T_n \models x_i$, and false otherwise. An hypothesis is said to explain a set of examples E whenever it both entails and is consistent with E.

In session n, having seen the labelled instances $E_{m_n} = \langle e_1, e_2, \ldots e_{m_n} \rangle$, $\mathcal{L}$ produces a hypothesis $\mathcal{L}(E_{m_n}, D_n)$ that explains E_{m_n}, using its current prior distribution over $\mathcal{H}$, D_n. The teacher stops the session after m_n labelled instances, if the learner's hypothesis $\mathcal{L}(E_{m_n}, D_n)$ has expected error less than ϵ (for some $0 \le \epsilon < 1$) for predicting the correct label of any $x \in X$ chosen according to D_X. This successful hypothesis is then labelled H_n. The learner then generates a new prior distribution D_{n+1} for session $n + 1$, using $r_{\mathcal{L}}$.

A repeat learner would be expected to show an improvement in performance after a number of sessions, by successively improving its approximation D_n of the teacher's distribution D_T over the target space. See Sect. 5.3 for a more precise description of this criterion.

5.2 Repeat Learning Under a Fixed Representation

The above framework can be extended to learning systems (such as ILP) that use a fixed representation during learning sessions.

The learning system is given an hypothesis language L that can describe target concepts in $\mathcal{H}$. We assume the existence of a universal linguistic bias generator G that, given a target space $\mathcal{H}$, and an hypothesis language L for it, returns a probability distribution $D_H = G(\mathcal{H}, L)$ over the target space. Any distribution consistent with Occam's razor can be taken as an example of such a generator. Such a distribution would assign a higher probability to hypotheses that can be expressed more simply in the hypothesis language.

It is assumed that the teacher has a predefined hypothesis language L_T, and that the bias generator gives the probability distribution $D_T = G(\mathcal{H}, L_T)$ over $\mathcal{H}$ for this language.

The learner has an initial hypothesis language L_1, giving the prior probability distribution $D_1 = G(\mathcal{H}, L_1)$ as before. The learning protocol for session n proceeds as before, but with the change that the learning algorithm's repeat–adjustment operator adjusts instead the hypothesis language L_n (using, for instance, predicate invention and retraction) to give language L_{n+1}, and thereby inducing a new distribution D_{n+1} over the target space.

The requirements for a repeat learner in this setting are the same as in Sect. 5.1, except that the performance improvement is achieved by successively improving the approximation L_n of the teacher's hypothesis language L_T.

5.3 A Criterion for Repeat Learning

A tentative set of conditions that a machine learning algorithm must satisfy in order to qualify as a repeat learning algorithm will now be described. The authors would like to make it clear that the necessity, sufficiency and satisfiability of these conditions have yet to be established. The conditions are related to the U–learnability criteria described in [8].

Let the distributions D_T, D_X have associated parameters $\nu_{D_T}, \nu_{D_X} \geq 0$ (for example, the parameters might be the greater of the mean and standard deviation of the distributions). The parameters may provide some indication of the difficulty of learning from the distributions.

Let $\text{LEARNTIME}(x) = x^c$ for some $c > 0$. Let $\text{IMPROVEMENT–DELAY}(x, y)$, $\text{LEARN–DELAY}(x, y)$, $\text{ERROR–BOUND}(x, y)$ be polynomial functions of x and y. Let X_m be an m-tuple of instances chosen randomly and independently from X according to D_X.

Define $E_{\mathcal{L}}(T, X_{m+1}, n) = 0$ in session n, if $\mathcal{L}$ correctly classifies (w.r.t T) instance x_{m+1}, given instances $\langle x_1, \ldots x_m \rangle$ labelled according to T, and $E_{\mathcal{L}}(T, X_{m+1}, n) = 1$ otherwise (where $X_{m+1} = \langle x_1, \ldots x_{m+1} \rangle$).

Time Complexity The average case time complexity of $\mathcal{L}$ in any learning session is bounded by $\text{LEARNTIME}(M)$, where M is the sum of $p(|x_i|)$ over the examples x_i seen to that point in that session. The time complexity of the repeat–adjustment operator r_L is unrestricted.

Correctness For all n, For all $m \geq \text{LEARN–DELAY}(\nu_{D_T}, \nu_{D_X})$:

$$\sum_{all(T_n, X_{m+1})} Pr_{D_T, D_X}(T_n, X_{m+1}) E_{\mathcal{L}}(T_n, X_{m+1}, n) < \text{ERROR–BOUND}(\frac{1}{m}, 1)$$

Improvement For all $n \geq \text{IMPROVEMENT–DELAY}(\nu_{D_T}, \nu_{D_X})$, For all $m \geq \text{LEARN–DELAY}(\nu_{D_T}, \nu_{D_X})$:

$$\sum_{all(T, X_{m+1})} Pr_{D_T, D_X}(T, X_{m+1}) E_{\mathcal{L}}(T, X_{m+1}, n) < \text{ERROR–BOUND}(\frac{1}{m}, \frac{1}{n})$$

6 Discussion

This paper has introduced a theoretical framework for machine learning a series of related concepts, which we call the *Repeat Learning* setting. This framework was extended to an ILP setting, and the possibility of using Predicate Invention under ILP to achieve the aims of the framework was discussed.

We have shown in experiment how Predicate invention under Repeat Learning can decrease the sample complexity requirements of an algorithm. However a comprehensive theoretical explanation of this is yet to be found. Surprisingly little experimental and theoretical evidence of the utility of Predicate Invention exists. The results of this paper indicate that Predicate Invention is useful under the Repeat Learning setting.

Many, indeed most, of the real–world domains in which ILP has been successful can be rephrased in the repeat learning setting. Consider, for instance, the Mutagenicity and Predictive Toxicology domains. Chemical bond and structure relationships learnt in early problems can be reused, and such relationships could potentially improve the accuracy of the algorithm in later problems.

Machine learning experiments in real–world domains aim to show that an algorithm is successful at learning a certain *type* of problem. This is only useful when there are other unsolved problems of the same type to which a successful algorithm can then be applied. Repeat Learning may be beneficial in such multiple–problem domains. There is clearly a need for further theoretical analysis of Repeat Learning in ILP.

7   FTP Site

The datasets used in the experiments described in this paper are available from anonymous ftp at: `ftp.cs.york.ac.uk/pub/ML_GROUP/Repeat/`

Acknowledgements

Thanks to David Page for vital input in discussions on this topic. This work was supported partly by the Esprit Long Term Research Action ILP II (project 20237), EPSRC grant GR/K57985 on Experiments with Distribution–based Machine Learning, an EPSRC Advanced Research Fellowship held by the second author and EPSRC postgraduate awards held by the first and third authors.

References

[1] J. Baxter. Theoretical models of learning to learn. In T. Mitchell and S. Thrun, editors, *Learning to Learn*. Kluwer, Boston, 1997.

[2] J. Goodacre. Inductive learning of chess rules using progol. Master's thesis, Oxford University, Oxford University Computing Laboratory, 1996.

[3] C. Ling. Inventing necessary theoretical terms in scientific discovery and inductive logic programming. Technical Report 302, Dept. of Comp. Sci., Univ. of Western Ontario, 1991.

[4] S. Muggleton. Predicate invention and utilisation. *Journal of Experimental and Theoretical Artificial Intelligence*, 6(1):127–130, 1994.

[5] S. Muggleton. Inverse entailment and Progol. *New Generation Computing*, 13:245–286, 1995.

[6] S. Muggleton. Learning from positive data. In *Proceedings of the Sixth Workshop on Inductive Logic Programming*, Stockholm, 1996.

[7] S. Muggleton and W. Buntine. Machine invention of first-order predicates by inverting resolution. In *Proceedings of the 5th International Conference on Machine Learning*, pages 339–352. Kaufmann, 1988.

[8] S. Muggleton and C. D. Page. A learnability model for Universal representations. In S. Wrobel, editor, *Proceedings of the 4th International Workshop on Inductive Logic Programming*, 1994.

[9] I. Stahl. Constructive induction in inductive logic programming: an overview. Technical report, Fakultat Informatik, Universitat Stuttgart, 1992.

[10] I. Stahl. Predicate invention in inductive logic programming. In L. De Raedt, editor, *Advances in Inductive Logic Programming*, pages 34–47. IOS Press, Ohmsha, Amsterdam, 1996.

[11] R. Wirth and P. O'Rorke. Constraints on predicate invention. In *Proceedings of the 8th International Workshop on Machine Learning*, pages 457–461. Kaufmann, 1991.

Normal Programs and
Multiple Predicate Learning*

Leonardo Fogel   Gerson Zaverucha

Coordenação dos Programas de Pós-Graduação em Engenharia
Universidade Federal do Rio de Janeiro - COPPE/UFRJ
Caixa Postal 68511, CEP 21945-970
Rio de Janeiro - RJ - Brasil
Phone: +55-21-590-2552
FAX: +55-21-290-6626
e-mail:{lfogel, gerson}@cos.ufrj.br

Abstract. We study the problem of inducing normal programs of multiple predicates in the empirical ILP setting. We identify a class of normal logic programs that can be handled and induced in a top-down manner by an intensional system. We propose an algorithm called NMPL that improves the multiple predicate learning system MPL and extends its language from definite to this class of normal programs. Finally, we discuss the cost of the MPL's refinement algorithm and present theoretical and experimental results showing that NMPL can be as effective as MPL and is computationally cheaper than it.

1 Introduction

Most ILP systems restrict their language to definite or semi-definite programs [6, 9]. The subsumption mechanism [10] introduces a syntactic notion of generality between definite clauses that can be used to prune the search space of hypotheses. These properties form the basis of most ILP systems that induce definite programs and also play an important role in the computation of heuristics. However, they do not hold for normal programs in general [4].

Recently, there has been increased interest in the multiple predicate learning problem [11] resulting in a number of systems, including MPL [11], MULT_ICN [8] and TRACY[not] [2]. This problem can be stated as follows: given background knowledge B containing definitions of predicates in normal or definite clauses and a training set E divided into positive E^+ and negative E^- examples (ground instances) of multiple predicates $p_1, ..., p_n$, the task is to find a normal or definite hypothesis H such that $B \cup H \vdash E^+$ and $\forall e^- \in E^-$, $B \cup H \not\vdash e^-$.

We improve the intensional system MPL that induces definite programs of multiple predicates. We propose an algorithm called NMPL which cuts much of MPL's computational cost and extends its language to normal programs. Since special care is needed because of the non-monotonicity of normal programs, we

---

* This work is part of the CNPq/ProTeM 3 project ICOM. The authors are partially supported by CAPES and CNPq, respectively.

propose a top-down mechanism for inducing normal clauses. Consequently, the gain heuristic needs to be changed.

The paper is organized as follows. In section 2, we discuss the pruning properties of subsumption, that do not hold for normal programs in general. In section 3, we identify a class of normal programs that obey these properties. In section 4, we propose a generic algorithm for inducing this class of normal programs, and training sets for cheaper computation of heuristics. In section 5, we present the NMPL algorithm. In section 6, we compare the two systems and, in section 7, we briefly conclude.

2 The search space of clauses

Our approach is based on the standard definitions of normal programs and SLDNF-resolution [7]. As well as other intensional systems, our algorithm is based on the following definition of coverage:

Definition 1 (Coverage [13]). Given background knowledge B, hypothesis H and example set E, we say that H covers an example $e \in E$ with respect to B if $B \cup H \vdash e$. The function covers(B, H, E) is defined as:
$$\text{covers}(B, H, E) = \{e \in E \mid B \cup H \vdash e\}$$

We also say that a clause C covers an example $e \in E$ if $B \cup H \cup \{C\} \vdash e$. Most ILP systems are based on the following definition of subsumption to search the space of clauses:

Definition 2 (Subsumption [10]). Let C and D be clauses. We say that C subsumes D if there is a substitution θ such that $C\theta \subseteq D$.

As pointed out by Lavrač and Džeroski [6], subsumption introduces a syntactic notion of generality. Given clauses C and D, we say that C is a generalization of D, denoted by $C < D$, if C subsumes D and D does not subsume C. In the same case, we also say that D is a specialization (or refinement) of C. They have also noted that for the task of inducing definite programs, subsumption can be used to prune large parts of the search space of clauses:

- when generalizing a clause C to D ($D < C$), all the examples covered by C will be also covered by D, since if $B \cup H \cup \{C\} \vdash e$ then $B \cup H \cup \{D\} \vdash e$.
- when specializing a clause C to D ($C < D$), any example not covered by C will not be covered by D either, since if $B \cup H \cup \{C\} \not\vdash e$ then $B \cup H \cup \{D\} \not\vdash e$.

The first (resp. second) property can be used to prune the search of more general (resp. specific) clauses when e is a negative (resp. positive) example. However, these two properties do not hold for normal programs [4]. Even if the clause being generalized (or specialized) is definite, subsumption can not be used to prune the search space if the given hypothesis is a normal program. For a simple example,

Example 1. Consider background knowledge $B = \{a(1), a(2), b(1), s(1,2)\}$, hypothesis $H = \{(p(X) \leftarrow q(X), s(X,Y), \neg q(Y))\}$ and example set $E = \{p(1), p(2)\}$. Consider clauses $C = q(X) \leftarrow a(X)$ and $D = q(X) \leftarrow a(X), b(X)$. Then, $C < D$ and $B \cup H \not\vdash p(1)$ and also $B \cup H \cup \{C\} \not\vdash p(1)$, but $B \cup H \cup \{D\} \vdash p(1)$.

These properties do not hold in the extensional coverage approach either [10]. Our first contribution in this paper is to identify a large class of normal programs that obey these properties, in an extended formulation:

- when generalizing a clause C to D $(D < C)$: if $B \cup H \not\vdash e$ and $B \cup H \cup \{C\} \vdash e$ then $B \cup H \cup \{D\} \vdash e$; if $B \cup H \vdash e$ and $B \cup H \cup \{C\} \not\vdash e$ then $B \cup H \cup \{D\} \not\vdash e$.
- when specializing a clause C to D $(C < D)$: if $B \cup H \not\vdash e$ and $B \cup H \cup \{C\} \not\vdash e$ then $B \cup H \cup \{D\} \not\vdash e$; if $B \cup H \vdash e$ and $B \cup H \cup \{C\} \vdash e$ then $B \cup H \cup \{D\} \vdash e$.

Consequently, for that class of normal programs, subsumption can be used to prune the search space of clauses. We identify it in the next section.

3 Pruning the search space of normal clauses

In this section, we do not distinguish between background knowledge and hypothesis, and denote by P the program $B \cup H$, on behalf of simplicity. Let us recall some useful definitions:

Definition 3 (Dependency [1]). Consider a program P.

- The *dependency graph* D_P *for* P is a directed graph with signed edges. Its nodes are the predicate symbols occurring in P. For every clause in P which uses predicate p in its head and predicate q in a positive (resp. negative) literal in its body, there is a positive (resp. negative) edge (q, p) in D_P.
- We say that p *depends positively* (resp. *negatively*) *on* q if there is a path in D_P from p to q with only positive edges (resp. at least one negative edge).
- We say that p *depends evenly* (resp. *oddly*) *on* q if there is a path in D_P from p to q with an even (resp. odd) number of negative edges.

Definition 4 (Strictness [1]). A program P is called *strict* if for no predicate symbols p and q of P, p depends both evenly and oddly on q.

Definition 5 (Call-consistency [12]). A program is called *call-consistent* if no predicate depends oddly on itself.

For an example, the program $P = \{(a \leftarrow b, \neg c), (b \leftarrow a, \neg c), (c \leftarrow \neg a)$ is strict and call-consistent. In fact, strictness and call-consistency are enough to attain our aim. We postulate an infinite 'universal language' (cf. Kunen [5]) in which all programs and queries are expressed, because it gives rise to simpler formulations of results.

Definition 6. Let p and q be n-ary predicate symbols. We denote by $p \geq \neg q$ the set of all ground instances of the clause $p(X_1, ..., X_n) \leftarrow \neg q(X_1, ..., X_n)$ with respect to that universal language.

Note that $p \geq \neg q$ is a ground program that can be interpreted propositionally. If p does not appear in the head of any clause in a program P, then, for ground terms $a_1, ..., a_n$, $P \cup (p \geq \neg q) \vdash p(a_1, ..., a_n)$ if and only if $P \cup (p \geq \neg q) \not\vdash q(a_1, ..., a_n)$. Thus, the reader can easily verify:

Proposition 7. Consider a normal program P, a ground atom A and a clause $C = H \leftarrow L_1, ..., \neg q(Y_1, ..., Y_m), ..., L_k$. Consider m-ary predicate symbols p_1 and p_2 that do not appear in P, C or A. Let $D = H \leftarrow L_1, ..., \neg p_1(Y_1, ..., Y_m), ..., L_k$. Then, $P \cup \{C\} \vdash A$ if and only if $P \cup \{D\} \cup (p_1 \geq \neg p_2) \cup (p_2 \geq \neg q) \vdash A$.

The intuition behind proposition 7 is that given a program P, strict and call-consistent, and a ground atom A, there exists a program P' in which every path from a node q to a node p in $D_{P'}$ has the same number of negative edges, and $P \vdash A$ if and only if $P' \vdash A$. It gives rise to a simpler proof of the following:

Proposition 8. Consider a program P strict and call-consistent, and ground atoms $A = p(a_1, ..., a_n)$ and $B = q(b_1, ..., b_m)$. Then,

1. If p depends oddly on q then $P \not\vdash A$ implies $P \cup \{B\} \not\vdash A$
2. If p depends evenly on q then $P \vdash A$ implies $P \cup \{B\} \vdash A$

Proof (1). Without loss of generality we can assume that every path in D_P from p to q has the same number of negatives edges, namely, $2n + 1$. Then the proof follows trivially by induction on n.

(2). Follows from (1) and the Closed World Assumption. □

The reader easily verifies that if p does not depend on q then $P \vdash A$ if and only if $P \cup \{B\} \vdash A$. Therefore, we take into account only predicates that have some dependency.

Proposition 9. Consider a program P, a clause $C = q(X_1, ..., X_m) \leftarrow L_1, ..., L_k$ and a ground atom $A = p(a_1, ..., a_n)$. Suppose $P \cup \{C\}$ is strict and call-consistent.

1. If p depends oddly on q then $P \not\vdash A$ implies $P \cup \{C\} \not\vdash A$.
2. If p depends evenly on q then $P \vdash A$ implies $P \cup \{C\} \vdash A$.

Proof (1). Suppose $P \cup \{C\} \vdash A$. Without loss of generality, we can assume $L_1 = \neg r$ and r does not appear in P. Following definition 3 and proposition 8, p depends evenly on r and $P \cup \{C\} \cup \{r\} \vdash A$. But C became irrelevant; consequently $P \vdash A$.

(2). Follows from (1) and the Closed World Assumption. □

Proposition 10. Consider a program P, clauses $C_1 = q(X_1, ..., X_m) \leftarrow L_1, ..., L_k$ and C_2 such that $C_1 < C_2$, and a ground atom $A = p(a_1, ..., a_n)$. Suppose $P \cup \{C_2\}$ is strict and call-consistent.

1. If $P \vdash A$ then $P \cup \{C_1\} \vdash A$ implies $P \cup \{C_2\} \vdash A$.
2. If $P \not\vdash A$ then $P \cup \{C_1\} \not\vdash A$ implies $P \cup \{C_2\} \not\vdash A$.

Proof (1). If p depends evenly on q, from proposition 9, $P \cup \{C_2\} \vdash A$. If p depends oddly on q, assume $P \cup \{C_2\} \not\vdash A$. From proposition 9, $P \cup \{C_2\} \cup \{C_1\} \not\vdash A$. Since $P \cup \{C_1\} \vdash \{C_2\}$, one has $P \cup \{C_1\} \not\vdash A$.

(2). Follows from (1) and the Closed World Assumption. □

Proposition 10 guarantees those pruning properties of subsumption for strict and call-consistent programs.

4 Training sets of normal programs

Our second contribution in this paper is to propose training sets for the top-down induction of strict and call-consistent programs. We discuss how these sets play an important role in the computation of the heuristics and, consequently, in the cost of the refinement algorithm.

Top-down systems usually search the hypothesis space using a refinement operator based on subsumption:

Definition 11 (Refinement operator [13]). Given a language $\mathcal{L}$, a refinement operator ρ maps a clause $C = A \leftarrow L_1, ..., L_k$ to a set of clauses $\rho(C) = \{D \in \mathcal{L} \mid D = A \leftarrow L_1, ..., L_k, L_{k+1}\}$.

When refining a clause C, a refinement operator considers only the literals that are syntactically relevant for being added to the body of C.

Definition 12. Given a clause $C = A \leftarrow L_1, ..., L_k$, a positive literal L_i is (syntactically) relevant if at least one variable of L_i appears in $A \leftarrow L_1, ..., L_{i-1}$. A negative literal L_i is relevant if every variable of L_i appears in $A \leftarrow L_1, ..., L_{i-1}$.

The following is a generic top-down algorithm [6] for the induction of definite programs, that performs a hill-climbing search based on the refinement operator.

Algorithm 1
Input: background knowledge B and example set E.
initialize $H := \emptyset$ and $T := E$ { training set }
repeat { covering }
  initialize $C := A \leftarrow$ and $T_c := T$ { local training set }
  repeat { refinement }
    find the best clause $D \in \rho(C)$
    assign $C := D$ and $T_c := \text{covers}(B, H \cup \{C\}, T_c)$
  until $T_c^- = \emptyset$
  assign $H := H \cup \{C\}$ and $T := T - T_c$
until $T^+ = \emptyset$
Output: hypothesis H.

Basically, the task of finding the best refinement of a clause C is driven by heuristics. For an example, consider that a clause $D \in \rho(C)$ covers $n^+(D)$ positive examples from the local training set T_c and $n^-(D)$ negative ones. A simple heuristic is the Laplace estimate $f(D) = \frac{n^+(D)+1}{n^+(D)+n^-(D)+2}$ [3]. Then, the clause $D \in \rho(C)$ with the greatest $f(D)$ is considered the best refinement of C.

In fact, the search of refinements is the most expensive task in ILP. But, an efficient management of the local training sets cuts its cost. Clearly, computing

$f(D)$, for each clause $D \in \rho(C)$, from the local training set T_c is much cheaper than computing it from the training set T, since $T_c \subseteq T$. Then, our effort is to propose training sets for strict and call-consistent hypotheses, and show that they can be managed in order to cut the cost of the heuristics.

The reader can verify that algorithm 1 works only for definite (or semi-definite) programs, since it does not take into account the non-monotonicity of normal hypotheses. The following algorithm is an extension to algorithm 1 that handles strict and call-consistent hypotheses.

Algorithm 2
Input: background knowledge B and example set E.
initialize $H := \emptyset$ and $T := E$
initialize $N := \emptyset$ {aux. training set }
repeat
   initialize $C := A \leftarrow$ and $T_c := T$
   initialize $N_c := N$ { aux. local training set }
   repeat { refinement }
     find the best clause $D \in \rho(C)$
     assign $C := D$ and $T_c := \text{covers}(B, H \cup \{C\}, T_c)$
     assign $N_c := N_c - \text{covers}(B, H \cup \{C\}, N_c)$
   until $T_c^- = \emptyset$
   assign $H := H \cup \{C\}$ and $T := (T - T_c) \cup N_c$
   assign $N := (N - N_c) \cup T_c$
until $T^+ = \emptyset$
Output: hypothesis H.

Algorithm 2 introduces a new training set N which is the set of examples from E covered by H, i.e. $N = \text{covers}(B, H, E) = E - T$, and a new local training set N_c which is the set of examples from N that are not covered by C, i.e. $N_c = N - \text{covers}(B, H \cup \{C\}, N)$, because of the non-monotonicity.

We now prove the soundness of algorithm 2, i.e. if algorithm 2 outputs a hypothesis H then $B \cup H \vdash E^+$ and $\forall e^- \in E^-$, $B \cup H \not\vdash e^-$, in order to ensure that the training and the local training sets are correctly handled.

Proposition 13. If algorithm 2 constructs a clause C then $T_c = \text{covers}(B, H \cup \{C\}, T)$ and $N_c = N - \text{covers}(B, H \cup \{C\}, N)$.

Proof. If $C = A \leftarrow$ then the proposition follows trivially. Consider $C < D$ and let $T_1 = \text{covers}(B, H \cup \{D\}, T)$ and $N_1 = N - \text{covers}(B, H \cup \{D\}, N)$. From proposition 10, $T_1 \subseteq T_c$ and $N_1 \subseteq N_c$. Then $T_1 = \text{covers}(B, H \cup \{D\}, T_c)$ and

$$N_1 \subseteq N_c - \text{covers}(B, H \cup \{D\}, N) \subseteq N - \text{covers}(B, H \cup \{D\}, N)$$
$$N_1 = N_c - \text{covers}(B, H \cup \{D\}, N) = N_c - \text{covers}(B, H \cup \{D\}, N_c)$$

After assigning $C := D$, the algorithm assigns:

$$T_c := \text{covers}(B, H \cup \{C\}, T_c) \quad \text{and} \quad N_c := N_c - \text{covers}(B, H \cup \{D\}, N_c)$$

which ensures the proposition holds for every clause C such that $(A \leftarrow) < C$. $\square$

Proposition 14. Algorithm 2 is sound.

Proof. We first prove that given H, one has $T = E - \text{covers}(B, H, E)$ and $N = \text{covers}(B, H, E)$. For $H = \emptyset$, it holds trivially. Consider $H \cup \{C\}$, then

$$(T - T_c) \cup N_c = (T - \text{covers}(B, H \cup \{C\}, T)) \cup (N - \text{covers}(B, H \cup \{C\}, N)) =$$
$$= (T \cup N) - (\text{covers}(B, H \cup \{C\}, T) \cup \text{covers}(B, H \cup \{C\}, N)) =$$
$$= E - \text{covers}(B, H \cup \{C\}, E)$$
$$(N - N_c) \cup T_c = \text{covers}(B, H \cup \{C\}, N) \cup \text{covers}(B, H \cup \{C\}, T) =$$
$$= \text{covers}(B, H \cup \{C\}, E)$$

After assigning $H := H \cup \{C\}$, the algorithm assigns:

$$T := (T - T_c) \cup N_c \text{ and } N := (N - N_c) \cup T_c = E - T$$

If the algorithm finishes ($T^+ = \emptyset$) then $N^+ = E^+$ and $N^- = \emptyset$ ($T_c^- = \emptyset$). $\square$

5 The NMPL algorithm

Our last contribution in this paper is to present an intensional top-down algorithm, called Non-monotonic Multiple Predicate Learner (NMPL), that is based on MPL and improves it in two ways: its refinement algorithm is cheaper than and can be as effective as MPL's one; it extends the function-free language of MPL from definite to strict and call-consistent programs.

NMPL
Input: background knowledge B and example set E.
$H := \emptyset$, $T := E$ and $N := \emptyset$
repeat
  $C := p_m(X_1, ..., X_{a_m}) \leftarrow$
  for i $= 1$ to n do
    $C_i := p_i(X_1, ..., X_{a_i}) \leftarrow$
    $T_i := T$ and $N_i := N$
  repeat
    find the best clause $D \in \rho(C)$
    let $D = p_m(X_1, ..., X_{a_m}) \leftarrow L_1, ..., L_k$
    assign $C := D$
    for i $= 1$ to n do
      $C_i := p_i(X_1, ..., X_{a_i}) \leftarrow L_1, ..., L_k$
      assign $T_i := \text{covers}(B, H \cup \{C_i\}, T_i)$
      assign $N_i := N_i - \text{covers}(B, H \cup \{C_i\}, N_i)$
  until $\exists i$ such that $T_i^- = \emptyset$
  let C_i be the best clause that $T_i^- = \emptyset$
  assign $H := H \cup \{C_i\}$
  assign $T := (T - T_i) \cup N_i$ and $N := (N - N_i) \cup T_i$
until $T^+ = \emptyset$
Output: hypothesis H.

Consider the system is provided example set E of predicates $p_1, ..., p_n$ of arities $a_1, ..., a_n$ respectively and let p_m be the predicate of the greatest arity $a_m = \max(a_1, ..., a_n)$. The refinement graph of H is constructed considering these n target predicates, since H has to be strict and call-consistent only with respect to them. The refinement loop initializes the $n + 1$ unit clauses:

$$C := p_m(X_1, ..., X_{a_m}) \leftarrow$$
$$\forall i = 1, ..., n, C_i := p_i(X_1, ..., X_{a_i}) \leftarrow$$

where $X_1, ..., X_{a_m}$ are distinct variables. The task of finding the best clause $D \in \rho(C)$ is driven by heuristics. Suppose $D = p_m(X_1, ..., X_{a_m}) \leftarrow L_1$; the system assigns:

$$\forall i = 1, ..., n, D_i := p_i(X_1, ..., X_{a_i}) \leftarrow L_1$$

with the corresponding bindings of the variables from the head to the body (which is a kind of head replacement of D). Let

$$T_{D_i} = \text{covers}(B, H \cup \{D_i\}, T_i) \quad \text{and} \quad N_{D_i} = N_i - \text{covers}(B, H \cup \{D_i\}, N_i)$$

T_{D_i} denotes the set of examples from T covered by D_i, and N_{D_i} denotes the set of examples from N not covered by D_i. Then, the heuristic for evaluating the refinement D of C is:

$$f(D) = \max_{i=1,...,n} \left(\frac{|T_{D_i}^+| + 1}{|T_{D_i}| + |N_{D_i}| + 2} \right)$$

based on the Laplace estimate [3]. The best refinement of C is the clause $D \in \rho(C)$ with the greatest $f(D)$.

For computing $f(D)$, for each clause $D \in \rho(C)$, the system considers only the corresponding clauses D_i such that $H \cup \{D_i\}$ is strict and call-consistent, and D_i has no irrelevant literals. Checking up on the strictness and call-consistency of $H \cup \{D_i\}$ takes $\mathcal{O}(n^3)$. If there is not any D_i that follows these conditions, the refinement D is dismissed.

The refinement loop finishes when it finds a clause D_i that covers only positive examples. Then it is added to the current hypothesis and the dependency graph is updated. The soundness of NMPL follows trivially from the soundness of algorithm 2.

6 Comparing NMPL with MPL

6.1 The refinement algorithm

Instead of refining a clause of the form $A \leftarrow L_1, ..., L_k$, MPL refines a clause of the form $\leftarrow L_1, ..., L_k$ and then adds a literal to its head.

Definition 15. Given a language $\mathcal{L}$, the *body refinement operator* ρ_B maps a clause $C = \leftarrow L_1, .., L_k$ to a set of clauses $\rho_B(C) = \{D \in \mathcal{L} \mid D = \leftarrow L_1, .., L_k, L_{k+1}\}$. The *head refinement operator* ρ_H maps a clause $C = \leftarrow L_1, .., L_k$ to a set of clauses $\rho_H(C) = \{D \in \mathcal{L} \mid D = A \leftarrow L_1, .., L_k\}$.

MPL's refinement procedure, called Findbest, is sketched as follows:

```
Findbest(B, H, E)
Beam := { true }
while improvement possible do
    select best Body from Beam
    BRefinements := ρ_B(Body)
    for all Bo ∈ BRefinements do
        assign val(Bo) := max{val(C) | C ∈ ρ_H(Bo)}
    Beam := b best bodies on Beam ∪ BRefinements
return best clause on Beam
```

Consider a clause $C = p_i(X_1, ..., X_{a_i}) \leftarrow L_1, ..., L_k$ and training set T. Let T_{p_i} be the set T restricted to the predicate p_i. Let $n_l^{\pm}(C) = \text{covers}(B, H \cup \{C\}, T_{p_i}^{\pm})$ and $n_g^{\pm}(C) = \text{covers}(B, H \cup \{C\}, T^{\pm} - T_{p_i}^{\pm})$. Then,

$$\text{val}(C) := w_1 \frac{n_l^+(C) + 1}{n_l^+(C) + n_l^-(C) + 2} + w_2 \frac{n_g^+(C) + 1}{n_g^+(C) + n_g^-(C) + 2}$$

Computing the heuristics for each body and head refinements of a given clause is costly because it has to be computed from the whole training set. Thus, the refinement algorithm of NMPL is cheaper than Findbest, since NMPL computes the heuristics with respect to the local training sets, which are subsets of the training sets, and for each iteration of its refinement loop, the new local training sets are subsets of the old ones, i.e. if $C < D$ then $T_D \subseteq T_C \subseteq T$ and $N_D \subseteq N_C \subseteq N$, and if we restrict the language to definite programs, as MPL does, we have $N_D = N_C = \emptyset$.

6.2 Experimental results

In order to show that NMPL can be as effective as MPL, we present here two experiments, performed using a preliminary implementation of NMPL in PRO-LOG. All the examples and background knowledge were extracted from [11].

Experiment 1 Aimed at learning the definitions of *ancestor, male-ancestor* (m_a) and *female-ancestor* (f_a) from *male, female* and *parent*. NMPL induced:

```
ancestor(X,Y) :- parent(X,Y).
ancestor(X,Y) :- parent(X,Z), ancestor(Z,Y).
m_a(X,Y) :- male(X), ancestor(X,Y).
f_a(X,Y) :- female(X), ancestor(X,Y).
```

Experiment 2 Aimed at learning the definitions of *male-ancestor* (m_a) and *female-ancestor* (f_a) from *father* and *mother*. NMPL induced:

```
m_a(X,Y) :- father(X,Y).
f_a(X,Y) :- mother(X,Y).
m_a(X,Y) :- father(X,Z), m_a(Z,Y).
```

```
f_a(X,Y) :- mother(X,Z), m_a(Z,Y).
m_a(X,Y) :- father(X,Z), f_a(Z,Y).
f_a(X,Y) :- mother(X,Z), f_a(Z,Y).
```

Some other experiments, concerning normal programs, are still being performed. They will be considered in future works.

7 Conclusions

We discussed the pruning properties of subsumption with respect to normal programs and proposed training sets for the top-down induction of strict and call-consistent hypothesis. We have also presented an algorithm for multiple predicate learning, called NMPL, which is based on MPL and that improves it in the following ways: the sets of training examples are iteratively constructed; the language of definite clauses is extended to normal clauses.

References

1. Apt, K. R. and Bol, R. N., Logic Programming and Negation: A Survey, *J. Logic Programming* 19, 20: 9-71 (1994).
2. Bergadano, F., Gunetti, D., Nicosia, M. and Ruffo, G., Learning Logic Programs with Negation as Failure, in: S. Muggleton (ed.), *Proceedings of the 5th International Workshop on Inductive Logic Programming*, 1995.
3. Džeroski, S. and Bratko, I., Handling Noise in Inductive Logic Programming, in: S. Muggleton (ed.), *Proceedings of the 2nd International Workshop on Inductive Logic Programming*, 1992.
4. Flach, P. A., A Framework for Inductive Logic Programming, in: S. Muggleton (ed.), *Inductive Logic Programming*, Academic Press, 1992, pp. 193-212.
5. Kunen, K., Signed Data Dependencies in Logic Programs, *J. Logic Programming* 7: 231-246 (1989).
6. Lavrač, N. and Džeroski, S., *Inductive Logic Programming: Techniques and Applications*, Ellis Horwood, 1994.
7. Lloyd, J. W., *Foundations of Logic Programming*, 2nd edition, Springer, Berlin, 1987.
8. Martin, L. and Vrain, C., MULT_ICN: an Empirical Multiple Predicate Learner, in: S. Muggleton (ed.), *Proceedings of the 5th International Workshop on Inductive Logic Programming*, 1995.
9. Muggleton, S. and De Raedt, L., Inductive Logic Programming: Theory and Methods, *J. Logic Programming* 19, 20: 629-679 (1994).
10. Plotkin, G. D., A Note on Inductive Generalization, in: B. Meltzer and D. Michie (eds.), *Machine Intelligence* 5, Elsevier North Holland, NY, 1970, pp. 153-163.
11. De Raedt, L., Lavrač, N. and Džeroski, S., Multiple Predicate Learning, in: *Proceedings of the 13th International Joint Conference on Artificial Intelligence*, Morgan Kaufman, 1993, pp. 1037-1042.
12. Sato, T., Completed Logic Programs and their Consistency, *J. Logic Programming* 9: 33-44 (1990).
13. Shapiro, E. Y., *Algorithmic Program Debugging*, MIT Press, 1983.

Strongly Typed Inductive Concept Learning

P.A. Flach, C. Giraud-Carrier and J.W. Lloyd

Department of Computer Science, University of Bristol
Merchant Venturers Building, Woodland Road, Bristol BS8 1UB, United Kingdom
{flach,cgc,jwl}@cs.bris.ac.uk   http://www.cs.bris.ac.uk/Research/MachineLearning/

Abstract. In this paper we argue that the use of a language with a type system, together with higher-order facilities and functions, provides a suitable basis for knowledge representation in inductive concept learning and, in particular, illuminates the relationship between attribute-value learning and inductive logic programming (ILP). Individuals are represented by closed terms: tuples of constants in the case of attribute-value learning; arbitrarily complex terms in the case of ILP. To illustrate the point, we take some learning tasks from the machine learning and ILP literature and represent them in Escher, a typed, higher-order, functional logic programming language being developed at the University of Bristol. We argue that the use of a type system provides better ways to discard meaningless hypotheses on syntactic grounds and encompasses many *ad hoc* approaches to declarative bias.

1. Motivation and scope

Inductive concept learning consists of finding mappings of individuals (or objects) into discrete classes. Individuals and induced mappings are represented in some formal language. Historically, attribute-value languages (AVL) have been most popular in research in machine learning. In an attribute-value language, individuals are described by tuples of attribute-value pairs, where each attribute represents some characteristic of the individuals (e.g., shape, colour, etc.). Although very useful, attribute-value languages are also quite restrictive. In particular, it is not possible to induce relations explicitly in that framework. In recent years, researchers have thus proposed the use of first-order logic as a more expressive representation language. In particular, the programming language Prolog has become the almost exclusive representation mechanism in inductive logic programming (ILP).

The move to Prolog alleviates many of the limitations of attribute-value languages. However, traditional application of Prolog within ILP has also caused the loss of one critical element inherent in attribute-value languages: the notion of type. Implicitly, each attribute in AVL is a type, which can take on a number of possible values. This characteristic of AVL makes it possible to construct efficient learners since the only way to define mappings of individuals to classes consists of constructing expressions (e.g., conjunctions) that extract a particular attribute (i.e., tuple projection) and tests its value against some value of that type. On the other hand, Prolog has no type system. All characteristics of individuals are captured by predicates. As a result, the way to construct mappings becomes rather unconstrained and a number of *ad hoc* mechanisms (e.g., linked clauses, mode declarations, determinacy, etc.) have to be introduced to restore the tractability of the learning problem.

A major aim of this paper is to demonstrate the usefulness of a strongly typed language for inductive concept learning, where we define a *strongly typed language* as one having a fully-fledged type system. We also propose that the natural extension of attribute-value learning to first- and higher-order consists in representing individuals by terms. Hence, individuals may have arbitrary structure, including simple tuples (as in the attribute-value learning case), lists, sets and indeed any composite type. This provides us with a unified view on

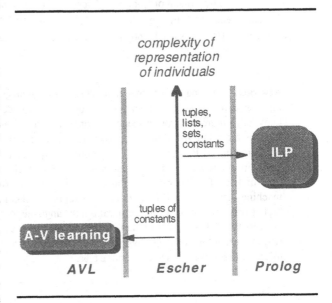

Fig. 1. The relation between attribute-value learning and ILP is illuminated by viewing it through a strongly typed language such as Escher. One of the main differences lies in the complexity of the terms representing individuals.

attribute-value learning and inductive logic programming, in which a typed language such as Escher[1] (a typed, higher-order, functional logic programming language being developed at the University of Bristol) acts as the unifying language (Fig. 1).

At Bristol, we have begun the implementation of a decision-tree learner, generalised to handle the constructs of the Escher language. Several of the illustrative examples below were run on this learner and the results produced are reported here. Full details about the learning system, its implementation, and the results of some larger-scale practical experiments will be reported elsewhere.

The paper is organised as follows. Section 2 describes Escher, the programming language which serves as a vehicle for the implementation of the aforementioned extension. Section 3 contains a number of illustrative learning tasks reformulated in Escher. In Section 4 we discuss the main implications of our approach for inductive logic programming, and Section 5 contains some conclusions.

---

[1] M.C. Escher® is a registered trademark of Cordon Art B.V., Baarn, Nederland. Used by permission. All rights reserved.

2. Elements of Escher

This section highlights the main features of the Escher language [3] and assumes familiarity with Prolog. We mainly deal with list-processing functions. It should be noted that the syntax of Escher is compatible with the syntax of Haskell (a popular and influential functional programming language). Consequently, Escher programs may look uncomfortably unfamiliar to Prolog aficionados (lowercase variables, constants starting with a capital), but we hope the reader will be able to abstract away from syntax.

The Escher definition of list membership is as follows (y : z stands for the list with head y and tail z, == is the equality predicate, and | | is disjunction).

```
member::(a,[a])->Bool;
member(x,[]) =
  False;
member(x,y:z) =
  (x==y) ||
  member(x,z);
```

The first statement defines the signature of member as a function taking a pair of arguments, an element and a list of elements (a is a type variable) and mapping them into the type Bool, which is a built-in type with data constructors True and False. The definition is inductive on the second argument. If this is the empty list, then the function maps to False; if it is non-empty, then the function maps to the truth-value of the disjunction in the last statement. Prolog programmers will recognise this last statement as essentially the Prolog definition of member.

Here is the Escher function to concatenate two lists:

```
concat::([a],[a])->[a];
concat([],x) =
  x;
concat(x:y,z) =
  x:concat(y,z);
```

As can be seen from the signature, concat is a function rather than a predicate. It corresponds to the Prolog append predicate with input-output mode append(+X,?Y,-Z). (Notice that the first argument must be instantiated in order to select the right statement.)

The Escher function corresponding to append(?X,?Y,+Z), with the list to be split as the third argument, looks as follows (&& stands for conjunction):

```
split::([a],[a],[a])->Bool;
split(x,y,[]) =
  x==[] && y==[];
split(x,y,u:w) =
  (x==[] && y==u:w) ||
  exists \v -> x==u:v && split(v,y,w);
```

Notice the explicit existential quantification of local variables ('exists \v ->' should be read 'there exists a v such that').

It is also possible to get the Escher equivalent of append(?X,?Y,?Z). In that case, the third argument is no longer used as the induction argument and the function is defined by a single statement.

```
append::([a],[a],[a])->Bool;
append(x,y,z) =
    (x==[] && y==z) ||
    exists \u v w -> x==u:v && z==u:w && append(v,y,w);
```

Notice the close correspondence with the Prolog definition.

Escher computations proceed by rewriting terms to simpler expressions. If s is the goal term and t is the answer term of a computation, then s==t is a logical consequence of the program. For instance, the goal term concat([1,2],[3]) reduces, via 1:concat([2],[3]) and 1:2:concat([],[3]), to the answer term [1,2,3]. The goal term split(x,y,[2,3]) reduces to the following answer term:

```
(x==[] && y==[2,3]) ||
    (x==[2] && y==[3]) ||
    (x==[2,3] && y==[])
```

From a Prolog perspective, Escher computations provide all answers at once. Note however that there is no backtracking, and no failure (the Escher equivalent of failure is to return the answer False).

Further features of Escher include facilities for representing (extensional and intensional) sets and a full range of set-processing functions. A set is identified with a predicate, its characteristic function. As an example of an intensional set, the set comprehension

```
{s | likes(Fred,s)}
```

where likes has the signature likes::(Person,Sport)->Bool, denotes the set of sports that Fred likes. Sets play a crucial role in the representation of ILP examples.

From an ILP perspective, Escher provides the following advantages over Prolog. First of all, no additional constructs such as ij-determinacy or integrity constraints are needed to specify that certain relations are functional. Escher can deal with functions and predicates in a unified way. Secondly, this leads to a more uniform schema for the function that is learned: if there are several statements making up the definition of a function, these are always mutually exclusive by virtue of a particular input argument. For instance, in the definition of member above we have two cases: either the second argument is the empty list (in which case member returns False) or it isn't, in which case we evaluate a disjunction. Notice that the Prolog definition of member does not allow clause indexing on the second argument.

The most important feature of Escher in the present context is its type system, which not only restricts possible instantiations of variables, but more importantly constrains the hypothesis language because every type carries with it a set of operations. For instance, projections are associated with tuple types; list membership, nth element selection and list length are associated with list types; set membership and cardinality are associated with set types; and so on. In the next section we illustrate this by representing various well-known learning tasks in Escher.

3. Representing learning tasks in Escher

We start with representing in Escher a typical attribute-value learning task which involves learning the concept of playing, or not playing, tennis, according to the weather [4]. In attribute-value learning, individuals are tuples (elements of a cartesian product) of atomic values. Translated to Escher, this means the definition of a tuple type, which is the domain of the function to be learned, and a data type for each attribute. In the following, the keyword data indicates the declaration of a type and the data constructors of that type, and type indicates a type synonym. We want to learn the definition of the function playTennis.

```
data Outlook = Sunny | Overcast | Rain;
data Temperature = Hot | Mild | Cool;
data Humidity = High | Normal | Low;
data Wind = Strong | Medium | Weak;

type Weather = (Outlook,Temperature,Humidity,Wind)

playTennis::Weather->Bool;
```

The examples each specify an input-output pair for the function to be learned:

```
playTennis(Overcast,Hot,High,Weak) = True;
playTennis(Sunny,Hot,High,Weak) = False;
...
```

In this setting, our learning system finds the following definition.

```
playTennis(w) =
    if (outlookP(w)==Sunny && humidityP(w)==High) then False else
    if (outlookP(w)==Rain && windP(w)==Strong) then False else True;
```

Here, outlookP is the projection function returning the value of the Outlook attribute, humidityP the projection function returning the value of the Humidity attribute, and so on. Their definitions follow in a straightforward way from the type definitions. For instance, outlookP could be defined as follows:

```
outlookP::Weather->Outlook;
outlookP(o,t,h,w) = o;
```

Clearly such definitions could be provided in a pre-processing stage.

It is worthwhile to reflect for a moment on how the hypothesis language is largely determined by the type definitions above. The induced function is of the form playTennis(w) = *Body*, where w is a variable of type Weather and *Body* is an if-then-else expression. What are the atomic expressions from which the boolean expression after the if can be built up? Initially we have only w to work on and, since w is of tuple type, the only associated operations are projections. Each projection returns a term of one of the four data types. Since the data types above are simple types without internal structure, the only operation available for, say, outlookP(w) is a test for equality with one of the constants of type Outlook.

Our next example concerns one of the Bongard problems [1]. We start with the appropriate type definitions.

```
data Shape = Circle | Triangle | Square | Inside(Shape,Shape);
data Class = Class1 | Class2;

type Diagram = {(Shape,Int)};

class::Diagram->Class;
```

A Bongard diagram consists of a set of tuples each of which consists of a shape together with the number of times that shape occurs in the diagram. The main difference with the previous attribute-value problem is that the `Shape` data type has a binary constructor `Inside`. This means that now we can construct, for a term s of type `Shape`, complex conditions which introduce new variables, such as

```
exists \t u -> s == Inside(t,u) && t == Circle && u == Triangle
```

Here are a few examples:

```
class({(Inside(Triangle,Circle),1)}) = Class1;
class({(Circle,1),(Triangle,1),(Inside(Triangle,Circle),1)}) =
                                                          Class1;
...
class({(Inside(Circle,Triangle),1)}) = Class2;
...
```

Our learning system finds the following definition.

```
class(d) =
    if (exists \p -> p 'in' d &&
                       (exists \s t -> shapeP(p) == Inside(s,t) &&
                                        s == Circle))
    then Class2
    else Class1;
```

Here `in` is a built-in predicate for set membership (the quotes make it infix). It follows that p is of type `(Shape, Int)`. The `shapeP` projection selects the first element of the pair, i.e. a shape, and tests whether it equals the term `Inside(Circle,t)`, for some t. Notice again how the Escher type definitions naturally generate the hypothesis space. The existential variables appear because

  (i) the top-level type is a set, from which we may select an element, and

  (ii) one of the data types defines a constructor.

Our third and final example involves mutagenicity [5]. An abstract view of a molecule is that it is a graph with atoms as nodes and bonds as edges. Below we represent this graph by the set of atoms and the set of bonds; in the next section we give an atom-centered representation. The type signature is as follows:

```
data Element = Br | C | Cl | F | H | I | N | O | S;
type Ind1 = Bool;
type IndA = Bool;
type Lumo = Float;
type LogP = Float;
type Label = Int;
type AtomType = Int;
type Charge = Float;
type BondType = Int;
type Atom = (Label,Element,AtomType,Charge);
type Bond = ({Label},BondType);
type Molecule = (Ind1,IndA,Lumo,LogP,{Atom},{Bond});
mutagenic::Molecule->Bool;
```

Notice the use of *labels* to model the complex geometric structure of individuals. Labels, here simply represented as integers, are used to name part of an individual (here: atoms) in order to be able to refer to it in other parts. The reason for labelling the atoms is that we need to record the bonds between individual atoms in the molecule. The last component of a molecule sextuple records the bond information.

Here is (part of) an example, classifying one particular molecule as mutagenic.

```
mutagenic(True,False,-1.246,4.23,
    {(1,C,22,-0.117),(2,C,22,-0.117),…,(26,O,40,-0.388)},
    {(({1,2},7),…,({24,26},2)}) = True;
```

So, for instance, in this molecule there is a bond between Carbon atom 1 and Carbon atom 2 of type 7. The following is a possible (partial) induced definition based on the theories induced by Progol.

```
mutagenic(m) =
    ind1P(m) == True ||
    lumoP(m) <= -2.072 ||
    (exists \a -> a 'in' atomSetP(m) && elementP(a)==C &&
            atomTypeP(a)==26 && chargeP(a)==0.115) ||
    (exists \b1 b2 -> b1 'in' bondSetP(m) && b2 'in' bondSetP(m) &&
            bondTypeP(b1)==1 && bondTypeP(b2)==2 &&
            not disjoint(labelSetP(b1),labelSetP(b2)) ||
    (exists \a -> a 'in' atomSetP(m) &&
            elementP(a)==C && atomTypeP(a)==29 &&
            (exists \b1 b2 ->
                    b1 'in' bondSetP(m) && b2 'in' bondSetP(m) &&
                    bondTypeP(b1)==7 && bondTypeP(b2)==1 &&
                    labelP(a) 'in' labelSetP(b1) &&
                    not disjoint(labelSetP(b1),labelSetP(b2)))) ||
    …;
```

The projection atomSetP is the projection onto the fifth component of a molecule. Similarly, labelSetP is the projection onto the first component of a bond. The predicate disjoint returns false if its arguments intersect and true otherwise. Notice the use of labels in the fifth disjunct to denote that there is a bond b1 from atom a to another atom, and a bond b2 from that atom to a third. The definition above is a direct translation of some clauses induced by Progol; we expect our learner will produce a similar result in the form of an if-then-else statement.

4. Discussion

We have seen how to use Escher as an ILP language through a number of examples. We will now discuss in more detail what we believe are the advantages of using a strongly typed language for learning. We will follow the traditional structure of an ILP task and discuss the representation of examples, hypotheses, and background knowledge.

Representation of examples. The view of attributes as types naturally leads to a representation of individuals by terms. This avoids naming individuals by constants, as is done in many ILP systems; instead, an individual is 'named' by the collection of all of its characteristics. The language of terms, and thus the example language, is fully determined by the type signature. Information about an individual is localised, and naming of subterms is only needed if we want to refer to them from other subterms, as in the mutagenesis example.

The representation of individuals by interpretations [2] is also motivated by localisation of examples. However, we believe that representing individuals by terms offers considerably more opportunities for localisation. For instance, we could easily adapt the representation of molecules to include all information about an atom, including the bonds it has with other atoms, in one subterm. We would have to adapt the types as follows:

```
type Bond = (Label,BondType);
type Atom = (Label,Element,AtomType,Charge,{Bond});
type Molecule = (Ind1,IndA,Lumo,LogP,{Atom});
```

The representation of an example then becomes

```
mutagenic(True,False,-1.246,4.23,
    {(1,C,22,-0.117,{(2,7),(6,7),(7,1)}),
    (2,C,22,-0.117,{(1,7),(3,7),(8,1)}), …,
    (26,O,40,-0.388,{(24,2)})}) = True;
```

While this representation has redundancy (each bond occurs twice), it has the advantage that all information pertaining to an atom is located in a single subterm.

One possible advantage of individuals as interpretations is that it may be easier to represent incomplete information by leaving things unspecified, while in our individuals-as-terms approach we would have to introduce explicit null values.

Representation of hypotheses. Given a type signature $f::X->Y$, Escher definitions that we learn have the form

```
f(x) = if E then s else t
```

where x is a variable of type X, s and t are either values of type Y or if-then-else expressions and E is a boolean expression. This is a very general format, and seems to be feasible as long as the number of classes in Y is limited. Learning such function definitions means instantiating E, s and t.

We believe that the use of a type system yields significant advantages when it comes to searching the hypothesis space because it helps us in ruling out useless hypotheses. More precisely, the construction of a boolean expression E is triggered by the available terms. Initially, the only variable we have is the head variable x of type, say, set. At this stage there are few options: we can use the card function to count the number of elements in the set, we can extract an element by means of in, or we can use background functions defined on sets. *Although the language may contain many more functions, they are not considered at this stage.* One possibility that will be considered is to instantiate E with (exists \y -> y 'in' x && E_1). Next, we consider the construction of E_1, for which our options are now slightly more numerous. On one hand we could extract another element of x, or we may proceed to consider y. In the latter case, we consider the type of y, which again gives us a limited number of choices. For instance, if y is a tuple, the only thing we can do is to project upon one of its components.

Top-down refinement approaches typically consider large parts of the search space. For instance, a naive refinement operator for Prolog may generate a new body literal with all new variables. Furthermore, at any point in the refinement process all available literals in the language will be considered for inclusion. While useless literals may be discarded later in the evaluation step, for instance because they fail to produce any information gain, the fact that they are generated by the refinement operator in the first place is wasteful. As sketched above, the use of a type system avoids the introduction of many useless literals altogether. Inductive hypotheses expressed in Escher are linked by definition: there is no possibility of introducing a literal `bondTypeP(b1)==7` unless the type of `b1` is determined by the preceding part of the rule. The notion of a non-linked clause seems more an artefact of using a non-typed language than anything else. Similarly, the need for syntactic biases such as mode declarations is subsumed by an appropriate type system. A type system is a powerful tool for expressing and employing declarative bias.

Types and their associated functions thus strongly, but not completely, constrain the hypothesis language. An important complexity dimension is given by the use of existential variables. In the case of attribute-value learning these are not allowed, and we might say in this case that the hypothesis language is completely determined by the types. Notice that when using functions in addition to predicates it is possible, without the use of variables, to represent 'relational' information such as the equality of the values of two attributes. The distinction between propositional and first-order learning tasks depends thus in part on the representation formalism. In fact, we would argue that the distinction between propositional learning and first-order learning is rather artificial. The number of existential variables provides another dimension, orthogonal to the complexity of the type system, along which to express the complexity of the learning task (*cf.* Fig. 1).

Representation of background knowledge. The use of a type system also suggests that background knowledge comes in flavours. First of all, with each complex type one needs *selector* functions for extracting subterms from terms of that type. For instance, projection functions come with tuple types; a set membership function comes with set types; a list membership function comes with list types; and so on. Without selector functions, the internal structure of the type could not be employed by the learner.

Secondly, there are generic, application-independent functions such as the standard set and list operations. Such functions are again closely associated with the types in the signature. The difference is that selector functions are automatically included in the hypothesis language, while this is optional for other background functions. In Escher, both selector and generic functions are provided in separate modules, and do not need to be defined by the user.

What remains are auxiliary functions that are neither useful outside the context of a particular learning task, nor to be easily found by the learner itself. In our view, such functions represent true background knowledge. The definitions of such background functions have to be provided by the user. Notice that if an ILP system does not represent individuals by terms, a significant part of what is conventionally called 'background knowledge' consists of descriptions of individuals, which are really artefacts of a flattened knowledge representation approach. In our approach this is avoided by representing all the knowledge about an individual in one term.

5. Summary and conclusion

If we were to summarise the previous discussion in one slogan, it would be: *attributes are types*. The reader may claim that many ILP systems use types. However, these are not the kinds of type system found in modern programming languages. Types are more than just labels attached to logical variables to prevent meaningless unifications, or to generate all possible instantiations of a variable. In a typed ILP language the type system provides many meaningful restrictions on the space of possible hypotheses. Escher is such a typed language, which in addition provides functions and higher-order constructs.

Related to the use of type systems, we would argue that individuals are properly represented by terms. This allows the learner to make full use of the type system, and it localises the information in a hierarchical way. Furthermore, we have argued that this viewpoint improves our understanding of the way in which ILP generalises attribute-value learning, by increasing the complexity of terms.

Many of the claims we make in this paper are rhetorical, and must be followed by experimental validation. We are currently working on the implementation of a decision-tree learner that employs Escher as an implementation and representation language to establish these claims.

Acknowledgements

Thanks are due to the other members of the Machine Learning Research group at the University of Bristol (Antony Bowers, Torbjørn Dahl, Claire Kennedy, Nicolas Lachiche, and René MacKinney-Romero) for their contributions to the ideas which led to this paper. Antony Bowers is implementing the learning system. Discussions with Nada Lavrac greatly helped to improved the presentation of the paper, as did the comments of the referees. This work was partially supported by EPSRC Grant GR/L21884 and by ESPRIT IV Long Term Research Project 20237 *Inductive Logic Programming 2*.

References

1. L. De Raedt & W. Van Laer. Inductive constraint logic. *Proc. 6th Int. Workshop on Algorithmic Learning Theory*, LNAI 997, pp.80–94, 1995.
2. L. De Raedt & L. Dehaspe. Clausal Discovery. *Machine Learning* 26(2/3):99–146, 1997.
3. J.W. Lloyd. Programming in an Integrated Functional and Logic Language. *Journal of Functional and Logic Programming*, 1998 (to appear).
4. T.M. Mitchell. *Machine Learning*. McGraw-Hill, 1997.
5. A. Srinivasan, S. Muggleton, R. King & M. Sternberg. Mutagenesis: ILP experiments in a non-determinate biological domain. *Proc. 4th Inductive Logic Programming Workshop*, GMD-Studien 237, 1994.

Function-Free Horn Clauses
Are Hard to Approximate

Richard Nock and Pascal Jappy

Laboratoire d'Informatique, de Robotique et de Microélectronique de Montpellier,
161, rue Ada,
34392 Montpellier, France
{nock,jappy}@lirmm.fr

Abstract. In this paper, we show two hardness results for approximating the best function-free Horn clause by an element of the same class. Our first result shows that for some constant $k > 0$, the error rate of the best k-Horn clause cannot be approximated in polynomial time to within any constant factor by an element of the same class. Our second result is much stronger. Under some frequently encountered complexity hypothesis, we show that if we replace the constant number of Horn clauses by a small, poly-logarithmic number, the constant factor blows up exponentially to a quasi-polynomial factor $n^{\log^k n}$, where n is the number of predicates of the problem, a measure of its complexity. Our main result links the difficulty of error approximation with the number of clauses allowed. We finally give an outline of the incidence of our result on systems that learn using ILP (Inductive Logic Programming) formalism.

1 Introduction and motivation

ILP is an active research branch at the crossroads of of Machine Learning and Logics. It aims at learning concepts expressed as (variously) restricted Horn Clause Programs from examples, and in the presence of background knowledge. Many experimental applications are available, that have been applied to domains such as biology, chess playing and natural langage analysis. Theoretical work has allowed to establish learnability results for some subclasses of first order Horn clauses. Early studies were undertaken in the Identification in the limit model [7], but most work has focused on Approximately Correct (PAC) learnability [15], [10] which is thought to better quantify the complexity of learning in terms of computational effort and number of examples required. In ILP, this latter problem is intractable for very general classes such as unconstrained Horn clauses (see [11] for a detailed presentation of computational hardness results). So, in order to achieve positive results, several restrictions of Horn Clause programs have been considered [13], [4], [5], and [6].

However, conflicts between PAC results and practical ones have led researchers to look for other learnability models [12]. In a previous paper, we highlighted divergences between PAC and robust learning [8] results for some of the main

ILP classes. Whereas PAC learning makes the strong assumption that any target concept can be represented in the hypothesis class $\mathcal{H}$, (which is very rarely acceptable in practice), robust learning studies the degradation in prediction performance of a hypothesis class $\mathcal{H}$ when it is not known a priori whether it contains the target concept's class. This makes this model a stricter one but it is closer to practical requirements. The commonpoint to both PAC and robust learning models is the sufficiency of worst case analyses to obtain negative results. Our result in [9] states that, even when considering a simple subclass of ILP formalism and even when looking for a single Horn clause, no polynomial-time algorithm can produce a formula whose error comes close to the error of the optimal single Horn clause. In this paper, we go further in worst-case analyses. We show that the condition on the error can be replaced by a much weaker one without losing negative results. We show that no polynomial-time algorithm can produce a formula approximating the error of the optimal one to within very large factors. The rest of this paper is organised as follows: in section 2, we present the ILP background we need for our results, and the link between ILP and structural complexity. In section 3 and 4 we prove that approximating function-free Horn clause is hard. Finally, in section 5, we highligh some relevant subclasses of ILP formalism for which our results are valid.

2 An ILP approximation problem

For a complete formalization of the ILP background needed for this article, we refer the reader to [9]. Given a Horn clause langage $\mathcal{L}$ and a correct inference relation on $\mathcal{L}$, an ILP learning problem can be formalized as follows. Assume a background knowledge $\mathcal{BK}$ expressed in a langage $\mathcal{LB} \subseteq \mathcal{L}$, and a set of examples $\mathcal{E}$ in a langage $\mathcal{LE} \subseteq \mathcal{L}$. The goal is to produce a hypothesis h in a hypothesis class $\mathcal{H} \subseteq \mathcal{L}$ consistent with $\mathcal{BK}$ and $\mathcal{E}$ such that h and the background knowledge cover all positive examples and none of the negative ones. The choice of the representation langages for the background knowledge and the examples, and the inference relation greatly influence the complexity (or decidability) of the learning problem. A common restriction for both $\mathcal{BK}$ and $\mathcal{E}$ is to use ground facts. As in [11], we use θ-subsumption as inference relation. Its main drawback being that it does not allow the use of background knowledge, other subsumption relations have been defined to do so, in particular generalized subsumption [2], and are thus preferred in ILP. We now state a useful lemma

Lemma 1 *Learning a Horn clause program from a set of ground background knowledge $\mathcal{BK}$ and ground examples $\mathcal{E}$, the inference relation being generalized subsumption, is equivalent to learning the same program with θ-subsumption, and empty background knowledge and examples defined as ground Horn clauses of the form $e \leftarrow b$, where $e \in \mathcal{E}$ and $b \in \mathcal{BK}$.*

This lemma allows us to incorporate the background knowledge in the new examples (and is thus empty). Examples and clauses are defined by predicates. To the variables of these predicates that are in the clauses built correspond constant symbols in the examples. θ-subsumption relative to the examples aims at finding adequate substitutions of variables with constant symbols. It can be defined in a general way as follows.

Definition 1 (θ-subsumption) *A clause C_1 θ-subsumes a clause C_2 if there exists a substitution θ such that $C_1\theta \subseteq C_2$.*

Our ILP problem can be presented as an optimization problem as follows, respecting the formalization of [8] :

> **Name** : Opt(Weighted-Approx($g(.)$-function-free Horn clauses)).
> **Instance** : A set of examples $\mathcal{E} = S^+ \cup S^-$, an integer weight $w(x_i) > 0$ for each example $x_i \in S^+ \cup S^-$.
> **Feasible Solutions** : $h \in g(.)$-function-free Horn clause.
> **Cost Function** : $\sum_{(x \in S^+ \wedge h(x)=0) \vee (x \in S^- \wedge h(x)=1)} w(x)$.

$g(.)$ is a function defining the maximum size (clause number) of the function-free Horn clauses constructed. It is worthwhile remarking that a machine learning algorithm is ran practically on a set of examples often called the "learning sample", and aims at finding a low-error formula, without prior knowledge on the concept from which these examples were taken. Therefore, what does such an algorithm is trying to find a feasible solution to the previous problem having a low cost. Proving lower bounds on the costs of polynomial-time algorithms for this problem is therefore of practical interest.

3 Result on k-function-free Horn clauses

In this section we state and prove a first non-approximability result, dealing with small-sized function-free Horn clauses.

Theorem 1 *If $NP \not\subset P$, $\forall k \geq 3$, Opt(Weighted-Approx(k-function-free Horn clauses)) is not approximable to within any constant $d > 0$.*

We make a reduction from a minimization problem previously studied in [8]:

> **Name** : Opt(Aggravated 3-SAT).
> **Instance** : A set of variables $U = \{x_1, \overline{x}_1, ..., x_n, \overline{x}_n\}$, a collection of 3-clauses over U, a subset $U' \subseteq U$, an assignment satisfying all clauses.
> **Feasible Solutions** : An assignation of the variables of U satisfying all clauses.
> **Cost Function** : The number of variables from U' assigned to **True** .

The satisfiability constraint implies that a solution always exists; the difficulty of the problem therefore relies only is the minimization of the cost function, and not in finding feasible solutions, which would be an artifact of the problem's hardness. We use the following result on Opt(Aggravated 3-SAT):

Theorem 2 [8] *If $NP \not\subset P$, Opt(Aggravated 3-SAT) is not approximable to within any constant $d > 0$.*

In order to prove our result, we need to obtain an intermediate inapproximability result for the following minimization problem:

Name : Opt(Aggravated k-Colorability).
Instance : A graph $G = (X, E)$. A subset $X' \subset X$. A vertex $x \in X \backslash X'$. A trivial k-Colorability of G.
Feasible Solutions : A valid k-Colorability of G.
Cost Function : The number of elements of X' having the same color as x.

Due to space limitations, undetailed proofs can be found in [14].

Theorem 3 *If $NP \not\subset P$, Opt(Aggravated k-Colorability) is not approximable to within any constant $d > 0$.*

Proof sketch. The reduction is made from the problem Opt(Aggravated 3-SAT). $C = \{C_1, ..., C_p\}$ denotes the set of 3-clauses instance of Opt(Aggravated 3-SAT). We transform it into a new set $C' = \{C'_1, ..., C'_p, C'_{p+1}, C'_{p+2}, C'_{p+3}, C'_{p+4}\}$ in the following way : let $L = U = \{x_1, \overline{x}_1, ..., x_n, \overline{x}_n\}$ stands for the variables set of the 3-SAT instance. Let $L' = \{x_1, \overline{x}_1, ..., x_n, x_{n+1}, \overline{x}_{n+1}, x_{n+2}, \overline{x}_{n+2}, x_{n+3}, \overline{x}_{n+3}\}$ be our new set of variables, and define $\forall 1 \leq i \leq p, C'_i = C_i \vee x_{n+1}, C'_{p+1} = \overline{x}_{n+1} \vee x_{n+2} \vee x_{n+3}, C'_{p+2} = \overline{x}_{n+2} \vee x_{n+3}, C'_{p+3} = x_{n+2} \vee \overline{x}_{n+3}$, and $C'_{p+4} = \overline{x}_{n+2} \vee \overline{x}_{n+3}$. The length of each new clause in C' is either 2, 3 or 4. We now state a number of facts useful to prove theorem 3. We let $[n]$ denote the set $\{1, 2, ..., n\}$.

Fact 1 *C' satisfies two properties : (1) if C' is satisfiable, x_{n+1}, x_{n+2} and x_{n+3} are all **False** ; (2) C is satisfiable iff C' is satisfiable.*

The graph G we construct, instance of Opt(Aggravated k-Colorability), has the modular structure which we now describe.

Step 1: each of the $2n + 6$ variables of L' is represented by a vertex in G:

$$\{x_1, \overline{x}_1, ..., x_n, \overline{x}_n, x_{n+1}, \overline{x}_{n+1}, x_{n+2}, \overline{x}_{n+2}, x_{n+3}, \overline{x}_{n+3}\}$$

We call these "variable vertices". We then place $n + 3$ edges $(x_i, \overline{x}_i), \forall i \in [n+3]$ in G. Each couple of variable vertices $(x_i, \overline{x}_i), i \in [n]$ represent the two possible truth assignment of the variables $x_i, \overline{x}_i$ of U: either **True** for x_i (and **False** for $\overline{x}_i$), or **False** for x_i (and **True** for $\overline{x}_i$).

Step 2: for each clause $C'_i, i \in [p+4]$, we create a corresponding subgraph H_i. Each of these subgraphs uses a basic buiding block shown in figure 1 (K_k is the complete graph on k vertices). In this figure, at least either of a or b is a variable vertex, and y is a new vertex. $\forall i \in [p+4]$, each clause C'_i of size 2, 3 or 4 is represented in G by a subgraph H_i using 1, 2 or 3 basic building blocks respectively. As shown in figure 1, to each clause C'_i corresponds a distinct vertex noted $y_{6,i}$. The only vertices shared by these subgraphs $H_i, i \in [p+4]$ are variable vertices.

Step 3: for each clause $C'_i, i \in [p+1]$, we create a corresponding subgraph H'_i isomorphic to H_i. $\forall i \in [p+1]$, the only vertices shared by H_i and H'_i are the variable vertices corresponding to C'_i. Vertices $y_{6,i}$ in H_i are renamed $y'_{6,i}$ in H'_i. Let $\chi(x)$ denote the color of any vertex x of G.

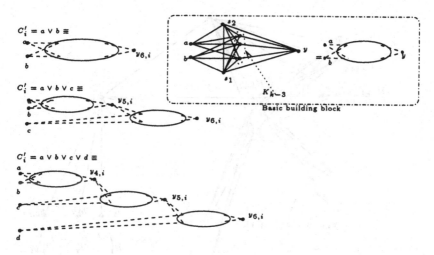

Fig. 1. Basic building block for $H_i, i \in [p+4]$, and subgraphs H_i generated by 2-, 3- and 4-clauses.

Fact 2 $\forall i \in [p+4], \forall j \in [p+1]$, for any valid k-coloring of the vertices of H_i (resp. H'_j), there exists one which gives to $y_{6,i}$ (resp. $y'_{6,j}$) a color shared by either

- a or b if C'_i (resp. C'_j) is of size 2.
- a or b or c if C'_i (resp. C'_j) is of size 3.
- a or b or c or d if C'_i (resp. C'_j) is of size 4.

Fact 3 $\forall i \in [p+4], \forall j \in [p+1]$, any valid k-coloring of the vertices of H_i (resp. H'_j) assigning the same color to each variable vertex of the clause C'_i (resp. C'_j), forces $y_{6,i}$ (resp. $y'_{6,j}$) to have this color.

Step 4: The subgraphs constructed in steps 1, 2 and 3 are linked to a subgraph W according to figure 2. This terminates the construction of G which now contains $6pk + 8k + 2n + 6$ vertices and is therefore of polynomial size. We have:

Fact 4 $\chi(x_{n+1}) = \chi(v_2)$ and $\chi(\overline{x}_{n+1}) = \chi(v_1)$.

Fact 5 In a valid k-coloring of G, let $\chi_1, ..., \chi_{k-2}$ denote the set of colors used to color K_{k-2} in W, and $\chi_1, ..., \chi_k$ the total set of colors. We have

$$\forall i \in [n+3], \{\chi(x_i), \chi(\overline{x}_i)\} = \{\chi_{k-1}, \chi_k\} = \{\chi(v_1), \chi(v_2)\}$$

Fact 6 $\forall i \in [p]$, let $C'_i = x_{i_1} \vee x_{i_2} \vee x_{i_3} \vee x_{n+1}$ denote a 4-clause of C'. We have

$$(\chi(x_{i_1}) = \chi(v_1)) \vee (\chi(x_{i_2}) = \chi(v_1)) \vee (\chi(x_{i_3}) = \chi(v_1))$$

We now let X' in the instance of Opt(Aggravated k-Colorability) denote the set of variable vertices built from U'. Recall that to one variable in U' corresponds one variable vertex. Therefore, X' does not contain any of the variables from

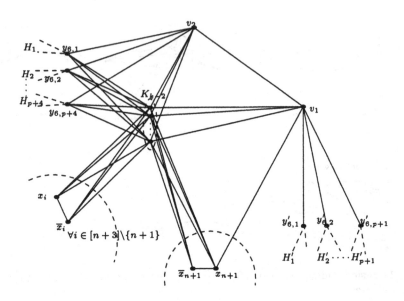

Fig. 2. The subgraph W of G.

the set $\{x_i, \overline{x}_i\}_{i\in\{p+1,p+2,p+3,p+4\}}$. We fix the special vertex to v_1. Proof of the reduction of theorem 3 can be found in [14]. $\qquad\square$

We now prove theorem 1 using the following reduction. For any graph G instance of Opt(Aggravated k-Colorability), we create a set of examples $\mathcal{E}$ described over a set of predicates $a_i(.), i \in [n]$, and constant symbols $\{l_i\}, i \in [n]$; $\{m_{i,j}\}, (i,j) \in E$; $\{s_{i,x}\}, i \in X'$ (there are $n + |E| + |X'|$ constant symbols). We let x denote the special vertex of the instance of Opt(Aggravated k-Colorability).

- $S^+ = \{q(l_i) \leftarrow \wedge_{j\neq i}a_j(l_i) : 1 \le i \le n\}$. The weight of these positive examples is $w^+ = n$.
- $S_1^- = \{q(m_{i,j}) \leftarrow \wedge_{k\notin\{i,j\}}a_k(m_{i,j}) : (i,j) \in E\}$. The weight of these negative examples is $w^- = w^+ = n$.
- $S_2^- = \{q(s_{i,x}) \leftarrow \wedge_{k\notin\{i,x\}}a_k(s_{i,j}) : (i,x) \notin E \wedge i \in X'\}$. The weight of these negative examples is $w'^- = 1$.

The proof of theorem 1 follows from the proof of the two following propositions:

Proposition 1 *From any k-function-free Horn clauses making t errors on $S^+ \cup S_1^- \cup S_2^-$, we can build in polynomial time a feasible solution to Opt(Aggravated k-Colorability) which gives the same color as x to at most t elements of X'.*

Proof. Suppose that $t \ge n$. In that case, we can use the trivial coloring of the instance of Opt(Aggravated k-Colorability). Since $X' \subset X$, there are trivially at most $t \ge n$ elements of X' colored by the same color as x.

Suppose now that $t < n$. In that case, any element of weight n is well classified. Let $\{h_1, h_2, ..., h_k\}$ denote the set of clauses solution to Opt(Weighted-Approx(k-function-free Horn clauses)). We can suppose without loss of generality that any predicate is absent of at most one clause. Otherwise, we can add this predicate to all clauses but one (in which it is absent), and this does not increase the number of errors since it only forces all positive examples to θ-subsume exactly one clause among the k. The colorability assigned is the following one : $\forall i \in [n], \forall j \in [k]$, if $a_i(.) \not\subset h_j$, then give color j to vertex x_i.

This is a valid k-colorability, otherwise some examples of weight n would be misclassified. The t errors are made on examples of weight 1. These examples represent distinct vertices having the same color as x. Note that a single clause is responsible for all the errors : $h_{\chi(x)}$.

Proposition 2 *Any feasible solution to Opt(Aggravated k-Colorability) which gives the same color as x to at most t elements of X' can be transformed in polynomial time into a feasible solution to Opt(Weighted-Approx(k-function-free Horn clauses)) which makes at most t errors over the examples.*

Proof. The k clauses of the solution to Opt(Weighted-Approx(k-function-free Horn clauses)) are defined by:

$$\forall j \in [k], h_j \equiv q(X) \leftarrow \wedge_{i \in [n] : \chi(x_i) \neq j} a_i(X)$$

These clauses do not make errors on examples of weight n. The only errors made are on examples of weight 1 corresponding to vertices having the same color as x. Note that in our construction, only one clause makes all the errors : $h_{\chi(x)}$.

Theorem 1 now follows from propositions 1 and 2.

4 Result on function-free Horn clauses having polylogarithmic size

Let QP denote the class of problems admitting quasi-polynomial time deterministic algorithms. A function of n is quasi-polynomial iff $f(n) \leq n^{\log^c n}$ for some constant c. Many results have introduced the class QP, such as for example [1], to point out the fact that hard-to-solve or approximate problems (such as Opt(Aggravated 3-SAT), and therefore Opt(Weighted-Approx(k-function-free Horn clauses))) might not even admit quasi-polynomial time approximation algorithms. We are going to use this fact to prove our next result. We now prove theorem 4 below.

Theorem 4 *If $NP \not\subset QP$, $\forall d > 0$ a constant, Opt(Weighted-Approx(log^{d+2} n-function-free Horn clauses)) is not approximable to within $n^{\log^d n}$.*

In order to do this, we highlight a correlation between the size of the formula and its error rate. To that effect, we multiply $\log^{d+2} n = K$ instances of Opt(Weighted-Approx(k-function-free Horn clauses)) by concatenating the tail of the examples to form new ones, thus described over a set of $n \times K$ predicates (plus the inferred predicate $q(.)$). Each predicate taken from the initial set serves to create exactly K new predicates. This can be viewed as making set products among the set of tails of the examples of the instance of Opt(Weighted-Approx(k-function-free Horn clauses)) we used to prove theorem 1. One of these examples could be represented $e.g.$ as follows:

$$q(l'_i) \leftarrow \left(\wedge_{j=1;j\neq i}^{j=n} a_{j,1}(l'_i) \right) \wedge \left(\wedge_{j=1;j\neq i}^{j=n} a_{j,2}(l'_i) \right) \wedge ... \wedge \left(\wedge_{j=1;j\neq i}^{j=n} a_{j,K}(l'_i) \right)$$

The subscript in $a_{i,j}(.)$ denotes the jth copy of the initial predicate $a_i(.)$. The example represented has each of its K predicate parts coming from the copy of an initial example from S^+ (we shall write that this example comes from $(S^+)^K$). The new examples are described as follows :

- S_K^+ is the subset $(S^+)^K$. Their weight is n^K.
- $S_{1,K}^- = (S^+ \cup S_1^-)^K \backslash S_K^+$. their weight is n^K.
- $S_{2,K}^- = (S_2^-)^K$. their weight is 1.

Due to the increase in the number of examples, the initial set of $n + |E| + |X'|$ constant symbols is replaced by a new larger set of size $(n + |E|)^K + |X'|^K$. Note that this new set of examples is created in quasi-polynomial time. For the sake of brevity, we let c_* denote the minimal error of a feasible solution to Opt(Weighted-Approx(k-function-free Horn clauses)), and c'_* the minimal error of a feasible solution to Opt(Weighted-Approx(K-function-free Horn clauses)).

Proposition 3 $c_* < n$

Proof follows from the fact that the instance of Opt(Aggravated k-Colorability) which serves to build the instance of Opt(Weighted-Approx(k-function-free Horn clauses)) is always k-colorable. Proposition 3 comes from the construction technique of proposition 2 : any example of weight n is well classified, and there are at most $n-1$ examples of weight 1. According to propositions 1 and 2, we can suppose that each predicate is absent from at most one clause. Let $c_*(c_{\chi(x)})$ denote the minimal error of the clause that does not contain the predicate $a_x(.)$ corresponding to the special vertex of the instance of Opt(Aggravated k-Colorability). From propositions 1 and 2, proposition 3 can be refined :

Proposition 4 $c_* = c_*(h_{\chi(x)})$

Proposition 5 $c'_* \geq (c_*)^K$.

Proof. Whenever an example from the set $S_K^+ \cup S_{1,K}^-$ is badly classified, proposition 3 gives the result: $c'_* \geq n^K > (c_*)^K$. Suppose that all examples from the set $S_K^+ \cup S_{1,K}^-$ are well classified. Any error is necessarily due to an example of the set $S_{2,K}^-$. The only type of clause that can cause these errors is a clause of type $q(X) \leftarrow P_1 \wedge P_2... \wedge P_K$ where $\forall j \in [K]$, P_j is a clause described over the set of predicates $\{a_{i,j}\}_{i\in[n]}$ such that P_j makes errors on S_2^-. Since the error of each P_j is at least $c_*(h_{\chi(x)})$, which is c_* (proposition 4), the error of the conjuction ($\wedge$) is at least the product of the minimal error of each part, $(c_*)^K$. The overall error of the set of clauses is thus at least equal to this quantity.

Proposition 6 *Let h denote a feasible solution to $Opt(Weighted\text{-}Approx(K\text{-}$ function-free Horn clauses)), whose error is a. Then we can find a feasible solution to $Opt(Weighted\text{-}Approx(k\text{-}function\text{-}free$ Horn clauses)) whose error is no more than $a^{\frac{k}{K}}$.*

Proof. Recall that the graph we constructed from the instance of the problem Opt(Aggravated 3-SAT) is always k colorable. Therefore, there always exist a set of k-function-free Horn clauses consistent with $S^+ \cup S_1^-$ (proposition 2), having error $< n$. In h, whenever an example from the set $S_K^+ \cup S_{1,K}^-$ is badly classified, proposition 3 gives the result since the error of h is at least $c_*' \geq n^K$. Suppose that all examples from the set $S_K^+ \cup S_{1,K}^-$ are well classified. Any error is necessarily due to an example of the set $S_{2,K}^-$. The only type of clause that can cause these errors is a clause of type $q(X) \leftarrow P_1 \wedge P_2 ... \wedge P_K$ where $\forall j \in [K]$,

1. P_j is a subset of predicates described over the set of predicates $\{a_{i,j}\}_{i \in [n]}$, and
2. the clause isomorphic to $q(X) \leftarrow P_j'$ described over the set $\{a_i\}_{i \in [n]}$, obtained by replacing each $a_{l,j} \in P_j$ by a_l in P_j', makes errors on S_2^-.

Note that the error of the conjuction ($\wedge$) is the product of errors of each part $P_j, j \in [K]$ on S_2^-. So, the part P_* over $P_1, ..., P_K$ leading to the least number of errors on S_2^- makes an error that is at most $a^{\frac{k}{K}}$. Now, construct the set h' of $(k-1)$-function-free Horn clauses of proposition 2 with all clauses except $h_{\chi(x)}$, and add (for $h_{\chi(x)}$) the clause corresponding to the part P_* (it is $q(X) \leftarrow P_*'$ as described in point 2 above). The overall error of h' does not exceed $a^{\frac{k}{K}}$.

Proposition 7 $c_*' \leq (c_*)^K$

The proof of this proposition follows simply if we calculate the K-time cross-product of the solution realizing the cost c_*. We obtain a set of k^K clauses, and the construction can be realized in quasi-polynomial time.

From this, it comes that $c_*' = (c_*)^K$. We now prove theorem 4 *ad absurdum*. Suppose that Opt(Weighted-Approx($\log^{d+2} n$-function-free Horn clauses)) is approximable to within $n^{\log^d n}$. In quasi-polynomial time, from any instance of Opt(Weighted-Approx(k-function-free Horn clauses)), we build an instance of Opt(Weighted-Approx(K-function-free Horn clauses)) following the procedure described at the beginning of this section. We can find an element of K-function-free Horn clauses whose error does not exceed $(Kn)^{\log^d(Kn)} c_*'$ (hypothesis). Thus, we can find a solution to Opt(Weighted-Approx(k-function-free Horn clauses)) whose cost is approximately no more than $\left((Kn)^{\log^d(Kn)} c_*'\right)^{\frac{1}{K}}$ (proposition 6). But (using propositions 5 and 7)

$$\left((Kn)^{\log^d(Kn)} c_*'\right)^{\frac{1}{K}} = \left((Kn)^{\log^d(Kn)} c_*'\right)^{\frac{1}{\log^{d+2} n}} \leq (Kn)^{\frac{1}{\log(Kn)}} c_* = \mathcal{O}(c_*)$$

This contradicts theorem 1, since we obtain an approximation of Opt(Weighted-Approx(k-function-free Horn clauses)) to within a constant factor.

5 Consequences on learnability

In this paper, we have essentially presented two structural complexity results. Their purpose, is to prove that Horn Clauses display very severe error rates when used for learning in complex domains, and they extend our previous results [9]. It should be noted that as in this previous work, in order to obtain general properties, we have studied general function-free Horn-clauses but the proofs of our theorems are made in such a manner (using simple ILP formalisms) as to remain valid for the more specialized classes encoutered in ILP. So, both our non-approximability results also apply to many subsets that have led to theoretical studies in the PAC-learning model. Classes for which this result applies are subclasses of the following classes where the number of clauses is limited to the values of theorems 1 and 4 : ij-determinate non recursive Horn clauses [13] where i and j are any integer constants satisfying $i \geq 0$ and $j > 0$, and l-local Horn clauses [3] where l is any integer constant satisfying $l > 0$.

References

1. S. Arora. Probabilistic checking of proofs and hardness of approximation problems. Technical Report CS-TR-476-94, Princeton University, 1994.
2. W. Buntine. Generalized subsumption and its applications to induction and redundancy. *Artificial Intelligence*, 36:149–176, 1988.
3. W.W. Cohen. Pac-learning nondeterminate clauses. In *Proceedings of the Twelfth National Conference on Artificial Intelligence, AAAI'94*, pages 676–681, 1994.
4. W.W. Cohen. Pac-learning recursive logic programs: Efficient algorithms. *Journal of Artificial Intelligence Research*, 2:501–539, 1995.
5. W.W. Cohen. Pac-learning recursive logic programs: Negative results. *Journal of Artificial Intelligence Research*, 2:541–571, 1995.
6. S. Dzerovski, S.H. Muggleton, and S. Russel. Pac-learnability of determinate logic programs. In *Proceedings of COLT-92*, pages 128–137, 1992.
7. E.M. Gold. Language indentification in the limit. *Information and Control*, 10:447–474, 1967.
8. K-U. Höffgen and H.U. Simon. Robust trainability of single neurons. In *Proc. of the 5 th International Conference on Computational Theory*, 1992.
9. P. Jappy, R. Nock, and O. Gascuel. Negative robust learning results for horn clause programs. In *Proceedings of ICML'96*, pages 258–265, 1996.
10. M. Kearns, M. Li, L. Pitt, and L.G. Valiant. On the learnability of boolean formulae. In *Proceedings of STOCS'87*, pages 285–294, 1987.
11. J.U. Kietz and S. Dzeroski. Inductive logic programming and learnability. *Sigart Bulletin*, 5:22–32, 1994.
12. S.H. Muggleton. Bayesian inductive logic programming. In *Proceedings of the Seventh Workshop on COmputational Learning Theory*, 1994.
13. S.H. Muggleton and C. Feng. *Efficient induction of logic programs*. Inductive Logic Programming. Academic Press, New York, 1992.
14. R. Nock and P. Jappy. On the hardness of approximating function-free horn clauses. Technical Report LIRMM-RR-98017, LIRMM, 1998.
15. L.G. Valiant. A theory of the learnable. *Association for Computing Machinery Communications*, 27:1134–1142, 1984.

DOGMA: A GA-Based Relational Learner

Jukka Hekanaho

Turku Centre for Computer Science
and
Åbo Akademi University
Department of Computer Science
Lemminkäisenkatu 14 A, SF-20520 Turku, Finland
hekanaho@abo.fi

Abstract. We describe a GA-based concept learning/theory revision system DOGMA and discuss how it can be applied to relational learning. The search for better theories in DOGMA is guided by a novel fitness function that combines the minimal description length and information gain measures. To show the efficacy of the system we compare it to other learners in two relational domains.

1 Introduction

Genetic Algorithms (GAs) are stochastic, general purpose search algorithms that have been applied to a wide range of Machine Learning problems. They work by evolving a population of chromosomes, each of which encodes a potential solution to the problem at hand. The task of a GA is to find a highly fit chromosome through the application of different selection and perturbation operators. In this paper we apply GAs to the process of extracting relational classification knowledge from a set of examples. In our case the chromosomes encode rules in a generalized first order logic language. Systems utilizing the search mechanism of GAs have recently been successfully applied to propositional concept learning, e.g. [9,3,7,13]. However, only a few GA-based systems perform relational learning , e.g. [7,1], and even they have been applied sparingly to relational domains. In this paper we describe a GA-based system DOGMA [10,11] that is capable of relational concept learning and theory revision. We also describe a new fitness function that combines the minimal description length principle [19] and an information gain measure [17]. Furthermore, we evaluate DOGMA in two relational domains, confronting its behavior with other relational learners.

2 Background

GA-based systems in rule-based concept learning may be divided into two main streams based on their knowledge representation. The Michigan type systems, e.g. [9], use a fixed length chromosome representation. Most often a chromosome represents a single rule and hence these systems have to develop special methods in order to deal with disjunctive concepts. In the Pittsburgh approach, e.g. [3, 13], the situation is reversed. These systems use chromosomes of varying length, where each chromosome is a total solution and encodes a set of rules. Therefore these systems can adapt to disjunctive concepts naturally, at the cost of having more complex chromosomes and genetic operators. DOGMA (Domain Oriented Genetic MAchine) combines the two approaches. It supports two distinct levels, with accompanying operators. On the lower level DOGMA uses Michigan type fixed length genetic chromosomes, which are manipulated by mutation and crossover operators. This lower level is similar to another GA-based learner RE-GAL [7]. On the higher level the chromosomes are combined into genetic families, through special operators that merge and break families. Just like in the Michigan approach the chromosomes represent single rules, whereas the genetic families, which compete à la Pittsburgh, encode rule sets that express classification theories. In addition, DOGMA incorporates special stochastic operators which induce knowledge from a given background theory, allowing theory revision to be performed. However, in this paper we don't utilize this part of DOGMA but use it as a pure inductive learner. For details about the background knowledge and theory revision in DOGMA we refer to [10, 11].

3 Knowledge Representation

DOGMA learns non-recursive relational concepts expressed in a generalized first order logic language. The rule language $\mathcal{L}_1$ of DOGMA is similar to the language used in REGAL [7] and to Michalski's VL_{21} language [15]. Since DOGMA always learns one target class at a time, we may drop the consequent of the rule and concentrate on the antecedent. A rule is a conjunction of internally disjunctive predicates, $P(X_1, \ldots, X_n, [v_1, \ldots, v_m])$, where the X_i's are variables and $[v_1, \ldots, v_m]$ denotes a disjunction of constants v_i. The symbol $*$ may be used to collapse a set of values. For example, let us assume that a feature of distance ranges over $0, \ldots, 5$. If the values from 2 to 5 are rarely used we might collapse them to $*$ and define the predicate $dist$ for values $[0, 1, *]$; then the formula $dist(X, Y, [0, *])$ equals $dist(X, Y, [0, \neg(0 \lor 1)])$.

Each example is composed of a set of objects whose properties are described in the example. This means that to derive relations like $on(X, Y, [yes])$ we have to define them in terms of the original attributes. For example, $on(X, Y, [yes, no])$ could be defined to yield yes if the position of X is greater than the position of Y and no otherwise. So far only intensional definitions of relations are allowed. The framework can, however, easily be extended with extensional definitions of relations. We say that a rule $\phi(X_1, \ldots X_n)$ covers an example e iff $\forall X_i. \exists obj_i \in e. \phi(obj_1, \ldots, obj_n)$ is true.

3.1 The Language Template

The formulae in $\mathcal{L}_1$ are mapped into bitstrings using a *language template* Λ that defines the structure and complexity of bitstring formulae. Λ acts as a language bias, defining the hypothesis space of the GA. Each predicate in Λ is in most general form, containing all possible values $[v_1, \ldots, v_k]$ (possibly with $*$) that the predicate can take. Therefore, each predicate in Λ is tautologically true. As an example consider the language template Λ in Figure 1. Every possible concept description is obtained by deleting a part of Λ. For example:

$$size(X, [s, m]) \wedge shape(Y, [tr]) \wedge ontop(X, Y, [yes]) \qquad (1)$$

is obtained by deleting the shape literal of variable X and some internal disjunctions from the template.

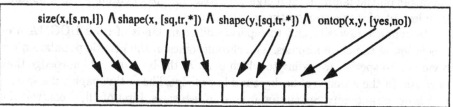

Fig. 1: A language template with the corresponding bitstring

Formulae are mapped to bitstrings by setting a bit to 1 if the corresponding predicate value is present in the literal, otherwise the bit is set to 0. Thus a 1 in the bitstring means that the corresponding value belongs to the internal disjunction of its predicate, while a 0 expresses absence. Consequently, a substring corresponding to all the values of a predicate consisting of only 0's is illegal and is automatically rewritten as a substring of 1's. For example, if formula (1) is mapped to a bitstring using the language template of Figure 1, then the first, second, fourth, fifth, sixth, eighth and eleventh bits of the bitstring are set to 1.

3.2 Expressing disjunctive concepts

The language $\mathcal{L}_1$ uses internal disjunctions but doesn't include higher level disjunctions for relating different rules. In order represent this kind of higher level disjunctions we extend our language to the language $\mathcal{L}_m$ that consists of maximally m disjunctive $\mathcal{L}_1$ formulae. At the level of bitstrings each $\phi \in \mathcal{L}_m$ is represented by a set of fixed length bitstrings.

In addition to internally disjunctive predicates, $\mathcal{L}_m$ may also have *necessary constraints*. These are predicates without internal disjunction, like $equal(X, Y)$, which represent facts that must hold for every concept. The necessary constraints are used to constrain the hypothesis space and can be added to the language template as a form of background knowledge.

There are two other extensions to the language representation scheme; k-CNF and contiguous rules. A k-CNF rule has an upper bound k on the number of internally disjunctive terms in the literals. For example a 1-CNF rule has only 1 term in the internal disjunction of a literal. Therefore a 1-CNF rule corresponds to a Horn clause. In contiguous rules each internal disjunction can only have contiguous values, where the order of the values is given by the language template. Contiguous rules are useful when applied to a predicate describing an ordered property.

4 The Genetic Algorithm

DOGMA follows the metaphor of competing families by keeping Michigan style genetic operators that work on fixed length chromosomes, while lifting fitness and selection on the level of Pittsburgh style families. A single chromosome encodes a rule in $\mathcal{L}_1$ and a family encodes a classification theory in $\mathcal{L}_m$. The operators on the family level merge and break groups of chromosomes, building families out of single cooperating chromosomes.

To enhance diversity and to separate different kinds of rules DOGMA uses speciation of the chromosomes. The chromosomes in the genetic population are divided into species according to which parts of the background knowledge they may use. In the absence of background knowledge, like in this paper, the speciation is done randomly. Speciation is used in two ways. First of all, it controls the mating of chromosomes of different species. This is achieved through a parameter that controls the ratio of interbreeding between chromosomes of different species. Secondly, speciation controls the composition of the families. Chromosomes of the same species can't be merged into the same family, i.e. the families are symbiotic. Since merged chromosomes in a family are evaluated together, this puts different genetic pressures on different species.

4.1 Genetic Operators

The genetic operators, working with genetic chromosomes, are *mating, mutation, crossover*, and *seeding*. The crossover operators are inherited from REGAL. We use four different crossovers; the well-known two-point and universal crossovers as well as a generalizing and a specializing crossover. The last two operators are specifically designed keeping in mind the specific requirements of concept learning.

Recall that a bitstring representing a formula is built up of substrings corresponding to each predicate in the language template Λ. Given two parent bitstrings s_1 and s_2 the generalizing crossover works as follows. It first selects randomly a set of predicates from Λ and locates the corresponding substrings in s_1 and s_2. Next, it produces the offsprings by doing a bitwise or operation on the located bits of s_1 and s_2. The specializing crossover works like the generalizing one, but instead of a bitwise or it performs a bitwise and.

The seed operator is similar to the seed used by Michalski in the Star methodology [15]. It generates a formula (= bitstring) covering at least one randomly selected positive training example. Seeding works by first generating a random bitstring, which is then changed minimally so that it covers the selected example. The seed operator is used both while creating the initial population of DOGMA and during the run. This ensures that the GA can start off with some meaningful chromosomes and that it keeps a diverse population.

4.2 Family Operators

The remaining operators work on the family level. The *break operator* splits randomly a family into two separate families. The counterpart of break is *join*, it merges two families of symbiotic chromosomes into a single family. Because of the symbiotic requirements join puts at most one chromosome of each species into the new combined family. If there are two chromosomes of the same species then one is deleted. The operator is made a bit more sophisticated by adding directed joining and seeding into it. When a family is about to be joined, a random uncovered positive example is chosen and join searches for a suitable family that covers this example. A family is suitable if it has a chromosome of a new species that covers the example. If no suitable family is found then a suitable single chromosome family is made with the seed operator. Finally the families are joined together. In addition to join, we use another family building operator called *make-family*. This is a global operator that builds a family by selecting the best chromosomes of different species from the population.

5 Combining MDL and Information Gain

GA methodology emphasizes the separation of the search mechanism and the particular fitness function used to rank the chromosomes. In concept learning this separation fits like a glove because the overwhelming diversity of learning problems makes it difficult, or even impossible, to construct a model selection criterion that would always give the best possible result. Whatever criterion is used to rank concepts, it adds a bias towards a class of concepts, which inevitably leads to unsatisfactory learning behavior in domains where the bias is unjustified [20]. As a result DOGMA incorporates several model selection criteria. In this study we'll use a fitness function that combines the *Minimal Description Length* (MDL) principle and an *information gain* measure.

To use the MDL we have to define an encoding for the examples and for all theories in $\mathcal{L}_m$. The encoding we use is similar to the scheme used by Quinlan in [18]. Next, to turn the MDL into a fitness function we compare the MDL against the total exception length, i.e. against the MDL of an empty theory $T_\emptyset$ that covers no examples. Given a set of examples E and a classification theory T the MDL fitness is defined as follows:

$$f_{MDL}(T, E) = 1 - \frac{MDL(T, E)}{W_\emptyset * MDL(T_\emptyset, E)}. \tag{2}$$

Here $W_\emptyset \geq 1$ is a weight factor that guarantees that even fairly bad theories have a positive fitness. The default value of $W_\emptyset$ is 1.2. Unfortunately however, f_{MDL} cannot be used directly as a fitness function in DOGMA. The problem stems from the fact f_{MDL} underrates theories that are almost consistent and very incomplete. This leads to a prevalence of fairly large, but very inconsistent rules, since these are mostly preferred by the f_{MDL} to small and almost consistent rules. The dominance of inconsistent rules will, however, quite fast push the whole GA population to become overly general and very inconsistent. As a consequence the GA will spend a lot of its resources in searching the very inconsistent part of the hypothesis space. Hence we need to adjust the fitness function so that it promotes small and almost consistent rules. We do this through an information gain measure. The information gain of a theory T compared to another theory T_{def} measures how much information is gained in the distribution of true and false positives of T compared to the distribution of T_{def}.

$$Gain(T_{def}, T, E) = log_b(t_T^+ + 1) \times (Info(T_{def}, E) - Info(T, E)),$$

where E is a set of examples and t_T^+ denotes the number of true positives of theory T. $b \geq 1$ is the base of the logarithm, with a default value of 1.2. The theory T_{def} that we compare theories against is a default theory that classifies all examples as positives. To derive a fitness function out of the gain information we compare it against the maximal gain, i.e. against the gain of a (hypothetical) theory T_{max} that classifies all examples correctly. The gain fitness is defined as

$$f_G(T, E) = W_G \times \frac{Gain(T_{def}, T, E)}{Gain(T_{def}, T_{max}, E)},$$

where $W_G > 0$ is a parameter that can be used to adjust the gain level. Its default value is 1.2. The combined MDL and gain fitness f_{MG} simply selects the minimum of the two fitnesses. In practice, f_{MG} with the default values has the effect that f_G is preferred in case of specific small rules which classify only a few examples. f_G is also used when the rules have too many false positives. In all other cases f_{MDL} is the minimum of the two functions. The effect of f_G is therefore to guide the learning in the beginning when the system is seeding quite specific initial rules and to constrain f_{MDL} from overrating too general rules.

6   Evaluation of Relational Learning

To show the efficacy of DOGMA we evaluate the system in two relational domains and compare the results to other relational learners. For a more detailed discussion of the test setup and of the GA parameters used we refer to [12].

6.1   Musk

Dietterich et.al [5] investigate how several learning algorithms perform in the task of predicting the musk-odor of a molecule. Since a molecule can be in a number of different states, or conformations, the problem is not a simply propositional but involves inference over multiple instances.

We have discretized the conformation features with the MDL-based discretizer in the $\mathcal{MLC}$++ package [14]. The language template Λ is defined as:

$$P_1(X, [v_{1_1}, \ldots, v_{1_n}]), \ldots, P_{166}(X, [v_{166_1}, \ldots, v_{166_n}]),$$

where each predicate P_i corresponds to a feature in a molecules conformation. The values v_{i_j} refer to the discretized feature values. Notice that as the discretization is done separately for each fold the discretized feature values vary from fold to fold. As a language bias we restrict the hypotheses to 1-CNF rules.

In Table 1 we compare our results on the clean1 dataset with the ones obtained by Dietterich et.al in [5] and by the relational decision tree learner TILDE [2]. Dietterich et.al hypothesized that a suitable representation language in the musk domain consists of so called axis-parallel hyper-rectangles (APR) and designed several special APR algorithms for this task. The algorithms that can take the multiple instance problem into account are marked with an * in Table 1.

Table 1. Results from a 10-fold crossvalidation of the clean1 musk-odor data

Algorithm	Errors	Performance %
*Iterated-discrim APR	7	92.4
*GFS elim-kde APR	8	91.3
*DOGMA	9	90.2
GFS elim-count APR	9	90.2
*TILDE	12	87.0
GFS all-positive APR	15	83.7
All-positive APR	18	80.4
Backpropagation	23	75.0
C4.5	29	68.5

As can be seen in Table 1 the general propositional learners that cannot handle the many-to-one problem of conformations perform poorly. DOGMA makes 9 prediction errors in the crossvalidation and is among the top four algorithms. The average time to learn a class in a crossvalidation fold was 68.1 CPU minutes, measured on a Sun Ultra 2 Model 2170. Also TILDE performs quite well, although slightly worse than DOGMA and the top three APR algorithms. The success of the APR algorithms can, at least partially, be explained by the fact that they are specialized to this problem, both through their language bias and their search strategy.

6.2 Relational Chess

Our second domain is the illegal white-to-move situation in chess end-game [16, 17, 6]. This has been a popular domain in the ILP literature, mainly because the data has also versions which are corrupted by different types of noise.

In the original ILP formulation [16, 6] the problem is presented through a six-place predicate $illegal(WKf, WKr, WRf, WRr, BKf, BKr)$, specifying the file and rank of white king, white rook, and black king, respectively. For example consider $\langle illegal(8, 5, 5, 4, 1, 4), \oplus \rangle$, it represents an illegal chessboard configuration where a white king is in position $(8, 5)$, a white rook in position $(5, 4)$, and a black king in position $(1, 4)$.

The background knowledge is represented either by two or four relations. In FOIL [17] the relations $adjacent(X, Y)$ and $less\_than(X, Y)$ are used. These indicate that the file or rank of X is adjacent to or less than the file or rank of Y. In many other ILP systems, e.g. mFOIL [6], the corresponding relations are typed so that there are separated relations for files and ranks. In addition many systems use a built-in equality relation.

In DOGMA the problem is posed as $illegal(WK, WR, BK)$, where WK, WR, and BK are the white king, the white rook, and the black king. Each example is made of three objects describing the positions of the three chess pieces. In DOGMA we use the four typed predicates plus two additional predicates eq_file and eq_rank. In addition we use necessary constraints that define the type of the chess piece in question, see the language template in Table 2.

Table 2. The learning setup for the illegal chess endgame problem in DOGMA

Language Template
$white\_king(X) \land white\_rook(Y) \land black\_king(Z) \land$
$less\_file(X, Y, [y, n]) \land less\_rank(X, Y, [y, n]) \land adj\_file(X, Y, [y, n]) \land$
$adj\_rank(X, Y, [y, n]) \land eq\_file(X, Y, [y, n]) \land eq\_rank(X, Y, [y, n]) \land$
$less\_file(X, Z, [y, n]) \land less\_rank(X, Z, [y, n]) \land adj\_file(X, Z, [y, n]) \land$
$adj\_rank(X, Z, [y, n]) \land eq\_file(X, Z, [y, n]) \land eq\_rank(X, Z, [y, n]) \land$
$less\_file(Y, Z, [y, n]) \land less\_rank(Y, Z, [y, n]) \land adj\_file(Y, Z, [y, n]) \land$
$adj\_rank(Y, Z, [y, n]) \land eq\_file(Y, Z, [y, n]) \land eq\_rank(Y, Z, [y, n])$

We used the same datasets and performed the same experiments as in [6], where FOIL and mFOIL were tested on data that was corrupted through different levels of noise. For each noise level the systems were trained on five set, each containing 100 examples. The classification accuracy was then tested on 5000 randomly generated examples. The noise levels are 0%, 5%, 10%, 15%, 20%, 30%, 50%, and 80%. For further details about the data we refer to [6].

Table 3. Results in the illegal chess domain. D, F and m stand for DOGMA, FOIL and mFOIL, respectively. The results show the accuracy percentages of each system under different kinds of noise

Noise type	Arguments			Class			Arguments and class		
Noise level	D	F	m	D	F	m	D	F	m
0%	97.31	94.82	95.57	–	–	–	–	–	–
5%	94.36	91.64	91.87	92.47	94.23	94.26	92.75	89.28	89.64
10%	88.70	80.45	84.59	90.64	90.07	92.02	80.23	76.94	80.79
15%	83.37	76.81	80.06	88.86	88.31	89.96	78.07	72.88	76.58
20%	80.86	73.79	76.49	88.77	87.53	88.37	74.16	71.02	74.74
30%	72.72	71.19	74.04	87.14	84.54	86.01	67.08	66.14	69.65
50%	61.84	63.25	68.64	77.13	71.86	79.20	56.20	61.33	66.27
80%	56.42	57.58	66.30	53.72	60.65	65.04	52.85	57.88	61.73

We summarize the results in Table 3. When only the arguments are noisy we notice that DOGMA has the best performance when the noise level is under 20%. When the noise level rises to 50% or more mFOIL outperforms both DOGMA and FOIL. In the case of a noisy class variable all the systems perform equally well up to a noise level of 30%. For the highest noise level mFOIL performs best. Once again, when both the arguments and the class variable are noisy, mFOIL learns the best rules for the very noisy sets (at least 50% noise). For noise levels below 20% DOGMA is slightly better than mFOIL. Overall we notice that noise in the class variable alone has the smallest effect on the learning performances of the systems. Learning is most difficult when both the arguments and the class variable are noisy. The average computation time for learning a class from a set of 100 examples was 1.26 CPU minutes, measured on a Sun Ultra 2 Model 2170.

7 Conclusions

We have described how the GA-based learner DOGMA can be applied to relational learning. We have also compared experimentally the system to other learners. Furthermore, we have discussed the difficulties of directly applying MDL in GA-based search. As a result we derived a novel fitness function by combining the MDL and information gain.

Unlike most rule-based systems we use a separate language for describing the examples and the hypotheses. The examples are sets of objects and the formulae are described using a logical language $\mathcal{L}_m$. In our setting the extension of a formula must be derived using a separate built-in matcher, that bridges the gap between the example and hypothesis formalisms. As described in [8], the representation we use can also easily be viewed in terms of relational algebra and object oriented databases. Furthermore, the extension of a formula can be calculated using relational algebra. This shows that our setting can take advantage of relational database systems and is extendible towards large volumes of data. As such the setting is also be extendible to relational data mining. In fact, Claudien [4] uses learning from interpretations to perform relational data mining by learning characteristic rules. Such rules are more special than the discriminant ones and aim at characterizing certain properties of the concept. DOGMA could also be applied to this task, given a fitness function that promotes the search of characteristic rules.

GAs make a clear separation between the search method and the criterion to be optimized. This facilitates the implementation of different fitness functions which encode different preference criteria. Hence GAs could be used to test the utility of different preference criteria used in relational concept learning.

References

1. S. Augier, G. Venturini, and Y. Kodratoff. Learning first order logic rules with a genetic algorithm. In *Proc. of the 1st International Conference on Knowledge Discovery and Data Mining*, pages 21–26, Montreal, Canada, 1995. AAAI Press.

2. H. Blockeel and L. De Raedt. Top-down induction of logical decision trees. Technical Report CW 247, Dept. of Computer Science, K.U.Leuven, January 1997.

3. K. A. De Jong, W. M. Spears, and F. D. Gordon. Using genetic algorithms for concept learning. *Machine Learning*, 13:161–188, 1993.

4. L. De Raedt and L. Dehaspe. Clausal Discovery. *Machine Learning*, 26:99–146, 1997.

5. T. G. Dietterich, R. H. Lathrop, and T. Lozano-Pèrez. Solving the multiple-instance problem with axis-parallel rectangles. *Artificial Intelligence*, 89(1-2):31–71, 1997.

6. S. Džeroski. Handling imperfect data in inductive logic programming. In *Proc. of the 4th Scandinavian Conference on Artificial Intelligence*, pages 111–125. IOS Press, 1993.

7. A. Giordana and F. Neri. Search-intensive concept induction. *Evolutionary Computation*, 3(4):375–416, 1995.

8. A. Giordana, F. Neri, L. Saitta, and M. Botta. Integrating multiple learning startegies in first order logics. *Machine Learning*, 27:209–240, 1997.

9. D. P. Greene and S. F. Smith. Competition-based induction of decision models from examples. *Machine Learning*, 13:229–257, 1993.

10. J. Hekanaho. Background knowledge in GA-based concept learning. In *Proc. of the 13th International Conference on Machine Learning*, pages 234–242, 1996.

11. J. Hekanaho. GA-based rule enhancement concept learning. In *Proc. of the 3rd International Conference on Knowledge Discovery and Data Mining*, pages 183–186, Newport Beach, CA, 1997. AAAI Press.

12. J. Hekanaho. DOGMA: A GA-Based Relational Learner. Technical Report 168, TUCS Technical Report series, March 1998. URL:http://www.tucs.fi/publications/techreports/.

13. C. Z. Janikow. A knowledge-intensive genetic algorithm for supervised learning. *Machine Learning*, 13:189–228, 1993.

14. R. Kohavi, G. John, R. Long, D. Manley, and K. Pfleger. MLC++: A machine learning library in C++. In *Tools with Artificial Intelligence*, pages 740–743. IEEE Computer Society Press, 1994. URL: http://www.sgi.com/Technology/mlc/.

15. R. S. Michalski. A theory and methodology of inductive learning. In R. S. Michalski, J. G. Carbonell, and T. M. Mitchell, editors, *Machine Learning: An Artificial Intelligence Approach*, volume I, pages 83–134, Palo Alto, CA, 1983. Tioga Press.

16. S. Muggleton, M. Bain, J. Hayes-Michie, and D. Michie. Experimental comparison of human and machine learning formalisms. In *Proc. of the 6th International Workshop on Machine Learning*, pages 113–118. Morgan Kaufmann, 1989.

17. J. R. Quinlan. Learning logical definitions from relations. *Machine Learning*, 5:239–266, 1990.

18. J. R. Quinlan. MDL and categorical theories (continued). In *Proc. of the 12th International Conference on Machine Learning*, pages 464–470, Tahoe City, CA, 1995. Morgan Kaufmann.

19. J. Rissanen. *Stochastic Complexity in Statistical Inquiry*. World Scientific, River Edge, NJ, 1989.

20. C. Schaffer. Overfitting avoidance as bias. *Machine Learning*, 10:153–178, 1993.

Generalization under Implication by λ-Subsumption

Zdravko Markov

Faculty of Mathematics and Informatics, University of Sofia,
5 James Bouchier Str., 1164 Sofia, Bulgaria
Email: markov@fmi.uni-sofia.bg

Abstract. The present paper discusses a generalization operator based on the λ-subsumption ordering between Horn clauses introduced by the author elsewhere. It has been shown that λ-subsumption is strictly stronger than *θ-subsumption* and a local equivalent of *generalized subsumption*. With some language restrictions it is decidable and possesses some other useful properties. Most importantly it allows defining a non-trivial upper bound of the λ-subsumption generalization hierarchy without the use of negative examples. Consequently this allows solving a version of the ILP task with positive-only examples.

1   Introduction

The basic problem that most of the approaches in Inductive Logic Programming (ILP) face is how to make the search in the space of clauses more efficient. Usually for this purpose the search space is structured as a subsumption hierarchy by some generality ordering. Two types of orderings are mostly used – θ-subsumption and logical implication. In contrast to implication θ-subsumption is decidable. This is the basic reason for its wide use in the practical ILP algorithms. However θ-subsumption is a weaker generality ordering than implication, i.e. it expresses fewer relations between clauses than logical implication does. As a consequence the θ-subsumption generalization operators may overgeneralize.

In the present paper we introduce a generalization operator based on the λ-subsumption ordering defined originally in [4]. It has been shown that λ-subsumption is strictly stronger than *θ-subsumption* and a local equivalent of *generalized subsumption* (a weaker version of implication introduced in [2]). Thus the new λ-subsumption-based generalization operator can avoid the problem of overgeneralization. Furthermore with some language restrictions it is decidable and possesses some other useful properties. Most importantly it allows defining a non-trivial upper bound of the λ-subsumption generalization hierarchy without the use of negative examples. Consequently this allows solving a version of the ILP task with positive-only examples.

The paper is organized as follows. The next section outlines the basic notions of λ-subsumption. Section 3 introduces the new λ-subsumption-based generalization operator. Its use for learning from positive-only examples is described in Sections 4 and 5. Section 6 discusses related work and Section 7 contains concluding remarks.

2   λ-Subsumption

This section outlines the basic definitions of λ-subsumption used further in the paper. In-depth discussion of these notions can be found in [4].

Definition 1 (λ-model of an expression). *Let E be a closed first order expression and λ – a substitution. Denote by λ_x the substitution λ, where the binding x/t is removed, i.e. $\lambda_x = \lambda \setminus \{x/t\}$. Now considering the expression $E\lambda_x$ as a function of x we can use the λ-notation to represent its semantics. That is, we have the function $f(x) = \lambda x E \lambda_x$, which maps terms (instances of x) onto truth values $\{T, F\}$ w.r.t. some Herbrand interpretation I. The set of all terms which map onto T w.r.t. I form the λ-calculus model of $\lambda x E \lambda_x$:*

$$\|\lambda x E \lambda_x\| = \{t | \exists \sigma, \lambda x E \lambda_x \sigma(t) = T \text{ in } I\}, \tag{1}$$

where σ is a substitution grounding $E\lambda$.

The intuition behind the notion of λ-model is to express explicitly the allowable instances of a variable in an expression with respect to some *partial interpretation*, determined by the substitution λ. Furthermore following the usual notion of Herbrand models we can introduce an ordering relation on expressions by using set operations between their λ-models. The basic idea is to consider the λ-models of the expressions with respect to some variables that they share. Then a λ-*model-based ordering* can be defined in a model-theoretic manner by *set inclusion*. Thus, given two expressions the problem is to find a substitution λ instantiating some variables which both expressions share. Clearly in the general case the choice of λ is non-deterministic which makes the formal definition of an ordering relation impossible. This problem is easily solved in the case of *Horn clauses* where the clause head can play the role of a pattern defining the variables needed for the calculation of the λ-models. Thus given a ground atom we can compare clauses covering this atom in some interpretation I.

Definition 2 (λ-subsumption of clauses). *Let C and D be clauses with identical heads ($C_{head} = D_{head}$) and λ – a grounding substitution for C_{head} and D_{head}. Clause C λ-subsumes clause D, denoted $C \geq_\lambda D$, if for any Herbrand interpretation I such that $C_{head}\lambda$ and $D_{head}\lambda$ are true in I:*

$$\|\lambda x \ C_{body}\lambda_x\| \supseteq \|\lambda x \ D_{body}\lambda_x\|, \forall x \in C_{head} \tag{2}$$

λ-Subsumption is also applicable if $C_{head} \neq D_{head}$. In that case a special kind of *flattening* (described in [4]) is used to transform C and D into clauses with identical heads.

The connection between λ-subsumption and *θ-subsumption* and between λ-subsumption and a weaker version of logical implication – *generalized subsumption* ([2]) has been studied in [4]. The basic result is that λ-subsumption is *strictly stronger* than θ-subsumption and a *local equivalent* of generalized subsumption.

3 Generalization under λ-subsumption

Hereafter we shall often use the notion of a clause covering a ground atom defined as follows. A clause C *covers* ground atom A in interpretation I if there exists a substitution θ such that $C_{head}\theta = A$ and $\exists(C_{body}\theta)^1$ is true in I.

Given a ground atom A let us denote by S_A the space of all clauses that cover A in interpretation I. Now we shall define a generalization operator which allows to move upward within this space.

Definition 3 (λ-Generalization operator). *Let A be a ground atom and C – a clause which covers A in I. Then the λ-generalization of C denoted $\lambda(C)$ is a clause obtained in one of the following ways:*

(a) $\lambda(C) = C\theta^{-1}$, where θ^{-1} is some inverse substitution.

(b) $\lambda(C) = (C \vee \neg L)\theta^{-1}$ for some θ^{-1} (including also $\theta = \emptyset$), where L is a ground literal which is true in I and there is a term t such that $t \in C$ and $t \in L$.

The purpose of the λ-operator is to express the idea of generalization by relaxing the constraints on the set of allowable terms for a predicate argument. This is done by replacing a ground argument with a variable (applying an inverse substitution) and eventually adding a new literal containing this variable (thus introducing some constraints on its possible instances). Table 1 illustrates this process showing two consecutive applications of the λ-generalization operator beginning with the fact member(b, [a,b]).

C / $\lambda(C)$	t	L	θ^{-1}
member(b,[a,b])	b	member(b,[b])	{b/X}
member(X,[a,b]) :– member(X,[b])	[b]	[a,b]=[a|[b]]	{[a,b]/L,[b]/Y,a/Z}
member(X,L) :– member(X,Y), L=[Z|Y]			

Table 1. Examples of λ-generalization (θ^{-1}, L and t are according to Definition 3)

There is a special case of applying the λ-operator when more than one body literals are needed to impose the necessary constraints on a variable. This is achieved through definition 3 (b) with $\theta = \emptyset$. Here is an example of a chain of clauses obtained by λ-generalization illustrating this case: $C_1 = p(a)$, $C_2 = \lambda(C_1) = p(a) :– q(a)$, $C_3 = \lambda(C_2) = p(a) :– q(a),r(a)$, $C_4 = \lambda(C_3) = p(X) :– q(X),r(X)$.

Further we shall show that the λ-generalization operator is an *upward refinement operator* ([10, 12]).

Proposition 1 (Properties of λ-generalization). *Let A be a ground atom and S_A – the set of all clauses that cover A in interpretation I. Then:*

---

[1] $\exists F$ is a shorthand for $\exists V_1 ... \exists V_n F$, where $V_1, ..., V_n$ are all the variables occurring in formula F.

1. *The λ-generalization operator never returns strictly smaller elements of S_A w.r.t. λ-subsumption, i.e. $\lambda(C) \geq_\lambda C, \forall C \in S_A$.*
2. *The λ-generalization operator is weakly complete[2]. That is, for any $C \in S_A$ there exists a chain of clauses $C_1, C_2..., C_n$ $(n \geq 0)$ such that $C_1 = \lambda(A), C_2 = \lambda(C_1), ..., C_{n-1} = \lambda(C_{n-2}), C_n = C = \lambda(C_{n-1})$.*

Proof. (1) (a) $\lambda(C) = C\theta^{-1}$. This means that $\lambda(C)$ θ-subsumes C and thus $\lambda(C) \geq_\lambda C$ by Theorem 4. $\square$

(b) $\lambda(C) = (C \vee \neg L)\theta^{-1}$. Thus $(C \vee \neg L)\theta^{-1}$ θ-subsumes $C \vee \neg L$ and by Theorem 4, $(C \vee \neg L)\theta^{-1} \geq_\lambda (C \vee \neg L)$. Let $C = C_{head} : -C_{body}$ and λ be a substitution such that $C_{head}\lambda = A$. Then by the definition of λ-subsumption, $\|\lambda x \ (C_{body} \wedge L)\theta^{-1}\lambda_x\| \supseteq \|\lambda x \ (C_{body} \wedge L)\lambda_x\|$ for all $x \in C_{head}$. Because L is ground and true in I, the λ-model of $C_{body} \wedge L$ is the same as the λ-model of C_{body}, i.e. $\|\lambda x \ (C_{body} \wedge L)\lambda_x\| = \|\lambda x \ C_{body}\lambda_x\|$ for all $x \in C_{head}$. Thus $\|\lambda x \ (C_{body} \wedge L)\theta^{-1}\lambda_x\| \supseteq \|\lambda x \ C_{body}\lambda_x\|$. Taking into account that $C \vee \neg L = C_{head} : -C_{body} \wedge L$ by Definition 2 we get $(C \vee \neg L)\theta^{-1} \geq_\lambda C$, i.e. $\lambda(C) \geq_\lambda C$. $\square$

(2) Let $C \in S_A$. If $C_{body} = \emptyset$ (i.e. $C = C_{head}$) by the definition of covers, there exists a substitution θ such that $C_{head}\theta = A$, i.e. $C = A\theta^{-1}$. By Definition 3 (a), $\lambda(A) = C$. $\square$

If $C = C_{head} : -L_1, L_2, ..., L_n$ $(n > 0)$ then there exists a substitution θ such that $C_{head}\theta = A$ and $L_i\theta$ are ground and true in I for $i = 1, ..., n$. Without loss of generality we can assume that every literal L_i has at least one variable in common with C_{head} or with the previous literals $L_1, ..., L_{i-1}$ (otherwise such a literal can be removed without affecting the λ-models of C). Let this variable be v_i for $i = 1, ..., n$. Let us denote by θ_i the substitution obtained by removing the bindings $v_{i+1}/t_{i+1}, ..., v_n/t_n$ from θ, i.e. $\theta_i = \theta \backslash \{v_{i+1}/t_{i+1}, ..., v_n/t_n\}$. Let also $C_i = (C_{head} : -L_1, ..., L_i)\theta\theta_i^{-1}$ for $i = 1, ..., n$. That is, C_i contains the first i body literals of C, where the common terms with the rest of the literals in C $(t_{i+1}, ..., t_n)$ are not variabilized. Thus we can represent the chain of clauses $C_1, ..., C_n$ iteratively by the formula $C_i = (C_{i-1} \vee \neg L_i\theta)\theta_i^{-1}$, where $L_i\theta$ is ground and true in I by the construction of C, $t_i \in C_{i-1}$ and $t_i \in L_i\theta$ by the construction of C_i and θ_i. According to Definition 3 (b) the latter means that $C_i = \lambda(C_{i-1})$, where $C_1 = \lambda(A)$ and $C_n = C$. $\square$

Another desirable property of a refinement operator is its *local finiteness* ([12]). This property is present if the set of clauses the operator induces from any clause is *finite* and *computable*. The λ-generalization operator is locally finite if the language is restricted to function-free logic programs (Datalog) because the number of inverse substitutions θ^{-1} and the number of literals L used to construct a λ-generalization of a clause are finite. Every literal L is also computable because in Datalog implication is decidable.

---

[2] Weak completeness is a weaker version of *completeness*. The latter is defined as follows: for any two clauses $C \geq D$ belonging to a *partially ordered set* w.r.t. relation $\geq$, there exists a chain of clauses $C = C_0, C_1, ..., C_n = D'$, such that C_i is produced by applying the refinement operator to C_{i-1} for $i = 1, 2, ..., n$ and $D' \sim D$.

4 Learning from positive-only examples

4.1 Locally consistent clauses

Viewing a Horn clause as implication in a *model-theoretic* manner leads to the conclusion that every model of the clause body should be also a model of the clause head. In terms of λ-models this is expressed in the following way: for clause C, substitution λ and interpretation I, such that $\exists C_{head}\lambda$ is true in I, the following should hold:

$$\|\lambda x\ C_{body}\lambda_x\| \subseteq \|\lambda x\ C_{head}\lambda_x\|, \forall x \in C_{head} \qquad (4)$$

The substitution λ can be determined by a ground atom A covered by C in I, i.e. $C_{head}\lambda = A$. Thus A also determines the λ-models $\|\lambda x\ C_{head}\lambda_x\|$ for $\forall x \in C_{head}$. We call the later λ-*extension* of A w.r.t. C or *head λ-model of C w.r.t.* A.

Let us consider again the set of clauses S_A covering ground atom A in interpretation I. For each clause $C \in S_A$ we can define the corresponding head λ-model and thus by using condition (4) we can determine the *correctness* of C w.r.t. the part of I determined by the substitution λ. Furthermore the head λ-model can play the role of a natural upper bound in the λ-subsumption chain of clauses induced by the λ-generalization operator. Table 2 illustrates this. All

No.	C	(4)
1 √	member(b,[a,b])	not applicable (no vars in C_{head})
2	member(X,[a,b])	$U_{member} \subseteq \{a, b\}$
3 √	member(X,[a,b]) :− member(X,[b])	$\{b\} \subseteq \{a, b\}$
4	member(X,[a,b]) :− member(X,[b,c])	$\{b, c\} \subseteq \{a, b\}$
5	member(b,L)	$U_{member} \subseteq \{L|b \in L\}$
6 √	member(b,L) :− L=[Z|[b]])	$\{L|b \in L, L \neq [b|\_]\} \subseteq \{L|b \in L\}$
7 √	member(X,L) :− member(X,[b]), L=[Z|[b]]	$\{b\} \subseteq \{a, b\}$, $\{L|L = [\_|[b]]\} \subseteq \{L|b \in L\}$
8 √	member(X,L) :− member(X,Y), L=[Z|Y]	$\{b\} \subseteq \{a, b\}$, $\{L|b \in L, L \neq [b|\_]\} \subseteq \{L|b \in L\}$

Table 2. Check for correctness according to condition (4)

clauses shown in Table 2 cover the atom member(b,[a,b]) in the intended interpretation of the member predicate. The third column of the table shows the instances of condition (4) for the corresponding clause in the second column. When the latter is correct the clause is marked by √ in the first column. The graph shown in Figure 1 describes the λ-generalization hierarchy of the clauses. The arrows of the graph represent applications of the λ-generalization operator. It is important to note that the set of examples used for building the λ-extension

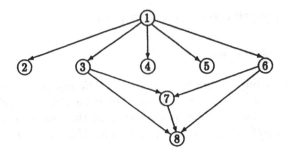

Fig. 1. λ-Generalization hierarchy of the clauses in Table 2

of member(b,[a,b]) is not the coverage of clause 8 (the target clause). Furthermore *no negative examples* are needed to check the clauses for correctness. In other words the λ-approach to correctness is different from the traditional ones based on completeness (covering all positive examples) and consistency (not covering negative examples). This is the basic motivation to introduce the notion of *locally consistent* ([4]) clause.

Definition 4 (locally consistent clause). *Clause C is locally consistent w.r.t. interpretation I if there exists a ground atom A which is true in I, C covers A in I and condition (4) holds for λ such that $C_{head}\lambda = A$.*

4.2 The λ-ILP algorithm

Hereafter we replace the *strong consistency* ($BK \cup H \not\models E^-$) condition in the standard ILP task with the newly introduced local consistency. Thus the task we address is as follows: Let BK (Background Knowledge) and H (Hypothesis) be logic programs, and E (Examples) – a set of ground facts. The conditions for construction of H are:

1. *Necessity: $BK \not\models E$*
2. *Weak consistency: $BK \cup E \cup H \not\models \Box$*
3. *Sufficiency: $BK \cup H \models E$*
4. *Local consistency: $\forall C \in H$, C is locally consistent w.r.t. some interpretation I such that E and BK are true w.r.t I.*

An algorithm for solving this task (proposed in [4]) is as follows:

1. Choose an example $E_i \in E$.
2. Find a clause $C_i \in S_{E_i}$, which is correct in terms of condition (4), where λ is such that $C_{head}\lambda = E_i$.
3. Remove from E the instances covered by C_i.
4. If $E \neq \emptyset$ then go to 1.
5. Remove all clauses λ-subsumed by other clauses. The remaining clauses form the hypothesis H conforming to the requirements of the λ-ILP task.

Hereafter we propose a bottom-up approach to finding clause C_i in step 2 of the algorithm. The basic advantage of the approach is that it is *complete*. This completeness can be achieved only with a *complete search algorithm* to search through the λ-generalization hierarchy beginning with the fact E_i and applying the λ-operator at each node to produce its successors.

The branching factor of the λ-generalization graph is typically very high. It depends mainly on the number of examples and on the size of the model of the background knowledge. Therefore the search algorithm must provide means to restrict the number of tested nodes. For this purpose we use a *hill-climbing* strategy with an evaluation function based on the number of ground terms as literal arguments in the clause. Thus the successors of a node are selected among its λ-generalizations with *minimal number of ground arguments*. This minimizes the branching factor of the successive nodes in the graph because the ground terms in the clause play the role of "links" to the next literals added by the λ-operator. Thus the smaller the number of ground terms, the fewer the links and consequently different literals to be added to the clause.

The *stopping criterion* employed is based on *information compression* and uses the encoding of Horn clause theories proposed in [3]. Thus for clause C we define $compression(C) = L(cov(C)) - L(C)$, where $cov(C)$ is the set of ground atoms that C covers and L is the code length function as defined in [3]. Clearly the value of $compression(C)$ depends greatly on the number of examples supplied. Thus the direct use of the condition $compression(C) > 0$ is not appropriate. Therefore we use an approach similar to that taken in Progol ([5]) – choosing a clause with *maximal compression*.

Formally the procedure discussed above is as follows:

1. $C_i = E_i$.
2. $S_i = \{C | C = \lambda(C_i), C$ is correct according to condition (4)$\}$.
3. If there is a clause $C \in S_i$ with maximal compression (in the sense described above) then stop and return C.
4. Otherwise let C_i be the clause in S_i containing *minimal number of ground terms* as literal arguments. Go to step 2.

5 Empirical Evaluation

The described algorithm was tested on the data sets used to test the former λ-ILP algorithm [3] based on heuristic top-down search ([4]). These sets include some of the most popular relational, recursive and propositional data used to test ILP systems. The experiments showed that the recent version of the algorithm overcomes the limitations of the former approach which were basically due to its incompleteness. Despite the very good results, we do not present these experiments here because they are described in [4] and most importantly to avoid the subjective evaluation of the fact that the learning data are manually chosen

---

[3] The previous λ-ILP system is available by anonymous ftp from ftp.gmd.de, directory /MachineLearning/ILP/public/software/lilp.

(though a formal criterion for this was presented also in [4]). Instead we employ the standard approach with randomly chosen data and perform comparative experiments with the Progol4.2 system[4].

Three domains have been chosen – appending lists (recursive functional relation), animal taxonomy (propositional) and family relationships (relational, non-recursive). The domain of four-element lists without repetition was used for generating random samples from the complete set of 261 positive examples of append. The test set contained 522 examples – all the positives and the same size random sample from the set of 274364 negatives. The animal taxonomy domain (the data supplied with the Progol4.2 package) contained 16 instances of animals belonging to 4 different classes and described with 8 attributes. Random samples from a set of 16 positives were used for learning. The test set contained 96 examples – the set of 48 negatives and the same size random sample from the positives. The family domain was the one used by Quinlan to test FOIL ([8]) – 56 examples over 12 individuals and 12 relationship types (husband, wife, mother, father, daughter, son, brother, sister, uncle, aunt, nephew, niece). The father relation described with 6 positives and 138 negatives was chosen as a target relation. The test set contained 276 examples – all the negatives and the same size random sample from the positives. Experiments were carried out with a series of 2, 4, 8, 16, 32 and 64 positive examples. For each size 10 samples were generated randomly and each one used to learn the target relation with Progol (supplied with proper mode and type declarations) and with the λ-ILP system. Then the predictive accuracy was estimated on the test set and averaged over the 10 trials. The results of all experiments are shown in Table 3.

	Append		Animals		Family	
Training set size	Progol	λ-ILP	Progol	λ-ILP	Progol	λ-ILP
2	59.83	60.07	50.20	56.35	75.11	73.37
4	67.87	68.20	50.10	60.42	81.74	92.28
8	68.22	75.51	50.31	68.02	100.0	100.0
16	69.73	77.85	94.89	84.27	100.0	100.0
32	68.96	84.92	98.54	90.73	100.0	100.0
64	80.46	98.66	99.89	99.27	100.0	100.0

Table 3. Predictive accuracy of learning from positive data – Progol vs. λ-ILP

6 Discussion

On the theoretical side the presented approach can be discussed within the framework of *refinement operators*. The first study of refinement operators was

---

[4] We used the public domain version obtained from ftp.comlab.ox.ac.uk

done by Shapiro [10]. His system MIS can learn clauses of the target program in an incremental manner by specialization of previously removed too general clauses. Top-down refinement of clauses is also the approach taken in the system FOIL ([8]) where special information-based heuristics are used to guide the search in the specialization hierarchy. Other systems (e.g. the recent one Progol [5]) use generalization operators and search preference criteria. A common feature of most of these approaches is that their refinement operators are based on θ-subsumption. As we mentioned before this choice could lead to overgeneralization or overspecialization which is normally avoided by using strong biases. In contrast our approach is based on λ-generalization which is a stronger generality ordering than θ-subsumption and thus allows the direct use of the operator in the search process with a limited use of heuristic guidance.

On the application side the approach can be related to the ILP approaches to learning from positive-only examples. Within this area generally two directions can be distinguished. The first one comprises the approaches, which assume some form of completeness within the example set. One form of completeness explored is for functional relations. That is, given the input arguments of the relation the outputs should be also presented in the example set. This idea is used in the systems FILP ([1]), INDICO ([11]) and more recently in FFOIL ([9]) to avoid the explicit specification of negative examples. A more general approach within this direction not restricted to functional relations is proposed in [13]. The second direction within the area of learning from positive examples is the Bayesian one. The Progol4.2 system ([6]) can learn from positive-only examples assuming that the learner knows the prior distributions of the hypotheses and the examples. As pointed out in [6] this is not a very strong assumption since there are means to estimate both distributions. Practically this means however that in some cases large[5] number of examples must be supplied and most importantly, they must be generated by a specially designed stochastic logic program ([7]) which uses a priori knowledge about the domain.

7 Conclusion

The presented in the paper approach can be roughly classified into the completeness-based approaches to learning from positive data. However the form of completeness it supposes is a very weak restriction on the training data. Furthermore the approach shows a potential for learning from randomly selected data which is a feature difficult to achieve within the Bayesian approaches.

Although the presented λ-ILP algorithm compares well to the best up-to-date system within this area - Progol4.2, more experimental work is needed to show the strong and the week points of the approach as a whole. The experiments done so far (discussed here and in ([4]) showed a good performance of the algorithm in recursive domains. This is a natural consequence of the fact that the approach

---

[5] Though there are domains where Progol can learn from very few positive examples, this is mainly due to the mode declarations it uses rather than due to the prior knowledge of the distribution of the examples.

is based on inverse implication instead of on θ-subsumption. In this direction an in-depth comparison to the ILP approaches addressing especially the induction of recursive clauses is needed. Further work will be also directed towards finding better strategies to search the λ-generalization hierarchy. For this purpose some constraint programming techniques could be used to explore the resemblance of the λ-models of clauses and the variable domains in CSP. On the theoretical side the existence and the computability of a least general generalization (lgg) under λ-subsumption will be investigated too.

Acknowledgements

I owe many tanks to the anonymous referees for the valuable comments and suggestions for improvement of the paper. This work was partially supported by a PECO contract between INRIA Rhone-Alpes and IIT-Sofia.

References

1. Bergadano, F., Gunetti, D. Functional Inductive Logic Programming with Queries to the User, in: *Proceedings of ECML-93*, LNAI, Vol.667, Springer-Verlag, 1993, 323-328.
2. Buntine, W. Generalized Subsumption and Its Application to Induction and Redundancy, *Artificial Intelligence*, Vol. 36 (1988), 149-176.
3. Conklin, D., Witten, I. Complexity-Based Induction, *Machine Learning*, Vol. 16 (3), 1994, 203-225.
4. Markov, Z. λ-Subsumption and Its Application to Learning from Positive-only Examples, in: *Muggleton (ed.), Proceedings of ILP-96, Selected Papers*, Lecture Notes in Artificial Intelligence, Vol.1314, Springer, 1997, 377-396.
5. Muggleton, S. Inverse Entailment and Progol, *New Generation Computing*, 13 (1995), 245-286.
6. Muggleton, S. Learning from positive data, in: *Proceedings of ILP-96*, Department of Computer and Systems Science, Stockholm University/Royal Institute of Technology, Report No.96-019, August, 1996, 225-244.
7. Muggleton, S. Stochastic Logic Programs, in: L.De Raedt (ed.), *Advances in Inductive Logic Programming*, IOS Press, 1996, 254-264.
8. Quinlan, J.R. Learning logical definitions from relations, *Machine Learning*, 5 (1990), 239-266.
9. Quinlan, J.R. Learning First-Order Definitions of Functions, *Journal of Artificial Intelligence Research*, 5 (1996), 139-161.
10. Shapiro, E.Y. *Algorithmic program debugging*, MIT Press, 1983.
11. Stahl, I., Tausend, B., Wirth, R. Two Methods for Improving Inductive Logic Programming Systems, in: *Proceedings of ECML-93*, LNAI, Vol.667, Springer-Verlag, 1993, 41-55.
12. Van der Laag, P.R.J. *An Analysis of Refinement operators in Inductive Logic Programming*, Ph.D. thesis, Tinbergen Institute Research Series, No.102, Amsterdam, 1996.
13. Zelle, J., Thompson, C., Califf, M., Mooney, R. Inducing Logic Programs without Explicit Negative Examples, in: Luc De Raedt (Ed.), *Proceedings of ILP-95*, Scientific report, Department of Computer Science, K.U. Leuven, September, 1995, 403-416.

Prolog, Refinements and RLGG's

Claude Sammut

School of Computer Science and Engineering
University of New South Wales
Sydney 2052 Australia
claude@cse.unsw.edu.au
http://www.cse.unsw.edu.au/~claude

Abstract. Cohen's [1] refinement rules provide a flexible mechanism for introducing intentional background knowledge in an ILP system. Whereas Cohen used a limited second order theorem prover to implement the rule interpreter, we extend the method to use a full Prolog interpreter. This makes the introduction of more complex background knowledge possible. Although refinement rules have been used to generate literals for a general-to-specific search, we show how they can also be used as filters to reduce the number of literals in an RLGG algorithm. Each literal constructed by the LGG is tested against the refinement rules and only admitted if a refinement rule has been satisfied.

1 Introduction

Most current ILP systems use some form of declarative bias to restrict the search space of the learner. Cohen [1] introduced *refinement rules* as a flexible way of specifying the form of literals that may be introduced into the head and body of the clause being constructed. His refinement rules are written in a second order language. This allows the rules to be expressed very succinctly. A disadvantage of this scheme is that the theorem prover is quite limited in its capabilities. In this paper we show how the language of the refinement rules can be based on a full Prolog interpreter with some simple second order extensions. We also show how this system can be used to achieve the same effects as lazy modes in Srinivasan's work with Progol [10].

In his FLIPPER system, Cohen [1] used refinement rules to generate literals for a general-to-specific search similar to FOIL's [6]. We show how the same kind of rules can be used to produce a saturated clause [8] [7] that can be used either in a general-to-specific search or in a specific-to-general search as used by Plotkin [5] or by Muggleton [2] in GOLEM. The crucial observation here is that the refinement rules can be used to filter literals that are created by Relative Least General Generalisation [5].

Learning based on the RLGG has fallen out of favour, mainly because the Least General Generalisation of two clauses often creates a very large number of redundant literals that must be avoided or removed by a variety of heuristics. However, the RLGG remains a useful technique, especially when a specific-to-general search is most suitable for a particular problem. It is well suited to learning tasks in which we are interested in obtaining a *characteristic* rather than a *discriminant* concept description. For example, in computer vision we may wish to learn to describe objects that appear in an image. In this case, it may not be useful to learn to simply distinguish between, say, a cup and a table because this does not capture the properties of the cup itself. For this reason, we are interested in obtaining generalisations of the training set that are as specific as possible.

In the following section, we review the basic ideas behind refinement rules. We then show how the refinement rule interpreter can be implemented as an extension to Prolog. Sections 4 and 5 demonstrates how refinement rules can be used in conjunction with an RLGG algorithm to limit the number of literals generated.

2 Refinement Rules and Generalisation

In this section, we briefly summarise some of the key ideas introduced by Cohen. Like FOIL, FLIPPER is a covering algorithm that creates a new clause by starting with a head and an empty body. New literals are introduced into the body of the clause to specialise it. The efficacy of the literal is tested, as in FOIL, by information gain. Where FLIPPER differs from FOIL is the way in which it constructs new literals. Literals are generated by refinement rules. Two types of refinement rule may be defined. A *head rule* has the form:

$$\langle A, Pre, Post \rangle$$

where A is a positive literal, Pre is a conjunction of literals and $Post$ is a set of positive literals. A body rule has the form:

$$\langle \leftarrow B, Pre, Post \rangle$$

where B is a positive literal and Pre and $Post$ are as above.

There must only be one head rule stating that A should be used to create the head of the clause being learned, provided that the condition Pre is satisfied. After A has been constructed, the literals in $Post$, are asserted into a temporary database. There may be any number of body rules to generate literals for the body of the clause under construction. The preconditions are tested using a function-free second order theorem prover.

Cohen gives an example of refinement rules that he used for the king-rook-king illegal problem:

$$DB_0 = \{rel(adjacent), rel(equal), rel(less\_than)\}$$

$illegal(A, B, C, D, E, F) \leftarrow$
  where $true$ asserting $\{row(A), col(B), ..., row(E), col(F)\}$

$\leftarrow R(X, Y)$
  where $rel(R), CommonType(X), CommonType(Y)$ asserting $\emptyset$

DB_0 is an initial database that contains information that the refinement operation can use. In this case, the database starts with a list of the relations that refinement is allowed to use in building a clause. Expressions of the form,

where ⟨*preconditions*⟩ asserting ⟨*postconditions*⟩

inform the system about the conditions that must be true before the rule can be applied and the conditions which must apply afterward. The post conditions are added to DB. In this example, the first refinement rule indicates that the head of the clause should be *illegal*(A, B, C, D, E, F) and the arguments are rows or columns. Rules of the form, ← *BodyLiteral*, tell the system the form of literals that may be added to the body of the clause being learned. In this example, the rule indicates that literals like *adjacent*(X, Y), *equal*(X, Y) and *less_than*(X, Y) are legal as long as X and Y are of the same type.

3 Using Prolog to Interpret Refinement Rules

Refinement rules have been embedded in the *iProlog* interpreter [9] so that Prolog itself is used to evaluate the rules rather than using a special purpose theorem prover. In *iProlog*, the above example is written as:

```
rel(adjacent).        type(row).
rel(equal).           type(col).
rel(less_than).
```

```
illegal(A, B, C, D, E, F)
    where true asserting row(A), col(B), ..., row(E), col(F).
```

```
(:- R(X, Y))
    where rel(R), type(CommonType), CommonType(X), CommonType(Y).
```

Note that *iProlog* has been extended to allow the predicate symbol to be a variable. So that minimal changes can be made to Prolog we insist that the predicate variable must be bound before execution. Thus, we must add the literal *type*(*CommonType*), to first bind *CommonType*. Thus, Cohen's language is more powerful in the sense that his theorem prover will search for an appropriate predicate for *CommonType*, however, in *iProlog*, we now have the full power of Prolog to specify intentional background knowledge. We will illustrate this with an example from image processing [11].

The task is to learn to recognise various blood vessels from x-ray angiograms of the cerebral vasculature. After preprocessing, the image is reduced to a skeleton of line segments, each of which represents a segment of a blood vessel. For example, the following predicates describe an internal carotid artery:

```
internal_carotid_artery(mb1, 1).
segment(1, mb1, n, 40, 130, [2]).
```

```
segment(2, mb1, w, 40, 144, [3]).
segment(3, mb1, nw, 35, 135, [4, 5]).
segment(4, mb1, n, 40, 50, [6, 7]).
segment(6, mb1, ne, 20, 170, [8, 9]).
segment(5, mb1b1, e, 10, 100, []).
segment(7, mb1b2, w, 5, 125, []).
segment(8, mb1b3, e, 18, 90, []).
segment(9, mb1b4, n, 15, 100, []).
```

The blood vessel *mb1*, which is an Internal Carotid Artery, starts with segment number 1. Each segment is described by an atom with the following arguments: the segment's segment number, the identifier of the blood vessel to which the segment belongs, the direction of the segment (north, north-east, east, south-east, *etc*), the diameter of the segment, the grey-level intensity of the segment and finally, a list of segments that branch from the end of this segment. A segment's start and end points are where there is a branch or a bend in the blood vessel.

In the following example, we will use the refinement rules, not to generate literals for a general-to-specific search, but to create a saturated clause. The head rule is:

```
internal_carotid_artery(VesselName, StartingSegment)
    where
        true
    asserting
        vessel_name(VesselName),
        seg_list(VesselName, [StartingSegment]).
```

Refinement rules are invoked in a forward chaining manner. The head rule matches the predicate *internal_carotid_artery(mb1, 1)*. Since there are no preconditions, the head of the new clause is created and the predicates

$$vessel\_name(VesselName) \text{ and } seg\_list(mb1, [1])$$

are asserted into the database. This enables the following body rule to construct literals for the segments of the blood vessel:

```
(:- segment(SegId, VesselName, Dirn, Diam, Inten, SegList))
    where
        seg_list(VesselName, S),
        member(SegId, S)
    asserting
        seg_list(VesselName, SegList),
        diameter(VesselName, SegId, Diam),
        intensity(VesselName, SegId, Inten).
```

For each match of the template and for each solution to the preconditions, a new segment literal is created and the corresponding post-conditions are asserted. We use the *seg_list* predicate to ensure that all segment literals that are generated are "linked", meaning that there is a path from the starting segment to every other segment that appears in the clause. We use the *diameter* and *intensity* predicates to specify the type and origin of the value found in the segment literal.

After execution of this rule, the clause is:

```
internal_carotid_artery(mb1, 1) :-
        segment(1, mb1, n, 40, 130, [2]),
        segment(2, mb1, w, 40, 144, [3]),
        segment(3, mb1, nw, 35, 135, [4, 5]),
        segment(4, mb1, n, 40, 50, [6, 7]),
        segment(6, mb1, ne, 20, 170, [8, 9]).
```

Intentional background knowledge is required if we wish to include in the concept description which segment has, say, the maximum diameter. This is a little tricky because the refinement rule must scan all of the segments to find the maximum value. First, we require a predicate that can find the maximum value of a measurement. We use the second order extension to make this predicate generic for different types.

```
max(M, V, S, X) :-
        findall(M(V, S, N), M(V, S, N), L),
        max(L, M(V, S, X)).

max([X], X) :- !.
max([M(V, SA, A)|B], M(V, S, X)) :-
        max(B, M(V, SY, Y)),
        (A > Y -> S = SA, X = A; S = SY, X = Y).
```

This can be read as: the maximum value of measurement M in blood vessel, V, occurs in segment, S, and has value, N. The predicate can be invoked from the body rule:

```
(:- max(M, V, S, N))
    where
        measurement(M),
        vessel_name(V),
        max(M, V, S, N).

measurement(diameter).
measurement(intensity).
```

A corresponding rule can be defined for the minimum value. After execution of these rules, the following literals are added to the clause:

```
        max(diameter, mb1, 1, 40)
        max(diameter, mb1, 2, 40)
```

```
max(diameter, mb1, 4, 40)
max(intensity, mb1, 6, 170)
min(diameter, mb1, 6, 20)
min(intensity, mb1, 4, 50)
```

Using Prolog to scan all examples gives us the same capability as Srinivasan's lazy evaluation [10] to accumulate values to pass to a predicate that performs some kind of "global" data analysis. In the case of Srinivasan and Camacho, this was a regression algorithm. *iProlog* includes a number of other data analysis tools (see [9]).

We now describe in some detail how refinement rules are evaluated.

3.1 Evaluating Refinement Rules

A head rule has the form:

$$\text{Literal where } precondition \text{ asserting } postcondition.$$

where *precondition* is any legal Prolog expression as would appear in the body of a clause. *Postcondition* is a conjunction of literals that will be asserted into Prolog's data base.

Training examples are given as ground unit clauses in Prolog's data base. When the refinement rules are invoked by a call to the *refine* built-in predicate, the head rule is invoked. A new clause is created such that *Literal* is the head of the clause, provided that the preconditions are satisfied. The preconditions are tested by invoking the Prolog interpreter to try to find a proof in exactly the same way that it would execute a Prolog program. Often the precondition for a head rule is simply true. Once the clause has been created, each literal in the postcondition is asserted, temporarily, into Prolog's data base. All postconditions are retracted after the refinement process has completed execution.

A body rule has the form:

$$(\text{:- } Template) \text{ where } precondition \text{ asserting } postcondition.$$

Note that the parentheses are needed simply so that the Prolog parser does not confuse this with a syntactically incorrect clause.

Once the head rule has completed execution, the refinement rule interpreter begins cycling through each body rule in text order. The following actions are performed:

1. The preconditions and the template are conjoined to form a single conjunction of literals, C.
2. C is tested by running it as a query to the Prolog interpreter.
3. If C is satisfied, the postconditions are temporarily asserted into Prolog's data base.
4. The literal resulting from satisfying $Template$ is added to the body of the clause.

5. If there is more than one solution to the query C, backtracking finds all solutions and therefore generates more than one literal to add to the clause.

Note that all literals added to the body of the new clause must be calls to defined Prolog predicates.

Like a forward chaining rule interpreter, the refinement rule interpreter repeats its cycle until no more new literals can be found. The result of this process is a saturated clause based on one of the training examples. This may be used as the "bottom" clause in a Progol-style search [3]. If the refinement process is applied to all of the positive training examples, the resulting set of clause can be used to form LGG's as with Plotkin [5] or in GOLEM [2].

The biggest problem with LGG's is that many redundant literals are usually created. In the next section we will see how refinement rules can be used to *filter* the LGG, eliminating unwanted literals.

4 Constrained RLGG's

We follow an approach similar in spirit to the constrained atoms of Page and Frisch [4]. Since refinement rules impose restrictions on the form of literals that can be generated through saturation, it is reasonable to apply the same restrictions to literals constructed by generalisation. Thus, we modify Plotkin's LGG algorithm to filter literals so that whenever an LGG of two literals is found, it is tested against the refinement rules. If no refinement rule is satisfied, the new literal is discarded. As a result, the RLGG's do not grow to impractical sizes.

Assuming the new literal is L, the refinement test proceeds as follows:

1. Search the list of refinement rules $\langle X, Pre, Post \rangle$ (for the head literal) and $\langle \leftarrow X, Pre, Post \rangle$ (for the body literals) to find a rule where X unifies with L. If no match is found, the test fails.
2. If a matching refinement rule has been found for L, invoke the Prolog interpreter to test the preconditions, Pre. If the proof fails, the refinement check fails.
3. If the preconditions are met, temporarily assert L into Prolog's data base. This is necessary so that subsequent tests of other literals can refer to L.
4. Assert the postconditions.
5. Return with a success.

One further variation of the LGG algorithm is required. When inverse substitutions are created and variables are inserted into the terms, each variable is temporarily bound to a unique dummy constant. This is necessary so that when L is asserted into the data base, it has constant values consistent with the variable bindings of other literals in the clause, rather than unbound variables that match anything.

To illustrate how refinement rules can reduce the number of literals in an RLGG, let us continue with the medical imaging example. Suppose we have the following two training instances:

```
internal_carotid_artery(mb1, mb1_1).
segment(mb1_1, mb1, n, 40,  130, [mb1_2]).
segment(mb1_2, mb1, w, 40,  144, [mb1_3]).
segment(mb1_3, mb1, nw, 35, 135, [mb1_4, mb1_5]).
segment(mb1_4, mb1, n, 40,  50, [mb1_6, mb1_7]).
segment(mb1_6, mb1, ne, 20, 170, [mb1_8, mb1_9]).
segment(mb1_5, mb1b1, e,  10,  100, []).
segment(mb1_7, mb1b2, w,   5,  125, []).
segment(mb1_8, mb1b3, e,  18,   90, []).
segment(mb1_9, mb1b4, n,  15,  100, []).

internal_carotid_artery(pk2, pk2_1).
segment(pk2_1, pk2, n, 35, 70, [pk2_2]).
segment(pk2_2, pk2, ne, 40, 100, [pk2_3]).
segment(pk2_3, pk2, w, 40, 120, [pk2_4]).
segment(pk2_4, pk2, n, 50, 40, [pk2_5, pk2_6]).
segment(pk2_5, pk2, nw, 45, 50, [pk2_7, pk2_8]).
segment(pk2_7, pk2, ne, 20, 120, [pk2_9, pk2_10]).
segment(pk2_6, pk2b1, e,  10,  150, []).
segment(pk2_8, pk2b2, w,   5,  175, []).
segment(pk2_9, pk2b3, e,  16,  130, []).
segment(pk2_10, pk2b4, n, 14,  140, []).
```

Using the refinement rules described in section 3, we obtain the following two saturated clauses. Note that at this point we have not yet created any variables but retain all constants.

```
internal_carotid_artery(mb1, mb1_1) :-
        segment(mb1_1, mb1, n, 40, 130, [mb1_2]),
        segment(mb1_2, mb1, w, 40, 144, [mb1_3]),
        segment(mb1_3, mb1, nw, 35, 135, [mb1_4, mb1_5]),
        segment(mb1_4, mb1, n, 40, 50, [mb1_6, mb1_7]),
        segment(mb1_5, mb1b1, e, 10, 100, []),
        segment(mb1_6, mb1, ne, 20, 170, [mb1_8, mb1_9]),
        segment(mb1_7, mb1b2, w, 5, 125, []),
        segment(mb1_8, mb1b3, e, 18, 90, []),
        segment(mb1_9, mb1b4, n, 15, 100, []),
        max(diameter, mb1, mb1_4, 40),
        max(intensity, mb1, mb1_6, 170),
        min(diameter, mb1, mb1_6, 20),
        min(intensity, mb1, mb1_4, 50).

internal_carotid_artery(pk2, pk2_1) :-
        segment(pk2_1, pk2, n, 35, 70, [pk2_2]),
        segment(pk2_2, pk2, ne, 40, 100, [pk2_3]),
        segment(pk2_3, pk2, w, 40, 120, [pk2_4]),
        segment(pk2_4, pk2, n, 50, 40, [pk2_5, pk2_6]),
```

```
segment(pk2_5, pk2, nw, 45, 50, [pk2_7, pk2_8]),
segment(pk2_6, pk2b1, e, 10, 150, []),
segment(pk2_7, pk2, ne, 20, 120, [pk2_9, pk2_10]),
segment(pk2_8, pk2b2, w, 5, 175, []),
segment(pk2_9, pk2b3, e, 16, 130, []),
segment(pk2_10, pk2b4, n, 14, 140, []),
max(diameter, pk2, pk2_4, 50),
max(intensity, pk2, pk2_7, 120),
min(diameter, pk2, pk2_7, 20),
min(intensity, pk2, pk2_4, 40).
```

Since there are 9 segment literals in the first clause and 10 in the second, a simple LGG of these clauses would result in 90 segment literals in the new clause. However, using the same refinement rules as filters on the LGG, we obtain:

```
internal_carotid_artery(_0, _1) :-
    segment(_1, _0, n, _2, _3, [_4]),
    segment(_4, _0, _5, 40, _6, [_7]),
    segment(_7, _0, _8, _9, _10, [_11 | _12]),
    segment(_11, _0, n, _13, _14, [_15, _16]),
    segment(_15, _0, _17, _18, _19, [_20, _21]),
    segment(_16, _22, _23, _24, _25, []),
    segment(_20, _26, _27, _28, _29, _30),
    segment(_21, _31, _32, _33, _34, []),
    max(diameter, _0, _11, _13),
    min(intensity, _0, _11, _14).
```

which is a considerable improvement on the unconstrained LGG.

5   A Small Trial

It is unlikely that we will ever have a large number of x-ray images as training examples since it is very time consuming for radiologists to provide fully labelled images. Therefore the mode of operation in this application is more one of "programming by example" than data mining. A small trial has been conducted on a sample of 10 x-ray images of the internal carotid artery and 11 negative examples obtained from images of different blood vessels or images from different views.

Apart from the predicates already described, the background knowledge includes the concepts of left and right turns (i.e. changes in direction from one segment to the next); left and right branches (i.e. different blood vessels emanating from the example vessel) and counting predicates providing the number of turns and branches.

The refinement rules were applied to all 10 positive examples, obtaining 10 saturated clauses. The constrained LGG of these clauses produced the following clause:

```
internal_carotid_artery(_0, _1) :-
        segment(_1, _0, n, _2, _3, [_4 | _5]),
        left_turns(_0, _6),
        right_turns(_0, _7),
        left_branches(_0, 2),
        right_branches(_0, 2).
```

This describes a blood vessel that has an initial segment heading North. It has some left and right turns and exactly two left branches and two right branches. While the size of the training set is extremely small, this trial demonstrates that refinement rules can be effective in constraining the LGG to produce a concise and understandable concept description.

Acknowledgments

Much of the motivation for this work came from the medical imaging application described here. Thanks to Tatjana Zrimec for providing the x-ray images, the preprocessing software and the domain knowledge needed for this problem. Thanks also to Mike Bain for many helpful discussions on refinement rules.

References

1. Cohen, W.: Learning to classify English text with ILP methods. In L. de Raedt (Eds.), Advances in Inductive Logic programming. IOS Press (1996) 124–143
2. Muggleton, S., Feng, C.: Efficient induction of logic programs. In First Conference on Algorithmic Learning Theory. Omsha, Tokyo (1990)
3. Muggleton, S.: Inverse Entailment and Progol. New Generation Computing 13 (1995) 245–286.
4. Page, C. D., Frisch, A. M.: Generalization and Learnability: A study of constrained atoms. In S. Muggleton (Eds.): Inductive Logic Programming. Academic Press (1992) 29–61
5. Plotkin, G. D.: A further note on inductive generalization. In B. Meltzer and D. Michie (Eds.): Machine Intelligence 6. Elsevier, New York (1971)
6. Quinlan, J. R.: Learning Logical Definitions from Relations. Machine Learning 5 (1990) 239–266
7. Rouveirol, C., Puget, J.-F.: Beyond Inversion of Resolution. In Proceedings of the Seventh International Conference on Machine Learning. Morgan Kaufmann (1990)
8. Sammut, C. A., Banerji, R. B.: Learning Concepts by Asking Questions. In R. S. Michalski Carbonell, J.G. and Mitchell, T.M. (Eds.): Machine Learning: An Artificial Intelligence Approach, Vol 2. Morgan Kaufmann, Los Altos, California (1986) 167–192
9. Sammut, C.: Using background knowledge to build multistrategy learners. Machine Learning 27 (1997) 241–257
10. Srinivasan, A., Camacho, R.: Experiments in numerical reasoning with Inductive Logic Programming. Journal of Logic Programming (in press)
11. Zrimec, T., Sammut, C.A.: A Medical Image Understanding System. Engineering applications of Artificial Intelligence 10(1) (1997) 31–39.

Learning Structurally Indeterminate Clauses

Jean-Daniel Zucker, Jean-Gabriel Ganascia

LIP6-CNRS, Université Paris VI, 4, Place Jussieu
F-75252, Paris Cedex 05, FRANCE
{Jean-Daniel.Zucker,Jean-Gabriel.Ganascia}@lip6.fr

Abstract. This paper describes a new kind of language bias, *S-structural indeterminate clauses*, which takes into account the meaning of predicates that play a key role in the complexity of learning in structural domains. *Structurally indeterminate clauses* capture an important background knowledge in structural domains such as medicine, chemistry or computational linguistics: the specificity of the component/object relation. The REPART algorithm has been specifically developed to learn such clauses. Its efficiency lies in a particular change of representation so as to be able to use propositional learners. Because of the indeterminacy of the searched clauses the propositional learning problem to be solved is a kind of Multiple-Instance problem. Such reformulations may be a general approach for learning non determinate clauses in ILP. This paper presents original results discovered by REPART that exemplify how ILP algorithms may not only scale up efficiently to large relational databases but also discover useful and computationally hard-to-learn patterns.

1. Introduction

In this article we address the problem of data mining a relational database describing Chinese characters. Chinese characters, or sinograms, are each a wealth of knowledge. Each of them has its own history during which, its graphical representation, its meaning and its pronunciation have all evolved. Today, there are 20,000 graphical signs, each of which has one or more meanings and, in Mandarin alone, with one or more pronunciations. The inherent structural aspect of Chinese characters makes their comparison heavily combinatorial. The basic interest of using KDD techniques to mine a large relational Database of Chinese characters is to go beyond the purely statistical approaches that have dominated computer analysis of Chinese characters [1]. Concretely, the linguists and teachers we are working with are searching for patterns or rules that could help better understand Chinese characters and facilitate their teaching as a second language. The kind of knowledge phoneticians are interested in discovering relates, for example, the pronunciation of characters with any of their properties or the property of their components or subcomponents: *"If a character X contains a component X1 such that X1 is not the key (i.e. the component used to semantically index the characters in dictionaries) then X and X1 may have the same initial (i.e. their pronunciation share some similarity)"*.

We have designed a database (DB) of Chinese characters represented as ground facts (See Table 1) also referred as O the set of *observations*. Background Knowledge *BK* on Chinese characters is represented by definite clauses. The data mining oriented ILP framework we consider is related to that of *characteristic induction from closed observations* used in CLAUDIEN [2]. More details on our KDD environment may be found in [3]. When "all observations are completely specified" w.r.t. to Background Knowledge, we shall refer to them as *closed observations*. Like in De Raedt and Dehaspe's framework, the data mining task is to look for interesting or valid regularities as definite clauses "that reflect what is in the data" [2]. A rule similar to that mentioned above may be reformulated as a clause C1:

$$C1 = init(X,I) \leftarrow carCompo(X,X1), key(X,X1,false), init(X1,I)$$

Table 1. Ground facts describing the Chinese character 爱

car(car14)	final(car14_c1,ua)	carGraphem(car14_c2,car14_c2_g1)
gb(car14,631)	ton(car14_c1,3)	grapheme(car14_c2_g1,g26)
carCompoNB(car14,3)	pinyin(car14_c1,zhua3)	—Third component 友
carGraphNB(car14,4)	graphemNB(car14_c1,1)	
carTradForm(car14,true)	carGraphem(car14_c1,car14_c1_g1)	carCompo(car14,car14_c3)
freq(car14,312)	grapheme(car14_c1_g1,g271)	gb(car14_c3,3956)
meaning(car14,love)	position(car14_c1,car14_c2,above)	absposition(car14_c3,bas)
init(car14,none)	position(car14_c1,car14_c3,above)	key(car14,car14_c3,false)
medial(car14,ai)	position(car14_c2,car14_c3,below)	init(car14_c3,y)
ton(car14,4)	—Second component 爫	final(car14_c3,ou)
pinyin(car14,ai4)	carCompo(car14,car14_c2)	ton(car14_c3,3)
—First component 爫	gb(car14_c2,4567)	pinyin(car14_c3,you3)
carCompo(car14,car14_c1)	absposition(car14_c2,middle)	graphemNB(car14_c3,2)
gb(car14_c1,4289)	key(car14,car14_c2,false)	carGraphem(car14_c3,car14_c3_g1)
absposition(car14_c1,upper)	ppcmini_mode(car14,car14_c2,_)	graphem(car14_c3_g1,g16)
key(car14,car14_c1,true)	ppcm_point(car14,car14_c2,_)	carGraphem(car14_c3,car14_c3_g2)
init(car14_c1,zh)	graphemNB(car14_c2,1)	grapheme(car14_c3_g2,g41)

The concrete task we are addressing raises two main related problems. The first one is that the clauses that are of interest include *nondeterminate* clauses that are known to be computationally hard to learn. The second problem is that our database of thousands of Chinese characters contains more than **200,000 ground facts** and that mining such a database requires scaling up learning algorithms. To solve the first problem, we propose to introduce a new type of restriction on clauses, *S-structural indeterminacy*, that takes into consideration the very *meaning* of the predicates. With this type of restriction it is possible to capture important background knowledge in structural domains, the specificity of the component/object relation. To solve the second problem, we have developed an efficient algorithm that changes the representation of nondeterminate clauses by allowing the use of propositional logic learning algorithms that solves the multiple-part problem.

The rest of the paper is organized as follows. The following section characterizes the role of determinacy in the complexity of learning clauses. The third section introduces the language bias of S-structural indeterminate clauses. The fourth section presents an ILP algorithm called REPART, which efficiently learns such clauses by reformulating the problem in propositional logic. It also presents original results discovered by REPART. Section five concludes and outlines possible lines of research opened up by this work.

2. Learning clauses efficiently: the role of determinacy

The ability to scale up to large numbers of facts is closely related to the complexity of learning. One main dimension to control this complexity is the choice of the restrictions on the hypothesis space searched [4]. The representation of this restriction knowledge is called *declarative bias*. Current ILP systems distinguish at least two kinds of declarative bias: *semantic* bias and *syntactic* bias [5]. Syntactic bias imposes restrictions on the *form* of clauses allowed in the hypotheses whereas semantic bias imposes restrictions on the *interpretation* of hypothesis. Depth, maximum arity, linkedness, schemata, are typical syntactic bias [6]. As for semantic bias, there are different types of restriction such as *modes* [7] and clause *determinacy* [7-9].

A well known language bias, ij-determinism [8], combines both syntactical (depth i and arity maximum j) and semantic restrictions (determinacy). This strong language bias is known to be PAC-learnable [10] and several ILP systems, such as GOLEM [8], LINUS [11] or GRENDEL [12], do learn ij-determinate clauses efficiently. Let us recall the definition of a determinate clause $C = H \leftarrow B_1, B_2, ..., B_k$ where H is the *head* and B_i are literals of the *body* of the clause.

Definition 1 : *A literal B_i is **determinate** in a definite clause $C = H \leftarrow B_1, B_2, ..., B_k$ (with respect to BK and O) if for every possible substitution σ that unifies H with some $o \in O$ such that $BK \vdash (B_1 \wedge .... \wedge B_{i-1}) \sigma$, there is at most one substitution θ so that $BK \vdash B_i \sigma \theta$. A clause is **determinate** if all of its literals are determinate.*

Unfortunately, in our domain like many other structural domains, the clauses of interest are not necessarily determinate. C1 for example is not a determinate clause with respect to our characters database. Indeed for $\sigma = \{X = car14\}$, of the three possible substitutions θ (one for each component of the character) $\theta1 = \{X1 = car14\_c1\}$, $\theta2 = \{X1 = car14\_c2\}$ and $\theta3 = \{X1 = car14\_c2\}$, both $\theta2$ and $\theta3$ are such that $BK \vdash (carCompo(X, X1) \wedge key(X, X1, false) \wedge init(X1, I)) \sigma \theta$. The clause C1 is a typical nondeterminate clause. It has the same nature as the clause parent(P) ← child(P,C) stating that P is a parent if there exists C such that C is a child of P in a database where some parents may have more than one child and if there are no other predicates [9].

Building algorithms that efficiently learn nondeterminate clauses is still an open problem. One of the early ILP systems that was not restricted to ij-determinate clauses is FOIL [13]. However, FOIL is short-sighted and may fail to learn determinate clauses because nondeterminate literals such as carCompo(X,X1) are likely not to bring any information gain (because not discriminant) [14, 15]. The FOCL system using *relational cliché* is an ad-hoc solution to avoid the problem of local minima of information gain [16]. Different promising approaches also propose a new stochastic bias, either on the exploration of the search space of the concept, SFOIL[15], or on the subsumption itself, STILL[17]. The genetic algorithm based REGAL system reports also good results [18]. To our knowledge, PROGOL is one of the most efficient system learning nondeterminate clauses. PROGOL allows the programmer to characterize very precisely the degree of indeterminacy using lists of *modes* [19]. Nevertheless, this approach requires both a good knowledge of the domain and of the PROGOL system.

To *bound the indeterminacy* of clauses, Cohen has proposed two kinds of restrictions: k-locality [9] and *l*-indeterminacy [20]. The first one is a syntactic restriction that strictly increases the expressiveness of constant depth clauses. Informally, a clause is k-local " *if the binding for any free variable affects the success or failure of only k literals* " [9]. Cohen has shown that the language of k-local clauses was PAC-learnable. However, the algorithm sketched by Cohen is "*relatively inefficient*" according to the author himself [9]. Nevertheless, since k-local clauses may be nondeterminate, Cohen's result is a solid hint that there are some restricted languages of nondeterminate rules for which there may exist tractable algorithms. The second restriction is a semantic one that bounds the degree of indeterminism. It is defined as follows:

Definition 2 [20]: *A clause $H \leftarrow B_1, B_2,..., B_n$ is called **l-indeterminate** (with respect to the set of observations O and the background knowledge BK) iff for every possible substitution σ that unifies H to some ground instance and for all i=1,...r there are at most l distinct substitutions θ such that $BK \vdash (B_1 \wedge B_2 \wedge .. \wedge B_i)\sigma\theta$.*

A *one-indeterminate* clause is by definition a *determinate* clause. Informally, a clause is *l*-indeterminate if there are at most *l* possible bindings that can be used to prove a clause or any of its prefixes. Using this definition, the clause C1 is 3-indeterminate w.r.t. BK and the sole example car_14 (cf. Table 1).

One particularity of *l*-indeterminacy, is that the order in which the literals appear may change the degree of indeterminacy. Let us consider the two following clauses:

C2=init(X,I) $\leftarrow$ carCompo(X,X1), key(X,X2,true), carCompo(X,X2).

C3=init(X,I) $\leftarrow$ carCompo(X,X1), carCompo(X,X2), key(X,X2,true).

The clause C2 is 3-indeterminate w.r.t. BK and example car_14 (cf. Table 1). On the contrary, the clause C3 is 9-indeterminate. The notion of *l*-indeterminacy is a semantic bias and depends very much on the database considered and on the order of literals. Although C2 is 3-indeterminate and C3 9-indeterminate w.r.t. BK and example car_14 (cf. Table 1), both C2 and C3 have the exact same interpretation model. Using such *l*-indeterminacy bias defines a hypothesis space that is therefore difficult to understand on real domains, it represents a problem in a KDD context. Moreover, as Cohen says, it remains to be seen if learning algorithms that are both well-understood and practically useful may be designed for such language bias [9].

3. A "meaningful" bias: Structurally Indeterminate clauses

Our approach is to introduce a language bias that takes into account the specificity of the component/object relation in structural domains to characterize degrees of indeterminacy. First the notion of *structural literal* is introduced

Definition 3 *A literal p(X,Y) is said to be **structural** iff p means that X is in a component/object relation with Y (p is said to be a structural predicate). A literal is said **functional** otherwise.*

The literal carCompo(X,X1) for example is a structural literal, given that carCompo means that X1 is in a component/object relation with X. Defining a structural clause involves grouping structural literals together. This aggregation should be done with respect to the meaning of the structural literals. At this time, it should be noted that the component/object relation possesses three axiomatizable properties. It is *irreflexive*, *antisymmetric* and *transitive* [21]. As such, component/object is an *order* relation. Let us consider a structural predicate pof. The first property expresses the fact that X cannot be a part of X (pof(X,X) cannot be true). The property of *antisymmetry* expresses the fact that if X is composed of Y, then Y cannot be composed of X (if pof (X,Y) then ¬pof(Y,X)). The third property of transitivity states that if pof(X,Y) and pof(Y,Z) then pof(X,Z). This property is used to define the notion of set of structural literals compatible with the meaning of their associated predicates (i.e. component/object).

Definition 4: *A set of structural literals is structurally compatible iff their transitive closure for the component/object relation does not contain any reflexive or symmetric structural literals.*

This simply means that if the predicates p1 and p2 are two predicates with a component/object meaning, the clause H ← p1(X,X1), p2(X1,X2), p1(X,X3) is structurally compatible whereas H ← p1(X,X1), p2(X1,X2), p1(X2,X) is not because the transitive closure of {p1(X,X1), p2(X1,X2), p1(X2,X)} is {p1(X,X1), p2(X1,X2), p1(X2,X))} which contains p(X,X). Let us note that this definition is independent of the semantics of the literals (in the sense of model interpretation) but depends on the meaning of the predicate. We shall now define *structural clauses* as linked clauses whose body contains *exclusively* structural literals. A clause is *linked* if all its variable are linked. A variable v is *linked* in a clause C iff v occurs in the head of C or there is a literal l in C that contains the variable v and w (different from v) and w is linked. Let us notice that this of structural clauses definition is independent of the database and characterizes a kind of indeterminacy since structural literals may be non determinate.

Definition 5: *A linked clause H ← B_1, B_2,..., B_n is said structural iff B_1, B_2,..., B_n is a set of fully variabilized compatible structural literals.*

As an example of this definition, the following clauses are structural clauses:

S1= final(X,F) ← carCompo(X,X1)   S'1= init(X,I) ← carCompo(X,X1)
S2= Final(X,F) ← carCompo(X,X1),carCompo(X,X2),carGraphem(X1,X3)

Let us now introduce a useful definition that we shall use to characterize a class of nondeterminate clauses that contain in their body all kinds of literals and not only structural ones.

Definition 6: *A clause C is said to be S-structural if S is the most specific structural clause that θ-subsumes C.*

Informally, if C is S-structural, the clause S captures the structural part of the clause. Given a clause C, the structural clause S such that C is S-structural is simply obtained by variabilizing the structural literals and removing the non structural ones. For example, the following clauses C4 and C5 are both *S1-structural clauses*:

$$C4 = Final(X,F) \leftarrow carCompo(X,X1), absposition(X1,right), Init(X1,j)$$
$$freq(X,U) init(X,F), medial(X, M), tone(X,T)$$

$$C5 = Final(X,F) \leftarrow carCompo(X,X1), position(X1,X2,left)$$
$$key(X1,X2,false) final(X,F)$$

We may now introduce a new kind of restriction on clause indeterminacy:

Definition 7: *A clause C is said to be S-structural indeterminate if all of its free variables appears in structural literals.*

Informally, if C is S-structural indeterminate, it means that all the free variables in C are linked by structural relations. C4 for example is S1-structural indeterminate. On the other hand C5 is not S1-structural indeterminate because the free variable X2 does not appear in a structural literal. Note that by adding the literal carCompo(X,X2), C5 becomes S2-structural indeterminate.

The previous definitions introduce a new kind of indeterminacy that has a few interesting properties. First, it is well adapted to the kind of indeterminacy found in structural domains. Second, unlike k-locality, it is not directly related to the number of literals in a clause (a S-structural indeterminate clause is still S-structural indeterminate when adding an unlimited number of constrained literals). Finally, it is defined independently of the database (as opposed to *l*-indeterminate clauses). We have developed the REPART algorithm to learn S-structural clauses. This algorithm is an adaptation and a formalization in ILP of the REMO algorithm [22].

4. REPART: an ILP algorithm for learning nondeterminate clauses

Our approach to learning S-structural indeterminate clauses is based on a change of representation that allows propositional learners to be used. The idea of incorporating efficient propositional learners in relational learners is not new. LINUS and DINUS [11] incorporated ASSISTANT—an ID3-like algorithm— and NEWGEM— an AQ-like algorithm— in a hierarchical deductive DATALOG database. REPART is based on the same general principle. It reformulates each observation in a propositional representation (phase 1), then it perforsm an induction from these observations (phase 2) and finally maps back the results as clauses (phase 3). However, the indeterminacy of the searched clauses greatly modify each phase.

4.1. Propositional representation of S-structural clauses

Given the structural predicates, the first step of phase 1 of the REPART algorithm consists in selecting a structural clause S. The second step is to build a propositional representation (also refereed as propositionalization [23]) so that S-structural indeterminate clauses may be induced.

Let us consider C_s, the *most specific fully variabilized S-structural indeterminate clause* w.r.t. to Background Knowledge. S being by definition fully variabilized, C_s is the clause S U D' where D' is the set of all the possible fully variabilized functional literals that may be defined using the background predicates. Using definition 6, any S-structural indeterminate clause C may be represented as C= Sθ U D where D represents a set of functional literals, i.e. that do not introduce any free variable that is not in Sθ. Therefore, by definition of C_s, there exists θ' such that $C \subseteq C_s\theta'$. In other words, any S-structural indeterminate clause C may be represented as a subset of instantiated literals of C_s. In REPART, the second step of phase 1 consists in building C_s and a set of attributes to describe each different literals of C_s. Each attribute corresponds to either a literal of the structural clause S or a literal of D'.

Let us illustrate this step on our reference example. To represent S'1-structural indeterminate clause, REPART first creates: attributes A1, A2, A3 and A4 to represent the two literals init(X,I) and carCompo(X,X1) of S'1. Then, it creates attribute A5,..., A30 to represent each possible literal that may be built using the variables X and X1 (that appear in the structural literal carCompo(X,X1)) and the existing predicates and functions: key(X,X1), init(X1), ..., gb(X1) (cf. Table 3 below).

4.2. Propositional reformulation of the observations

Once the attribute value representation is defined, REPART reformulates the closed observations into attribute/value vectors. For each **closed** observation o in O, and each substitution θ such that $C_s \theta$–subsumes o, a vector representing $C_s\theta$ using the attributes defined in 4.1 is created. In LINUS or DINUS, for each observation o there is a **unique such substitution** θ. The reformulation is therefore "*quite straightforward*" [11]. In REPART, unlike LINUS, by definition of indeterminate clauses, there is a **variable number of substitutions** θ (see for example $\theta2$ and $\theta3$ in section 2).

Table 3. Propositional representation of two observations: 爱 and 掂

| | Attributes representing the structural clause S'1 | | | | Attributes representing relations between variables appearing in S'1 | | | | |
| | init(X, I) | | carCompo(X,X1) | | key(X,X1) | init(X1) | | | gb(X1, Y) |
	A1	A2	A3	A4	A5	A6	....	....	A29	A30
$\theta1$	car14	f	car14	car14_c1	true	—			car14	4289
$\theta2$	car14	f	car14	car14_c2	false	zh			car14	—
$\theta3$	car14	f	car14	car14_c3	false	y			car14	3956
$\theta'1$	car534	ch	car534	car534-c1	true	—			car534	4989
$\theta'2$	car534	ch	car534	car534-c2	false	d̄			car534	1161

4.3. Solving the multiple-part problem to induce S-structural indeterminate clauses in the propositional representation

After the reformulation in propositional logic, to each initial observation corresponds many feature vectors. In this representation, *subsuming an observation o* corresponds to cover *one of the instances* coming from the reformulation of o. The search for S-structural clauses may be recast in this propositional representation as the search for rules that cover at least **one** instance per observation. The learning task is not longer to induce an hypothesis that is consistent with all the feature vectors reformulated but the multiple-part problem:

Definition 8 [22]: *The multiple-part problem consists in finding a description that covers at least **one** reformulated example of each positive initial learning example and **no** reformulated examples of any negative initial learning example.*

This reformulated problem is closely related to what Dietterich recently termed the *multiple-instance problem* [24]. In this latter problem, each *example* is represented by different alternative feature vectors (instances) where only one of instances may be responsible for the observed classification. CHARADE is originally a k-DNF propositional learner that may be used either for concept learning or to detect all empirical correlation between conjunctive descriptions which can be observed on all the examples of a training set. REPART uses a variant of the CHARADE [25] algorithm extended to solve the multiple-part problem [3].

4.4. Results

The REPART algorithm has been tested on a database containing the descriptions of 3285 Chinese characters. Table 4 presents several clauses judged to be interesting by the phoneticians out the thousands of rules found by REPART. Each clause is representative of a family of interesting rules. For each discovered rule the number of Chinese characters to which the association rule applies is given (the rule *coverage*). The accuracy of all rules found is 100%. In the different results reported below in Table 4, the language restriction used is [S3=H ← carCompo(X,X1), carGraphem(X1,X2)]-structural indeterminate clauses.

Table 4: A few original rules discovered by REPART

R1: pinyin(X,zh,u,_,T)← carCompo(X,X$_1$), freq(X, =1000), gb(X$_1$, 4276) Coverage=[5] This rule states that under certain conditions of frequency of the considered characters, the component 主 "gives" its full pronunciation to the character it composes.

R2: init(X,I)← carCompo(X,X$_1$), frequency(X, =1000), init(X$_1$, I), gb(X$_1$, 2484) Coverage=[13] This rule states that the component 民 "gives" always its initial to the character it composes.

R3: tone(X,T)← carCompo(X,X$_1$), tone(X$_1$, T), gb(X$_1$, 1716) Coverage=[13] This rule states that the component 会 "gives" its final to the character it composes if it is not a simplified character.

R4: init(X,labial)← carCompo(X,X$_1$), gb(X$_1$, 709) Coverage=[27] This rule states that the component 包 "gives" a fuzzy initial belonging to labials (b, p, f or m) to a character it composes.

5. Conclusion

The work presented here addresses the problem of data mining nondeterminate clauses in relational databases. This type of clause is known to be hard to learn, especially in the case where the number of examples is very high. To deal with this problem we have refined the definition of bounded *l*-indeterminacy by introducing a new language bias (S-structural indeterminate clauses) that takes into account the specificity of the component/object relation found in structural domains such as medicine, chemistry or Chinese characters. The efficiency of REPART, that learns S-structural indeterminate clauses from thousands of ground facts, lies in a change of representation. This particular change of representation allows REPART to use multiple-instance propositional learners [22]. The original results found by REPART go beyond traditional computational analysis of Chinese characters, thus exemplifying how ILP algorithms may not only scale up efficiently to large relational databases but also discover expressive hard to learn patterns.

Our current researches include using S-structural indeterminate language bias in other domains such as the mutagenesis problem [7]. Although data mining systems have a less operational criterion of success than concept learning, comparison with systems such as CLAUDIEN [2] is also planned. On a more theoretical level, it remains to be proved that S-structural indeterminate clauses are PAC-learnable. This should be facilitated by Cohen's results on PAC-learnability of nondeterminate clauses [20]. The language restriction we have introduced in this article captures important knowledge in structural domains that plays a key role in the complexity of learning. This type of language restriction based on the *meaning* of predicates represents a new direction of research for more "meaningful" bias in ILP. Indeed, what we have done for component/object relations may be generalized to predicates that have a clear meaning and whose properties may be axiomatized. We believe that reformulations to Multiple-instance problem may be a general approach for learning clauses with fixed patterns of indeterminacy.

Acknowlededgements

We deeply thank the anonymous reviewers for their constructive critics and useful suggestions that helped us improve the text. We also express our gratitude to Stan Matwin for his encouragement to recast our work within an ILP framework.

References

1. Suen, C., Computational Analysis of Mandarin. Interdisciplinary System Research. 1972: Birkhäuser.
2. De Raedt, L. and L. Dehaspe, Clausal discovery. Machine Learning Journal, 1996. 26(3): p. 99-145.
3. Zucker, J.-D., J.-G. Ganascia, and I. Bournaud, Relational Knowledge Discovery in a Chinese Characters Database. Applied Artificial Intelligence, 1998. 12(5) to appear.

4. Kietz, J.-U. and S. Wrobel, Controlling the Complexity of Learning in Logic through Syntactic and Task-Oriented Models, in Inductive Logic Programming, S. Muggleton, Editor. 1992, Harcourt Brace Jovanovich: London. p. 335-359.
5. Muggleton, S. and L. De Raedt, Inductive Logic Programming: Theory and Methods. Journal of Logic Programming, 1994. 19(20): p. 629-679.
6. Nédellec, C., C. Rouveirol, H. Adé, F. Bergadano, and B. Tausend, Declarative Bias in ILP, in Advances in Inductive Logic Programming, L. De Raedt, Editor. 1996, IOS Press. p. 82-103.
7. Srinivasan, A., S. Muggleton, M.E. Sternberg, and R.D. King. Mutagenesis: ILP experiments in a non-determinate biological domain. in Fourth International Workshop on Inductive Logic Programming (ILP-94). 1994. Bonn, Germany.
8. Muggleton, S. and C. Feng, Efficient Induction of logic program, in Inductive Logic Programming, S. Muggleton, Editor. 1992, Harcourt Brace Jovanovich: London. p. 281-298.
9. Cohen, W. Pac-learning Nondeterminate Clauses. in Twelth National Conference on Artificial Intelligence. 1994.
10. Dzeroski, S., S. Muggleton, and S. Russell. Pac-learning of determinate logic programs. in of the Workshop on Computational Learning Theory. 1992. Pittsburgh, Pennsylvania.
11. Lavrac, N. and S. Dzeroski, Inductive Logic Programming: Techniques and Applications. Artificial intelligence. 1994: Ellis Horwood.
12. Cohen, W. Rapid Prototyping of ILP Systems Using Explicit Bias. in IJCAI Workshop on inductive logic programming. 1993.
13. Quinlan, J.-R., Learning Logical Definitions from Relations. Machine Learning, 1990(5): p. 239-266.
14. Silverstein, G. and M.J. Pazzani. Relational clichés: Constraining constructive induction during relational learning. in 8th IWML. 1991: Morgan Kaufmann.
15. Pompe, U., I. Kokonenko, and T. Makse. An application of ILP in a musical database: Learning to compose the two-voice contrepoint. in Data Mining with Inductive Logic Programming. 1996. Bari, Italy.
16. Pazzani, M.J., C.A. Brunk, and G. Silverstein. A knowledge intensive approach to relational concept learning. in 8th IWML. 1991: Morgan Kaufmann.
17. Sebag, M. and C. Rouveirol. Tractable Induction and Classification in First Order Logic. in Fifteenth International Joint Conference on Artificial Intelligence, IJCAI'97. 1997. Nagoya, Japan: Morgan Kaufmann.
18. Giordana, A., F. Neri, L. Saitta, and M. Botta, Integrating multiple learning strategies in first order logics. Machine Learning, 1997. 27: p. 209-240.
19. Muggleton, S. and A. Srinivasan, Mode-directed inverse resolution, in Machine Intelligence, Michie et al. Editors. 1994, Oxford University Press.
20. Cohen, W. Learnability of Restricted Logic Programs. in IJCAI, Workshop on ILP. 1993. Chambery, France.
21. Chaffin, R. and D. Herrmann, The nature of semantic relations, in Relational Models of the Lexicon, M. evens, Editor. 1988, Cambridge University Press: Cambridge. p. 289-334.
22. Zucker, J.-D. and J.-G. Ganascia. Changes of Representation for Efficient Learning in Structural Domains. in International Conference in Machine Learning. 1996. Bari, Italy: Morgan Kaufmann.
23. Kramer, S. Stochastic propositionalization of non-determinate background knowledge. in IJCAI-97 Workshop on Frontiers of Inductive Logic Programming, 1997. 1997. Nagoya, Japan.
24. Dietterich, T., R. Lathrop, and T. Lozano-Perez, Solving the Multiple-Instance Problem with Axis-Parallel Rectangles. Artificial Intelligence, 1996. 89(1-2).
25. Ganascia, J.-G. CHARADE: A rule System Learning System. in the tenth International Jointed Conference in Artificial Intelligence. 1987. Milan, Italy.

Completing Inverse Entailment

Stephen Muggleton

Department of Computer Science
University of York
Heslington, York, YO1 5DD
United Kingdom

Abstract. Yamamoto has shown that the *Inverse Entailment* (IE) mechanism described previously by the author is complete for Plotkin's relative subsumption but incomplete for entailment. That is to say, an hypothesised clause H can be derived from an example E under a background theory B using IE if and only if H subsumes E relative to B in Plotkin's sense. Yamamoto gives examples of H for which $B \cup H \models E$ but H cannot be constructed using IE from B and E. The main result of the present paper is a theorem to show that by enlarging the bottom set used within IE, it is possible to make a revised version of IE complete with respect to entailment for Horn theories. Furthermore, it is shown for function-free definite clauses that given a bound k on the arity of predicates used in B and E, the cardinality of the enlarged bottom set is bounded above by the polynomial function $p(c+1)^k$, where p is the number of predicates in B, E and c is the number of constants in $B \cup \overline{E}$.

1 Introduction

In [5] Yamamoto shows that the mechanism of *Inverse Entailment* (IE) introduced in [2] is complete for Plotkin's relative subsumption, but incomplete for entailment. In this paper it is shown that enlarging the bottom set leads to completeness of IE with respect to entailment for Horn theories.

This paper is organised as follows. The next section gives formal definitions used in the rest of the paper. Some useful properties of Herbrand models of Horn theories are proved in Section 2.3. Section 3 introduces the definitions of IE and and the revised bottom set. A useful model intersection property of Horn theories is also proved. The definitions are applied to the example Yamamoto uses to show the incompleteness of IE. The main completeness theorem is proved in Section 4. The results are summarised and an open problem is discussed in Section 5.

2 Preliminaries

It is assumed the reader is familiar with first-order logic and logic programming (see [4]).

2.1 Clauses and clausal theories

A positive literal is an atom, a negative literal is the negation of an atom. A clause is a finite set of literals, and is treated as a universally quantified disjunction of those literals. A finite set of clauses is called a clausal theory and is treated as a conjunction of those clauses. A Horn clause is a clause containing at most one positive literal. Non-definite Horn clauses are called goals. A Horn theory is a clausal theory containing only Horn clauses. A definite clause is a clause containing exactly one positive literal. A definite clause program is a clausal theory containing only definite clauses. A clause C can be written as

$$a_0; ..; a_m \leftarrow b_1, .., b_n$$

where the a_i are the positive literals and the b_j are the negative literals. In this case C^+, C^- denote the clauses consisting of the positive and negative literals of C respectively.

A clause is said to be function-free whenever it does not contain functions of arity 1 or more. A clausal theory is said to be function-free whenever all its clauses are function-free.

A unique Skolem constant c_v will be assumed to be associated with every variable v. If F is a first-order formula then $N(F)$ is formed by replacing each variable x in F by the Skolem constant c_x and each Skolem constant c_y by the associated variable y. If l is a literal then $\bar{l}$ is formed by removing all occurrences of double negation ($\neg\neg$) in $\neg N(l)$. Thus $\bar{\bar{l}} = l$ for all literals l. If $C = \{l_1, ..l_n\}$ is a clause then $\overline{C}$ is the Horn theory $\{\{\overline{l_1}\}, .., \{\overline{l_n}\}\}$.

Definition 1. Subsumption. *Let C and D be clauses. C subsumes D, denoted $C \succeq D$, if and only if there exists a substitution θ such that $C\theta \subseteq D$.*

2.2 Herbrand models

Suppose T is a clausal theory. $B(T)$ will denote the Herbrand Base of T (see [4] for a definition of $B(T)$). As usual, Herbrand interpretations and Herbrand models of T are represented by subsets of $B(T)$. $M \subseteq B(T)$ is a Herbrand model of T if and only if it is a model of all the clauses in T. M is a Herbrand model of a clause $C \in T$ if and only if there does not exist a ground substitution θ and a clause $D = C\theta$ such that $D^+ \subseteq B(T) \setminus M$ and $D^- \subseteq M$. $\mathcal{M}(F) = \{M_1, M_2, ..\}$ will be used to denote the Herbrand models of T. When $\mathcal{M}(T)$ is non-empty $M(T)$ denotes $\bigcap_i M_i$. If $M(T)$ is a model of T then it will be known as the least Herbrand model of T. According to Herbrand's theorem T is satisfiable if $\mathcal{M}(T)$ is non-empty and unsatisfiable otherwise.

The following is a restatement of Proposition 6.1 in [1] Theorem 2.14 in [4] and Proposition 7.13 in [3].

Theorem 1. Model intersection property. *Let P be a definite clause program and $\mathcal{M} = \{M_1, M_2, ..\}$ be a non-empty set of Herbrand models of P. Then $\bigcap_i M_i$ is a Herbrand model of P.*

2.3 Herbrand models of Horn theories

The following Lemma is a generalisation of Theorem 1 to Horn theories[1].

Lemma 1. Horn theory model intersection property. *Let $T = T_0 \cup T_1$ be a satisfiable Horn theory in which T_0, T_1 are the non-definite and definite subsets of T respectively. Let $\mathcal{M} = \{M_1, M_2, ..\}$ be a non-empty set of Herbrand models of T. Then $M = \bigcap_i M_i$ is a Herbrand model of T.*
Proof. *Assume false. Then there exists T for which $\mathcal{M}$ is non-empty and M is not a model of T. M must either not be a model of T_0 or not be a model of T_1. However, every model in $\mathcal{M}$ is a model of T_1 since $T \models T_1$ and thus according to Theorem 1 M is a model of T_1. It follows that M must not be a model of T_0. Thus there must exist a ground instance of a clause in T_0:*

$$\leftarrow a_1, .., a_n$$

for which $a_1, .., a_n$ are all in M. Then $a_1, .., a_n$ are in every model in $\mathcal{M}$. But this means that no element of $\mathcal{M}$ is a model of T, which contradicts the assumption that $\mathcal{M}$ is non-empty. This completes the proof.

Corollary 1. Least Herbrand model of Horn theories. *Let T be a satisfiable Horn theory. $M(T)$ is the least Herbrand model of T.*
Proof. *Follows directly from Lemma 1 and the definitions of satisfiability and least Herbrand model.*

3 IE and the enlarged bottom set

The following is a variant on the definition of the bottom set used by Yamamoto in describing IE.

Definition 2. Enlarged bottom set. *Let B be a Horn theory, E be a clause, such that $F = (B \cup \overline{E})$ is satisfiable (ie. $B \not\models E$)). The enlarged bottom set of E under B is denoted $BOT(B, E)$ and is defined as follows.*

$$BOT^+(B, E) = \{a | a \in B(F) \setminus M(F)\}$$
$$BOT^-(B, E) = \{\neg a | a \in M(F)\}$$
$$BOT(B, E) = BOT^+(B, E) \cup BOT^-(B, E)$$

Note that the cardinality of $BOT(B, E)$ can be infinite. However, this will not be the case when B, E are function-free.

Remark 1. **Cardinality of $BOT(B, E)$ (function-free case).** Let B be a Horn theory and E be a clause, such that $F = (B \cup \overline{E})$ is satisfiable. Suppose F contains p predicate symbols with maximum arity k and c is the number of constants in F. The cardinality of $BOT(B, E)$ has an upper bound of $p(c+1)^k$.
Proof. Follows from the fact that for each of the p predicate symbols there are at most $(c+1)^k$ different atoms that can be constructed from the at most $c+1$ constants in $B(F)$.

---

[1] Lemma 1 is not found in logic programming theory texts such as [1, 4, 3].

Below we give a revised definition of IE similar to that in [5], but based on the enlarged bottom set.

Definition 3. IE based on enlarged bottom set. *Let B be a Horn theory and E be a clause, such that $B \not\models E$. A clause H is derived by IE from E under B if and only if there exists a clause $H' \subseteq BOT(B, E)$ such that $H \succeq H'$.*

The following example demonstrates the construction of $BOT(B, E)$ for a function-free version of the example Yamamoto uses to demonstrate the incompleteness of IE.

Example 1. **Yamamoto's example.**

$$B = \left\{ \begin{array}{l} even(0) \leftarrow \\ even(y) \leftarrow s(x, y), odd(x) \end{array} \right\}$$

$$E = odd(z) \leftarrow s(y, z), s(x, y), s(0, x)$$

$$\overline{E} = \left\{ \begin{array}{l} \leftarrow odd(c_z) \\ s(c_y, c_z) \leftarrow \\ s(c_x, c_y) \leftarrow \\ s(0, c_x) \leftarrow \end{array} \right\}$$

$$B(B \cup \overline{E}) = \left\{ \begin{array}{l} even(0), even(c_x), even(c_y), even(c_z), odd(0), \\ odd(c_x), odd(c_y), odd(c_z), s(0, 0), s(0, c_x), .., s(c_z, c_z) \end{array} \right\}$$

$$M(B \cup \overline{E}) = \{ even(0), s(c_y, c_z), s(c_x, c_y), s(0, c_x) \}$$

$$BOT(B, E) = even(c_x); even(c_y); ..; odd(c_x) \leftarrow even(0), s(c_y, c_z), s(c_x, c_y), s(0, c_x)$$

Note that $BOT(B, E)$ is subsumed by the following clause H.

$$odd(u) \leftarrow s(v, u), even(v)$$

Thus H can be derived by IE from E under B. H is a function-free version of the one which Yamamoto showed could not be derived by the original definitions of IE.

4 Completeness

Below is the main completeness result for clauses derived using IE.

Theorem 2. Horn theory completeness of IE. *Let B be a Horn theory, E be a clause, such that $F = (B \cup \overline{E})$ is satisfiable (ie. $B \not\models E$)). $G = (B \cup H \cup \overline{E})$ is unsatisfiable (ie. $B \cup H \models E$) and $B(G) = B(F)$ only if H is derived by IE from E under B.*

Proof. *Assume false. Then G is unsatisfiable and $B(G) = B(F)$ and (according to Definition 3) there does not exist $H' \subseteq BOT(B, E)$ such that $H \succeq H'$. Since F is a satisfiable Horn theory according to Corollary 1 $M(F)$ is its least Herbrand model. But $M(F)$ cannot be a Herbrand model of G since G is unsatisfiable, and therefore there must be a ground substitution θ such that $H^+\theta \subseteq (B(F) \setminus M(F))$ and $H^-\theta \subseteq M(F)$. Therefore letting $H' = H\theta$ clearly $H \succeq H'$ and $H' \subseteq BOT(B, E)$. This contradicts the assumption and completes the proof.*

It is worth drawing attention to the "only if" in the theorem above. For some clauses H derived by IE from E under B it is not the case that $B \cup H \models E$. In example 1, the following is such a clause.

$$odd(u) \leftarrow s(v, u), s(w, v), even(w)$$

5 Discussion

Yamamoto [5] demonstrated the incompleteness of the mechanism of IE described in [2]. This paper defines an enlargement of the bottom set definitions of [2,5]. In fact this enlargement is a generalisation of the use of sub-saturants in [2]. Although the enlarged bottom set is infinite in the non-function-free case, a polynomial bound to the cardinality of the enlarged bottom set is provided in the case of function-free Horn background theories. Example 1 shows how the enlarged bottom set deals with a function-free form of the example Yamamoto used to show the incompleteness of IE. Finally a completeness result is given for definite clauses for the revised version of IE.

It is an open question as to whether a further generalisation of this approach would be complete for arbitrary clausal background theories.

Acknowledgements

The author would like to thank his wife Thirza and daughter Clare for their support during the writing of this paper. Thanks also to David Page, James Cussens, Alan Frisch, Akihiro Yamamoto and Koichi Furukawa for relevant discussions on this topic. This work was supported partly by the Esprit Long Term Research Action ILP II (project 20237), EPSRC grant GR/K57985 on Experiments with Distribution-based Machine Learning and an EPSRC Advanced Research Fellowship held by the author.

References

1. J.W. Lloyd. *Foundations of Logic Programming*. Springer-Verlag, Berlin, 1987. Second edition.
2. S. Muggleton. Inverse entailment and Progol. *New Generation Computing*, 13:245–286, 1995.
3. S-H. Nienhuys-Cheng and R. de Wolf. *Foundations of Inductive Logic Programming*. Springer-Verlag, Berlin, 1997. LNAI 1228.
4. U. Nilsson and J. Maluszynski. *Logic, Programming and Prolog*. Wiley, New York, 1995. Second edition.
5. A. Yamamoto. Which hypotheses can be found with inverse entailment? In N. Lavrac and S. Dzeroski, editors, *Proceedings of the Seventh International Workshop on Inductive Logic Programming*, pages 296–308. Springer-Verlag, Berlin, 1997. LNAI 1297.

Distances and Limits on Herbrand Interpretations

Shan-Hwei Nienhuys-Cheng

`cheng@cs.few.eur.nl`

Department of Computer Science
Katholieke Universiteit Leuven & Erasmus Universiteit Rotterdam

Abstract. A notion of distances between Herbrand interpretations enables us to measure how good a certain program, learned from examples, approximates some target program. The distance introduced in [10] has the disadvantage that it does not fit the notion of "identification in the limit". We use a distance defined by a level mapping [5] to overcome this problem, and study in particular the mapping T_Π induced by a definite program Π on the metric space. Continuity of T_Π holds under certain conditions, and we give a concrete level mapping that satisfies these conditions, based on [10]. This allows us to prove the existence of fixed points without using the Banach Fixed Point Theorem.

1 Introduction

Logic and analysis are two important branches of mathematics. The flavors of approaching the problems in these two branches are quite different. The most striking difference is that the approach in logic is so black and white (true or false) and analysis uses often real numbers as values. In analysis we can use the concepts of limit and approximation. Is there any use at all for limits in logic?

The fixed points of a mapping are important in applications. For example, the Brouwer Fixed Point Theorem can be used to characterize some topological spaces. Numerical equations are often solved by using fixed points. In logic the least Herbrand model of a definite program is actually a fixed point [7]. In semantics one can use fixed points to characterize the declarative semantics of some programming languages ([1],[8]).

There are usually two approaches to fixed points in literature. The choice often depends on the structure of the domain where the mapping is defined. If the mapping is defined on a complete lattice or a complete partially ordered set, then we consider the possibility that it may have more than one fixed point (e.g. [7]). If the domain is a complete metric space, then the *Banach Fixed Point Theorem* often applies, which says that a contraction has precisely one fixed point. This approach is used by Fitting [5]. However, in this article we want to consider the fixed points as limits of some sequences in the metric space without using the Banach Theorem.

In this article we define metrics on the set of Herbrand interpretations. This is motivated by the *model inference problem* [11]. This problem illustrates the limit concept in a metric space in Inductive Logic Programming. Suppose we have a first order logic language with $\mathcal{B}$ as Herbrand base. Consider some Herbrand interpretation $M \subseteq \mathcal{B}$ which is called the target interpretation. If the elements in M are given as positive examples and the elements in set $\mathcal{B} \setminus M$ as negative examples, our aim is to use these examples to find a definite program Π whose least Herbrand model M_Π is M. If we find such a program Π, then we say Π is *correct with respect to* M. However, such a correct program may not exist ([9]), and we may settle for an approximation. Even a correct program does exist, it may require so much work to find it, that an approximation is more feasible. Moreover, we are ususaly not supplied with the whole sets M and $\mathcal{B} \setminus M$ as examples. Instead we are given a proper subset E^+ of M as positive examples and a proper subset E^- of $\mathcal{B} \setminus M$ as negative examples Using these we try to find a correct program Π with respect to examples (i.e. $\Pi \models E^+$ and $\Pi \not\models e$ if $e \in E^-$). This Π can be used to predict the truth values of new examples. This is the basic idea of machine learning. A good quality Π will be a good "approximation" of a correct program. We would like to have an estimation of the quality of Π. In other words, we would like to estimate the closeness of M_Π, the least Herbrand model of Π, to M even if we do not know M completely.

These reasons were also the motivation to define a distance between Herbrand interpretations by Nienhuys-Cheng[10]. That paper defines a distance on the set of all expressions $\mathcal{E}$ (ground atoms and ground terms). This distance induces a *Hausdorff* metric on the set of all subsets of expressions. Since an Herbrand interpretation can be considered as a subset of ground expressions, we have a distance between Herbrand interpretations.

What does it mean to *learn* something? Shapiro [20] introduced the criterion of *identification in the limit*. Suppose we have some (unknown) target interpretation M. Examples $e_1, e_2, \ldots$ are given one by one. Each example is a ground atom labeled with its M-truth-value. After each new example e_i, the learner has to output a hypothesis program Π_i that is correct for the examples seen up to that point. The learner solves the problem of its sequence of programs converges to a correct program: after some n, the hypotheses do not change any more ($\Pi_n = \Pi_{n+1} = \ldots$) and have M as least Herbrand model. We then say the learner has *identified* M in the limit. To make this conform to the metric approach, we would like to have a distance d such that $\lim_{i \to \infty} d(M_{\pi_i}, M) = 0$. Unfortunately, the distance d defined in [18] does not have this desired property, as we will show in Section 3.

Fitting[5] uses a level mapping ([7, 2]) to define a metric on valuations. This distance can be translated into a distance between Herbrand interpretations. [5] discusses the fixed point of a mapping T_Π on a metric space induced by a normal program Π. A similar mapping is also given in chapter 2 of Lloyd[7] where the least Herbrand model of a definite program is considered as a fixed point of T_Π. [5] considers only the level mapping and the mapping T_Π based on some special program Π. In these concrete cases T_Π is a contraction so the Banach Fixed Point Theorem works. If we want to develop more general theories then we should consider an unknown definite program Π. This is particularly true in

ILP where a correct program is yet to be found. The mapping T_Π may not be a contraction. We try to find more general theories about such metric spaces. For example, some models of Π or fixed points of T_Π are the limits of some special sequnces in the metric space. We can use the limit concept in such metric spaces to explain the concept of identifying the target in the limit. We can prove that T_Π is continuous on the metric space if Π satisfies some conditions.

This article consists of three parts. Only proofs of more important results will be given. The first part of the article contains some preliminaries about metric spaces and some results of [10] and [5]. The second part is about metric spaces based on some level mappings and about T_Π, in particular the case that the level mapping satisfies some condition. There really is a level mapping which satisfies the conditions. For this we use the depth of a expression tree defined in [10] for the level mapping. Then we can apply the results of the second part. This level mapping and the induced metric will be discussed in the last part of this article.

2 Preliminaries about Metric Spaces

Definition 1. Given a set V, a binary function $d : V \times V \to \mathbf{R}$ is called a *metric* or *distance* if 1. $\forall x, y \in V$, $d(x, y) \geq 0$. Moreover, $d(x, y) = 0$ iff $x = y$. 2. $d(x, y) = d(y, x)$. 3. $d(x, y) + d(y, z) \geq d(x, z)$.

Remark For an arbitrary metric space (V, d) we can and we will always suppose that the metric is bounded by 1. If d does not have the property, we can define a new metric d' by $d'(x, y) = min(d(x, y), 1)$. Then d' is bounded by 1.

Definition 2. Let a metric space (V, d) and $\epsilon > 0$ be given. For $x \in V$, the *open ϵ-ball* $B(x, \epsilon)$ *centered at* x is the set $\{y \mid d(x, y) < \epsilon\}$. A set $T \subseteq V$ is called *open* if for every $x \in T$, there is an open ball centered at x in T. A set $T \subseteq V$ is *closed* if $V \setminus T$ is open. The sets V and $\emptyset$ are both open and closed.

Definition 3. Let (V, d) be a bounded metric space and $C(V)$ be the set of all closed subsets of V. For non-empty $T \in C(V)$ and $x \in V$, let $d(x, T) = \text{glb}_{y \in T} d(x, y)$ (greatest lower bound). For non-empty $S, T \in C(V)$, let $\rho(S, T) = \text{lub}_{x \in S} d(x, T)$, and $h(S, T) = \max(\rho(S, T), \rho(T, S))$. Furthermore, define $h(\emptyset, \emptyset) = 0$ and $h(\emptyset, T) = 1$ if $T \neq \emptyset$. It can be shown that h is a metric (*Hausdorff metric*[3]) on $C(V)$.

Definition 4. Let V, W be metric spaces and $f : V \to W$ be a function. f is *continuous at* x if for every open ball $B(f(x), \epsilon)$ centered at $f(x)$, there is an open ball $B(x, \delta)$ centered at x such that $f(B(x, \delta)) \subseteq B(f(x), \epsilon)$. f is *continuous* if f is continuous at every point $x \in V$. A sequence $\{x_n\}$ in a metric space (V, d) converges to x, written as $\lim_{n \to \infty} x_n = x$ if for every $\epsilon > 0$, there is an N such that if $n \geq N$, then $d(x_n, x) < \epsilon$.

Definition 5. A sequence $\{x_n\}$ in a metric space (V, d) is a *Cauchy sequence* if for every $\epsilon > 0$, there is a natural number N such that $d(x_n, x_m) < \epsilon$ if $n, m \geq N$. A metric space is *complete* if every Cauchy sequence converges to a point in the space.

Definition 6. Let a metric space (V, d) be given. For a function $f : V \to V$, x is a *fixed point* of f if $f(x) = x$. A mapping $f : V \to V$ is called a *contraction* if there is a number $k : 0 \leq k < 1$ such that $d(f(x), f(y)) \leq k \cdot d(x, y) \, \forall x, y \in V$.

Lemma 7. *Let (V, d) be a complete metric space and $f : V \to V$. If there is a constant k such that $\forall x, y \in V$, $d(f(x), f(y)) \leq kd(x, y)$, then f is continuous.*

Corollary 8. *A contraction is continuous.*

Lemma 9. *Let $f : V \to W$. If f is continuous, then $f(x) = \lim_{n \to \infty} f(x_n)$ for every sequence $\{x_n\}$ such that $\lim_{n \to \infty} x_n = x$.*

Lemma 10. *Let (V, d) be a complete metric space and f be a contraction on V. Then for arbitrary $x \in V$, $x, f(x), f^2(x), \ldots$ is a Cauchy sequence. The limit of this sequence is a fixed point of f.*

Theorem 11. (Banach) *Let (V, d) be a complete metric space and $f : V \to V$ be a contraction. Then f has a unique fixed point.*

3 Metric defined by [10]

In this section we will briefly review the metric introduced in [10] and the results given there. We will also explain why this metric is not suitable to explain identification in the limit (see [11]).

Definition 12. An *expression* is a ground term or a ground atom. An expression e has a tree structure. We can express this structure by coding the *positions* of symbols in e in the following way: **1.** The leftmost symbol in e has $\langle 1 \rangle$ as its position. **2.** If $\langle a_1, a_2, \ldots, a_n \rangle$ is the position of a predicate or function symbol p occurring in e, and p has $k > 0$ arguments, then the leftmost symbol of the i-th argument has $\langle a_1, \ldots, a_n, i \rangle$ as its position in e.

For an expression e, the *depth* of a symbol occurrence is the length of its position. The *depth* of an expression e, denoted by $depth(e)$, is the depth of the symbol in e with the greatest depth.

Example 1. Consider $e = p(g(b), f(a, g(b)))$ and $e' = p(g(b), f(a, b))$. Then $e(\langle 1 \rangle) = p$, $e(\langle 1, 1, 1 \rangle) = b$ and $e(\langle 1, 2, 2, 1 \rangle) = b$. The depth of e is 4 and the depth of e' is 3. Expressions e and e' are the same to depth 2.

3.1 A metric on expressions

Let $\mathcal{E}$ denote the set of all expressions in a first-order language. We introduce a metric d, bounded by 1, on $\mathcal{E}$ such that $d(s, t)$ can be used to measure the difference between s and t. Differences between terms that occur at low depth are given more "weight" than differences at higher depth.

Definition 13. We define $d : \mathcal{E} \times \mathcal{E} \to \Re$ as follows. **1.** $d(e, e) = 0, \forall e \in \mathcal{E}$ **2.** If $p \neq q$, then $d(p(s_1, \ldots, s_n), q(t_1, \ldots, t_m)) = 1$ **3.** $d(p(s_1, \ldots, s_n), p(t_1, \ldots, t_n)) = \frac{1}{2n} \sum_{i=1}^{n} d(s_i, t_i)$

Example 2. $d(g(f(a), g(a, b)), g(f(b), b)) = \frac{1}{2 \cdot 2}(d(f(a), f(b)) + d(g(a, b), b))$
$= \frac{1}{4}(\frac{1}{2}d(a, b) + 1) = \frac{1}{4}(\frac{1}{2} + 1) = \frac{3}{8}$.

Theorem 14. $(\mathcal{E}, d)$ *is a metric space. Every subset of $\mathcal{E}$ is closed.*

Since every subset in $\mathcal{E}$ is closed, the Hausdorff metric h induced by d is a metric defined on the set of all subsets of $\mathcal{E}$. In particular h is defined on the set of all Herbrand interpretations $\mathcal{I}$.

Example 3. Let $\mathcal{B} = \{p(a), p(f(a)), p(f^2(a)), p(f^3(a)), \ldots\}$. Let $S = \{p(a), p(f^2(a)), p(f^4(a)), \ldots\}$ and $M = (S \cup \{p(f^{99}(a))\}) \setminus \{p(f^{100}(a))\}$. Then $d(f^{99}, S) = \frac{1}{2^{100}}$ and $d(p(f^{100}(a)), M) = \frac{1}{2^{101}}$. Thus $h(S, M) = \frac{1}{2^{100}}$. Now consider a program Π, with the following clauses: $p(a)$ and $p(f^2(x)) \leftarrow p(x)$. Then $M_\Pi = S$. Suppose the target interpretation is M. Then the model inference problem is approximately solved using Π, where the "quality" of the approximation can be measured by $h(M_\Pi, M) \leq \frac{1}{2^{100}}$.

Example 4. Let $M = \{p(a), p(f^2(a))\}$ be the target interpretation. Let $p(a)$, $p(f(a)), p(f^2(a)), p(f^3(a)), \ldots$ in $\mathcal{B}$ be given one by one as positive or negative examples. For every $i \geq 2$, suppose a learner finds $\Pi_i = \{p(a), p(f^2(a)), p(f^i(a))\}$. Then the least Herbrand model of Π_i is $M_i = \{p(a), p(f^2(a)), p(f^i(a))\}$. It is correct w.r.t. examples $e_1, e_2, \ldots, e_{i-1}$. However, $d(p(f^i(a)), M) = 1/8$ and $h(M, M_i) = 1/8$ for all $i \geq 2$. That means $d(M_i, M) \not\to 0$ even $i \to \infty$. If we define a distance, we would also like the distance between the target interpretation and the least Herbrand models of the programs confirms this concept. That means $\lim_{i \to \infty} h(M, M_{\Pi_i}) = 0$. This example shows that the Hausdorff metric does not satisfy this requirement.

4 Metric Space Induced by a Level Mapping

Fitting[5] defines metrics on the set of *valuations* (Herbrand interpretations) by level mappings. In that article some examples of such metric spaces are given. The related program Π in such an example induces a mapping T_Π on the metric space. In the examples T_Π is a contraction, so it has a unique fixed point. We want to investigate some properties in the complete metric spaces induced by level mappings in general. That means the program is unknown and T_Π is not always a contraction. Some properties of T_Π and the fixed points of T_Π are approached from the limit concept in metric spaces.

4.1 $\mathcal{I}$ as a metric space

Definition 15. Let $\mathcal{B}$ be the Herbrand base of a logical language. A *level mapping* is a function $\| \| : \mathcal{B} \to \mathbf{N}$ (natural numbers). We use $|A|$ to denote $\|(A)\|$, i.e. the image of A. It is called the *level of A.*

Given a level mapping $\|$ we can define a metric on the set of all Herbrand interpretations as follows: $d(I, I) = 0$ for every interpretation I. If $I \neq J$, then $d(I, J) = 1/2^n$ if $A \in I \cap J$ for all $|A| \leq n - 1$ and there is an $A \in I \triangle J = (I \setminus J) \cup (J \setminus I)$ such that $|A| = n$.

Theorem 16. ([5]) *The function d defined above is a metric on the set of all Herbrand interpretations $\mathcal{I}$.*

Lemma 17. ([5]) *The metric space $(\mathcal{I}, d)$ is complete.*

4.2 A mapping T on $\mathcal{I}$ induced by a program

Let $\mathcal{I}$ be the set of all Herbrand interpretations and Π be a definite program. Then Π induces a mapping $T_\Pi : \mathcal{I} \to \mathcal{I}$ as follows If $I \in \mathcal{I}$, then $T_\Pi(I) = \{A \in \mathcal{B} | \exists$ a ground instance of a clause in $\Pi : A \leftarrow A_1, \ldots, A_m$ such that every $A_i \in I\}$. We will often use T instead of T_Π.

Proposition 18. T *is monotonic, i.e. if $I \subseteq J$, then $T(I) \subseteq T(J)$.*

Proposition 19. *An interpretation I is a model of Π iff $T(I) \subseteq I$.*

Corollary 20. *Every fixed point of T is a Herbrand model of Π.*

For a model I of Π, we will prove that $J = \bigcap_i T^i(I)$ is a model of Π. For proving this we do not need to consider the metric. However, we would like to know if $J = \lim_{i \to \infty} T^i(I)$ in the metric space $(\mathcal{I}, d)$. This can be proved in special situations as given in Corollary 24.

Theorem 21. *Let I be a model of Π, we have $I = T^0(I) \supseteq T(I) \supseteq T^2(I) \supseteq \ldots$. Let $J = \bigcap_i T^i(I)$. Then J is also a model of Π.*
Proof If I is a model of Π, then $T(I) \subseteq I$ by Proposition 19. By Proposition 18, we have $T^i(I) \subseteq T^{i-1}(I)$ for all $i \geq 1$. Now consider $J = \bigcap_i T^i(I)$. We want to prove $T(J) \subseteq J$. Let $A \in T(J) = T(\bigcap T^i(I))$. That means there is an instance of a clause in $\Pi : A \leftarrow A_1, \ldots, A_m$ such that every $A_i \in J$. This implies also for every j, $A_i \in T^j(I)$. Thus $A \in T^{j+1}(I)$ for all j and $A \in J$.

Corollary 22. $\bigcap_i T^i(\mathcal{B})$ *is a model of Π.*

Theorem 23. *Suppose for every n, the set of $A \in \mathcal{B}$ with $|A| = n$ is finite. Let $I_0, I_1, I_2, \ldots$ be a sequence of interpretations such that $I_{i+1} \subseteq I_i$ for all i. Then $\lim_{i \to \infty} I_i = \bigcap_i I_i$, i.e. $\lim_{i \to \infty} d(I_i, \bigcap_j I_j) = 0$.*
Proof If for some k, $I_k = I_{k+1} = \ldots$, then we have also $J = I_k = I_{k+1} = \ldots$. Apparently $d(I_i, J) = 0$ for all $i \geq k$. Thus $\lim_{i \to \infty} d(I_i, J) = 0$.

Now suppose for every i there is a j such that $j > i$ and $I_j \subset I_i$ (thus $I_i \neq I_j$). For simplicity we assume that $I_0 \supset I_1 \supset I_2 \supset \ldots$. For every i, there is $A_i \in I_i \setminus J$ such that $d(J, I_i) = 2^{-|A_i|}$. It is clear $|A_1| \leq |A_2| \leq \ldots$. We claim that for every A_i, there is a j such that $j > i$ and $|A_i| < |A_j|$. First we prove that for every A_i, there is a $j > i$ such that $A_i \neq A_j$. Suppose this is not true. Then $A_i = A_j \in I_j$ for all $j \geq i$. That means $A_i \in J$ by the definition of J. This contradicts $A_i \in I_i \setminus J$. Now we claim that for every A_i, there is $j > i$ such that $|A_j| > |A_i|$. If it is not so, then $|A_i| = |A_{i+1}| = \ldots$. That means there are infinite A_i with the same level. This contradicts the given condition. Thus for some $i_1 < i_2 < i_3 < \ldots$, we have $|A_{i_1}| < |A_{i_2}| < |A_{i_3}| < \ldots$, hence the sequence $|A_i|$ is unbounded and the sequence $2^{-|A_1|}, 2^{-|A_2|}, \ldots$ converges to 0. Hence $\lim_{i \to \infty} I_i = J$.

Corollary 24. *Let $(\mathcal{I}, d)$ be the metric space induced by a level mapping $\|\ \|$ and I be a model of Π. If for every n, the set of $A \in \mathcal{B}$ such that $|A| = n$ is finite, then the sequence $I \supseteq T(I) \supseteq T^2(I) \supseteq \ldots$ converges to $J = \bigcap T^i(I)$ in $(\mathcal{I}, d)$.*

Consider the special interpretation $\emptyset$. The sequence $\emptyset, T(\emptyset), T^2(\emptyset), \ldots$ needs special attention. The following theorem (also in [7]) can be proved here diretly by proving that $\bigcup_i T^i(\emptyset)$ is a subset of every Herbrand model. We need also to prove it is the limit of the sequence $T^i(\emptyset)$ in metric space $\mathcal{I}$.

Theorem 25. *For a given definite program Π, let $J = \bigcup_i T^i(\emptyset)$. Then J is the least Herbrand model of Π.*

Theorem 26. *Suppose for every n, the set of $A \in \mathcal{B}$ with $|A| = n$ is finite. Let Π be a definite program and let T be induced by Π. Then $\lim_{i \to \infty} T^i(\emptyset) = \bigcup_i T^i(\emptyset)$ in the metric space $(\mathcal{I}, d)$.*

Proof Let $I_0 = \emptyset$, $I_i = T^i(\emptyset)$ if $i > 0$ and $J = \bigcup_i I_i$. Since $\emptyset \subseteq T(\emptyset)$, we have $I_0 \subseteq I_1 \subseteq I_2 \subseteq \ldots$. If $I_i = I_{i+1}$ for some i, then $I_i = I_{i+1} = \ldots$ and $J = I_i = I_{i+1} = \ldots$. Thus $d(J, I_j) \to 0$ if $j \to \infty$.

We can now suppose $I_0 \subset I_1 \subset I_2 \ldots$. There is $A_i \in J \setminus I_i$ such that $d(I_i, J) = 2^{-|A_i|}$. It is clear $|A_1| \leq |A_2| \leq \ldots$. We claim that for every A_i, there is $j > i$ such that $|A_j| > |A_i|$. Suppose not. Let us consider $J_i = \mathcal{B} \setminus I_i$. Then $J_0 \supset J_1 \supset J_2 \supset \ldots$. The set $J' = \bigcap J_i$ is the limit of $\{J_i\}$ by Theorem 23. Since $J' = \bigcap J_i$, we have $\mathcal{B} \setminus J = J'$ i.e. $\bigcap J_i = \bigcap(\mathcal{B} \setminus I_i) = \mathcal{B} \setminus \bigcup I_i$. Since $A_i \in J \setminus I_i$, then $A_i \in (\mathcal{B} \setminus I_i) \setminus (\mathcal{B} \setminus J) = J_i \setminus J'$. We can use the same proof of Theorem 23 to prove that $|A_i|$ indeed increases. (The I_i is replaced by J_i and J is replaced by J' in the proof). That means $2^{-|A_i|}$ decreases and $\lim_i d(J, I_i) = 0$.

The empty set is often a model of a program which does not contain a unit clause, so both Theorem 21 and Theorem 25 are applicable. Does the empty set have some special property?

Proposition 27. *Given a program Π and its induced mapping T, then $\emptyset$ is a model of Π iff $T(\emptyset) = \emptyset$, i.e. $\emptyset$ is a fixed point of T.*

As we have seen that $\bigcap_i T^i(\mathcal{B})$ is also a model of Π. We would like to know if it is also a fixed point of T. This can be proved in certain situations. We use the following lemma which is a generalization of Lemma 10.

Lemma 28. *Given a continuous mapping $T : V \to V$ where V is a complete metric space, if $x, T(x), T^2(x), \ldots$ is a Cauchy sequence, then this sequence converges to a fixed point.*

Proof Let $y = \lim_{i \to \infty} T^i(x)$. By the continuity of T and Lemma 9, we have $T(y) = T(\lim_i T^i(x)) = \lim_i T^{i+1}(x) = y$.

Theorem 29. *Suppose for every n, the set of ground atoms with level n is finite. Suppose also T is continuous. Then $\bigcap T^i(\mathcal{B})$ is the greatest fixed point of T and $\bigcup T^i(\emptyset)$ is the smallest fixed point of T.*

Proof (of the first part) As we have seen $\mathcal{B} \supseteq T(\mathcal{B}) \supseteq T^2(\mathcal{B}) \ldots$. By Corollary 24 we know $J = \bigcap T^i(\mathcal{B}) = \lim_i T^i(\mathcal{B})$. Since every convergent sequence is also a Cauchy sequence, so J is also a fixed point by Lemma 28. Now consider an arbitrary fixed point I. Then $I \subset \mathcal{B}$. By the monotonic property of T, we have $I = T^i(I) \subseteq T^i(\mathcal{B})$ for all i. Thus $\bigcap T^i(I) \subseteq \bigcap T^i(\mathcal{B})$. Since $\bigcap T^i(I) = I$ so $I \subseteq \bigcap T^i(\mathcal{B}) = J$.

Lemma 30. *If interpretations I and J coincide in all ground atoms with levels less than n, then $d(I, J) \leq 1/2^n$.*

Identify the target interpretation in the limit Let M be the target interpretation and we are looking for a correct program Π such that the least Herbrand model of Π is M. Let $\mathcal{B}$ be ordered as $e_1, e_2, e_3, \ldots$ according to its levels, i.e. $|e_i| \geq |e_j|$ if $i > j$. Let $e_1, e_2, \ldots$ be given one by one as positive or negative examples. Suppose we can find programs $\Pi_1, \Pi_2, \ldots, \Pi_n, \ldots$ such that Π_i is correct with respect to $e_1, \ldots, e_i$. We want to show that $\lim_{i \to \infty} M_{\Pi_i} = M$. If the Herbrand base is finite (for example, function free language), there are only finite possible examples $e_1, e_2, \ldots, e_n$. Then every $\Pi_i, i \geq n$ is correct with respect to the target interpretation. We can say $\lim_{i \to \infty} M_{\Pi_i} = M$ because $d(M_{\Pi_i}, M) = 0 \, \forall i \geq n$. On the other hand, if $\mathcal{B}$ is infinite and for every n the set of A with $|A| = n$ is finite, then for every level n, there is an atom with level larger than n. Now we would like that for every $\epsilon > 0$, there is N such that $d(M_i, M) \leq \epsilon$ if $i \geq N$. Let us choose an k such that $\epsilon > 1/2^k$. Let N satisfy that $|e_i| > k$ if $i \geq N$. Now M_{Π_i} coincides with M for all ground atoms with level less than or equal to k. That means $d(M_{\Pi_i}, M) < 1/2^k$ by the lemma above. Thus $M_{\Pi_i} \to M$. This limit process is consistent with the concept of identifying the target concept in the limit given by [11].

5   A new level mapping

There are two ways to approach the fixed points in literature. One is based on complete partial ordered sets (CPO) and lattices. In this situation one considers mappings with more than one fixed point (see [4]). Another way uses metric spaces and the Banach theorem (see [5]). In this situation we consider a contraction which has only one fixed point. We want to combine these two approaches in this section: the function T is investigated on a metric space $(\mathcal{I}, d)$ and it is not necessarily a contraction. Thus T may have more than one fixed point.

Definition 31. Every ground atom has a tree structure and the depth of the tree can be considered as the level of the atom (Definition 12). Thus we have a level mapping $|| : \mathcal{B} \to \mathbf{N}$. Let d be the distance on the set of Herbrand interpretations induced by this level mapping. We consider a logic language with finite number of function symbols. Then for every level, there is only finite number of ground atoms with this level.

Example 5. Let us consider a definite program Π which contains only the following clause $p(f(x)) \leftarrow p(x)$. The induced Herbrand base is $\mathcal{B} = \{p(a), p(f(a)), p(f^2(a)), \ldots\}$. We have $|p(f^n(a))| = n + 2$. Let $I \in \mathcal{I}$. For $n > 0$, then $p(f^n(a)) \in T(I)$ iff $p(f^{n-1}(a)) \in I$. Consider $I, J \in \mathcal{I}$. Suppose $d(I, J) = 2^{-k}$. Then I and J coincide in level less than k. There is an A with $|A| = k$ and $A \in I \triangle J$. We assume $A \in I \setminus J$. So $A = p(f^{k-1}(a)) \in I$ and $B = p(f^k(a)) \in T(I)$. Moreover, $A \notin J$ so $B \notin T(J)$. Thus $d(T(I), T(J)) = 2^{-(k+1)}$. This means that T is a contraction. This example can serve as a motivation for Lemma 32.

Example 6. Consider the following program $\Pi: p(f(x)) \leftarrow p(x)$ and $q(a) \leftarrow q(x)$. Then both $I = \emptyset$ and $J = \{q(a)\}$ are fixed points of T induced by Π. We conclude that T is not a contraction because it has more than one fixed point.

Example 7. Consider program with only one clause $p(x) \leftarrow p(f^n(x)), n \geq 0$. If x is substituted by a ground term t with level k, then $p(t)$ is a ground atom of level $k + 1$. Suppose $p(f^n(t)) \in I \setminus J$. Then $p(t) \in T(I) \setminus T(J)$. This means $d(T(I), T(J)) \geq d(I, J)$. On the other hand, $d(T(I), T(J)) \leq 2^n \cdot d(I, J)$. This example serves as a motivation for Lemma 36

Lemma 32. *Let Π be a given definite program. Suppose every clause $C : A \leftarrow A_1, \ldots, A_m$ in Π has the following property: For every i, if t is a term in A_i, then t is also a term in A. Then $d(T(I), T(J)) \leq d(I, J)$.*

Proof Suppose $d(I, J) = 2^{-k}$. Suppose there is B such that $d(T(I), T(J)) = 2^{-|B|}$. That means there is a ground instance $B \leftarrow B_1, \ldots, B_m$ of a clause $C : A \leftarrow A_1, \ldots, A_m$ such that for some j we have $B_j \in I$ and $B_j \notin J$. Then we have $|B_j| \geq k$. If term t is in A_j, then t is in A, thus $|B| \geq |B_j|$. This implies $|B| \geq k$. Thus $d(T(I), T(J)) \leq 2^{-k} = d(I, J)$.

Definition 33. Given a level mapping $||$, a program Π is *recurrent* (see [2]) w.r.t. $||$ if it satisfies the following condition: For every ground instance $B \leftarrow B_1, \ldots, B_m$ of a clause in Π we have $|B| > |B_i|$ for all i.

Proposition 34. *Given a level mapping $||$, if Π is recurrent w.r.t. $||$, then $d(T(I), T(J)) \leq d(I, J)$.*

The following theorem is an immediate consequence of Lemma 7, Lemma 32 and Proposition 34

Theorem 35. *Let Π be a given definite program which is either recurrent or every clause $C : A \leftarrow A_1, \ldots, A_m$ in Π has the following property: For every i, if t is a term in A_i, then t is also a term in A. Then T is continuous.*

Lemma 36. *Let Π be a given definite program. Suppose every clause $C : A \leftarrow A_1, \ldots, A_m$ in Π has the following property: If t is a term in A, then for every i, t is also a term in A_i. Then there is K such that $d(T(I), T(J)) \leq 2^K \cdot d(I, J)$ for all $I, J \in \mathcal{I}$.*

Proof Let A be a given atom which may contain variables. Then we can use $|A|$ to denote the length of the tree structure of the atom A. For every clause $C : A \leftarrow A_1, \ldots, A_m$ in Π, by the assumption given for a clause in Π, we have $|A| \leq |A_i|$ for all i. Let $M_C = \max\{|A_i| - |A| | A_i$ in the body of $C\}$. Then $|A_i| \leq |A| + M_C$. Let $K = \max\{M_C | C \in \Pi\}$. We will prove this K satisfies the inequality stated in the lemma. Suppose $d(I, J) = 2^{-k}$ and there is B such that $d(T(I), T(J)) = 2^{-|B|}$. Then there is a clause $C : A \leftarrow A_1, \ldots, A_m$ such that a ground instance of this clause $C\theta : B \leftarrow B_1, \ldots, B_m$ has the property that for some j, $B_j \in I \setminus J$. This implies $|B_j| \geq k$. Since $K + |A| \geq |A_j|$, we have $K + |A\theta| \geq |A_j\theta|$ by the given property of Π. This means $K + |B| \geq |B_j|$. Thus $K + |B| \geq k$ or $|B| \geq k - K$. This means $d(T(I), T(J)) \leq 2^{-(k-K)} \leq 2^K \cdot d(I, J)$.

The following theorem is a direct consequence of Lemma 36 and Lemma 7. Moreover, Theorem 38 is a direct consequence of Corollary 24 and Theorem 26.

Theorem 37. *Let Π be a given definite program. Suppose every clause $C : A \leftarrow A_1, \ldots, A_m$ in Π has the following property: If term t is in A, then for every i, t is in A_i. Then T is continuous.*

Theorem 38. *Let the level mapping $\| \| : B \to \mathbf{N}$ be defined by the depth of the expression trees and let d be the distance on $\mathcal{I}$ induced by $\| \|$. Then $\lim_{i \to \infty} T^i(\emptyset) = \bigcup T^i(\emptyset)$ and $\lim_{i \to \infty} T^i(I) = \bigcap_{i \to \infty} T^i(I)$ in $(\mathcal{I}, d)$ if I is a model of Π.*

Example 8. Consider the definite program $\Pi = \{p(a), p(f^2(x)) \leftarrow p(x)\}$. Let $I_0 = I = \emptyset$ and $I_i = T^i(I)$. Then $I_1 = \{p(a)\}$, $I_2 = \{p(a), p(f^2(a))\}$ and $I_i = \{p(a), p(f^2(a)), \ldots, p(f^{2i}(a))\}$. The least Herbrand model is $J = \bigcup_i T^i(\emptyset) = \{p(f^{2i}(a)) | i \geq 0\}$. Since $p(f^{2i+2}(a)) \in J \setminus I_i$, we have $d(J, I_i) = 1/2^{2i+4}$ which goes to 0 when $i \to \infty$. Thus $\lim_{i \to \infty} I_i = J$.

Remark In the last section we have shown that identifying the target in the limit given by [11] is consistent with the limit concept in a metric space $\mathcal{I}$ defined by a level mapping with some property. Now we have a concrete example of a metric space where the correct programs w.r.t. the given examples identifies the target interpretation in the limit.

6 Conclusion

To define a metric in the set of Herbrand interpretation is mathematical interesting. With such a metric d we can consider an interpretation J as an approximation of an interpretation I if $d(I, J)$ is small. This is particularly interesting for ILP when we want to find an almost correct program with respect to examples or a target interpretation. However, the metric defined in [10] can not explain the idea of identifying the target concept in the limit in model inference. This is improved by a metric defined by a level mapping if we require that the level mapping satifies some simple condition. However, using level mappings such as [5] has also some disadvantages. The level mapping and hence the metric are defined by some program. The mapping T_Π induced by a program Π should be a contraction. Thus it has a unique fixed point. This is not suitable for ILP when the programs are unknown. We should define level mappings independent of the programs. Since the examples are given as input so we know the levels of these examples. With the levels of examples we can estimate the closeness of a correct program w.r.t. the given examples to a target program. We can also talk about the concept of limit in this space of Herbrand interpretations. This is especially interesting when we consider some important models or fixed points. The condition needed for our level mappings is fortunately satisfied when we use depth of an expression to define the level.

References

1. J. W. de Bakker, E. de Vink, *Control Flow Semantics*. MIT press, 1996.
2. M. Bezem Characterizing Termination of Logic Programs with Level Mappings p.69-80, *Proceedings of the North American Conference on Logic Programming*. MIT press, Cambridge, MA, 1989.
3. J. Dieudonné. *Foundations of Modern Analysis*. Academic Press, 1969.
4. B.A. Davey and H.A. Priestley. *Introduction to Lattices and Order*. Cambridge University Press, 1990.
5. M. Fitting. Metric methods, three examples and a theorem. *Journal of Logic Programming*, 1994;21:p.113-127.
6. A. Hutchinson. Metrics on Terms and Clauses. In: M. Someren, G. Widmer, editors. *Proceedings of the 9th European Conference on Machine Learning (ECML-97)*, p.138-145, Springer-Verlag, 1997.
7. J. W. Lloyd. *Foundations of Logic Programming*. Springer-Verlag, Berlin, second edition, 1987.
8. S. H. Nienhuys-Cheng and A. de Bruin. Kahn's fixed-point characterization for linear dynamic networks. In: *Proceedings of SofSem97*. Lecture Notes in Computer Science, Springer-Verlag, 1997.
9. S. H. Nienhuys-Cheng and R. de Wolf. *Foundations of Inductive Logic Programming*, LNAI Tutorial 1228, Springer-Verlag, 1997.
10. S. H. Nienhuys-Cheng. Distance between Herbrand interpretations: A measure for approximations to a target concept, In: *Proccedings of ILP97*, Lavrač and Džeroski (eds), Springer-Verlag, 1997.
11. E. Y. Shapiro. *Inductive inference of theories from facts*. Research Report 192, Yale University, 1981.

Relational Distance-Based Clustering

Mathias Kirsten* and Stefan Wrobel*

German National Research Center for Information Technology,
SET.KI,
Schloß Birlinghoven,
D-53757 Sankt Augustin,
email: {mathias.kirsten,stefan.wrobel}@gmd.de

Abstract. Work on first-order clustering has primarily been focused on the task of *conceptual* clustering, i.e., forming clusters with symbolic generalizations in the given representation language. By contrast, for propositional representations, experience has shown that simple algorithms based exclusively on distance measures can often outperform their concept-based counterparts. In this paper, we therefore build on recent advances in the area of first-order distance metrics and present RDBC, a bottom-up agglomerative clustering algorithm for first-order representations that relies on distance information only and features a novel parameter-free pruning measure for selecting the final clustering from the cluster tree. The algorithm can empirically be shown to produce good clusterings (on the mutagenesis domain) that, when used for subsequent prediction tasks, improve on previous clustering results and approach the accuracies of dedicated predictive learners.

1 Introduction

Clustering is one of the fundamental unsupervised learning tasks, and has been intensively studied for propositional representations, both in statistics and in Machine Learning. For relational, first-order representations, there has been a lot less research, but here also, existing work (e.g. [20], [1], [10], [3] has shown the application potential of clustering for tasks where class information is sparse, expensive to obtain, or unavailable. However, up to now, work in ILP has mostly concentrated on the task of *conceptual* clustering, i.e., restricting cluster formation to clusters with symbolic generalizations in the given representation language. By contrast, in propositional learning and especially in statistics, experience has shown that simple algorithms based exclusively on distance measures can be very successful and often outperform their concept-based counterparts.

In this paper, we therefore build on recent advances in the area of first-order distance metrics (see e.g. [2], [12], [4]) and present RDBC, a bottom-up agglomerative clustering algorithm for first-order representations that relies on distance information only. The algorithm features a novel parameter-free pruning measure for turning the hierarchical cluster tree into a single-level cluster

* Partially supported by ESPRIT IV Long Term Research Project ILP II (No. 20237).

partitioning of the data. Experiments in two real-world domains have shown that the algorithm is capable of producing clusterings of good quality. When used for subsequent prediction (in the mutagenicity domain), the clustering results (obtained without class information) show an improvement on previous first-order clustering results, and are almost on a par with the accuracies of dedicated prediction learning systems.

The paper is organized as follows. In section 2, we introduce the basic idea of distance-based clustering and briefly review the first-order similarity metric used in our work. In section 3, we present the RDBC algorithm, including its pruning measure that selects a single-level set of clusters from the induced clustering hierarchy. Results from empirical experiments are reported in section 4. In the related work section, we discuss other first-order clustering systems, and in particular the relationship of RDBC to KBG [1], Cola-2 [10] and C0.5 [3] which have used distance functions within conceptual clustering. We conclude with a summary and some pointers to future work.

2   Distance-Based Clustering

For propositional representations, most clustering algorithms are based on elementary distance properties of the instance space. Two general classes of algorithm can be distinguished. In the first group, a continuous instance space with a Euclidean distance metric is assumed (typically, the R^n), and algorithms make use of the properties of this space in using operations such as moving cluster centers or averaging cluster elements into prototypes. For first-order representations, this group of algorithms cannot easily be used, since the space of first-order expressions cannot be interpreted as a continuous space. Thus, in first-order distance-based clustering, we need to rely on algorithms that assume only the availability of a distance (or similarity) measure between elements in the instance space, i.e., a function that when given two elements of that space, returns a distance (similarity) value, typically normalized to the interval of 0 to 1.

We can thus define the task of similarity based clustering as follows.

Given:

- a set of *instances* I
- a *similarity function* $sim : I \times I \to \mathbb{R}$

Find:

- a set of clusters $C \subseteq P(I)$
- that maximizes given *quality criteria*

In this definition, three components need to be defined more precisely, instances, similarity function and quality criteria.

Firstly, whereas in propositional learning, an instance is simply a feature vector, in first-order clustering, a little more needs to be said. Here, we follow the basic approach first introduced in [1] of using sets of ground facts as descriptions of instances. We will refer to a set of facts that describe an instance as a *case*. A case is a very similar notion to the models used in the "learning from interpretations" setting [7], however, the facts of a case do include the instance identifier. If the given problem is not already structured into a set of cases, we use the case generation approach introduced for RIBL to generate cases based on predicate mode declarations and a depth bound (see [12] for details).

Secondly, a suitable similarity function needs to be selected. Fortunately, recent work in ILP has produced distance measures that have already proven their power within predictive learning. Here, we use the distance measure of RIBL2.0 [4]. This distance measure uses the idea (first introduced in [2] and somewhat modified for RIBL [12]) of computing distances by recursively comparing the components of first-order instances until one can finally fall back on propositional comparisons on elementary features. The RIBL2.0 version used for this work in addition is capable of handling non-flat representations, i.e., instance descriptions involving lists and other terms (see [4] for details).

Finally, there are a large number of quality measures that could be applied to the result of clustering. Here, we have chosen to base clustering on the most basic quality criteria, namely maximizing average intra-cluster similarity (average similarity of elements within a cluster).

We can thus refine the above definition to precisely describe the learning task of RDBC as follows.

Given:

- a set of instances I, with each instance a ground atom
- background knowledge B, with B a set of ground atoms
- a declaration D specifying argument types and modes as well as the arity for all predicates in I and B.
- a case generator $case_{RIBL} : I \to C := I \times B^*$
- a similarity function $sim_{RIBL} : C \times C \to \mathbb{R}$ that computes the similarity of two cases

Find:

- a set of clusters $C \subseteq P(I)$
- that maximizes average intra-cluster similarity.

3   The RDBC algorithm

Finding a clustering that is guaranteed to be optimal in terms of the chosen quality measure is an infeasible task, so the available distance-based clustering algorithms use heuristic strategies. One of the most basic distance-based clustering algorithms is "Average Linkage" bottom up clustering (c.f. [9]). This method starts out with the list of cases as one-element clusters, and iteratively groups the two most similar clusters into a new cluster. Removing both and inserting their union instead, we do this all over again until eventually the cluster list contains only a single cluster (see Figure 1).

```
cluster(C, S) : ListOfClusters
var C : List of (nested) clusters
    S : Similarity matrix

begin
    (Cₓ, C_y) := find_nearest_neighbor_pair(C, S);
    C_new := {(Cₓ, C_y)} ∪ C \ {Cₓ, C_y}
    if length(C_new) > 1 then
        return(cluster(C_new, S));
    else
        return(C_new);
    endif

end
```

Fig. 1. Basic clustering algorithm of RDBC

This is the representation of a binary tree whose leaves are the cases C, whereas the internal nodes contain the similarity values of the corresponding two subtrees, respectively the two (sets of) cases. Figure 2 shows a sample cluster hierarchy from the mutagenicity domain described in section 4.1.

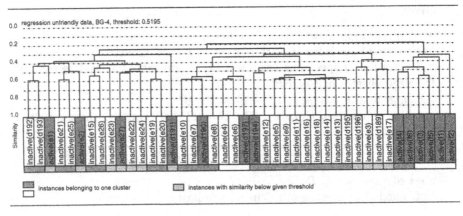

Fig. 2. Sample cluster hierarchy on the mutagenicity data

For the 'Average Linkage' method similarity between clusters is defined as :

$$sim(C_i, C_j) = \frac{1}{n_{C_i} n_{C_j}} \sum_{k=1}^{n_{C_i}} \sum_{l=1}^{n_{C_j}} sim_{RIBL}(Inst_k, Inst_l)$$

with n_C being the number of instances in cluster C, $Inst_k$ belonging to cluster C_i, $Inst_l$ belonging to C_j, and $sim_{RIBL}(Inst_k, Inst_l)$ denoting the similarity function inherited from RIBL.

Thus, the chosen agglomerative approach renders a similarity-based hierarchy of cases, in which similarity between subtrees increases as we move from root towards the leaves. For many applications, such a hierarchical tree is all that is required. If however, the clustering task requires the selection of a single set of clusters, we need a technique for turning the tree into such a set. Since we are trying to optimize intra-cluster similarity, it is natural to base cluster selection from the tree on this criterion. We therefore decided to use a search procedure that "cuts up" the tree according to growing intra-cluster similarity thresholds, and selects the threshold and corresponding group of clusters that maximizes average intra-cluster similarity. More precisely, the quality of a set of clusters C is defined as:

$$qual(C) = \frac{\sum_{C \in C} sim_{intra}(C)}{|C|},$$

where $sim_{intra}(C)$ denotes the intra-cluster similarity of a cluster C.

$$SIM := \{sim_{intra}(C) \mid C \in C\},$$

and for any element $s \in SIM$, let

$$C(s) := \{C \in C \mid sim_{intra}(C) \geq s \text{ and } sim_{intra}(parent(C)) < s\}.$$

The chosen clustering is $C_{chosen} := argmax_{s \in SIM} \, qual(C(s))$.

4   Experimental results

For an empirical evaluation of our system, we have conducted experiments on two different domains. The first of these is the well-known mutagenicity domain [18] used in many ILP papers for comparative evaluation. In this domain, in addition to performing clustering, we have also used the clustering results for subsequent prediction as done in [3]. While not a direct measure of cluster quality and thus a problematic criterion, this at least gives a comparable numerical estimate. As a second domain, we have used the mRNA signal structure domain introduced in [5].

4.1   Mutagenesis data

The goal of the mutagenicity application [17] is to predict the mutagenicity of chemical compounds. The data contains twentyone extensionally defined predicates. These predicates encode class information (i.e. wether a compound is active or inactive in terms of mutagenicity), some aspects of molecule structure (i.e. bond- and atom-types, as well as atom charge), non-structural knowledge about the molecules (logp and lumo values), specifically chosen data, based on chemical knowledge of mutagenicity, generic structual knowledge about elementary chemical concepts (like groups, connected rings, ring length), and the numerical mutagenicity value for all compounds.

We have conducted several experiments using different background knowledges BG1-BG4 [17]. BG-1 and BG-2 contain structural information only, in BG-1 without, in BG-2 with numerical information about atom charge. BG-3 adds to BG-2 the non-structural knowledge from logp and lumo. Finally, BG-4 includes the twelve predicates extensionally describing generic structural knowledge.

Experiments All clustering experiments described in this section were conducted in an unsupervised manner, i.e., not making class information available to RDBC. To evaluate the usefulness of RDBC's results for prediction, we have used the same procedure as described in [3], computing the average *logm* values for an entire cluster, and assigning a cluster class based on whether this number was positive (positive cluster) or negative (negative cluster). The observed class of an instance was then compared to the predicted class of its cluster. However, we have used the leave-one-out-approach for both the regression-unfriendly and the regression-friendly datasets. As seen in table 1, the results compare favorably with previous published results on this problem; in fact, the results of RDBC are close to the results obtained by predictive learners. (Results for PROGOL are taken from [19] and from [17] for FOIL, FOIL's results for the unfriendly datasets were not available; results for C0.5 are unsupervised results from [3].)

	Regression unfriendly				Regression friendly				
	Progol	TILDE	C0.5	RDBC	Progol	FOIL	TILDE	C0.5	RDBC
BG-1	N/A	83%	76%	78.6%	N/A	83%	75%	73%	83.0%
BG-2	N/A	83%	74%	78.6%	N/A	75%	75%	81%	84.0%
BG-3	83%	79%	71%	78.6%	82%	83%	85%	79%	82.4%
BG-4	83%	N/A	N/A	78.6%	88%	82%	N/A	N/A	83.0%

Table 1. Classification accuracy yielded by RDBC, C0.5, TILDE, and Progol on the mutagenesis data

In another experiment, we have tested the hypothesis, originally put forth in [11] that unclassified instances contain information that helps later prediction. To this end, we have completely removed the test instances from the clustering run, and readded them to the "closest" (least average distance) cluster after clustering and clustering selection were complete. The results are shown in table 2 and confirm the hypothesis: missing the unclassified instance causes accuracies to drop slightly.

4.2 mRNA signal structure detection

mRNA molecules transmit the genetic information from the DNA to the protein-making machinery of the cell (ribosome). Such mRNA molecules can contain interesting substructures, so called signal structures.

	Regression unfriendly	Regression friendly
BG-1	71,4%	78,2%
BG-2	71,4%	79,8%
BG-3	71,4%	81,9%
BG-4	78,5%	83,0%

Table 2. RDBC accuracy without unclassified test instances

So far the domain contains 66 classified signal structures, composed of 15 IRE (s_ire), 15 TAR (s_tar), 2x15 SECIS (in the following refered to as s_secis1 and s_secis2) and 6 HISTONE (s_histone). See [4] for further details. The aim of our clustering was then to find clusters correlated to the 5 original classes of signal structures given in the data.

Using all 66 instances for clustering, RDBC returned the ten clusters shown in Figure 3. While some of the actual classes were rediscovered by RDBC (s_tar, s_ire, s_histone, and s_secise2), mainly the clustering of s_secise1 appears to be hard. Whereas the mixed cluster number 8 made up of s_secise1, and s_secise2 may be caused by a folding which those instances have in common, cluster 6 is hard to explain. In addition the misplaced instances s_secise1(5) and s_secise1(10) in cluster 2 would better fit into cluster 5.

To further evaluate the quality of RDBC's results, we used the computed clusters for prediction. Two experiments were conducted and the prediction accuracy was determined via a leave-one-out-approach. In both experiments class information was not used during the clustering stage. In the first experiment all instances except the test instance were available for building the clusters. The test instance's class was then determined by a majority vote over instances of the most similar of the obtained clusters (according to the distance measure). In contrast to that, for the second setup we included the test instance during clustering. As in the first experiment, we employed majority voting for determining the test instance's class.[1] Table 3 gives the accuracies obtained by our two experiments together with RIBL2.0's original result as reported in [4].

	RIBL	RDBC with test instance	RDBC without test instance
	97.0%	87.9%	83.3%

Table 3. RIBL's and RDBC's accuracies on the mRNA domain.

---

[1] In nine cases the majority vote resulted in a draw between two equally frequent classes. We resolved this by assigning the class of the instance most similar to our test instance. For this nearest-neighbor voting only instances of the cluster belonging to one of the two equally frequent classes were taken into account.

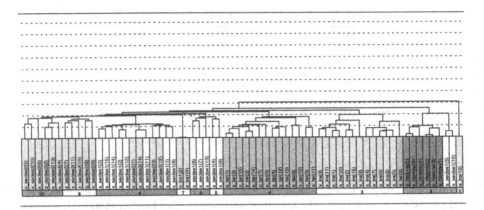

Fig. 3. Sample cluster hierarchy on the mRNA data. Shaded bars at the bottom mark the clusters found by RDBC.

5 Related Work

RDBC is related to a number of previous first-order clustering systems, namely KBG [1], COLA-2 [10] and C0.5 [3]. As pointed out in the introduction, these systems are *conceptual* clustering systems, i.e., they form clusters by considering possible descriptions in the given representation language, whereas RDBC is purely similarity-based.

Given this, RDBC is closest in spirit to KBG. KBG [1] forms clusters bottom-up based on a similarity metric that is a predecessor of the RIBL2.0 [4] similarity metric used in RDBC. Besides the modifications detailed in [12], the main difference is that KBG's metric lacks the ability to handle lists and terms. With respect to clustering, KBG uses a "threshold" algorithm which forms overlapping clusters, whereas RDBC, as detailed above, uses simple average linkage agglomerative clustering. Furthermore, to form a hierarchy (DAG) KBG replaces the elements of bottom-level clusters with generalized variants, resulting in a conceptual clustering. Finally, KBG does not feature a cluster selection step as in RDBC, but transforms the cluster hierarchy into a hierarchical set of rules.

Similar comments apply to SPRITE, the clustering system used within the characteristic description learner COLA-2 [10], since it is a modified variant of KBG. However, the ideas developed in COLA-2 for selecting clusters from a hierarchy for prediction tasks could be usefully applied to further improve the accuracy of RDBC results when used for prediction; in our experiments in this paper, we have used the simplest possible selection function.

C0.5 finally is a first-order top-down clustering system based on the use of logical decision trees. Instead of selecting split literals based on their predictive accuracy or entropy, C0.5 selects the split literal which maximizes the distance between the two resulting subsets (clusters) of examples. However, in contrast to RDBC, C0.5 uses a user-provided propositional distance measure in making its literal choices. Another difference is in the stopping/selection criterion that is used: C0.5 selects clusters that contain at least a user-specified number of elements, whereas RDBC uses a parameter-free search procedure to select the final clusters from all levels of the cluster tree.

6 Conclusion

In this paper, we have presented a first-order clustering system named RDBC that forms clusters bottom-up in an agglomerative fashion based on similarity only. The similarity metric used is the one introduced for RIBL2.0 [4], which means that RDBC can handle representations involving lists and other arbitrary terms. The empirical results presented above indicate that RDBC finds good clusterings; if used for prediction, accuracies compare favorably to previous approaches and even approach the accuracies of predictive learners in the mutagenesis domain. Even though this is encouraging, using accuracies on a prediction task to compare clustering systems is not a direct indication of cluster quality for other purposes, so future work should be investigating the direct measures of cluster quality available in the clustering literature. As for algorithmic aspects, the clustering algorithm selected here is the simplest possible, and more elaborate methods, such as the one used in KBG and SPRITE, should be examined. Furthermore, three other distance measures for first order logic domains have been proposed. These are described in [13], [15], and [16], and may be well worth a try. It would also be useful to try the similarity metric and cluster selection techniques used here in the context of a top-down strategy as employed in C0.5. In addition, the cluster selection technique introduced here which is only one way of generating and evaluating candidate clustering. An alternative worth investigating would be a strictly top-down search procedure. Finally, to feed each cluster into a first order learner like Foil [6], Progol [14], or Claudien [8] may provide us with sensible conceptual descriptions for each cluster and while maintaining the performance of the instance-based approach (as discussed in [12]).

References

1. G. Bisson. Conceptual clustering in a first order logic representation. In *Proc. European Conference on Artificial Intelligence (ECAI-92)*, 1992.
2. G. Bisson. Learning in fol with a similarity measure. In *AAAI-92 Proc. Tenth Natl. Conference on Artif. Intelligence*, 1992.
3. H. Blockeel and L. De Raedt. Using logical decision trees for clustering. In N. Lavrač and S. Džeroski, editors, *Inductive Logic Programming (Proc. 7th Int. Workshop ILP-97)*, pages 133 – 140, Berlin/New York, 1997. Springer Verlag.
4. U. Bohnebeck, T. Horvath, and S. Wrobel. Term comparisons in first-order similarity measures. In D. Page, editor, *Proc. 8th Int. Workshop on Inductive Logic Programming (ILP98)*, Madison, WI, USA, July 1998. to appear.

5. U. Bohnebeck, W. Sälter, O. Herzog, M. Wischnewsky, and D. Blohm. An Approach to mRNA Signalstructure Detection through Knowledge Discovery. In *Proceedings of GCB'97*, pages 125–126, 1997.

6. R. M. Cameron-Jones and J. R. Quinlan. Efficient top-down induction of logic programs. *SIGART Bulletin*, 5(1):33 – 42, 1994.

7. L. De Raedt, editor. *Advances in ILP: Proc. Fifth Int. Workshop on Inductive Logic Programming (ILP-95)*. IOS Press, Amsterdam, 1996. To appear.

8. L. De Raedt and L. De Haspe. Clausal discovery. *Machine Learning*, 26:99ff., 1997.

9. W. Dillon and M. Goldstein. *Multivariate analysis*, pages 157–208. John Wiley & Sons, Inc., 1984.

10. W. Emde. Inductive learning of characteristic concept descriptions. In S. Wrobel, editor, *Proc. Fourth International Workshop on Inductive Logic Programming (ILP-94)*, 53754 Sankt Augustin, Germany, 1994. GMD. GMD-Studien Nr. 237. .

11. W. Emde. Inductive learning of characteristic concept descriptions from small sets of classified examples. In F. Bergadano and L. D. Raedt, editors, *Machine Learning: ECML-94, European Conference on Machine Learning, Catania, Italy, April 1994, Proceedings*, pages 103 – 121, Berlin, New York, 1994. Springer-Verlag. Also as Arbeitspapiere der GMD No. 821. .

12. W. Emde and D. Wettschereck. Relational instance based learning. In L. Saitta, editor, *Machine Learning - Proceedings 13th International Conference on Machine Learning*, pages 122 – 130. Morgan Kaufmann Publishers, 1996. .

13. A. Hutchinson. Metrics on Terms and Clauses. In M. Someren and G. Widmer, editors, *Machine Learning: ECML-97 (Proc. Ninth European Conference on Machine Learning)*, volume 1224 of *LNAI*, pages 138–145. Springer Verlag, 1997.

14. S. Muggleton. Inverse entailment and Progol. In K. Furukawa, D. Michie, and S. Muggleton, editors, *Machine Intelligence 14*, pages 133 – 188. Oxford Univ. Press, Oxford, 1995.

15. S.-H. Nienhuys-Cheng. Distance Between Herbrand Interpretations: A Measure for Approximations to a Target Concept. In N. Lavrač and S. Džeroski, editors, *Inductive Logic Programming (Proc. 7th Int. Workshop ILP-97)*, volume 1297 of *LNAI*, pages 213–226. Springer Verlag, 1997.

16. M. Sebag. Distance induction in first order logic. In N. Lavrač and S. Džeroski, editors, *Inductive Logic Programming (Proc. 7th Int. Workshop ILP-97)*, LNAI, pages 264 – 272, Berlin/New York, 1997. Springer Verlag.

17. A. Srinivasan, S. Muggleton, and R. King. Comparing the use of background knowledge by inductive logic programming systems. In *Proceedings of the 5th International Workshop on Inductive Logic Programming*, 1995.

18. A. Srinivasan, S. Muggleton, R. King, and M. Sternberg. Mutagenesis: Ilp experiments in a non-determinate biological domain. In S. Wrobel, editor, *Proc. Fourth Int. Workshop on Inductive Logic Programming (ILP-94)*, pages 217 – 232, Schloß Birlinghoven, 53754 Sankt Augustin, Germany, 1994. GMD (German Natl. Research Center for Computer Science). Order from teuber@gmd.de.

19. A. Srinivasan, S. Muggleton, M. Sternberg, and R. King. Theories for mutagenicity: a study in first-order and feature-based induction. *Artificial Intelligence*, 85:277 – 299, 1996.

20. K. Thompson and P. Langley. Incremental concept formation with composite objects. In *Proc. of the Sixth Int. Workshop on Machine Learning*, pages 371 – 374, San Mateo, CA, 1989. Morgan Kaufman.

A Framework for Defining Distances Between First-Order Logic Objects

Jan Ramon and Maurice Bruynooghe

Katholieke Universiteit Leuven, Department of Computer Science
Celestijnenlaan 200A, B-3001 Heverlee, Belgium
{janr,maurice}@cs.kuleuven.ac.be

Abstract. Several learning systems, such as systems based on clustering and instance based learning, use a measure of distance between objects. Good measures of distance exist when objects are described by a fixed set of attributes as in attribute value learners. More recent learning systems however, use a first order logic representation. These systems represent objects as models or clauses. This paper develops a general framework for distances between such objects and reports a preliminary evaluation.

1   Introduction

In learning systems based on clustering (e.g. TIC [3], KBG [1]) and in instance based learning (e.g. [12, ch.4], RIBL [10]), a measure of the distance between objects is an essential component. Good measures exist for distances between objects in an attribute value representation (see e.g. [12, ch. 4]). Recently there is a growing interest in using more expressive first order representations of objects and in upgrading propositional learning systems into first order learning systems (e.g. TILDE [2], ICL [7] and CLAUDIEN [5]). The upgrading of clustering and instance based learning systems requires to develop a measure for the distance between first order objects, either described as clauses or as models of first order theories.

Some proposals for distance measures between atoms and clauses exists (e.g. [13] and [11]). They use Hausdorff metrics to extend distances between atoms into distances between sets of atoms (clauses or models). This has two drawbacks. Firstly, the value of the Hausdorff metric depends very much on the most extreme value in both sets. Secondly, the similarity due to occurrences of the same subterm (constant, variables, ...) in different atoms of the same clause has no influence on the value. Other authors (e.g. [10], [1]) use rather ad-hoc measures of similarity which do not comply with all axioms of a distance, in particular with the triangle axiom $(d(x,z) \leq d(x,y) + d(y,z))$.

Attribute value systems also allow to compute a prototype [12, ch. 4] of a set of similar objects. A prototype is an object such that the sum of (or the sum of squares of) the distances between each object and the prototype is minimal. So far this notion has not been upgraded to first order representations.

In this paper we develop a framework for distances between clauses and distances between models. The framework can be parametrised by a measure for the distance between atoms. It is general enough to be applied both for distances between clauses and distances between models. It takes into account subterms common to distinct atoms of a set of atoms in the measurement of the distance between sets. Moreover, for a constant number of variables, the complexity of the distance computation is polynomially bounded by the size of the objects. Initial experiments show that the framework can be the basis of good clustering algorithms.

We recall some basic concepts about distances, prototypes, and logic in section 2. In section 3, we briefly discuss the Hausdorff distance. Next, we propose a framework that is a generalisation of three polynomial time computable similarity measures proposed by Eiter and Mannila. We also introduce another instance of this framework which is a distance, while still polynomially computable. We also define a normalised distance and a polynomially computable binary prototype on sets. We instantiate the general schema with a distance between sets of atoms (either clauses or models) in section 4. Section 5 contains some results from initial experiments. We end with a brief discussion in section 6.

[14] is a full version of this paper including all proofs.

2 Preliminaries

Definition 1 (distance). *Given a set of objects O, a distance function d (also called a metric) is a mapping $O \times O \rightarrow \mathbb{R}$ such that for all x, y, $z \in O$:*

1. *$d(x, y) \geq 0$ and $d(x, y) = 0 \Leftrightarrow x = y$*
2. *$d(x, y) = d(y, x)$ (symmetry)*
3. *$d(x, z) \leq d(x, y) + d(y, z)$ (triangle inequality)*

Example 1 (Manhattan and Euclidian distance). Let $x = (x_1, \ldots, x_n)$ and $y = (y_1, \ldots, y_n)$ be elements of the n-dimensional Euclidian space E_n. With $c_1, \ldots, c_n$ some positive real constants (weights), the (weighted) manhattan distance (d_m) and the (weighted) euclidian distance (d_e) are defined as: $d_m(x, y) = \sum_{i=1}^{n} c_i |x_i - y_i|$ and $d_e(x, y) = (\sum_{i=1}^{n} c_i (x_i - y_i)^2)^{1/2}$.

Definition 2 (prototype).
Let $S = \{o_1, \ldots, o_n\}$ with $o_i \in O$. p is a prototype of S in O for the distance d iff $p \in O$ and $\sum_{i=1}^{n} d(p, o_i)^2 = \min_{x \in O} \sum_{i=1}^{n} d(x, o_i)^2$. A function $\mathcal{P}_d : 2^O \rightarrow O$ is a general prototype function for d if it maps each set of objects on a prototype for it. A function $\mathcal{P}_d : O \times O \rightarrow O$ is a binary prototype function for d if it maps each set of two objects on a prototype for it.

We also recall some preliminaries from logic. We consider terms built from an enumerable set $\mathcal{V}$ of variables, a set $\mathcal{C}$ of constants, and a set $\mathcal{F}$ of functors with arity > 0. A *term* is either a variable, a constant or of the form $f(t_1, \ldots, t_n)$ with f/n a functor of arity n and $t_1, \ldots, t_n$ terms. An *atom* is of the form $p(t_1, \ldots, t_n)$ with p/n an n-ary predicate symbol and $t_1, \ldots, t_n$ terms. A *literal* is an atom or its negation. A *clause* is a set of literals. A program is a set of clauses. A Herbrand interpretation (and also a Herbrand model) of a program can be described by a set of ground atoms (the atoms mapped to *true* by the interpretation). We denote the set of all terms (ground terms) by T (T_g). The sets of all atoms (ground atoms) is denoted by $\mathcal{A}$ ($\mathcal{A}_g$).

A is more general than B ($A \succeq B$) if there exists a substitution θ such that $A\theta = B$. The *lgg* (Least General Generalisation) of two atoms A and B are defined as follows: $lgg(A, B) = G$ iff $G \succeq A$ and $G \succeq B$ and $\forall L, L \succeq A$ and $L \succeq B : L \succeq G$.

Definition 3 (renaming substitution). *A renaming substitution is a substitution of the form $\{x_1 \to y_1, \ldots, x_n \to y_n\}$ such that $\{x_1, \ldots, x_n\}$ is a permutation of $\{y_1, \ldots, y_n\}$. With E an expression and θ a renaming substitution, $E\theta$ is a variant of E. Being variant of is an equivalence relation.*

Example 2. $\{xt \to xt1, xc \to xc1, xt1 \to xc, xc1 \to xt\}$ *is a renaming substitution. $r(xt1, xc1)$ is a variant of $r(xt, xc)$.*

Finally, we recall some special binary relations.

Definition 4. *A relation $f \subseteq A \times B$ between two sets A and B is a surjection if $\forall (a, b), (c, d) \in f : (a = c \Rightarrow b = d)$ and $\forall b \in B, \exists a \in A : (a, b) \in f$ (Fig. 1). A surjection f between A and B is fair if $\forall x, y \in B : \big| |f^{-1}\{x\}| - |f^{-1}\{y\}| \big| \leq 1$, so f maps the elements of A on elements of B as evenly as possible. A linking $f \subseteq A \times B$ is a relation such that $\forall a \in A, \exists b \in B : (a, b) \in f$ and $\forall b \in B, \exists a \in A : (a, b) \in f$, so all elements of A are associated with at least one of B and vice versa. A matching f between A and B is a relation such that $\forall (a, b), (c, d) \in f : (a = c \Leftrightarrow b = d)$, so each element of A is associated with at most one element of B and vice versa.*

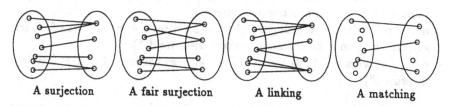

| A surjection | A fair surjection | A linking | A matching |

Fig. 1. Examples of relations between two sets.

3 Distances between sets of points

The Hausdorff distance. Well known is the Hausdorff distance (e.g. [13]). Given X, a set of points, and d, a distance function between points, $d_h : 2^X \times 2^X \to \mathbb{R}$ is defined as:

$$d_h(A, B) = \max \left(\max_{a \in A} (\min\{d(a, b)|b \in B\}), \max_{b \in B} (\min\{d(a, b)|a \in A\}) \right)$$

While this function has all the properties of a distance function, it does not take into account much information about the points in the sets (it is determined by the distance of the most distant element of both sets to the nearest neighbour in the other set). Therefore, it is not very well suited for applications in first order logic, where it is plausible that two sets of atoms that differ only (but perhaps very strongly) in one atom are very similar. So it is very desirable to have a better distance function.

Manhattan distances based on optimal mappings. Eiter and Mannila [9] discuss a family of Manhattan measures between sets which we can formulate as instances of the following scheme:

$$d^{\beta}(A, B) = \min_{r \in m^{\beta}(A,B)} \left\{ \left[\sum_{(x,y) \in r} d(x, y) \right] + \frac{\#(B \setminus r(A)) + \#(A \setminus r^{-1}(B))}{2} . M \right\}$$

where m^{β} is a function that maps each pair $(A, B) \in 2^X \times 2^X$ to a relation between A and B (a subset of $A \times B$), M is a positive constant, $r(A) = \{b | (a, b) \in r \wedge a \in A\}$, and $r^{-1} = \{(b, a) | (a, b) \in r\}$ and $\#(S)$ denoting the cardinality of a set S.

This means that one sums the distances of the pairs of elements which are in r and adds a penalty $M/2$ for each element that does not match with an element from the other set. Therefore, to obtain a measure which works well in practice, one should take for M a large value ideally at least as large as the maximal distance between 2 points.

The authors discuss three instantiations:

- $m^{\beta} = m^s$ with —assuming $\#(A) \geq \#(B)$— $m^s(A, B)$ the set of all surjections from A to B (surjection-measure d^s).
- $m^{\beta} = m^{fs}$ with —assuming $\#(A) \geq \#(B)$— $m^{fs}(A, B)$ the set of all fair surjections from A to B (fair surjection-measure d^{fs}).
- $m^{\beta} = m^l$ with $m^l(A, B)$ the set of all linkings between A and B (linking-measure d^l).

They show that these measures can be evaluated in polynomial time, but are not distance functions (the triangle inequality is violated). Using matchings ($m^{\beta} = m^m$ with $m^m(A, B)$ the set of all matchings between A and B) one obtains another instantiation. In this case, the formula simplifies into:

$$d^m(A, B) = \min_{r \in m^{\beta}(A,B)} \left\{ \left[\sum_{(x,y) \in r} d(x, y) \right] + \frac{\#(B) + \#(A) - 2\#(r)}{2} . M \right\}$$

We prove in [14] the following theorems:

Theorem 1. $d^m(A, B)$ *is a distance function.*

Theorem 2. *If the time to compute the distance between two points is bounded by a constant, then the time to compute $d^m(A, B)$ is bounded by a polynomial in the sum of the sizes of A and B.*

Proposition 1. *If $d(a, b)$ is invariant for renaming substitutions i.e. $d(a, b) = d(a\theta_r, b\theta_r)$ for all atoms a and b and for all renaming substitutions θ_r then $d^m(A, B)$ is invariant for renaming substitutions.*

We can develop also a similar scheme for Euclidian measures (the square of the distances between elements in the relation m is used). Our result also holds for this scheme.

Normalised matching distances. In some applications it is desirable to work with distances in the interval $[0, 1]$. Having a distance between points which is in this interval, one can obtain such a distance between sets of points. M can be set to 1 when $d(x, y)$ is bounded by 1 and the general formula for distances between sets can be simplified into:

$$d^m(A, B) = \sum_{(x,y)\in m_{AB}} d(x, y) + \frac{\#(B) + \#(A) - 2\#(m_{AB})}{2}$$

where m_{AB} is the matching which results in the minimal value.
In [14] we show that

$$d^{m,n}(A, B) = \frac{2\sum_{(a,b)\in m_{AB}} d(a, b) + \#A + \#B - 2\#m_{AB}(A)}{\sum_{(a,b)\in m_{AB}} d(a, b) + \#A + \#B - \#m_{AB}}$$

is a good distance, bounded from above by 1.

Proposition 2. *If $d(a, b)$ is invariant for renaming substitutions then $d^{m,n}(A, B)$ is invariant for renaming substitutions.*

Prototype functions for matching distances Not only distances, but also prototypes can be extended to sets of objects. For prototypes, however, the situation is not so favorable as for distances, as the complexity of prototype functions for sets seems to grow exponentially in the number of objects. Nevertheless, we can give a binary prototype function for euclidian distance that is computable in polynomial time.

Given a prototype function $p : X \times X \to X$ that computes the prototype of two elements, we define a measure $e(x, y) = d(x, p(x, y))^2 + d(p(x, y), y)^2$. Given 2 sets A and B we select the matching r such that

$$\sum_{(x,y)\in r} e(x, y) + \frac{M}{2}(\#A + \#B - 2\#r)$$

is minimal. This can be done in polynomial time when the computation of $p(x, y)$ is bounded by a constant because computing $e(x, y)$ for all pairs x and y requires $(\#(A)\#(B))$ steps. Finding the best one of all matchings r is also polynomially bounded (the proof of this is similar to the proof of Theorem 2). Let

$p_0(A, B) = \{p(x, y) | (x, y) \in r\}$. Then we define

$$p(A, B) = \text{if } \#A < \#B \text{ then } p_0(A, B) \cup (A \setminus r^{-1}(B))$$
$$\text{else } p_0(A, B) \cup (B \setminus r(A)).$$

Lemma 1. *The set $p(A, B)$ is a prototype of the sets A and B for the distance d^m. If the time to compute a prototype of two points is bounded by a constant, then the time to compute $p(A, B)$ is polynomially bounded in the sum of the sizes of A and B.*

The proof is in [14].

4 Distances between sets of atoms

In the previous section, we developed functions for measuring the distance between two sets of points which, contrary to the Hausdorff distance, return a value which depends on all points in the two sets. In our application of interests, our "points" are atoms and the sets are sets of atoms. Simply taking a existing distance function between atoms and applying the distance functions of the previous section is not what we aim at as it ignores the similarity between different atoms in a set.

Example 3. Let $A = \{r(xt1, xc1), p(xt1, x), q(xc1, x)\}$, $B = \{r(xt2, xc2), p(xt2, y), q(xc2, y)\}$ and $C = \{r(xt4, xc3), p(xt3, y), q(xc1, v)\}$ be sets of atoms. Applying any of the distance functions of the previous section, one obtains $d(A, B) = d(A, C)$. However, A is, up to renaming, equivalent to B while different from C. Note that A and B are renamings of $lgg(A, B)$, while A is not a renaming of $lgg(A, C)$.

We want to adjust the distance functions of the previous sections with a factor accounting for the recurrence of terms in different atoms of the same set. Our approach is to generalise the two sets so that their distance becomes smaller, to add factors accounting for the complexity of the substitutions needed to return to the original set and to set the cost of a renaming to 0.

In what follows, d^m can be any correct distance function between sets of atoms based on a distance function d between atoms. Let Θ be a set of substitutions, and let *cost* be a function mapping a set of substitutions to a positive number. A family of potential distances between sets of atoms A and B is:

$$d^{\Theta}_{cost}(A, B) = \min_{\theta_a, \theta_b \in \Theta; X, Y \in \mathcal{A}} d^m(X, Y) + cost(\theta_a) + cost(\theta_b)$$

where $A = X\theta_a$, $B = Y\theta_b$.

With appropriate choices for Θ and *cost* one can obtain that d^{Θ}_{cost} is a distance function[1]. However we have to be careful to obtain computationally feasible

---

[1] With only the empty substitution in Θ and with zero cost function we obtain d^m.

solutions (we want to measure the distance between sets consisting of hundreds of atoms). We should somehow limit the number of generalisations and thus the class of candidate substitutions. One possible choice which is in agreement with the intuitions sketched in the above example is to allow only renaming substitutions.

Restricting the substitutions to Θ_r, the set of all renaming substitutions, and setting the cost of substitutions to 0, we obtain a function which, as desired, returns 0 for sets of atoms which are variants of each other.

Theorem 3. *If d^m is invariant under renaming substitutions, then*

$$d_0^{\Theta_r}(A, B) = \min_{\theta_a, \theta_b \in \Theta_r; X, Y \in A} d^m(X, Y) \ \text{where} \ A = X\theta_a, \ B = Y\theta_b$$

is a distance function on sets of atoms.

The proof is in [14].

Example 4. Let $A = \{r(xt1, xc1), p(xt1, x), q(xc1, x)\}$ and $C = \{r(xt4, xc3), p(xt3, y), q(xc3, v)\}$. The distance is minimal with $X = \{r(xt, xc), p(xt, x), q(xc, x)\}$ and $Y = \{r(xt, xc), p(xt3, x), q(xc, y)\}$. X and Y differ on one position in the p atom and one position in the q atom, so the distance will be non-zero.

5 Results in practice

We present some preliminary empirical results for distances defined with the presented framework.

Our experiments are in the learning from interpretations setting (see also [6], [4]) where examples correspond to models (sets of atoms) of the theory to be learned.

5.1 Mutagenesis

As a first experiment, we did simple instance based learning on the mutagenesis database [16]. Using a k-nearest-neighbours method (k=5,7,9 and 11 give the same result), we tried to predict the classes of all examples. In a first (propositional) experiment using only the numerical attributes lumo and logp in an euclidian distance, 77% of the examples was predicted correctly. Next, we performed the same experiment with only structural data (so we did not make use of the numerical attributes). As instance of our scheme we chose the manhattan, unnormalised, matching distance with renaming substitutions based on the distance between atoms defined in [13]. We treat the constants giving arbitrary names to the objects within an example, as variables. This allows us to recognise the similarity between examples using renaming substitutions. We obtained 83%. This is significantly better than what we obtained using the propositional data which correlates very well with mutagenicity. This shows that this distance (and mainly the renaming substitution component) performs well on purely structural data.

5.2 Diterpenes

The diterpene database is described in [8], where also some experimental results with FOIL, RIBL, TILDE and ICL are reported. These are all classification systems (which make use of information that assigns a class to each example in the training set during the building of the decision tree).

TIC (see [3]) is a clustering system based on TILDE. Clustering does not make use of class information during the building of the decision tree. TIC uses a distance measure for choosing the best tests. Unfortunately, until now only euclidian distances (on the propositional part of the data) could be used. Using a first order measure much better results can be reached. We extended TIC such that our new distances can be used. We used for the atom-level a variant of the atoms distance of [13] which assigns a value in the interval $[0, 1]$ to the distance between numerical components. For the second level, we used the distance based on matchings (d^m) as well as the similarity measures d^l and d^s from [9]. The diterpene database does not contain variables, so we do not need a third level for our distance.

The following table summarises the obtained results (the evaluation method for TIC is explained in [3]): The first column gives the system used, the second gives the results using only the attribute-value part of the data and the third gives the results using all data.

We see that, for the second level the distance d^m performs better than the similarity measures d^s and d^l.

This result obtained by TIC which does not use class information is comparable to that of good classification systems which do use class information during the induction of the tree. It also shows that the use of a first order distance measure is superior to attribute-value measures, and that it is possible to construct distance measures for first order models which perform well in practice.

System	Propositional	First order
FOIL	70.1%	78.3%
RIBL	79.0%	91.2%
TILDE	78.5%	90.4%
ICL	79.1%	86.0 %
TIC	78.2%	
TIC - matchings (d^m)		84.8%
TIC - linkings (d^l)		77.6%
TIC - surjections (d^s)		79.3%

6 Discussion

We developed a scheme for distances between clauses in three levels. At the first level one chooses a distance between atoms, e.g. [11], [13] or [15]. The second level upgrades this distance to a distance between sets of atoms. We developed a scheme for similarity between sets of points and an instance which is a real distance function, computable in polynomial time. We developed also a binary prototype function for sets of points. Prototype functions for atoms, based on the distances in [13] and [11] are described in [14].

At the third level, we developed a distance function $d_0^{\Theta r}(A, B)$ which takes into account the "similarity" of the atoms in the sets by computing the minimal distance between a variant of A and a variant of B.

We did clustering experiments using instances of this scheme, i.e. distance functions between models. We obtained promising results, much better than when data are represented in an attribute value setting, and comparable to other first-order learners.

Acknowledgements

Maurice Bruynooghe is supported by the Fund of Scientific Research, Flanders. This work is supported by the European community Esprit project no. 20237, Inductive Logic Programming 2.

References

1. G. Bisson. Conceptual clustering in a first order logic representation. In *Proceedings of the 10th European Conference on Artificial Intelligence*, pages 458–462. John Wiley & Sons, 1992.
2. H. Blockeel and L. De Raedt. Top-down induction of first order logical decision trees. *Artificial Intelligence*, 1998. To appear.
3. H. Blockeel, L. De Raedt, and J. Ramon. Top-down induction of clustering trees. In *Proceedings of the 15th International Conference on Machine Learning*, 1998.
4. L. De Raedt. Logical settings for concept learning. *Artificial Intelligence*, 95:187–201, 1997.
5. L. De Raedt and L. Dehaspe. Clausal discovery. *Machine Learning*, 26:99–146, 1997.
6. L. De Raedt and S. Džeroski. First order jk-clausal theories are PAC-learnable. *Artificial Intelligence*, 70:375–392, 1994.
7. L. De Raedt and W. Van Laer. Inductive constraint logic. In *Proceedings of the 5th Workshop on Algorithmic Learning Theory*, volume 997 of *Lecture Notes in Artificial Intelligence*. Springer-Verlag, 1995.
8. S. Džeroski, S. Schulze-Kremer, K. R. Heidtke, K. Siems, D. Wettschereck, and H. Blockeel. Diterpene structure elucidation from 13C NMR spectra with inductive logic programming. *Applied Artificial Intelligence: Special Issue on First-Order Knowledge Discovery in Databases*, 1998. To appear.
9. T. Eiter and Mannila H. Distance measures for point sets and their computation. *Acta Informatica*, 34, 1997.
10. W. Emde and D. Wettschereck. Relational instance based learning. In *Proceedings of the 1995 Workshop of the GI Special Interest Group on Machine Learning*, 1995.
11. A. Hutchinson. Metrics on terms and clauses. In *Proceedings of the 9th European Conference on Machine Learning*, Lecture Notes in Artificial Intelligence, pages 138–145. Springer-Verlag, 1997.
12. P. Langley. *Elements of Machine Learning*. Morgan Kaufmann, 1996.

13. Shan-Hwei Nienhuys-Cheng. Distance between herbrand interpretations: A measure for approximations to a target concept. In *Proceedings of the 7th International Workshop on Inductive Logic Programming*, Lecture Notes in Artificial Intelligence. Springer-Verlag, 1997.

14. J. Ramon and M. Bruynooghe. A framework for defining distances between first-order logic objects. Technical Report CW 263, Department of Computer Science, Katholieke Universiteit Leuven, 1998. http://www.cs.kuleuven.ac.be/-publicaties/rapporten/CW1998.html.

15. J. Ramon, M. Bruynooghe, and W. Van Laer. Distance measures between atoms. Technical Report CW 264, Department of Computer Science, Katholieke Universiteit Leuven, 1998. http://www.cs.kuleuven.ac.be/publicaties/rapporten/-CW1998.html.

16. A. Srinivasan, S.H. Muggleton, R.D. King, and M.J.E. Sternberg. Mutagenesis: ILP experiments in a non-determinate biological domain. In S. Wrobel, editor, *Proceedings of the 4th International Workshop on Inductive Logic Programming*, volume 237 of *GMD-Studien*, pages 217–232. Gesellschaft für Mathematik und Datenverarbeitung MBH, 1994.

Detecting Traffic Problems with ILP

Sašo Džeroski[1], Nico Jacobs[2], Martin Molina[3], Carlos Moure[3],
Stephen Muggleton[4], Wim Van Laer[2]

[1] J. Stefan Institute, Jamova 39, SI-1000 Ljubljana, Slovenia
[2] K.U.Leuven, Celestijnenlaan 200A, B-3001 Heverlee, Belgium
[3] Universidad Politecnica de Madrid, E-28660 Boadilla del Monte, Madrid, Spain
[4] Department of Computer Science, University of York, York, YO1 5DD, UK

Abstract. Expert systems for decision support have recently been successfully introduced in road transport management. These systems include knowledge on traffic problem detection and alleviation. The paper describes experiments in automated acquisition of knowledge on traffic problem detection. The task is to detect road sections where a problem has occured (critical sections) from sensor data. It is necessary to use inductive logic programming (ILP) for this purpose as relational background knowledge on the road network is essential. In this paper, we apply three state-of-the art ILP systems to learn how to detect traffic problems and compare their performance to the performance of a propositional learning system on the same problem.

1 Introduction

Expert systems for decision support have recently been successfully introduced in road transport management. Some of the proposals in this direction are TRYS [5], KITS [4] and ARTIST [9]. From a general perspective, the goal of a real time traffic expert system for decision support is to advise traffic management center operators by proposing control actions to eliminate or reduce problems according to the global state of traffic. To assess the global state of traffic, the system periodically receives readings from sensors on the road, which measure magnitudes such as speed (Km/h), flow (veh/h) and occupancy (percentage of time that the sensor is occupied by vehicles), as well as information about the current state of control devices, such as traffic signals at intersections, traffic signals at sideway on-ramps, CMS (Changeable Message Signs), etc. The system interprets sensor data, detects the presence of a problem, gives the possible cause and proposes recommendations about how to solve or reduce it.

The usual approach to building traffic expert systems is to use knowledge based architectures that support the strategies of reasoning followed by operators. This approach requires to develop knowledge bases using symbolic representations (such as rules, frames, or constraints) that include specific domain knowledge of transport management corresponding to the city for which the system is developed. Among other things, knowledge on detecting specific traffic problems is necessary.

On the other hand, traffic management centers have databases that include basic information about different traffic scenarios, such as congestions at certain locations caused by lack of capacity due to accidents or excess of demand (rush hours). This data, collected from sensors on the road, can be used to either generate or improve the knowledge base for problem (incident) detection of the expert system. The paper explores the possibility to use inductive learning techniques (in particular ILP-inductive logic programming) to generate knowledge on traffic problem detection from historical data that contains parameters recorded by sensors.

The learning experiments described in this paper take place within the context of the traffic management expert system TRYS [5], developed for the cities of Madrid and Barcelona. The system uses knowledge distributed in a collection of knowledge bases that use different representations and address specific tasks (such as data abstraction, incident detection, problem diagnosis, prediction of behaviour, and recommendation of control actions). The knowledge for incident (traffic problem) detection has been formulated by domain experts in a first-order frame-based representation, i.e., in the concept description language CONCEL. Therefore, ILP is a suitable tool for learning to detect traffic problems in this context.

Overall, two kinds of input are available to the learning process. The first type is background knowledge on the road network, which is present in and used by the TRYS system. An object oriented representation is used to capture the different types of road sections, the relations among them, and the placement of sensors on individual road sections. The second type is sensor readings on three basic quantities describing traffic behaviour: speed, flow and occupancy. Both types of input will be described in more detail in Section 2. The goal of the learning process is to identify critical sections (where problems have occurred) by using sensor readings and road geometry. Technically speaking, a critical section is a section of the road which constrains the road capacity the most, e.g., because an accident has occured just after this section in the immediate past. In the paper, the term accident critical section refers to such a section and not to a section where accidents occur frequently.

Let us note at this point that in practice real sensor data are available. However, we have used simulated data in our experiments for three reasons. The first is that real sensor data were not immediately available because of management reasons. The second is missing sensor data from broken sensors (which amounts to approximately 20% of the sensors). Finally, using a simulator makes it possible to easily generate a wide range of different traffic problems (including accidents that should not be artificially produced in the real world).

We used AIMSUN (Advanced Interactive Microscopic Simulator for Urban and Non-Urban Networks) [1], a software tool able to reproduce the real traffic conditions of any urban network on a computer. AIMSUN follows a microscopic simulation approach. It means that the behaviour of each individual vehicle in the network is continuously modelled throughout the simulation time period it remains inside the system (i.e., the traffic network), according to several vehicle behaviour models. A model of the urban-ring of the city of Barcelona was developed using this simulator. This model includes exactly the same variables that the real information system records using sensors and was calibrated using information from the real system. Using this model, a collection of examples (including accidents and congestions due to rush hours) were produced for the learning experiments presented in the paper.

The remainder of the paper is organized as follows. Section 2 describes in some detail the background knowledge on the road network and the sensor data used in TRYS. Section 3 describes the particular dataset used in our experiments. Section 4 presents the results of applying three ILP systems to this dataset, and Section 5 concludes with a discussion.

2 Road network and sensor data

In TRYS [5], the road network is represented in an object oriented fashion. The basic object in the road network representation is the section. A section refers to a cross-section of the road and typically has an array of sensors associated to it. There exist several types of sections, such as off-ramp, on-ramp or highway. Relations between sections, such as previous and next, are included in the TRYS knowledge base. The complexity of road structures makes it possible for a section to have more than two previous or next sections.

A link describes a logical group of sections. For instance, the section just before and just after an off-ramp, together with the off-ramp itself, form an off-ramp-link. There are about ten different types of links. TRYS also uses other concepts like nodes, problem areas and measurement points, but these were not used in our experiments.

The information about sections and links is static. Each section is of a certain type and is associated to a number of sensors (as many sensors as there are lanes at that cross-section of the road) and each link is of a certain type and links a predefined set of sections. These relationships can therefore be considered background knowledge for the learning process.

Sensors provide us with a continuous stream of information, sending five readings each minute that refer to the last minute and each of the four minutes preceding it. Typically, flow (number of cars that passed the sensor in the last minute) and occupancy (the proportion of time the sensor is occupied, in thousandths) are measured. Some sensors (which are actually double sensors) also measure the average speed of the cars that passed the sensor during the last minute. The measurements of sensors related to a single section are aggregated: flow is summed across lanes, while occupancy and velocity are averaged across lanes. Saturation is a derived quantity defined as the ratio between the flow and the capacity of a section: the latter depends on the number of lanes and is part of the background knowledge.

The TRYS system stores its information in two formats: in CONCEL format, which is a frame-based format, and in Prolog format. The Prolog format is object-oriented and consists mainly of facts about the predicates instance and value. For use in ILP, we transformed these facts in the following fashion:

facts of the form `instance(Instance,Class)` are translated to facts of the form `Class(Instance)` and facts of the form `value(Instance,Attribute,Value)` are translated to `Attribute(Instance, Value)`. For example, the fact `valor('RLTL_Ronda_Litoral_en_Rambla_Prim',tipo,carretera)` is transformed to `tipo('RLTL_Ronda_Litoral_en_Rambla_Prim',carretera)`.

3 The dataset and the methodology

After conducting preliminary experiments with CLAUDIEN [7] on a handful of simulated accidents and congestions, we proceded to create a larger dataset [10]. A dataset containing 66 examples of congestion and 62 examples of accidents on different locations (off-ramp, on-ramp and highway sections) was generated using the AIMSUN simulator. The learning task was formulated as a classification task, with three possible classes `accident`, `congestion` and `noncs` (noncritical section). Each section at a particular moment of time was treated as an example, classified into one of the above classes. In this way we obtained a dataset consisting of 5952 examples altogether.

The background knowledge consisted of facts on sensor values as well as facts on road geometry. More precisely, the background knowledge predicates `velocidadd(Time,Section,Value)`, `ocupaciond(Time,Section,Value)`, and `saturaciond(Time,Section,Value)` were available. These predicates discretize the continuous sensor measurement values, so `Value` takes one of three discrete values: `alta` (high), `media` (medium), and `baja` (low).

As far as road geometry was concerned, the predicates `tipo(Section,Type)` and `secciones_posteriores(Section1,Section2)` were available. The first gives the type of a section, which can be `carretera` (highway), `calle` (street), `rampa_abandono` (off-ramp), `rampa_incorporacion` (on-ramp), `via_secundaria_abandono` and `via_secundaria_incorporacion`. The second predicate captures the relational structure of the road network: it states that `Section2` follows `Section1`. Note that this is a many to many relation.

The class distribution is very skewed, as the frequency of the majority class is 97.85%. Despite showing the potential of ILP to learn to detect traffic problems, preliminary experiments with TILDE [2] on this dataset [10] did not yield satisfactory performance. The skewed distribution was identified as one of the main reasons for this.

To alleviate this problem, we randomly sampled 128 of the 5824 noncritical sections. In all experiments presented in the remainder of the paper, we used the dataset comprising 66 examples of congestion, 62 examples of accidents, and 128 examples of noncritical sections.

From the dataset of 256 examples, we created 10 folds. Each of the ILP systems considered was applied on the entire dataset and the rules produced were shown to the domain experts. Also, the time taken to induce a hypothesis from the 256 examples dataset was recorded. Each of the systems was then applied to the 10 folds, where the induced hypotheses were tested on unseen cases and the overall accuracy recorded.

```
class(accident) :- section(A), timemoment(B), tipo(A,carretera),
  secciones_posteriores(C,A), velocidadd(B,C,baja). % [29,0,0]
class(accident) :- section(A), timemoment(B),
  ocupaciond(B,A,alta), saturaciond(B,A,baja),
  secciones_posteriores(A,C), velocidadd(B,C,alta). % [36,0,0]
class(accident) :- section(A), timemoment(B), velocidadd(B,A,baja),
  secciones_posteriores(C,A), ocupaciond(B,C,alta). % [27,0,0]
class(accident) :- section(A), timemoment(B), ocupaciond(B,A,alta),
  saturaciond(B,A,baja), secciones_posteriores(A,C), tipo(C,carretera),
  secciones_posteriores(C,D), ocupaciond(B,D,baja). % [22,0,0]

class(congestion) :- section(A), timemoment(B),
  tipo(A,rampa_incorporacion),
  secciones_posteriores(A,C), saturaciond(B,C,alta),
  secciones_posteriores(D,C), velocidadd(B,D,baja). % [0,31,0]
class(congestion) :- section(A), timemoment(B), tipo(A,rampa_abandono),
  secciones_posteriores(C,A), velocidadd(B,C,baja). % [0,30,0]

class(noncs) :- section(A), timemoment(B), velocidadd(B,A,alta),
  secciones_posteriores(C,A), velocidadd(B,C,alta). % [0,0,46]
class(noncs) :- section(A), timemoment(B), ocupaciond(B,A,baja),
  secciones_posteriores(C,A), velocidadd(B,C,alta),
  secciones_posteriores(D,C),velocidadd(B,D,alta). % [0,0,17]
class(noncs) :- section(A), timemoment(B),  tipo(A,carretera),
  secciones_posteriores(A,C),ocupaciond(B,C,alta),
  secciones_posteriores(C,D),ocupaciond(B,D,alta). % [0,0,26]
...
```

Fig. 1. An incomplete listing of the rules generated by ICL.

4 Experiments and results

Three ILP systems were applied to the problem formulated above. ICL [8] and TILDE [2] operate within the 'learning from interpretations' [6] setting, while PROGOL [11] operates in the 'learning from entailment' setting. This is the reason for the slightly different form of rules induced by the three systems, i.e., the appearance of the literals section(A) and timemoment(B) in the bodies of ICL and TILDE rules, which do not appear in the bodies of PROGOL rules.

While ICL and PROGOL learn clauses/rules, TILDE learns logical decision trees. The decision trees can be rewritten as decision lists, where the first rule in the list that applies to the example classified is taken. Decision lists can be viewed as lists of clauses, each followed by a Prolog cut (!).

The following settings were used: ICL used a minimal coverage of three examples, instead of the default one, and the default significance threshold of 90%. TILDE also used the limit of at least three examples in each leaf, as well as a lookahead of two.

```
accident(A,B) :- velocidadd(B,A,baja), saturaciond(B,A,baja). % [27,0,0]
accident(A,B) :- secciones_posteriores(C,A), tipo(A,carretera),
  velocidadd(B,C,baja). % [29,0,0]
accident(A,B) :- ocupaciond(B,A,alta), saturaciond(B,A,baja),
  secciones_posteriores(A,C), velocidadd(B,C,alta). % [36,0,0]

congestion(A,B) :- secciones_posteriores(C,A), tipo(A,rampa_abandono),
velocidadd(B,C,baja). % [0,30,0]
congestion(A,B) :- secciones_posteriores(A,C), saturaciond(B,C,alta),
  secciones_posteriores(D,C), velocidadd(B,D,baja). % [0,31,0]

noncs(A,B) :- velocidadd(B,A,alta), saturaciond(B,A,media). % [0,0,32]
noncs(A,B) :- saturaciond(B,A,alta), tipo(A,carretera). % [0,0,30]
noncs(A,B) :- secciones_posteriores(C,A), ocupaciond(B,C,baja). %[0,0,25]
noncs(A,B) :- ocupaciond(B,A,baja), saturaciond(B,A,baja),
  tipo(A,rampa_incorporacion). % [0,0,8]
noncs(A,B) :- ocupaciond(B,A,baja), secciones_posteriores(A,C),
  saturaciond(B,C,media). % [0,0,5]
noncs(A,B) :- ocupaciond(B,A,baja), secciones_posteriores(C,A),
  saturaciond(B,C,alta). % [0,0,11]
noncs(A,B) :- ocupaciond(B,A,baja), saturaciond(B,A,baja),
  secciones_posteriores(C,A), ocupaciond(B,C,media). % [0,0,11]
noncs(A,B) :- secciones_posteriores(C,A), saturaciond(B,C,alta),
  secciones_posteriores(C,D), velocidadd(B,D,media). % [0,0,12]
```

Fig. 2. The set of rules generated by PROGOL.

PROGOL used its default settings. Since it works with positive and negative examples only, a set of rules was induced for each of the three predicates accident(Section,Time), congestion(Section,Time), and noncs(Section, Time). Positive examples of one predicates were treated as negative examples of the other two predicates, e.g., positive examples for congestion(Section, Time) and noncs(Section,Time) were treated as negative examples for accident(Section,Time). To the rules induced, a classification procedure similar to the one of CN2 [3] and ICL was applied: all rules whose conditions apply to a testing example are taken and the number of training examples of each class covered by the rules are summed up. The class with the largest sum is assigned to the testing example.

In addition to the three ILP systems, the decision tree learning system C4.5 [12] was used for comparison. C4.5 only took into account sensor values for the focus section and could not access sensor values of neighboring sections. Since a section can have several previous and/or next sections, the problem cannot be transformed to propositional form easily without loss of information. The default parameters were used in C4.5.

The rules induced by each of ICL, PROGOL and TILDE are given in Figures 1, 2, and 3, respectively. The numbers in square brackets are the numbers of examples covered by the respective clauses / leaves. The second ICL rule and the first PROGOL rules for congestions thus cover 30 examples of the correct class and no examples of the other classes ([0,30,0]). For TILDE, the first leaf covers 36 examples, all of which represent accidents ([36 / 36]), and the last one covers 14 examples, 12 of which are noncritical sections ([12 / 14]).

In all three cases, two rules are used to characterize congestions. PROGOL uses three rules to characterize accidents and leaves eight accidents uncovered, while ICL and TILDE use four rules, resp. leaves, each.

Table 1 summarizes the accuracies of the four systems on unseen cases, as estimated by 10 fold crossvalidation. The numbers in brackets are the standard errors. For example, ICL achieves an average accuracy of 93.36% over the 10 folds with a standard error of 4.42%.

The running time (on a SUN SPARC Ultra 2) and the number of rules (res. leaves) for each system on the 256 examples dataset are also listed in the table. In terms of induction speed, ICL and TILDE are much faster than PROGOL in this particular domain. In terms of classification accuracy, all three algorithms perform at a similar level.

C4.5 is much faster than the three ILP systems. However, its accuracy is lower than the accuracies achieved by the ILP systems. The relational information on the road structure and the sensor values at neighboring sections allow ILP systems to achieve better classification of the focus section.

An important aspect of the suitability of the induced rules for use in an expert system is their comprehensibility to domain experts, in this case traffic engineers. The rules listed in Figures 1, 2, and 3 were inspected by the domain experts. Many of them were judged to be correct, but a substantial number were qualified as overly general, i.e., as potentially covering examples from other classes.

The TILDE decision tree and the corresponding rules fare the lowest in terms of comprehensibility: the dependence of rules in the decision list on rules above them makes them difficult to understand. On the positive side, only the first two accident rules/leaves produced by TILDE were judged to be correct, whereas all other accident rules were judged to be overly general. The two remaining accident leaves are expected to also cover noncritical sections.

Table 1. Performance of three ILP systems and one propositional system at detecting traffic problems.

System	Time	Accuracy	Rules
ICL	82s	93.36 (4.42) %	18
PROGOL	27min	93.75 (2.64) %	13
TILDE	28s	94.14 (3.63) %	12
C4.5	20ms	87.90 (5.34) %	14

Let us take a look at the first two accident rules/leaves by TILDE. The first states that there is an accident at section A if the saturation at A is low and the occupation at the section preceding A is high. The second states that there is an accident at section A if the saturation is low and the occupation is high at A, whereas the velocity at the next section is high.

```
section(A), timemoment(B)
secciones_posteriores(A,C), saturaciond(B,A,baja)?
+--yes: secciones_posteriores(D,A), ocupaciond(B,D,alta)?
|       +--yes: accident [36 / 36]
|       +--no:  ocupaciond(B,A,alta)?
|               +--yes: velocidadd(B,C,alta)?
|               |       +--yes: accident [15 / 15]
|               |       +--no:  secciones_posteriores(C,E),
|               |               ocupaciond(B,E,baja)?
|               |               +--yes: accident [3 / 3]
|               |               +--no:  noncs [4 / 4]
|               +--no:  noncs [13 / 13]
+--no:  tipo(A,carretera)?
        +--yes: secciones_posteriores(F,A), velocidadd(B,F,baja)?
        |       +--yes: accident [5 / 5]
        |       +--no:  noncs [73 / 75]
        +--no:  secciones_posteriores(G,A), velocidadd(B,G,alta)?
                +--yes: noncs [21 / 23]
                +--no:  secciones_posteriores(H,A), velocidadd(B,H,baja)?
                        +--yes: congestion [30 / 30]
                        +--no:  secciones_posteriores(A,I),
                                ocupaciond(B,A,alta)?
                                +--yes: secciones_posteriores(J,I),
                                        velocidadd(B,J,baja)?
                                |       +--yes: congestion [31 / 31]
                                |       +--no:  noncs [5 / 7]
                                +--no:  noncs [12 / 14]
```

Fig. 3. The logical decision tree generated by TILDE.

The first, second and fourth accident rules by ICL are expected to cover congestions as well, whereas the third accident rules and the second congestion rule are expected to also cover noncritical sections. The remaining ICL rules are judged to be correct. This includes all rules on noncritical sections and the first rule on congestions.

Let us take a look at the correct rule about congestions. It concerns a section A of type on-ramp (rampa_incorporacion). There is a congestion at such a section if the saturation at a following section C is high and the velocity at a section preceding C is low.

Finally, all PROGOL rules on noncritical sections are judged correct, as well as one rule on congestions which is identical to the ICL correct rule on congestions. As stated above, all PROGOL accident rules are considered overly general.

5 Discussion

We have presented an application of inductive logic programming in a novel domain, namely the domain of detecting traffic problems. The task addressed was to learn rules that identify road sections where accidents or congestions have occurred in the immediate past. As shown by a comparison to a propositional learning system, background knowledge on road geometry was essential, requiring the use of ILP for this task. While simulated data were used for our experiments, it should be noted that the simulator is very realistic and has been calibrated using real-world data.

We applied three different ILP systems to this problem and compared their performance in terms of efficiency of induction, accuracy on unseen cases and comprehensibility of induced rules. All three systems perform at roughly the same level as far as accuracy is concerned. TILDE performs best in terms of efficiency, but its rules are overall more difficult to understand. All three ILP systems are much slower than C4.5, but perform better in terms of classification accuracy.

The rules induced by PROGOL and ICL are very similar and receive similar comprehensibility marks from the domain experts. They also perform at the same level as far as accuracy is concerned. ICL is more efficient, however, and marginally the best choice of the three ILP systems considered.

Many of the rules were judged as overly general by the domain experts. A possible reason for this are errors in identifying the critical section in an area where an accident has occurred. The critical section is the one that constrains capacity the most, but in some cases a previous or a following section may have been stated as critical.

Regarding related work, several ILP systems have been compared to C4.5 on the problem of identifying accidents caused by young male drivers [13]. However, the data considered there is propositional. The ILP systems perform at approximately the same level as C4.5, while being much slower.

Much work remains to be done. Immediate further work concerns the use of nondiscretized sensor values. Since all three ILP systems considered can handle real values this should not be a problem. Exepriments are already underway.

A practical issue of utmost importance is the issue of using real sensor data instead of simulated data. Missing sensor values are a problem that has to be dealt with here and redundant rules will have to be built for this purpose.

Other issues to be addressed include mapping the induced problem detection rules into a frame-based representation with which experts are familiar and using the time series of sensor values instead of the current values only. The domain of traffic control also holds other challenges for machine learning techniques. Detecting traffic problems is only one step of the traffic management process: suggesting actions to alleviate the problems is the natural next step. Since examples of operator actions in response to detected problems exist, there is hope that the problem of suggesting appropriate actions for alleviating traffic problems can also be addressed using machine learning and inductive logic programming.

Acknowledgements This work was supported in part by the ESPRIT IV Project 20237 ILP2. Nico Jacobs is supported by the Flemish Institute for the Promotion of Scientific and Technological Research in Industry (IWT). Wim Van Laer is supported by the Fund for Scientific Research, Flanders.

References

1. Barcelo, J., Ferrer J.L., and Montero, L. (1989). *AIMSUN: Advanced Interactive Microscopic Simulator for Urban Networks. Vol I: System Description, and Vol II: User's Manual.* Departamento de Estadistica e Investigacion Operativa, Facultad de Informatica, Universidad Politecnica de Cataluna, Barcelona, Spain.
2. Blockeel, H., and De Raedt, L. (1997). Lookahead and discretization in ILP. In *Proc. 7th Intl. Workshop on Inductive Logic Programming*, pages 77–84, Springer, Berlin.
3. Clark, P. and Boswell, R. (1991). Rule induction with CN2: Some recent improvements. In *Proc. Fifth European Working Session on Learning*, pages 151–163. Springer, Berlin.
4. Cuena, J., Ambrosino, G., and Boero M. (1992). A general knowledge-based architecture for traffic control: The KITS approach. In *Proc. Intl. Conf. on Artificial Intelligence Applications in Transportation Engineering*. San Buenaventura, CA.
5. Cuena, J., Hernandez, J., and Molina, M. (1995). Knowledge-based models for adaptive traffic management systems. *Transportation Research: Part C*, 3(5): 311-337.
6. De Raedt, L. (1997). Logical settings for learning. *Artificial Intelligence*.
7. De Raedt, L., and Dehaspe, L. (1997). Clausal discovery. *Machine Learning*, 26: 99–146.
8. De Raedt, L., and Van Laer, V. (1995). Inductive constraint logic. *Proc. Sixth International Workshop on Algorithmic Learning Theory*, pp. 80-94. Berlin: Springer.
9. Deeter, D.L., and Ritchie, S.G. (1993). A prototype real-time expert system for surface street traffic management and control. In *Proc. 3rd Intl. Conf. on Applications of Advanced Technologies in Transportation Engineering*, Seattle, WA.
10. Džeroski, S., Jacobs, N., Molina, M., Moure, C. (1998). ILP experiments in detecting traffic problems. In *Proc. Eleventh European Conference on Machine Learning*. Springer, Berlin. To appear.
11. Muggleton, S. (1992). Inverse entailment and PROGOL. *New Generation Computing* 13: 245-286.
12. Quinlan, J.R. (1993) *C4.5: Programs for Machine Learning*. Morgan Kaufmann, San Mateo, CA.
13. Roberts, S., Van Laer, W., Jacobs, N., Muggleton, S., Broughton, J. (1998) A comparison of ILP and popositional systems on propositional traffic data. In *Proc. Eighth International Conference on Inductive Logic Programming*. Springer, Berlin. This volume.

A Comparison of ILP and Propositional Systems on Propositional Traffic Data

Sam Roberts[1]*, Wim vanLaer[2], Nico Jacobs[2], Stephen Muggleton[3], and Jeremy Broughton[4]

[1] Oxford University Computing Laboratory
Samuel.Roberts@comlab.ox.ac.uk
[2] Department of Computer Science, Katholieke Universiteit Leuven
{Wim.VanLaer,Nico.Jacobs}@cs.kuleuven.ac.be
[3] Department of Computer Science, University of York
stephen@cs.york.ac.uk
[4] Transport Research Laboratory, Crowthorne, Berkshire
JeremyB@E.TRL.CO.UK

Abstract. This paper presents an experimental comparison of two Inductive Logic Programming algorithms, PROGOL and TILDE, with C4.5, a propositional learning algorithm, on a propositional dataset of road traffic accidents. Rebalancing methods are described for handling the skewed distribution of positive and negative examples in this dataset, and the relative cost of errors of commission and omission in this domain. It is noted that before the use of these methods all algorithms perform worse than majority class. On rebalancing, all did significantly better. The conclusion drawn from the experimental results is that on such a propositional dataset ILP algorithms perform competitively in terms of predictive accuracy with propositional systems, but are significantly outperformed in terms of time taken for learning.

1 Introduction

ILP (Inductive Logic Programming) has been defined [10] as the intersection of Machine Learning and Logic Programming, and as such it represents an advance over propositional learning systems. ILP systems are able to handle complex relational data which are not representable propositionally, such as chemical structures (e.g. see [16]). However, there are many domains of interest which are representable propositionally, and ILP systems must also be able to handle these domains as effectively as a propositional learner if they are to become as widely used.

This paper presents an experimental comparison of two Inductive Logic Programming systems, PROGOL and TILDE, with C4.5, a standard propositional algorithm, on just such a domain, that of traffic accidents. The paper grew from previous work [17] and from applications of various systems to this data at an ILP Transport workshop held at the University of York on December 3rd, 1997.

---

* Corresponding author. Oxford University Computing Laboratory, Wolfson Building, Parks Road, Oxford OX1 3QD. Tel: +44 1865 273869. Fax +44 1865 273839.

2 Systems

2.1 PROGOL

PROGOL is a state of the art ILP system described in [11]. The user specifies a restricted language of first order expressions to be used as the hypothesis space H. Restrictions are stated using "mode declarations", which specify which predicates are to be used in the heads and bodies of learnt rules, and the types and formats of their arguments.

PROGOL uses a sequential covering algorithm to learn a set of rules from H which cover the examples. For each positive example e^+ not yet covered, PROGOL constructs the most specific hypothesis $\perp$ from H such that $B \wedge \perp \vdash e^+$, where B is background knowledge supplied. PROGOL then performs a general to specific search of the hypothesis space bounded by $\perp$. During this search, PROGOL looks for the hypothesis having minimum description length.

PROGOL has been used successfully in many domains, including finite element mesh design [8], mutagenesis [16], natural language [6] and road traffic accidents [17]. It is available by anonymous ftp from ftp.cs.york.ac.uk in the directory pub/ML_GROUP/progol4.4 and includes a manual written by the first author. Further information about PROGOL is available from the following URL:

$$\texttt{http://www.cs.york.ac.uk/mlg/}$$

2.2 TILDE

A main feature of TILDE [2, 3] is the representation of examples, which correspond to a small relational database (or Prolog knowledge base). In other words, an example consists of multiple relations and each example can have multiple tuples for these relations. This setting is known in the literature as *learning from interpretations* and was first introduced in [15]. This representation is a natural upgrade of the attribute-value representation where each example consists of a single tuple in a relational database. *Learning from interpretations* contrasts with the classical inductive logic programming setting *learning from entailment* which is employed by systems such as PROGOL and FOIL. Details about the relation between these different settings can be found in [14].

The setting *learning from interpretations* allows us to upgrade a propositional learner towards a relational learner. TILDE is a first-order upgrade of an existing attribute-value learning system, Quinlan's popular predictive C4.5 algorithm for decision tree induction [13]. Other examples of first-order upgrades are ICL, which upgrades the predictive production rule approach as incorporated in e.g. CN2 [5, 4] AQ [9], and WARMR [7], which extends APRIORI [1] to mine association rules in multiple relations.

TILDE learns a theory which discriminates as well as possible between (training) examples of different classes. The learnt theory can be used to classify new, unseen examples into one of the available classes.

TILDE (Top down Induction of Logical DEcision trees) builds a decision tree similar to C4.5, but with first order logic conjunctions of literals as tests in the nodes. Heuristics are used to choose the best test at each node. The resulting classification tree can also be outputted as a Prolog program or a logical program. TILDE can discretize numerical values and has look ahead ability (see [2]). TILDE is an efficient ILP-system that can handle large datasets (in experiments datasets up to 100 Mb were used).

More information on TILDE and ICL can be found at the following URL:

http://www.cs.kuleuven.ac.be/~ml/MLRG-E.shtml

2.3 C4.5

C4.5 [13] is an extension of Quinlan's ID3 system [12]. Decision trees are induced by growing them from the root downward, using a greedy algorithm to select the next best attribute for each new decision branch added to the tree. The complete hypothesis space is searched, with an inductive bias to prefer smaller trees. Extensions to ID3 include methods for avoiding overfitting data and for handling training examples with missing attribute values.

3 Data and Datasets

3.1 The Road Accident Reporting System in Great Britain

In Great Britain, the national database of police accident reports contains details of all road accidents involving personal injury of which the police become aware within 30 days. Each report contains:

- 1 Attendant Circumstances Record
- 1 Casualty Record for each injured person
- 1 Vehicle Record for each vehicle involved

The data are largely objective, such as road number or age of driver, and do not include details of why the accidents occurred. The potential contribution of such information to improved road safety has been recognised for several years, and recent research at the Transport Research Laboratory has developed a new system for recording these 'Contributory Factors'. It is hoped that this system will be adopted as a regular part of the UK national reporting system.

The new system was trialed with 8 police forces for 3 months in 1996, and the data analysed in this paper is the result of matching about half of the Contributory Factor reports with the accident records routinely collected by the police.

The new system is unique in dividing the factors into two groups: 'What went wrong' (known as Precipitating Factors) and 'Why?' (known as Contributory Factors). This approach leads reporting officers to structure their investigations: they work back from the actual accident to identify the principal failure or manoeuvre which led directly to the accident, select the appropriate Precipitating Factor from the list, then try to establish the reasons for this failure or manoeuvre. Up to four Contributory Factors can be entered, in order of diminishing importance, and each is marked as Definite, Probable or Possible. The trial showed that the police were able to operate the system with little training, and the data collected were of good quality.

3.2 Dataset

The dataset used for this study consists of 1413 accident reports, during the period from April until August 1996. It was studied previously in [17] to find rules for predicting accidents caused by young male drivers (a class of accidents of interest to traffic experts).

Accidents are given preclassified as positive or negative. Positive examples are those accidents which were caused by a young male driver.

Each of the above types of record (attendant circumstances, casualties, vehicles, and contributory factors) is represented by the following four predicates.

- acc_record/25
- cas_record/24
- veh_record/16
- caus_record/19

Seventeen fields were selected from these records for relevance to classifying accidents as caused by young male drivers, by experience from the previous study. The values of these fields for each accident form the background knowledge concerning the accidents.

4 Experimental Description

4.1 Learning task

The dataset of 1413 examples was split 10 times randomly and independently into training and test sets. The training sets contained 70% of the examples and the corresponding test set contained the remaining 30%. A second set of training sets was also constructed from the first by rebalancing (see section 4.2).

Using each algorithm in turn, and supplying identical background knowledge in each case, rules for predicting whether an accident was caused by a young male driver were learnt from each training set, and from each rebalanced training set. The time taken to learn was recorded, and the accuracy of the learnt rules was assessed on the corresponding test set.

4.2 Rebalancing

The data under discussion in this paper have two unusual properties. The first is that they are skewed towards negative examples; out of 1413 examples, only 255 (18%) are positive and 1158 (82%) negative. The second is that traffic experts are less concerned about errors of commission than errors of omission; it is more important to be able to predict when an accident *is* caused by a young male driver than when it is not. These properties, when combined, reduce the value of standard testing methods; accuracies and χ^2 figures obtained from contingency tables give too much weight to negative predictions. What is needed is a method of reweighting the influence of the positive examples on these results.

This effect can be reduced by rebalancing the training and test data. A training set can be rebalanced by the following method. All positive examples in the set are kept, along with an equal number of the negative examples in the set, randomly selected. Thus a rebalanced training set consists of 50% positive and 50% negative examples.

A test set can be rebalanced in a similar way, or the effect can be simulated easily by the following method. Say a set of rules has been tested on an unrebalanced test set T, giving the contingency table on the left of Table 1. We can construct a new contingency table from this by multiplying the left hand column by $\frac{1}{2P}$ and the right hand column by $\frac{1}{2(1-P)}$, where

$$P = \frac{A+C}{A+B+C+D}.$$

This ratio ensures that the totals for both contingency tables remain equal, and the new table gives the values which we would have obtained had we rebalanced T. Note that "accuracy" values obtained from the resulting table cannot correctly be regarded as such; rather they are an expression of benefit (1-cost, expressed as a percentage of maximum benefit) according to a non-symmetric cost matrix in which a higher cost is placed on errors of omission than commission. This is the same as the "stratified sampling" used by pollsters to rebalance the proportions of polled subjects to that expected in various categories of the voting population.

Table 1. Reweighting a contingency table to simulate a rebalanced test set. Here $P = \frac{A+C}{A+B+C+D}$.

	Actual			Actual	
Predicted	Positive	Negative	Predicted	Positive	Negative
Positive	A	B	Positive	$\frac{A}{2P}$	$\frac{B}{2(1-P)}$
Negative	C	D	Negative	$\frac{C}{2P}$	$\frac{D}{2(1-P)}$

5 Results

The results shown in Tables 2 and 3 show evaluations of rules learnt from original and rebalanced training sets. Note again that only figures for original training sets on original test sets can be regarded as accuracy values. The majority class (empty algorithm) is also shown.

Table 4 shows the mean times taken to learn from original and rebalanced training sets. Standard deviations are given in brackets where available. All times were measured on an i586 running Linux2.0.30.

Table 2. Evaluation of rules learnt from original training sets on original and rebalanced test sets.

Algorithm	Original	Rebalanced
PROGOL	80.78% ± 0.61%	55.25% ± 0.76%
TILDE	80.93% ± 0.60%	55.25% ± 0.76%
C4.5	81.64% ± 0.60%	54.49% ± 0.77%
Majority Class	81.95%	50%

Table 3. Evaluation of rules learnt from rebalanced training sets on original and rebalanced test sets.

Algorithm	Original	Rebalanced
PROGOL	66.79% ± 0.72%	58.42% ± 0.76%
TILDE	66.08% ± 0.73%	61.72% ± 0.75%
C4.5	68.47% ± 0.71%	62.57% ± 0.74%
Majority Class	81.95%	50%

Table 4. Mean times taken for learning from each training set. Figures in brackets are standard deviations.

Algorithm	Learning time (secs)	
	Original	Rebalanced
PROGOL	2249.7 (93.39)	579.4 (42.32)
TILDE	585.0 (98.85)	95.0 (13.54)
C4.5	3.09	0.8

6   Discussion

The clearest implication of the results is the difference in times taken for learning between the systems. PROGOL is around six times slower than TILDE, which is over 100 times slower than C4.5.

We now turn to the predictive accuracy results in Tables 2 and 3. Let us first consider rules learnt from original training sets (Table 2). When evaluated normally, C4.5 gives a greater accuracy than PROGOL and TILDE, though none of the differences between systems are significant. However, when evaluated on a rebalanced test set to give a more realistic appraisal of rules from the point of view of a traffic expert, the reverse is the case.

Note also that when tested on an unrebalanced test set no system exceeds the majority class prediction, while on rebalanced data they all do. This fact may be explained by noting that rebalancing is equivalent to assuming that the class value of each example in the training set has exactly one bit of information, an assumption made in the evaluation function of many machine learning systems, including PROGOL.

In Table 3 again the differences in prediction between systems is at best marginal. However, a comparison between Tables 2 and 3 shows that all the systems have significantly improved performance when tested on the same distribution they were trained on.

These results suggest that ILP systems, as well as being able to cope with a wider range of more structurally complex domains, can also compete on an even footing with propositional learning algorithms on their home ground.

7 Conclusions

This paper has presented an experimental comparison of three learning algorithms, two ILP and one propositional, on a propositional dataset. It has shown that, whilst being significantly slower, ILP systems can indeed perform as well as propositional learning systems in such a domain. This is especially true when methods of evaluation are used which reflect the understanding and values of domain experts more appropriately than simple contingency table analysis.

7.1 Further Work

The work contained in this paper has concentrated on a single ILP representation of the data. One of the strengths of ILP is the ability to use many alternative representations of data, which can raise or lower learning efficiency. For example, it is possible that grouping attributes (currently represented by two-place predicates) into bundles represented by, say, three, four, or five-place predicates might improve learning, particularly if the attributes were naturally related (e.g. in the traffic case, weather-related or road surface-related attributes). The potential gain from attribute grouping deserves further investigation.

We also hope to investigate learnability (e.g. PAC/Bayes) theory approaches to understand the non-differences in accuracy between systems, and to investigate theoretical approaches to analysing the increase in prediction rate due to rebalancing.

A further task is to investigate the use of expert-provided cost functions in place of the rebalancing scheme used.

8 Acknowledgements

Sam Roberts would like to thank Smith System Engineering for their support during this work, Stefan Wrobel for his work on MIDOS which unfortunately could not be included, and Stephen Muggleton for his help and encouragement. This work was supported by the Esprit Long Term Research Action ILP II (project 20237), EPSRC grant GR/K57985 on Experiments with Distribution-based Machine Learning, an EPSRC Case award held by Sam Roberts and an EPSRC Advanced Research Fellowship held by Stephen Muggleton. Nico Jacobs is supported by the Flemish Institute for the Promotion of Scientific and Technological Research in Industry (IWT). Wim Van Laer is supported by the Fund for Scientific Research, Flanders. Nico Jacobs and Wim Van Laer would like to thank Hendrik Blockeel, Luc Dehaspe and Luc De Raedt for their valuable comments and feedback.

References

[1] R. Agrawal, H. Mannila, R. Srikant, H. Toivonen, and A.I. Verkamo. Fast discovery of association rules. In *Advances in Knowledge Discovery and Data Mining*, pages 307–328. MIT Press, 1996.

[2] H. Blockeel and L. De Raedt. Lookahead and discretization in ILP. In *Proceedings of the 7th International Workshop on Inductive Logic Programming*, volume 1297 of *Lecture Notes in Artificial Intelligence*, pages 77–85. Springer-Verlag, 1997.

[3] H. Blockeel and L. De Raedt. Top-down induction of first order logical decision trees. Submitted, 1998.

[4] P. Clark and R. Boswell. Rule induction with CN2: Some recent improvements. In Yves Kodratoff, editor, *Proceedings of the 5th European Working Session on Learning*, volume 482 of *Lecture Notes in Artificial Intelligence*, pages 151–163. Springer-Verlag, 1991.

[5] P. Clark and T. Niblett. The CN2 algorithm. *Machine Learning*, 3(4):261–284, 1989.

[6] J. Cussens, D. Page, S. Muggleton, and A. Srinivasan. Using Inductive Logic Programming for Natural Logic Processing. In W. Daelemans, T. Weijters, and A. van der Bosch, editors, *ECML'97 – Workshop Notes on Empirical Learning of Natural Language Tasks*, pages 25–34, Prague, 1997. University of Economics. Invited keynote paper.

[7] L. Dehaspe and L. De Raedt. Mining association rules in multiple relations. In *Proceedings of the 7th International Workshop on Inductive Logic Programming*, volume 1297 of *Lecture Notes in Artificial Intelligence*, pages 125–132. Springer-Verlag, 1997.

[8] B. Dolsak and S. Muggleton. The application of Inductive Logic Programming to finite element mesh design. In S. Muggleton, editor, *Inductive Logic Programming*, pages 453–472. Academic Press, London, 1992.

[9] R.S. Michalski. A theory and methodology of inductive learning. In *Machine Learning: an artificial intelligence approach*, volume 1. Morgan Kaufmann, 1983.

[10] S. Muggleton. Inductive logic programming. *New Generation Computing*, 8(4):295–318, 1991.

[11] S. Muggleton. Inverse entailment and Progol. *New Generation Computing*, 13:245–286, 1995.

[12] J.R. Quinlan. Induction of decision trees. *Machine Learning*, 1(1):81–106, 1986.

[13] J.R. Quinlan. *C4.5: Programs for Machine Learning*. Morgan Kaufmann, 1993. Morgan Kaufmann series in machine learning.

[14] L. De Raedt. Induction in logic. In R.S. Michalski and J. Wnek, editors, *Proceedings of the 3rd International Workshop on Multistrategy Learning*, pages 29–38, 1996.

[15] L. De Raedt and S. Džeroski. First order *jk*-clausal theories are PAC-learnable. *Artificial Intelligence*, 70:375–392, 1994.

[16] A. Srinivasan, S. Muggleton, R. King, and M. Sternberg. Theories for mutagenicity: a study of first-order and feature based induction. *Artificial Intelligence*, 85(1,2):277–299, 1996.

[17] B. Williams, S. Roberts, and S. Muggleton. Use of ILP to investigate accident data: final report. Technical Report JA022D010-0.1, Smith System Engineering, Surrey Research Park, Guildford, Surrey GU2 5YP, September 1997.

Author Index

Lecture Notes in Computer Science

Lecture Notes in Artificial Intelligence (LNAI)